CANADIAN MUNICIPAL GOVERNMENT

The student who would understand the government of a country can only obtain a complete knowledge of it if he knows something of the government of its local subdivisions. Yet the Canadian student will find studies of Canadian local government almost non-existent. Similarly the citizen or municipal officer looking for details of the organization and operation of the several systems of local government in Canada needs, but has not yet had, one single source with all the information on the subject gathered together in readily available form. Mr. Crawford meets both needs in his excellent study, the sixth volume in the Canadian Government Series.

Since local government in Canada comes under provincial jurisdiction, there are ten distinct systems having many similarities and diversities. Mr. Crawford's aim is to show how various Canadian municipal systems function, rather than to present a critical analysis of existing institutions and practices. But first he discusses the necessity of local government, its practical and political importance, the degree of self-government involved in local government and the factors contributing to this, and the weak constitutional position of local government, a position offset by the needs of the community, needs which can be best met by local government and which assure the continuance of that government despite the tightening of central control by province and nation.

KENNETH GRANT CRAWFORD has been interested in both theoretical and the practical aspects of Municipal Government since he began his academic career at the University of Western Ontario. In 1944 he was appointed Director of the Institute of Local Government at Queen's University, a position he still holds. He is also Professor of Political Science at Queen's.

CANADIAN GOVERNMENT SERIES

EDITORS

R. MacG. Dawson, 1946–1958

J. A. Corry, 1958–1961

C. B. Macpherson, 1961–

1. *Democratic Government and Politics.* By J. A. Corry and J. E. Hodgetts
2. *The Government of Canada.* By R. MacGregor Dawson
3. *Constitutional Amendment in Canada.* By Paul Gérin-Lajoie
4. *The Canadian House of Commons: Representation.* By Norman Ward
5. *The Government of Prince Edward Island.* By Frank MacKinnon
6. *Canadian Municipal Government.* By Kenneth Grant Crawford
7. *Pioneer Public Service: An Administrative History of the United Canadas, 1841–1867.* By J. E. Hodgetts
8. *The Government of Nova Scotia.* By J. Murray Beck
9. *The Office of Lieutenant-Governor.* By John T. Saywell
10. *Politics in New Brunswick.* By Hugh G. Thorburn
11. *The Public Purse: A Study in Canadian Democracy.* By Norman Ward
12. *Procedure in the Canadian House of Commons.* By W. F. Dawson
13. *The Canadian General Election of 1957.* By John Meisel
14. *The Government of Manitoba.* By Murray S. Donnelly
15. *The Modern Senate of Canada.* By F. A. Kunz

CANADIAN MUNICIPAL GOVERNMENT

BY

KENNETH GRANT CRAWFORD
Professor of Political Science and
Director of the Institute of Local Government
Queen's University

TORONTO
UNIVERSITY OF TORONTO PRESS

Copyright Canada 1954

University of Toronto Press, Toronto & Buffalo

Reprinted 1955, 1958, 1961, 1964, 1967, 1968, 1970

Reprinted in paperback 2015

ISBN 978-0-8020-5022-9 (cloth)
ISBN 978-1-4426-3951-5 (paper)

Municipal institutions constitute the strength of free nations

Alexis de Tocqueville

FOREWORD

THE BOOKSHELF which is reserved for studies in Canadian politics will be found to contain a number which deal with government at the municipal level, a display of interest which, in view of the general neglect of the Canadian political field, may appear at first glance to be quite unnatural. There are no doubt several explanations for this, but the most obvious is the close relationship which inevitably arises between the municipality and the citizen's life and happiness. The local government protects the citizen's person; it educates his children, and provides them with playgrounds and recreational facilities; it gives him roads, sidewalks, sewers, water, and electricity; it guards his health from the onslaught of disease and his property from attack by fire and the marauder. In return for these amenities, it makes very substantial levies on his property for maintenance.

The passage of time has witnessed a steady increase in the duties which the municipality has been called upon to perform; and the modern trend towards the welfare state has powerfully accelerated this tendency as governments at a higher level have demanded that the local authorities assume more and more of the administrative load. The citizens have not only called upon their local governments to assume more functions but they have at the same time expected them to raise the standard of performance in those activities which have been long established. The rush of population to urban areas has further accentuated the problems confronting the municipalities: and such matters as slum clearance, insufficient housing, green belts and recreational facilities, new highways and transportation systems, maladjustments between industrial and residential areas, assessment and taxation problems, have created unparalleled demands for immediate and drastic action by various local government services. It would be strange indeed if this turmoil in social and economic life were not accompanied by an aroused interest in the machinery which is supposed to bring about better regulation and control.

Professor Crawford is exceptionally well qualified to deal with the subject of local government and the problems which are associated with it. He has acquired first hand experience as City Clerk in London, Ontario, as a member of the City Council of Kingston, and as Secretary-Treasurer of the Ontario Municipal Association. Mr.

Crawford is Professor of Political Science at Queen's University where he has also been the Director of the Institute of Local Government since its establishment in 1944. He is as well a member of the Provincial-Municipal Relations Committee of the Province of Ontario. It is not often that a theoretical knowledge of government can be so effectively joined with practical experience, and every chapter of this book bears witness to the happy consequences of this union.

R. MacGregor Dawson

PREFACE

THE STUDENT who would understand the government of a country can only obtain a complete knowledge of it if he knows something of the government at its local or municipal level. Numerous texts are available which deal with the local government of England, the United States, and other countries and with special aspects of their municipal organization, but few are available which explain the Canadian municipal system. While much information can be found in government reports, in periodical literature, and in the daily press, it is impossible for the general reader to collate this mass of fragmentary material. This book attempts to perform that function.

It has been said that an understanding of any system of government is the work of a lifetime. The problem confronting the student of local government, however, is that there are so many systems of municipal government, even within the one country, so many varieties within each system, and such a divergence of practices among individual municipalities that he becomes lost in a morass of detail. To discuss the detail of local government in all its units is impossible within a reasonably sized book. All that can be attempted is to outline something of the development of municipal government in Canada, the organization of the country into local units of government, and the municipal machinery provided in the various provinces.

As local government in Canada comes under the jurisdiction of the provinces, there are ten distinct systems. While they have many characteristics in common there are also diversities attributable to the history and development of particular provinces. Many other factors enter into the existing differences. In every province the powers and responsibilties of municipal authorities are subject to endless change due to provincial legislation, changing public opinion as to the function of government, and the continuous flow of new problems arising from increased urbanization.

Municipalities in Canada, or even within one province, range from those containing a few hundred people scattered over a large geographical area to those with hundreds of thousands concentrated within a few square miles. To generalize regarding such extremes means that many exceptions must be understood to be implied, though not stated. There is scarcely a general statement that can be made regarding local government which is not subject to a multiplicity of exceptions. The reader should keep constantly in mind that, when attempts are made to generalize for the sake of simplicity, there will be found to be numerous and glaring exceptions to the generalizations.

To keep the book within reasonable limits it has been necessary to omit many details of interest. The limitations of time and space have made it impossible, for example, to include a study of municipal services and their administration. Yet on the other hand much detail is required to provide a useful picture of the ten systems of local government. The author's aim has been to make available such facts as would enable the reader to obtain a general understanding of the functioning of the various Canadian municipal systems rather than to present a critical analysis of existing institutions and practices.

A work of this nature will inevitably, in view of the constant flow of new legislation, be in some respects out of date. The pursuit of complete accuracy and amendment in accordance with current legislation would permanently preclude publication. The author has chosen what he believes to be the lesser of the two evils.

The author would like to acknowledge with sincere thanks the generous financial support of the Canadian Social Science Research Council and the Publications Fund of the University of Toronto Press, without which the publication of this book would not have been possible.

He also wishes to acknowledge the courtesy of the following publishers and authors in granting permission to use extracts from their books: Clarke, Irwin and Company, *A History of Canada*, by Jean Bruchési; George Allen and Unwin Ltd., *Letters from Lord Sydenham to Lord John Russell*, edited by Paul Knapland; The Ryerson Press, Toronto, and Yale University Press, New Haven, *Canada and Her Great Neighbour*, by H. F. Angus; Mr. H. E. Manning, Q.C., *Assessment and Rating*; and Methuen and Co. Ltd., *English Local Government*, by Herman Finer.

K. G. C.

October, 1952
Kingston, Canada

CONTENTS

Foreword. *By* R. MacGregor Dawson		vii
Preface		ix
Contents		xi
Appendices		xii
Tables		xiii
I	Introduction	3
II	History of Municipal Government in Canada	19
III	Local Governments	48
IV	Municipal Councils	77
V	Council Organization and Operation	108
VI	Special Purpose Bodies	126
VII	Elections, By-Laws, and "Questions"	138
VIII	Municipal Administration	162
IX	Municipal Officers and Employees	177
X	Municipal Finance: Expenditures	191
XI	Municipal Finance: Tax Revenues	206
XII	Municipal Finance: Borrowings and Non-Tax Revenue	223
XIII	Assessment	261
XIV	Real Property Assessment	279
XV	Personal Property and Business Assessment	302
XVI	Taxation	315
XVII	Provincial-Municipal Relations	335
Index		371

APPENDICES

Statutory Requirements for:

The Creation of New Rural Municipalities 74

The Creation of Villages 75

The Creation of Towns and Cities 76

Basis of Election and Composition of Municipal Councils under General Legislation 106

Property and Residence Qualifications Required of Municipal Electors under General Provincial Legislation 159

Municipal Elections Schedule 160

Examples of Percentage and Unit or Flat Rate Provincial Grants towards Municipal Costs 259

Constitution of Municipal Assessment Appeal Courts or Courts of Revision 277

Appeal Procedure on Assessments beyond the Original Court of Revision 278

Real Property Assessments on Which Taxes are Levied in Certain Canadian Provinces (1950) 301

Business Taxes in Canadian Municipalities 313

Statutory Provisions re Penalties to be Imposed on Overdue Taxes 332

More Important Conditions for Redeeming Lands Sold at Tax Sales 333

TABLES

1. Percentage Distribution of Rural and Urban Population in Canada 11
2. Canadian Rural and Urban Population, 1951, by Provinces 12
3. Canadian Urban Population Growth in Various Population Concentrations, 1901–51 13
4. Total Expenditures of Dominion, Provincial, and Local Governments for Selected Years 1913 to 1948 59
5. Annual Governmental Expenditures, 1948 60
6. Municipally Organized Territory and Population in Canadian Provinces 60
7. Types of Municipalities in Canadian Provinces 61
8. Basic Units of Rural Government in Canadian Provinces 63
9. Municipalities in Canadian Provinces 66
10. County Council Personnel 80
11. Basis of Election of Councillors 83
12. Ward Population in Selected Cities 85
13. Remuneration of Members of Council in Certain Cities 103
14. Canadian Urban Municipalities in Which Formal Pension Plans Exist 189
15. Distribution of Major Municipal Expenditures in Certain Cities, 1949, as a Percentage of Total Expenditure 205
16. Percentage of Gross Revenues Derived from Various Sources in Twenty Canadian Cities (1949) 207
17. Sources of Government Tax Revenues, 1948 210
18. The More Common Types of Municipal Taxation in Canada 212
19. Taxable Municipal Assessments, 1948 215
20. Sales Tax Revenue in Some Quebec Cities 217
21. Municipal Amusement Tax Revenues 218
22. Limitations on Temporary Municipal Borrowings for Current Expenditures 225
23. Statutory Limitation on Interest Rates Payable on Municipal Debentures 227
24. Statutory Limitation of Debenture Terms 228
25. Statutory Municipal Debt Limits 230

26. Municipal Debenture Debt in Certain Provinces, 1945–8 240
27. Outstanding Municipal Debt (net), 1944 and 1948 241
28. Distribution of Municipal Bonded Debt, 1944 and 1948 241
29. Importance of Provincial Subsidies and Grants in Canadian Municipal Revenues 247
30. Some Municipal Enterprise Operations 252
31. Commonly Recurring "Miscellaneous" Revenues in 10 Canadian Cities, 1946 254
32. Basis of Valuation of Buildings and Improvements for Assessment in Provinces where Basis Differs from that for Land 281
33. Legal Basis of Assessment of Real Property for Taxation as Related to Value 282
34. Per Capita Taxable Assessments of Real Property in Various Classes of Municipalities in Certain Canadian Provinces 286
35. Per Capita Taxable Assessments of Real Property in Cities of 10,000 or Over (1950) 286
36. Real Property Exemptions for Taxation Purposes—1946 288
37. Real Property Exemptions in Certain Canadian Cities 289
38. Taxed Assessment of Buildings and Improvements as a Percentage of Assessed Values in Alberta and British Columbia Municipalities, 1946 290
39. Personal Property Assessment 305
40. Business Assessment and Taxation in Canadian Municipalities 312
41. Business Tax as a Percentage of Total Tax Revenue 313
42. Range of Business Tax as a Percentage of Total Tax Revenue in Cities 313
43. Statutory Municipal Tax Limits 317

CANADIAN MUNICIPAL GOVERNMENT

CHAPTER I

INTRODUCTION

LOCAL GOVERNMENT developed originally in the history of society to meet a need—a need to accomplish some purpose which could be more adequately achieved by action of the group than by action of the individual. As society became more complex the number of such needs increased. The functions of local authorities expanded as concentrations of population became greater. Under the constitution of most countries today local governments are subsidiary units, but historically some type of local government was, by force of circumstances, the first to be established. The purpose which originally called local governments into being—to meet a need—still exists, although such governments now assume different forms.

It is generally accepted that in Canada the purposes of local government are twofold. One is to carry out the duties imposed upon local authorities by the provinces which have created them, and to which they are ultimately answerable. The other is to carry out the wishes of the inhabitants of the area under their jurisdiction, within the scope and to the extent permitted by law. Opinions differ as to which of these two purposes should be dominant, though legally and constitutionally, if not politically, the priority of the former cannot be questioned.

PRACTICAL IMPORTANCE OF LOCAL GOVERNMENT

Experience through the ages has shown the necessity of dividing countries of any appreciable extent into subdivisions for the purposes of government and administration. The resulting units in some cases have been governed by a representative of the sovereign power, with little or no consideration for the wishes of the inhabitants. Other systems have provided for varying degrees of local self-government. The subdivisions then proved expedient as a means of bringing the governing authorities in closer contact with the people governed and in providing for rapid and practical solutions of the multitude of problems which clog the administrative machinery when all government is administered from one central point. Such a method permits problems which are of little concern to the central authority to be disposed of locally and usually with greater acceptability to the citizens concerned.

The universality of some form of local government, both in the past and in modern times, suggests that it is indispensable, particularly where the area under one authority is large. The maintenance of the national government is essential to the life of the nation but, in modern urban communities at least, the exercise of the functions of the local government is essential to human life itself. In the event of the collapse or destruction of a national government by conquest in modern times the first concern of the conqueror is to re-establish some form of local administration and to get it functioning. Even when there has been a collapse of a civilization, as in the Dark Ages, some form of local government has survived, for it is both fundamental and essential.

It would be difficult to overemphasize the importance of the local government in the everyday life of the citizens, more especially for those who live in urban centres. That is not to say that one level of government is necessarily more important than another, for all perform functions which are essential to complete the programme of governmental service demanded in a modern society. Yet few fully appreciate the vital part played by the local level of government. What Graham Wallas said of England might well be applied to a wider field, that

> "for the average English citizen the possibility of health, of happiness, of progress towards the old Greek ideal of 'beautiful goodness,' depends on his local government more than on any other factor in his environment." Yet so smoothly does the system work, and so accustomed are we to the existence of the conditions which alone make modern industrial civilization possible, that we tend to overlook the vast amount of hard work and hard thought which led to the creation of those conditions and which are involved in their efficient maintenance. "The city council's services," Sir Ernest Simon has said, "mean the difference between savagery and civilization."[1]

Because many of the services of the local government have been in operation throughout our lifetime, because its services have expanded gradually, unnoted by the citizen, and because those services function so efficiently, they are taken for granted as a natural condition of existence, like the air we breathe. When we turn the tap, we assume we will get water; when we call the fire department, we expect a prompt response; when the children are sent to school, we expect the school to be open; and when we drive our car, we expect to find the road surface reasonably smooth and free from holes. It is only on those rare occasions when turning the switch produces no heat in the stove,

[1] *A Century of Municipal Progress 1835–1935*, ed. by Harold J. Laski, W. Ivor Jennings and William A. Robson (London, 1935), p. 11.

when the street lights fail, or when the garbage collector neglects to call that we realize how essential to tolerable community living are the services of the local government and how bothersome is any failure in their functioning.

The importance of local government in the life of the citizen is not limited to the services it supplies or to the protection it gives him against a variety of hazards, ranging from fire to contagious diseases. To a great extent the urban citizen is what he is as a result of the living conditions and the institutions of the communities in which he has lived. In great part these have been determined by policies of the local government. The sanitary conditions, the purity of the water, milk and meat supply, the incidence of communicable diseases, the educational standards, the recreational facilities, and many of the cultural influences are in great part the product of local government policies. These are factors which, to an increasing extent, condition the development of the individual throughout his life. The business man and the industrialist, for example, seldom realize the extent to which their affairs are dependent upon the operations of municipal services and enterprises or the long-run effects of municipal educational, health, and welfare policies on the quality of their employees. A notable instance is the extent to which local health policies have practically eliminated diseases such as diphtheria, smallpox, and typhoid with consequent reduction in lost time of employees. One of the factors which makes possible industrial organization on a mass production basis is the application of scientific knowledge in the fields of sanitation, public health, and engineering by local units of government which permits the concentrations of population required to supply the large labour force and the mass markets indispensable to mass production.

These services could be supplied by some other unit of government but, as government functions are presently distributed, they are the responsibility of the local unit. At one time it would have been impossible for provincial or national authorities to perform such functions adequately owing to the time loss in the contacts between the central authorities and the local communities. Improvements in transportation and communications have reduced the difficulties imposed by time and distance, and it might be thought that a consequent reduction in the importance of the local units of government would result. In fact, owing to increasing urbanization with its multiplying problems and a changing public attitude respecting governmental functions, the expansion in the activities of local government has more than offset the effect of the reduced importance of the time and space factors.

Political Importance of Local Government

Canada is a democracy and the majority of its people prefer the democratic form of government to any other known form. Professor Corry has suggested[2] that an essential condition for an enduring democracy is the maintenance of a limited number of political parties. To this end the national parties must concentrate on policies of wide appeal which will draw support from diverse groups and individuals across the nation, and eliminate from party platforms those issues which tend to divide people rather than to bring them together. The greater the extent to which the divisive sectional and local issues can be divorced from the national political field, the less are the chances that issues will develop which will divert the allegiance of party supporters and result in the dangerous splintering of parties. It appears, therefore, that in the interests of a democratic form of government it is essential that the multitude of issues of local interest be disposed of locally. The existence of a network of municipal governments dealing with local affairs and ten provincial authorities dealing with matters of sectional interest tends to reduce the hazard of splintering in the national parties.

Undoubtedly the existence of strong units of local government adds political stability to the nation. Any person who has attempted to persuade a number of municipal councils to adopt a particular policy knows how long and tedious is the task. The obvious short cut is to have the desired policy imposed by a higher level of government which will make its local adoption compulsory. Thus, the more local authorities are permitted to settle matters of policy, the more deliberate will be the rate of change and, correspondingly, the more difficult it will be to effect drastic changes rapidly merely by capturing control at a higher level.

Students of government, when considering the political importance of local government in a democracy, emphasize the fact that the local unit serves as a training school for the electors and the elected in the practice of democracy. While this is a limited view, such claims are true and justify elaboration. Democracy, we are told, is the most difficult form of government to operate because for its continued and successful operation it requires intelligent participation by the mass of the adult population. They being busy with their private affairs can not or will not afford the time to give the study required to understand the complex issues of the modern state. They may then become

[2] J. A. Corry, *Democratic Government and Politics* (Toronto, 1946), chaps. vi, vii.

disillusioned by actions of their governing authorities which they do not understand and tend to become convinced of the futility of an individual trying to do anything about it.

However, the citizen is more likely to understand the issues under consideration at the local level and to have ideas about how they should be settled. The matters for decision are within the range of his experience; he knows the local conditions and can appreciate what is involved in working out a solution. The intricacies of price control, of constitutional niceties, or of Dominion-provincial relations are remote and to a great extent unintelligible to most citizens but they can readily decide the merits of a proposal to close gasoline stations at a fixed hour.

Moreover, in the local field the interval between decision and result is usually sufficiently short, and the result sufficiently evident, that the citizen can measure the result. His understanding of local issues, his more intimate knowledge of the members of his local government, and the direct impact of local government policies enable him to measure performance against promises. He thus acquires the ability to weigh conflicting programmes and proposals; he learns to discount extravagant election pledges; he develops a healthy scepticism which is his protection against the demagogue in politics; and, what is most important, he learns that according as he calls the tune, so must he pay the piper.

Municipal elections, which recur more frequently than national or provincial elections, also contribute towards the education of the citizen in the mechanics of voting and keep him in the habit of exercising the franchise. This benefit, of course, may be offset by the possibility of overworking the elector, as too frequent calls upon him to cast a ballot may result in his refusing to be bothered. Not the least of the values of experience in local government is that the citizen learns how effective the voter can be when he decides to reject at the polls a representative or policies he does not approve. It is a useful lesson to impress upon the minds of the people just who is ultimately in control under a democratic system of government. By training and experience in the sphere of local government the citizen learns to play his part in a self-governing community and he is better equipped to play his part as a member of the larger community of the province or nation.

Members of elected municipal bodies have an opportunity to prove themselves as representatives of the electors, to learn the techniques of public business in a democracy, and the art of working with others to obtain results. The electors, in turn, have an opportunity to try out as representatives their fellow citizens who, if acceptable in the local field, may be selected for the larger and more distant spheres, the province and the Dominion. The extent to which the local government serves as a training school for elected representatives is evidenced by the fact that of the 262 members of the 1952 Canadian House of Commons 77 have held municipal office.[8] In the Ontario Legislature, of a membership of 90, 19 have been councillors; 13, mayors; 13, reeves; 11, school trustees; and 4, members of other civic bodies. Of the 90, 46 have held elective municipal offices before becoming members of the Legislature.

The major political function of local government in a democracy, however, is not that of training citizens and elected representatives for the practice of democratic government in the provincial and national spheres; it is the actual exercise of democracy at the local level. There are many and varied definitions of democracy, but basically it means the conduct of government in accordance with the wishes of the governed. At no other level of government is this more nearly possible or more nearly attained than at the local level. Certain functions of government cannot be performed to advantage by authorities having a limited area of jurisdiction; more effective results can be obtained if some functions are the concern of one of the senior governments. But to the extent that functions can be exercised effectively locally, they are more likely to be exercised in accord with what the people want than if they are the responsibility of any other government. Such a claim on behalf of local government, of course, has little appeal for those who believe that a government should give the people what is good for them rather than what they want. They argue that decisions should be made on the basis of the larger community of the province or the nation where legislators and administrators with wider vision and experience, though more remote from the people concerned, can take a detached and objective view of what is for the greatest benefit for all.

No small part of the contribution which local government makes toward maintaining a democratic form of government lies in the constant resistance, sometimes apparently perverse and unreasonable, which it offers to the trend toward over-centralization in the higher levels of government. Even though at times the resistance of local authorities to the policies of higher levels of government may appear

[8]Mayors, 25; reeves, 15; councillors, 18; school trustees, 10; wardens, 4; members of other civic bodies, 5.

to be unreasonable and motivated by narrow self-interest it has somewhat the same value as the resistance of the Opposition in requiring the Government to justify its proposals and to weigh more carefully the implications of its policies before they are proposed.

Administrative Importance of Local Government

In Canada in 1949 there were 4,099 incorporated municipalities and the total of local "authorities" probably approaches 25,000.[4] The number of municipalities corresponds to 12,630 in England[5] and 119,416 in the United States.[6] The range of problems with which these authorities deal varies according to their population. The total of the decisions made and the problems dealt with is colossal. If all these decisions and adjustments had to be made by one central authority the organization required to handle the vast flow of work would be so huge as to be unmanageable and would probably break down under its own weight. The magnitude of the task and the administrative impossibility of dealing with it centrally compel decentralization. Local authorities may be rather rigidly controlled from the centre, as in France and increasingly in England, or they may be allowed considerable latitude, as in Canada; but it is imperative that a substantial measure of local decision be permitted if administrative congestion is to be avoided.

Decentralization relieves the pressure on the central authorities and leaves them free to deal with the sufficiently burdensome problems of national or provincial importance. If such relief is not provided, either the larger issues will be neglected, because of the mass of urgent local problems crying for disposition, or the local problems will get scant attention while the larger issues take precedence. In the latter case dissatisfaction is likely to be more widespread than in the former. The handling of local problems through local authorities permits them to be disposed of with greater despatch and acceptability to the people immediately concerned, for the local authorities have a more intimate knowledge of the local conditions and can provide greater flexibility in the application of policies than is possible for a central authority.

[4]H. Carl Goldenberg, in his study, *Municipal Finance in Canada* (Ottawa, 1939), p. 12, prepared for the Royal Commission on Dominion-Provincial Relations in 1939, lists the following municipal institutions in the Canadian provinces: counties 158, cities 111, towns 480, villages 1,032, rural municipalities 2,182, school districts 24,126; total 28,090. Since that date there has been a considerable reduction in the number of school districts in several of the provinces.

[5]J. H. Warren, *The English Local Government System* (London, 1946), chap. III.

[6]*Governments in the United States, 1951*, United States Department of Commerce, Bureau of Census, G-SS, no. 29 (March, 1952).

As the economy of Canada becomes more complex, there is increasing reliance on social and economic planning at the higher levels of government and the welfare of the community becomes more and more dependent upon the national and provincial policies and administration. The more the economy comes to depend on such planning, the more vulnerable it becomes to the consequences of any major errors. An organization of self-reliant local governing and administrative agencies serves as a useful cushion against the shock of what might otherwise be the disastrous results of such errors. A people or a community which has been schooled to leave the solution of all its problems to a remote level of government cannot be expected, on short notice, to marshal and organize local resources to meet the problems of an emergency.

The Effect of Urbanization on Local Government

Municipalities may be classified as rural, urban, or suburban, though there are differences of opinion as to just where the dividing line should be drawn. For 1951 census purposes in Canada the population of cities, towns, and villages of 1,000 or over, whether incorporated or unincorporated, as well as the population of all parts of census metropolitan areas was defined as urban and the population outside such localities as rural. Since the basis of incorporation of cities, towns, and villages is a matter under provincial control the distinction between rural and urban, for other than census purposes, is not the same for all the provinces.[7] There is no generally accepted degree of population concentration marking the suburban status, which is a stage in the transition from rural to urban in areas adjacent to urban centres.[8]

As the nation becomes more urbanized the importance of local government in Canada is continuously increasing. The functions of rural municipalities are important, but the range of services which a rural community requires of its local government is relatively restricted. On the other hand, the greater and more numerous hazards, such as those from fire, unsanitary conditions, traffic, and unemployment, against which the individual in urban centres must be protected create a greater need for community action. In addition, because of the social and economic problems of the more thickly populated industrialized areas there is a more pressing need for social services in the larger

[7]An illustration of the unsatisfactory nature of classification based on municipal status is the township of York, Ontario. It is classed municipally as rural but it has a population of 93,248 in an area of 5,050 acres—a population concentration of 18.4 to the acre compared with the city of Fort William with 4.2.

[8]Manitoba provides a statutory class of "suburban municipalities."

centres. For example, the means by which urban dwellers earn their living, in contrast to those in rural communities, results in a need for more services for urban citizens. Since their resources for existence depend on continued employment they may be unable to maintain themselves in periods of unemployment and in the years after employable age and must be assisted. The rural dweller in depressed times may have difficulty in obtaining cash income but to some extent, barring crop failures, he can eke out an existence for himself and family on the farm.

Tables 1 to 3 indicate the shift toward urban living in Canada. This trend is not peculiar to Canada, but has been proceeding throughout the Western world since early in the nineteenth century and has been most marked in the more industrialized countries. Its importance for this study lies in the increase in the demands upon local units of government which accompanies an increase in population concentration.

Over five and one-half million persons, approximately 40 per cent of the total population, live in the 106 urban centres of over ten thousand population. This high concentration of population in a relatively few centres, which has developed in a comparatively short period, has created many problems for municipal authorities. It partially explains why so much of the attention devoted to local government has been directed to the cities, for their problems have been the most acute. The urgency of the need to provide accommodation for this rapidly

TABLE 1

PERCENTAGE DISTRIBUTION OF RURAL AND URBAN POPULATION IN CANADA[a]

	Rural	Urban[b]
1871	80.42	19.58
1881	74.35	25.65
1891	68.20	31.80
1901	62.50	37.50
1911	54.58	45.42
1921	50.48	49.52
1931	46.30	53.70
1941	45.66	54.34
	43.48[c]	56.51[c]
1951	43.31	56.68
	38.41[c]	61.58[c]

[a]Tabulation based on tables in *Canada Year Book, 1952–53*, p. 144.

[b]As the distinction between rural and urban was changed for 1951 census purposes the distribution for 1941 and 1951 is shown on both bases. Prior to 1951 only persons living in incorporated cities, towns, and villages were classed as urban. For the 1951 census the population of cities, towns, and villages of 1,000 or over, whether incorporated or not, as well as the population of all parts of census metropolitan areas was classed as urban.

[c]On 1951 census definition basis.

TABLE 2

CANADIAN RURAL AND URBAN POPULATION, 1951, BY PROVINCES

	Rural	Urban	Urban[a]		Percentage increases[a] in urban population		
			Percentage	Rank	1921–31	1931–41	1941–51
Newfoundland	257,039	104,377	28.8(42.8)	9			10.4
Prince Edward Island	70,807	27,622	28.0(25.0)	10	6.7	19.4	2.4
Nova Scotia	344,865	297,719	46.3(53.6)	6	2.0	15.4	.04
New Brunswick	348,185	167,512	32.4(41.6)	8	3.6	11.2	1.1
Quebec	1,326,883	2,728,798	67.2(66.5)	1	37.1	16.3	3.9
Ontario	1,844,316	2,753,226	59.8(70.7)	2	22.8	11.5	− 1.8
Manitoba	392,112	384,429	49.5(56.6)	5	20.7	1.8	5.3
Saskatchewan	461,047	370,681	44.5(30.3)	7	32.8	1.4	11.6
Alberta	451,313	488,188	51.9(47.8)	4	24.9	10.0	13.4
British Columbia	550,158	615,052	52.7(68.0)	3	59.4	12.3	− 1.4

[a]The percentages, except those within brackets, are based on the 1941 census distinction between rural and urban population. Percentages in brackets are based on the 1951 census distinction.

TABLE 3

CANADIAN URBAN POPULATION GROWTH[a] IN VARIOUS POPULATION CONCENTRATIONS, 1901–51[b]

In urban centres of population	Number						Percentage of total population						Pop'n in thousands	Cumulative percentage of 1951 total
of	1901	1911	1921	1931	1941	1951	1901	1911	1921	1931	1941	1951	1951	
Over 500,000	0	1	2	2	2	2	0	6.5	12.9	13.9	13.6	12.1	1,697	12.11
300,000–500,000	0	2	0	0	0	1	0	11.7	0	0	0	2.4	344	14.57
200,000–300,000	2	0	0	2	2	3	8.8	0	0	4.4	4.3	4.6	646	19.18
100,000–200,000	0	2	4	3	4	4	0	3.2	5.9	3.9	5.0	4.0	572	23.27
50,000–100,000	3	3	5	7	7	9	3.3	3.4	3.8	4.5	4.4	4.2	588	27.47
25,000– 50,000	5	6	7	10	19	24	3.5	3.3	2.7	3.2	5.2	5.7	802	33.20
15,000– 25,000	3	13	19	23	20	34	1.0	3.3	4.2	4.4	3.2	4.5	636	37.74
10,000– 15,000	8	18	18	23	24	29	1.7	3.0	2.5	2.6	2.5	2.4	347	40.22
5,000– 10,000	37	46	54	68	74	100	5.1	4.4	4.3	4.4	4.4	5.1	720	45.36
3,000– 5,000	50	60	72	71	91	119	3.5	3.1	3.1	2.6	3.0	3.2	457	48.63
1,000– 3,000	187	251	293	324	337	409	5.9	5.9	5.6	5.3	4.8	4.9	698	53.61
Under 1,000			969	1072	1060	1049	4.4	3.7	4.2	3.9	3.4	3.0	429	56.68
			1443	1605	1640	1783	37.6	45.5	49.5	53.7	54.3	56.6	7,941	

[a]Based on tabulations in *Canada Year Book*, 1920, p. 100; 1943–44, p. 122; 1945, p. 113; 1952–53, p. 131.
[b]Years prior to 1951 do not include Newfoundland.

expanding population also explains, in part, the preoccupation of civic administration with developing the physical structure for expansion to the partial neglect of other but less pressing aspects of the community needs.

The growth of the larger urban centres has been accompanied by the problem, not peculiar to Canada, of the spill-over from the cities into the adjacent rural municipalities. As the city boundaries have not expanded at the same rate as the population there have developed the acute problems of the suburban or the metropolitan areas adjacent to cities such as Halifax, Saint John, Quebec, Montreal, Ottawa, Toronto, Hamilton, London, Windsor, Winnipeg, Vancouver, and Victoria, and, to a lesser degree, other smaller centres.

Local Government or Local Self-Government?

While some form of local government is found in most countries, there is great diversity in the extent to which it is local self-government. Even in countries which in the past have permitted a considerable degree of self-government there has been a narrowing of the scope of local decision and a tightening of control by the central authorities in recent years. With improved communications the possibilities of central control have vastly increased. In Canada the concentration of population, increased internal travel, scientific and technological advances, and the change in the national economy, from one predominantly agricultural to one of increasing industrialization, have compelled the senior governments to take an interest in many activities previously left solely to local discretion. "Canadian municipalities," Goldenberg states, "are neither organically nor in practice units or agents of the central (provincial) administration, although in a few particular fields of modern governmental activity some tendency in this direction may be discerned."[9] The trend is more marked in some provinces than in others, but in none of the provinces except Newfoundland has it reached the stage of centralized control and direction attained in England. Yet there is today no difficulty in discerning "some tendency in this direction"; and there has been a marked acceleration in the trend since the thirties.

The pressure upon the limited revenue sources of Canadian municipalities which has accompanied the expansion of their activities, in both rural and urban communities, has forced them to look to the provinces for financial help, and substantial assistance is now granted in some provinces. Inevitably increased provincial assistance will be

[9]Goldenberg, *Municipal Finance in Canada*, p. 2.

accompanied by increased provincial control. As continuing adjustments are made in the relationships between the Dominion and the provinces, especially in the fields of taxation and finance, attempts are being made to settle the problems of provincial-municipal financial relations. Pending a lasting settlement of Dominion-provincial relations the problem of provincial-municipal relations still has to be faced, though the basis of such an adjustment may be tentative and experimental, awaiting settlement between the senior governments.

Whether the Dominion will ultimately absorb more and more of the functions and powers of the provinces, or whether the provinces can maintain a place of importance in the national framework of government are questions to which only the future will provide the answer. The place of local government, its relative importance, and the extent of its powers of self-government in the future are also unpredictable. Yet it would seem reasonable to expect that, from the nature of many of its functions and in the light of historical experience, local government will survive and will retain a considerable degree of autonomy. Although they lack the protection of any assured constitutional position, the local urban units at least have one advantage over both the provincial and the national units of government in that their jurisdiction covers a group of people with a natural community of interest as contrasted with the somewhat artificial unity of the Dominion or even of most of the provinces.

Factors Which Influence the Character of Local Government

Many factors have an influence in determining the type of local government which develops in a country and the extent to which it is self-government. Some of the more important factors are the physical characteristics of the country, its location, and its political and constitutional development.

The need for local government occurs when people live in sufficiently close association that community problems arise or that it becomes feasible to join together as a group to attain certain mutually desired ends. People settle where the land resources are capable of satisfying their wants. Such settlement may be highly concentrated where the population is engaged in manufacturing, trade, or service industries and is likely to be more sparse where the population is engaged in extractive industries such as agriculture, mining, or lumbering.

The degree of concentration of population for those engaged in agriculture may be strictly limited by a number of physical factors among which are topography and climate. Thus land which has a fall in excess of fifteen feet in a hundred or where the annual rainfall is less than twenty inches is usually unsuitable for any agricultural purposes other than grazing. Where such conditions prevail, as is the case in 52 per cent of North America's land surface, the possibility of a heavily populated agricultural area is limited. Further limitations are imposed where the shortness of the frost-free season and the limited amount of sunshine restrict the possibilities of producing crops.[10] The effect of such influences on municipal developments in New Zealand is noted by Professor Brady.[11]

The system of local government which evolves in a country is, in part, determined by that country's location. In a country such as France, ease of access for invading armies from adjacent countries makes it imperative for national self-preservation that the whole governmental organization be highly centralized so that the entire resources of the nation can be mobilized promptly. Too much local independence and self-government might make for a slow response when time is vital. A country in a location such as that of England, long protected by the English Channel against sudden invasion, can afford to allow a much greater degree of local self-government. In Canada, the absence of any continuing threat of invasion, the sparse settlement in the early years of municipal development, and the difficulties of communication in provinces of wide expanse combined to permit the development of a considerable degree of self-government at the local level, once the principle of local self-government had been conceded.

Countries which are distant from their neighbours or cut off by natural barriers are not likely to be influenced by current municipal developments elsewhere. However, where there is extensive travel between countries, as between the United States and Canada, the continuous exchange of experience has a marked effect on the less populous country.[12] Topographical influences on local institutions are

[10] Ronald R. Renne, *Land Economics* (New York, 1947), chap. VII.

[11] Alexander Brady, *Democracy in the Dominions* (Toronto, 1947), p. 278: "An extensive network of municipal units was more feasible [in New Zealand] than in most areas of Australia and South Africa owing to closer land settlement, the product in turn of adequate rain. In this matter New Zealand resembles more clearly eastern Canada, especially Ontario. The abundant life of local institutions has been proportioned to the extent of the rainfall and the opportunities for close settlement."

[12] H. F. Angus, *Canada and Her Great Neighbour* (Toronto, 1938), p. 48: "From the establishment of Upper Canada, American influence upon the politics of the Province, especially upon the municipal government, has been persistent and crucial, though not always evident to the casual observer. The existing municipal institutions of Ontario were originally the product of the insistence of the

illustrated in Switzerland where the mountainous terrain has served as a protection against invasion and has also cut up the country internally. Among the results have been the large degree of local self-government and the marked diversity of its development in various sections within the nation. Similarly, in provinces such as Newfoundland or British Columbia the topography has had a marked effect on municipal developments.

Local government institutions are considerably influenced by past events in the national development. Thus, in France the sharp break with the past at the time of the Revolution made it feasible to create an orderly planned municipal system. In England, by contrast, there has been a continuous evolution of political institutions with no such abrupt break-away from the past and the local government institutions even today are complicated by age-long traditions, as exemplified by the structure of the government of the City of London. In newer countries such as the United States and Canada, the municipal institutions of which were in great part imported directly or indirectly from England, there was no long-established local tradition and it was relatively simple to establish an orderly system of municipal organization.

A democratic tradition, such as exists in England or Switzerland, makes for individual and community self-reliance and a demand for local independence. Yet, frequently local affairs have been overshadowed by the importance of pressing national issues, as in England prior to 1830, and in the United States in the years before the Civil War. When burning national issues are foremost in the minds of the people, legislators are prone to neglect the less appealing civic problems. Local government issues also may become involved in the politics of the larger field, as in Upper Canada at the time of the struggle between the radicals and the Family Compact.

The constitution of a country determines the level of government under which local government operates and the extent to which it is controlled by that government. In countries with a unitary national government, such as England and France, local governments come directly under the national government; where this is the case there is

---

Loyalist and part-Loyalist immigrants upon at least a modified form of the local government development in New England. And, at the present day, Ontario cities watch closely the practices and proceedings in the administration of cities on the other side of the border, and make such adaptations as their rulers think expedient. There is, however, a strong endeavour to avoid, in appearance at least, anything in the nature of direct imitation." It is worthy of note, however, that the United States vogue for the manager system of city government has only been followed in Ontario in three cities. This, of course, may be explained by the time lag between developments in the United States and their adoption in Ontario.

considerable uniformity within the municipal system. In federal states, such as the United States, Canada, or Switzerland, local government comes under the jurisdiction of the state or provincial authorities; there is therefore a greater variety of systems. Again, the legislatures of Canadian provinces are all-powerful in municipal matters in contrast to many state legislatures in the United States which are restricted, by the provisions of the state constitutions, in legislating on matters of local government.

The Constitutional Position of Canadian Local Government

The local governments in Canada are in a different constitutional position than either of the two senior levels of government. Each of the latter has an assured constitutional position and, subject to the mysteries of judicial interpretation, is protected by the allocation of powers under the British North America Act against encroachments on its sphere. It may be that from time to time by reason of crisis or emergency, such as depression or war, urgent need induces consent to encroachments by one government on the normal sphere of activity of the other; again, developments, unforeseen at the time of Confederation, may open up new fields of uncertain jurisdiction. Under normal conditions, however, the Dominion and the provinces each have an assured area of jurisdiction.

Such is not the case with the municipalities. They are creations of the provinces; their powers can be extended or contracted at will by the provincial legislatures or, in the extreme, they can quite legally be legislated out of existence, although politically this would not probably be practicable.[13] The protection of the municipalities lies, not in their legal or constitutional position, but rather in the needs of the people which must be met and the difficulty, especially in urban communities, of meeting those needs through the medium of any other level of government.

[13]Arthur Roberts, *The Municipal Review of Canada*, vol. XLIV, no. 2, Feb. 1948, p. 8: "The British North America Act says that—'In each province the legislature may exclusively make laws in relation to municipal institutions.' That does not mean that municipal government, otherwise called local government, is the creation of the province. It is not merely a privilege conceded by the legislature in its discretion, and which may at any time be withdrawn. It is a well-established part of our system of democratic government, part of our heritage from the Mother Land and of our freedom."

CHAPTER II

HISTORY OF MUNICIPAL GOVERNMENT IN CANADA

To UNDERSTAND existing municipal institutions it is necessary to know something of their history and development. That history and development varies from province to province, having been determined by such factors as the date and rate of settlement, the place of origin of the settlers, and the physical characteristics of the various provinces.

In Upper Canada there was a long and bitter struggle to wrest from a reluctant government the right of local self-rule; in Lower Canada a refusal by the people to use the system introduced by a distrusted government. In Nova Scotia and New Brunswick there was little popular interest in local self-government, while in Prince Edward Island the limited area enabled the legislature to handle local affairs except for a few urban centres.

The Prairie Provinces were opened for settlement many years after the struggle for local control had been won in the central provinces and they benefited by the experience of a quarter century of municipal government in those provinces; the question at issue was not whether local self-government should be permitted but rather the basis on which it should be established. In British Columbia, the problem of communications and the scattered nature of the early settlements, resulting from the mountainous nature of the province, determined the issue of the right of local self-government before it arose. On the other hand, there has been no popular demand for municipal organization in Newfoundland but rather a general resistance of any such proposals by the island's government, a resistance based on the widely held view that the provincial government is responsible for local services and a long-standing dread of the introduction of real property taxes.

ONTARIO AND QUEBEC

The French Régime, 1608–1760

There may be said to have been no municipal government in Canada during the French régime. This omission of provision for local institutions was in accord with the policy of the home authorities in France. During the eleventh century the kings of France had assisted cities and towns in their struggles against their feudal lords but as the feudal system weakened and as more power became centralized in the King, his erstwhile allies, the *communes*, found themselves bereft even of such rights and independence as they had previously acquired.[1] It was this later policy of almost unlimited central control which guided the authorities in New France.

There were one or two attempts to institute some local control in Canada. In the early years of the French régime there grew up a system of choosing *syndics d'habitations*, local officers elected by ballot in the larger centres to look after the interests of the people. Although the records relating to them are infrequent, it is known that *syndics* were elected in Quebec, Montreal, and Three Rivers in 1647 and that they had the right to attend the Council of the colony to express the sentiments of their communities. Frontenac, in 1663, provided for the election of a Board of Aldermen in the town of Quebec but an order soon came from France to put a stop to such a dangerous innovation. The *syndics*, too, were viewed with suspicion. In 1672 Colbert, in sending instructions to Frontenac, wrote: "It will be advisable when the colony is more vigorous than at present, to suppress by degrees the syndic who presents petitions in the name of the inhabitants as it seems better that everyone speak for himself, and no one for all."[2] At times meetings of the people were called for consultation on some matters,[3] but in general, throughout the period of the French régime, local matters were dealt with by the Intendant and the Council.

The British Régime

Following the conquest, in the years 1760-3, all government was vested in the military authorities. Subsequently, in the period 1763-91, Canada was governed by a Governor and Legislative Council. Little provision, however, was made for the establishment of local government. The Governor General in 1764 established Courts of Quarter Sessions, composed of justices of the peace, for the trial of less important matters. Provision was also made to permit the inhabitants in each parish to elect six men annually as *baillis* and *sous baillis*, whose functions were to inspect highways and bridges and to act as constables. If those elected were approved, they were appointed by the Governor General with the consent of his Council. Later, in 1777, in accordance

[1] *Canada and Its Provinces* (Toronto, 1914-17), Vol. XV, p. 287.

[2] J. G. Bourinot, *Local Government in Canada* (Baltimore, 1887), p. 12.

[3] ". . . it must not be forgotten that the *Canadiens* were not completely isolated from public affairs. In the eighteenth century, particularly, the leading men of the country were consulted and general assemblies of the citizens were held, in principle, twice a year. Moreover, many offices were elective, for example, church wardens for the temporal administration of the parishes, captains of militia, or syndics of the merchants' corporations." Jean Bruchési, *A History of Canada*, trans. R. W. W. Robertson (Toronto, 1950), p. 88.

with the desire of the British Government to continue the established institutions of the country to which the people were accustomed, the office of *grand voyer*[4] was re-established and the repair and maintenance of highways and bridges was again placed under his direction.

Thus the people had little to do with local administration. Only in church matters did they have any great responsibility. Until 1841 the "affairs of each parish were regulated by the Curé, the Seignior and the Captain of Militia, as in the days of the French government. . . . Indeed as we review the history of French Canada in all times, we can not pay too high tribute to the usefulness of the French Canadian clergy in the absence of the settled institutions of local government. In fact, it was only in ecclesiastical affairs that the people ever had an opportunity of exercising a certain influence. The old institution of the *fabrique*[5]—which still exists in all its vigor—enabled them to meet together whenever it was necessary to repair a church or presbytery."[6]

By the 1780's, however, the complexion of the population was changing, and the old system was no longer adequate. During the years of the War of Independence there was a continuous migration of Loyalists from the American colonies to Nova Scotia and Canada.[7] It is estimated that in 1782 and 1783 when this trek reached its peak about 10,000 arrived in the Saint John area on the Bay of Fundy, approximately 25,000 others settled in Nova Scotia, which had previously had a population of only about 13,000,[8] and approximately 20,000[9] were established in Canada, mostly west of Montreal, in ter-

[4]The office of *grand voyer* or road overseer was created as early as 1657. It was the duty of the *grand voyer* to visit parishes and, after notice, the inhabitants were required to meet him, bringing their tools, and under his direction to construct or repair the roads.

[5]"The communal belongings," Falardeau states, referring to the church building, the rectory, and the cemetery, "are called the *fabrique* and the moral person who legally owns and administers them is the *conseil de fabrique* (board of wardens.) This board of parochial wardens is composed *ex officio*, of the pastor, and of a small group of parishioners whose number may vary from place to place. It acts as a policy making and administrative body in all financial affairs relating to the parochial organization." Jean C. Falardeau, "The Parish as an Institutional Type," *Canadian Journal of Economics and Political Science*, vol. XV, 1949, p. 358.

[6]Bourinot, *Local Government in Canada*, p. 28.

[7]The term "Canada" as used here refers to the territory subsequently known as Upper and Lower Canada, now the provinces of Ontario and Quebec, and not the larger area now included in the Dominion of Canada.

[8]In 1763 the population was 13,374.

[9]Estimates of the number who came to Canada vary. Edgar McInnis in his *Canada: A Political and Social History* (New York, 1947) states (p. 165): "Loyalists, disbanded German Mercenaries, and new settlers from the United States together formed a population of some 10,000 in what was to become Ontario and the number continued to increase as the westward migration in the United States lapped over into Canada."

ritory which had been practically unsettled. These main settlements, in what was then known as the Province of Quebec, were in the vicinity of Kingston, along the north shore of Lake Ontario, and in the Niagara area.

It is useful to know something of the local government systems which had existed in the American colonies to understand the subsequent developments in the British colonies. Shortt[10] points out that two distinct types of local government, both of British origin, had developed in the American colonies, the New England type and the Southern type. The New England colonies had been settled largely by middle class people with a puritanic strain. Characterized by independence of thought, they had developed a vigorous form of local self-government, the central feature of which was the town meeting with its popularly elected local officials and its elected "select men" who had general oversight of town matters. Although such regulations as they enacted were subject to the approval of the Court of Quarter Sessions, in actual practice the inhabitants exercised local self-government.

In the population of the southern colonies "there was a wider range of social and intellectual types," including an aristocratic class as well as middle and lower classes, and "the superior white minority easily secured the right to rule in local as well as in more general matters." In these colonies, of which Virginia was an example, the counterpart of the old English Court of Quarter Sessions, operating on a county basis, administered local affairs and the chief county officers were appointed by the governor. "Inasmuch as the justices of the peace [who composed the Court] were all appointed by the governor-in-council, the local administration of Virginia was very slightly dependent upon the direct will of the people, and in this respect differed radically from the New England type."[11]

Approximately three-quarters of the Loyalists who came to Canada were from the colony of New York where the local institutions and practices were akin to the New England type rather than to the Southern type. Thus, from the beginning local government in Upper Canada was greatly influenced by New England experience.

Upper Canada—Ontario

The influx of English-speaking people into Canada caused many problems. One of the first tasks was to provide for the maintenance of law and order and for the settlement of minor disputes. A number of

[10] *Canada and Its Provinces*, vol. XVIII, p. 405.
[11] *Ibid.*

the ex-officers among the Loyalists in the western settlements were commissioned as magistrates for this purpose and subsequently, by an Ordinance of 1785, they were given limited civil jurisdiction. The Loyalists, who had been accustomed to more extended local autonomy in the colonies from which they had come, continuously petitioned for a system of local self-government in their adopted country. Nor were they content to be subject to the prevailing French civil law or to the system of land tenure provided by the Quebec Act, and as early as 1785 they petitioned the King to constitute the settlement above Montreal a separate district distinct from the Province of Quebec.[12]

Lord Dorchester, in an attempt to provide more adequate administration for the expanded settlements of the west, issued a proclamation on July 24, 1788, dividing the "Upper Country," previously a part of the District of Montreal, into four districts, appointing judges of the Court of Common Pleas, justices of the peace, a sheriff, a clerk for the Court of Common Pleas and of the sessions of the peace, and coroners for each district. The districts, from east to west, were known as Luneburg,[13] Mecklenburg, Nassau, and Hesse;[14] the dividing lines between these districts were north and south lines intersecting respectively the mouth of the Gananoque River, the mouth of the Trent River, and Long Point.[15] By 1800, owing to the expansion of settlement, the districts had been subdivided to provide for four additional districts, Johnstown, Niagara, London, and Newcastle.

The Courts of Quarter Sessions, which were composed of the justices of the peace of each of these districts, had limited legislative and administrative as well as judicial functions. They regulated the matter of domestic animals running at large, the conduct of licensed taverns, the appointment of minor officials, and the laying out and superintending of highways. As the population continued to increase, and the problems demanding local decision multiplied, more and more powers for the management of local affairs were added to the duties of the Court, for so long as there was no alternative provision for local government, the Court remained the only medium by which such matters could be handled. Over the years they were empowered to erect and manage court houses, gaols, and asylums, to lay out and improve highways, to make assessments for and to pay the wages of members of the House of Assembly, to make regulations to prevent accidental fires, to appoint

[12]*The Cambridge History of the British Empire* (Cambridge, 1930), vol. VI, p. 188.

[13]This name is sometimes spelled Lunenburg.

[14]Renamed by 32 Geo III, c. 7 (1792), Eastern, Midland, Home, and Western.

[15]The western limit of the most westerly district was the St. Clair River.

district or township constables, to fix the fees of gaolers, town or parish clerks, and pound keepers, to appoint street and highway surveyors and inspectors of weights and measures, to regulate ferries, to establish and regulate markets in certain towns, to grant certificates to sell liquor, and to permit dissenting clergy to solemnize marriages.[16] These district courts, composed of appointed magistrates, continued to exercise their local government functions, limited somewhat in a few of the towns, until 1841.

In the meantime continuing pressure from the Loyalists as well as others finally resulted in the passing of the Constitutional Act of 1791 which established Upper Canada as a separate province, with English civil law and a freehold system of land tenure. Governor Simcoe, on July 16, 1792, divided the districts into nineteen counties for the purpose of the militia and of electing representatives to the new parliament.[17] This is the first appearance of the county in Upper Canada but at this stage it had no municipal significance. It was not until 1849 that the county succeeded the district as a subdivision for municipal and judicial purposes.

The struggle for local self-government which extended over the next half century was in part explained by a conflict of views and in part by a competition for political power. In general, the governors who were stationed in Canada believed that the unrest in the American colonies, which had culminated in rebellion and independence, was the result of too much democracy, as represented especially in the spirit of the New England town meeting. They considered it their obvious duty to preserve for the Crown what remained of British North America and to restrict severely any radical or democratic tendencies. The Loyalists, on the other hand, accustomed to a considerable degree of local self-rule, wanted to deal with their local problems through their own elected bodies and felt, not without reason, that the sacrifices they had already made were sufficient evidence of their loyalty. They had not abandoned their land and sacrificed wealth and position only to be deprived in their new home of the institutions which they had been allowed previously under British rule.

At the same time the struggle for political power was going on with increasing bitterness between the Family Compact, composed of those holding appointed public office and the social and economic group which they represented, and the popular representatives of the mass of

[16]C. R. W. Biggar, *Municipal Manual* (Toronto, 1900), p. 3.

[17]The counties were named Glengary, Stormont, Dundas, Grenvill, Leeds, Frontenac, Ontario, Addington, Lenox, Prince Edward, Hastings, Northumberland, Durham, York, Lincoln, Norfolk, Suffolk, Essex, and Kent.

the people. The support of the demands for local autonomy by the latter group did little to incline those in power to make any concessions.

The importance which the early settlers attached to the establishment of some local control is indicated by the fact that the first bill introduced in the new provincial Parliament in 1792 was "To authorize town meetings for the purpose of appointing divers parish officers." It is of interest to note that on the same day another bill was introduced "To authorize the justices of the peace to appoint annually divers public officers," indicating the conflict of views as to the basis upon which local governmental authority should be founded. McEvoy, however, in his study of the Ontario township suggests that the demand for some local control was based more on expediency than upon any theoretical idea of the justification for self-government. He argues that municipal institutions developed as wealth increased and they became more necessary to meet a widened concept of the needs which local government should satisfy.[18]

This first bill introduced in the Parliament of Upper Canada did not pass, but in the following session, in 1793, it was enacted as The Parish and Town Officers Act.[19] It is described by Biggar[20] as "The germ of our democratic system of municipal institutions which has now so completely superseded the former oligarchic method of government through nominees of the Crown." By this Act any two justices of the peace[21] could authorize the constable of any parish, township,[22] or place to assemble the inhabitant householders, on the first Monday in March (later changed to the first Monday in January) each year, for the purpose of choosing a clerk, two assessors, a collector, a number of overseers of highways, fence viewers, a pound keeper, and two town wardens. (If there was a parish church with a duly appointed minister, he was to appoint one warden and the town meeting to elect the other. Under these latter conditions they were referred to as church wardens.) If the meeting failed to elect the required town officers they were to be appointed by the justices in sessions. It was the duty of the officials chosen by the meeting to carry out the laws of Parliament. The wardens constituted "a corporation to represent the whole inhabitants of the township or parish," with power to have a property in goods or chattels

[18]J. M. McEvoy, "The Ontario Township," *University of Toronto, Studies in Political Science*, First Series, no. 1, 1889, p. 16,

[19]33 Geo. III, c. 2.

[20]*Municipal Manual*, p. 3.

[21]In 1835, 5 Wm. IV, c. 8, the responsibility for convening the annual town meeting was placed upon the township clerk.

[22]Townships at this date had no municipal significance but were merely areas of land survey.

of or belonging to the parish, and to sue, prosecute, and defend on behalf of the inhabitants.

But the Parish and Town Officers Act of 1793 was far from allowing any real measure of local autonomy. At this time both the basis of assessment and the rates of taxation were determined by Acts of the provincial Parliament, not by local elected officials. Moreover, the officers appointed by the town meetings were responsible only to the justices of the peace or magistrates. In fact, "For years to come the Court of Quarter Sessions remained the only living centre of municipal affairs."[23] The only legislative powers given to the inhabitants' meeting were to determine the height of lawful fences and to decide if, and when, domestic animals should be allowed to run at large or be restrained. These were, of course, matters of serious concern at that period. Yet, "however small might be the authority actually granted, the very fact of their meeting and choosing officers and exercising the meagre powers given them gradually create in a people of strongly democratic tendencies a keen desire and greater ability for self-government. When they met discussion ensued, rules of doing public business were evolved, and men were constantly brought to think of the necessity and the advantage of local administration."[24]

As population increased and villages and towns developed the Quarter Sessions was given further powers to deal with markets, watching, paving, lighting, maintaining streets, the assize of bread, slaughter houses and nuisances, firemen and fire companies, and weights and measures. In time the problems of the urban communities became so pressing that the powers of the magistrates in such centres were transferred, in the thirties, to representative bodies called Boards of Police, elected by vote of the male resident householders.[25] These boards were given extensive powers of legislation dealing with the appointment of town officers, the making of assessments, the purchase of real property for town purposes, the establishment of fire companies, the provision of a water supply, the weighing of hay, and the measuring of wood. More extensive powers were granted to cities and towns which were incorporated as such by special Acts.[26] The municipal government of these incorporated municipalities was vested in a mayor and common coun-

[23]Adam Shortt, "Municipal Government in Ontario," *University of Toronto Studies, History and Economics*, vol. II, no. 2, 1903.

[24]McEvoy, "The Ontario Township," p. 16.

[25]Boards of Police were provided for in Brockville in 1832, Hamilton in 1833, Cornwall, Port Hope, Prescott, and Belleville in 1834, and Cobourg and Picton in 1837.

[26]Toronto, 1834; Kingston, 1838; Cornwall and Hamilton, 1846; Bytown, Dundas, London, and Brantford, 1847.

cil, the mayor being usually, but not always, chosen by and from the council.[27]

Biggar points out that "the contrast thus becoming continually more marked between the measure of local self-government accorded to the urban as compared with the rural elector was one which could not fail to produce in the latter a feeling of profound dissatisfaction—which indeed was not without cause."[28] McEvoy lists some specific causes of this discontent:

. . . a full and careful study of the "orders" of the different District Courts of Quarter Sessions, would do very much to explain and justify the irritation which was so prevalent during the time that these courts exercised their taxing and regulating authority. The Court of Sessions was composed of the magistrates of the District. . . . All the public funds available for the building of roads and bridges . . . were in the hands of these eight or ten men appointed for life by the government. In the matter of roads and bridges they were indifferent and incompetent; they neither knew the needs of the District nor were sufficiently anxious to supply them to make them at all fitted to open up a new country. In the matter of gaols and other public works these courts were invested with large authority. They procured plans and estimates for the building of gaols and court houses of whatever dimensions they deemed fit, erected these buildings and ordered the people to pay the expense thus incurred. Their Worships also ordered what fare the prisoners should get and contracted for the supply of provisions; they ordered what fees the District Officers should receive, they had control of public charity. . . . Besides this large statutory authority, they might venture upon almost any stretch of power; and no one was willing or able to make question of their actions. A body of public officers with such large and unrestricted powers would now be considered . . . somewhat dangerous, even if its members were annually subject to popular election. But the magistrates who exercised these enormous powers in Quarter Sessions were life appointees of the Government, and often had very meagre qualifications for public office. Many of them were old army officers, and most of them men of sufficient income to render them indifferent to the hardships and wants of the average hard working settler.[29]

There was little change in the municipal organization, however, until after the rebellion of 1837, following which Lord Durham was sent to Canada "to be our High Commissioner for the adjustment of certain important questions depending in the said provinces of Lower

[27]Considerable variation existed in this regard. The Kingston city council was composed of elected aldermen and common councilmen who in turn elected a qualified inhabitant as mayor; the Hamilton city council and the Cornwall, Bytown, and Brantford town councils consisted of elected councillors who elected the mayor from among themselves; the Dundas town councillors elected an additional member to the council and then elected one of the total number to be president; the London town council consisted of elected councilmen and an elected mayor.

[28]Biggar, *Municipal Manual*, p. 5.

[29]McEvoy, *"The Ontario Township,"* p. 20.

and Upper Canada respecting the form and future government of the said provinces" and "to enquire into and as far as may be possible to adjust all questions depending in the said Provinces of Lower and Upper Canada, or either of them, respecting the form and administration of the Civil Government thereof respectively."

Lord Durham, in his Report, emphasized the vital importance of establishing a good system of municipal institutions in the provinces. He felt that the management by the legislature of the business of every parish in addition to the common business of the country placed too much power in one single body and that the power of local assessment and the application of the resulting revenues should be entrusted to local management. In discussing local management and the distribution of funds for local purposes he advised that "it would be far better, in point of efficiency and of economy, that this power should be entrusted to municipal bodies of much smaller districts; and the formation of such bodies should, in my opinion, be an essential part of any durable and complete union."[30]

Following the issue of Durham's Report, Charles Poulett Thomson, afterwards Lord Sydenham, was sent to Canada as Governor to prepare the way for the union of Upper and Lower Canada which Durham had recommended and to carry it into effect. The draft of the Act of Union which he prepared and forwarded to England provided for a system of local government. "The establishment of Municipal Government by Act of Parliament," he wrote to the Colonial Secretary, "is as much a part of the future scheme of Government for the Canadas as the Union of the two Legislatures, and the more important of the two."[31] He believed that local government was essential to eliminate "jobbing" in the provincial legislature and that a principle should be laid down, that all purely local expenses be borne by the localities themselves, settled and voted by them, and that only great works be paid for out of the provincial funds. The establishment of municipal institutions in his opinion was important not only for the Canadas but for the effect in the other British North American colonies.[32]

[30]*Lord Durham's Report*, ed. by Sir C. P. Lucas (Oxford, 1912), vol. I, p. 238.

[31]Paul Knaplund, *Letters from Lord Sydenham to Lord John Russell* (London, 1931), p. 75.

[32]"Since I have been in these Provinces I have became more and more satisfied that the capital cause of the misgovernment of them is to be found in the absence of Local Government and the consequent exercise by the Assembly of powers wholly inappropriate to its functions. In both Nova Scotia and New Brunswick I was told that if Parliament laid down a system of Local Government for Canada, then it was likely that in these provinces too the Assembly would adopt it, but without that, it would be impossible to get it done." G. Poulett Scrope, *Life of Lord Sydenham* (London, 1893), p. 202.

However, when the Union Bill was discussed in the British Parliament the clauses concerning municipal affairs were opposed by some members and the Government, rather than endanger the bill, dropped these clauses. In September of 1840, therefore, Sydenham prepared an ordinance providing for municipal institutions in Lower Canada and had it passed by the Special Council administering the government of Lower Canada. In the Speech from the Throne at the opening of the first session of the United Parliament, at Kingston, on June 15, 1841, one of the subjects dealt with was the establishment of municipal institutions for Upper Canada. A bill, essentially the same as the Lower Canada Ordinance, was subsequently introduced by Mr. Harrison, the Provincial Secretary, but was opposed from all sides for divers reasons. Even Mr. Baldwin, whose name is associated with the Municipal Act of 1849, opposed the measure. The story is effectively told by Lord Sydenham in a letter to Lord John Russell dated August 28, 1841:

> The Tories opposed the measure because it gave too much power to the people; the radicals because it imposed checks on that power. And with many members the bill was most unpalatable though they did not like to avow the real motives of their dislike, because it is a death blow to their own jobbing for local purposes. The combination was so strong that on a most important clause in the Committee, that of the nomination of wardens by the Crown, we could only throw out an amendment making them elective by the casting vote of the Chairman; the Tories actually voting for their election by the people, in order to quash the bill . . . there could not have been the slightest chance of getting such a law for the whole Province if it had not already been enacted for Lower Canada.[33]

In spite of the combined opposition, however, the measure passed and the District Councils Act of 1841,[34] "To provide for the better internal government of that part of the Province which formerly constituted the Province of Upper Canada, by the establishment of Local or Municipal Authorities therein," became law. By this Act the inhabitants of each district were constituted a body corporate, its powers to be exercised by a council composed of a warden, appointed by the Governor and holding office at pleasure, and councillors elected by the "Inhabitant Freeholders and Householders" at their annual meeting. Each township was to elect one councillor; a township with more than 300 inhabitant freeholders and householders was entitled to two councillors. The councillors, who were required to be residents of the township they represented and possessed of land within the district, or an

[33]Knaplund, *Letters from Lord Sydenham to Lord John Russell*, p. 162.
[34]4-5 Vict., c. 10.

adjacent district, of a value of £300 over encumbrances, were elected for a three-year term, one-third retiring each year.

The Governor appointed the clerk of the council from a list of three persons submitted by the district council and he held office at the pleasure of the Governor. The district treasurer also was appointed by the Governor and was accountable to the council in matters within its scope and to the justices in other matters. The warden, with the "approbation" of the Governor, appointed the district surveyor but no person was to be so appointed until examined and declared qualified for office by the Provincial Board of Works or other competent persons to be named by the Government. It was the duty of the district surveyor to superintend the execution of all works undertaken by the district council, to take care of the fixed property of the district, to report on all estimates of proposed works, and to report annually to the warden. No public works were to be undertaken without an estimate being made by the district surveyor and if the estimated cost exceeded £300 it was to be reported on by the Provincial Board of Works.

Many of the administrative powers previously exercised by the justices, as well as the assets and liabilities of the district, were transferred to the district councils which were given jurisdiction over roads, bridges, the purchase and sale of district real estate, the defraying of the costs of the administration of justice, the establishment and maintenance of schools, the fixing of its officers' salaries, and the salaries and fees of township officers. The councils could meet their expenses by tolls or taxes on real or personal property or both, but such taxes were limited to two pence on the pound of assessed value. The basis of assessment for taxation was provided by statute.

The district councils were required to meet quarterly, and extraordinary meetings could be called on the order of the Governor. No by-law passed by a council was effective until thirty days after it had been filed with the Provincial Secretary, within which time the Governor, by Order-in-Council, could disallow it.[35] The Act provided that "at no meeting of any such council shall any matter be deliberated or determined on except such matters as fall within the scope of the powers and jurisdiction of such council." The Governor, with the advice and consent of the Executive Council, could dissolve all or any of the district councils.

Although the Municipal Act of 1849, commonly known as the Baldwin Act, is usually considered as the starting point of Ontario's present

[35]This power of disallowance remained in effect until legislation in 1849 provided that illegal municipal by-laws could be quashed by the courts.

system of local government, Biggar's statement that the District Councils Act of 1841 "established the municipal system in Upper Canada," in which he is supported by Sir Francis Hincks,[36] would appear to be more nearly correct. Despite the extent of the power retained in the hands of the Governor under the Act of 1841, the establishment of the district councils, with the powers granted to them, marked a definite break from the long-established system of local government by the justices of the peace and it preceded by almost fifty years the abandonment of this system in England. There was still much to be done. As McEvoy points out, officials such as the warden, clerk, surveyor, and treasurer, whose appointment required approval by the Crown, could exert an important influence at any parliamentary election.

McEvoy suggests that behind these provisions was an honest fear on the part of the provincial authorities "lest the people shall not use their powers even to their own advantage," that they "honestly doubted the people's ability to exercise sufficient discretion in the choice of their officers and the execution of their business."[37] There were, however, other considerations in the mind of the Governor. The Act applying to Upper Canada was, in respect to the appointment of these officers and in most other aspects, identical with the provisions of the Ordinance applying to Lower Canada. Because the people of Lower Canada had not had even the limited experience in handling their own affairs which those of Upper Canada had enjoyed, and because of the uncertainty of conditions in Lower Canada following the rebellion of 1837, the authorities felt it expedient to retain control in this somewhat radical experiment. Considering the personnel of the United Parliament and the opposition of the French Canadian population to the union, it would hardly have been realistic to expect the United Parliament to provide a system for Upper Canada which was less subject to the Governor's control than that which already applied in the other province. Moreover, while there was continuous agitation by councils against the principle of an appointive warden, the quality of the men appointed was high and their permanent tenure of office gave continuity and leadership in the early years of organization. In 1846, however, this source of discontent was removed when legislation was passed providing that thereafter wardens, clerks, treasurers, and surveyors were to be appointed by councils without any necessity for approval by the Governor in Council.[38]

[36]Sir Francis Hincks, *Reminiscences of His Public Life* (Montreal, 1884), p. 64.

[37]McEvoy, "The Ontario Township," p. 24.

[38]9 Vict., c. 40, 1846.

In 1843 Robert Baldwin, then Attorney General, introduced a general municipal Act "to provide for the incorporation of Townships, Towns, Counties and Cities in Upper Canada." The bill passed the Assembly but not the Legislative Council. The subsequent resignation of the Baldwin–La Fontaine Government a fortnight later delayed further action until 1849 when the second Baldwin–La Fontaine Government took office. Baldwin then introduced an Act "to provide by one general law for the erection of Municipal Corporations and the establishment of Regulations of Police, in and for the several Counties, Cities, Towns, Townships and Villages in Upper Canada."[39] This Act, which is known as the Baldwin Act, established the framework of the municipal system as it exists in Ontario, although in the intervening years numerous amendments have been made to meet changing conditions. At the same session the districts were abolished and the counties became territorial divisions of the province for municipal as well as judicial purposes.

A continuous and sometimes bitter agitation extending from 1793 to 1849 had thus evolved a uniform plan of municipal system for rural and urban communities. Within the scope allowed, and the scope was extensive, the municipalities had gained the right to local self-government with a minimum of parliamentary or executive control, the elected representatives being answerable in matters of policy to their electors and in matters of law to the courts. "Never," wrote Biggar,[40] "had the principle of local self-government been more fully carried out than in the Act of 1849." And he adds: ". . . the Baldwin Act and its lineal descendants have in their turn become the progenitors and paradigms of the Municipal Institutions Acts in force today in nearly every Province of the Dominion." That the plan was soundly conceived is evidenced by the fact that the system established in 1849 has sustained the strains of a rapidly changing economy for over one hundred years without substantial alteration in its basic features.

Lower Canada–Quebec

During the period from 1791 until the rebellion in 1837 local administration in Lower Canada continued to function much as it had done under the old French régime. The people had no power to assess themselves for local improvements and when a road or a bridge was needed they had to appeal to the legislature. The legislature, as a result, was preoccupied with a vast number of minor matters of local concern.

[39]12 Vict., c. 81. This Act came into effect January 1, 1850.
[40]Biggar, *Municipal Manual*, p. 9.

To the French-Canadian inhabitants of the rural areas such things as municipal institutions were unknown and they never complained of their lack. But it is surprising that the considerable number of Loyalists who came to Lower Canada from colonies accustomed to local government should have been content without it. According to Bourinot, however,

They appear to have quietly acquiesced in a state of things calculated to repress a spirit of local enterprise and diminish the influence of the people in the administration of public affairs. Indeed we have some evidence that the government itself was prepared for many years to discourage every attempt to introduce into Canada anything like the local system that had so long existed in New England. British statesmen probably remembered the strong influence that the town meetings of Boston had in encouraging a spirit of rebellion, and thought it advisable to stifle at the outset any aspirations that the Canadian colonists might have in the direction of such doubtful institutions. "I understand," wrote Mr. Richards in a report to the Secretary of State for the colonies, "that the Vermonters had crossed the line and had partially occupied several townships, bringing with them their municipal institutions; and that when the impropriety of electing their own officers was pointed out to them, they had quietly given them up and promised to conform to those of Canada."[41]

During this period, however, there did develop a demand for some adequate form of local administration and in 1830 the Assembly in Quebec "called attention to the deplorable conditions resulting from the lack of municipal institutions."[42] The need was urgent in the growing urban centres and in 1827 both Quebec and Montreal had urged the legislature to grant them charters of incorporation. Such charters were granted in 1832 for a period of four years but, owing to the unsettled political conditions, they were not renewed in 1836, nor were they restored until 1840.

Durham in his Report drew particular attention to the plight of these cities:

. . . the want of municipal institutions has been and is the most glaringly remarkable in Quebec and Montreal. These cities were incorporated a few years ago by a temporary provincial Act; of which the renewal was rejected in 1836. Since that time these cities have been without any municipal government; and the disgraceful state of the streets, and the utter absence of lighting, are consequences which arrest the attention of all, and seriously affect the comfort and security of the inhabitants.[43]

[41]Bourinot, *Local Government in Canada*, p. 26.
[42]Carl Wittke, *History of Canada* (Toronto, 1941), p. 96.
[43]*Lord Durham's Report*, p. 81.

And again, speaking of the Lower Province in general:

> . . . there is hardly a semblance of direct taxation in Lower Canada for general or local purposes. This immunity from taxation had been sometimes spoken of as a great privilege of the people of Lower Canada, and a great proof of the justice and benevolence of their government. The description which I have given of the singularly defective provision made for the discharge of the most important duties of both the general, and local government will, I think, make it appear that this apparent saving of the pockets of the people has been caused by their privation of many of the institutions which every civilized community ought to possess. A people can hardly be congratulated on having had at little cost a rude and imperfect administration of justice, hardly the semblance of police, no public provision for education, no lighting, and bad pavements in its cities, and means of communication so imperfect, that the loss of time and wear and tear caused in taking any article to market, may probably be estimated at ten times the expense of good roads.[44]

Lord Sydenham, as we have seen, fully agreed with Durham on the need for municipal government. Acting under Sydenham's direction, the Special Council which governed Lower Canada after the rebellion passed on December 29, 1840, an ordinance[45] providing for local government institutions. These were in all important respects the same as were provided for Upper Canada by the District Councils Act of 1841, already described. The ordinance divided Lower Canada into districts to be governed in local affairs by an appointed warden and elected councillors. Another ordinance[46] provided that in Lower Canada, on the warrant of the warden of the district, the inhabitant householders of the parishes and townships should be assembled annually to elect a clerk, three assessors who were to assess rates and taxes imposed by the legislature or other competent authority, a collector, a surveyor and overseer of highways, overseers of the poor, fence viewers, drain inspectors, and pound keepers. Parishes and townships with over 300 inhabitants were constituted corporate bodies, their powers to be exercised by the inhabitants at their annual meeting or at a special meeting convened under the authority of the Governor.

These measures were not popular in Lower Canada for several reasons. The ordinances gave the district councils power to levy taxes to provide for their operations, and taxes, other than customs duties, had been unknown for many years in Lower Canada. The fact that the provisions for local councils had been instituted by the Special Council in the post-rebellion period made the people suspicious of the motives

[44] *Ibid*, p. 102.
[45] 4 Vict., c. 4, Provincial Ordinances of Lower Canada.
[46] 4 Vict., c. 3, Provincial Ordinances of Lower Canada.

behind these innovations. Their popularity was not increased by the fact that they came at a time when Upper and Lower Canada were being united for the admitted purpose of offsetting French Canadian influence. Consequently the effective operation of the ordinances was nullified by the resistance of the people whom they were designed to serve.

Both ordinances were repealed, therefore, effective July 1, 1845.[47] The preamble of the repealing Act reads in part: "Whereas experience hath demonstrated that the ordinances hereinafter mentioned, are not and cannot be adapted to the present state of Lower Canada. . . ." The district councils were eliminated and the inhabitants of every parish or township, much smaller areas, were constituted as corporate bodies, their powers to be exercised by a parish or township council of seven councillors elected by the qualified inhabitants at an annual meeting on the second Monday in July. The councillors, elected for a three-year term, chose from among themselves a chairman or mayor. The council were to hold meetings quarterly, more often if necessary. They appointed officers, such as the secretary-treasurer, assessors, collectors, and road overseers and had the power to raise money by taxation up to a limit of three pence on the pound. The inhabitants of an area having the requisite population could petition the council to create villages and towns which were to have a government similar to that of the parish or township but with somewhat wider powers. Where undertakings required joint action by two or more parishes or townships, each council appointed two delegates who, with the delegates from the other councils concerned, decided the matters at issue; their decisions were binding on all the councils.

The Act of 1845 was to apply for two years and thence to the end of the next ensuing session of the provincial Parliament. By 1847 it was "deemed expedient to abolish parish and township municipalities . . . and substitute county municipalities in their stead."[48] The Act of that year repealed the previous legislation, and incorporated the inhabitants of every county or portion of a county (some eight counties were subdivided for this purpose), forty-six in all, with a county council composed of two councillors from each parish or township, elected for a term of two years at an annual meeting of the qualified inhabitants. If the meeting failed to elect councillors the Governor in Council could do so. These councils, from their own number, elected a chairman or mayor and appointed the necessary officers, who were to hold office for

[47] 8 Vict., c. 40, Provincial Statutes, Canada.
[48] 10 Vict., c. 7, Provincial Statutes, Canada.

two years. They had the power to raise money by taxation up to six pence on the pound on the annual value of property, which was to be taken as 6 per cent of the rental value. These county councils had the same power to create towns and villages as was previously exercised by the parish or township councils, and the village or town councils so created were to be composed, as previously, of seven councillors elected for a two-year term by the qualified inhabitants at their annual general meeting.

The system was again changed, this time to its present form, by the Lower Canada Municipal and Road Act, 1855,[49] which provided for incorporation of parishes, townships, towns, and villages with councils composed of seven councillors elected at an annual meeting of the qualified inhabitants. The mayor was elected by the councillors from their own number. The mayors of these local municipalities comprised the county council and they elected one of the mayors to be warden of the county. Both local and county municipalities could appoint necessary officers and levy taxes. There have been numerous amendments since that time but the basic framework of the system then established is still in effect.

The development of municipal institutions in Lower Canada was hindered by the lack of any popular demand for local self-government, particularly in the rural areas, by the lack of experience on the part of the inhabitants in the practice of local government, and by a suspicion of any innovation of the English minority. The tension existing between French and English was intensified following the events of 1837 just at the time when the demand for municipal institutions in Upper Canada made it expedient to make similar provision in Lower Canada. These factors, in part, explain the frequent changes in the system which were necessary to arrive at a form acceptable to the people and, as experience has demonstrated, suitable to the conditions of Lower Canada.

The Maritime Provinces

Nova Scotia

Governor Cornwallis, soon after his arrival in Nova Scotia in 1749, had issued commissions of the peace to the more influential settlers and by 1765 such commissions were general throughout the settled portions of the province.[50] In 1759 the province was divided for administrative purposes into five counties, Annapolis, Kings, Cumberland, Lunen-

[49] 17-18 Vict., c. 100, Provincial Statutes, Canada.

[50] Prior to the influx of the Loyalists the population of Nova Scotia was very small, approximately 13,000 in 1767; almost three times that number arrived from the United States in 1782 and 1783.

burg, and Halifax. Some of the first New Englanders to settle in the Maritimes came from Connecticut, Rhode Island, and Massachusetts to the Annapolis Valley in 1760 and later, taking up land from which the Acadian French had been expelled. They were accustomed to elect their own officers and manage their own affairs and, having been promised the privilege of local self-government, they started to do so again. The government at Halifax, however, did not favour the establishment of independent townships on the New England model and in 1765 the Council in Halifax confirmed the system of government by Sessions, which was already in existence, by an Act which fixed the form of local government in Nova Scotia and New Brunswick for over a century.[51] In spite of this legislation, however, the settlers persisted in dealing with their own problems and in 1770 the Governor in Council passed a resolution to the effect that "the proceedings of the people in calling town meetings for discussing questions relative to law and government and such other purposes are contrary to law, and if persisted in, it is ordered that the parties be prosecuted by the attorney-general."

Even with respect to the larger urban centres there was reluctance to grant the right of running their own affairs, for although the provincial Assembly had, in 1790, requested the Lieutenant-Governor to grant a charter to the town of Halifax, it was not until 1841 that it was incorporated. The business of local finance and police in both counties and towns was caried out "through the clumsy machinery of the grand jury and sessions"[52] until 1879. The magistrates met in General Sessions of the Peace in each county annually, semi-annually, or, as in Halifax, four times a year. The grand jury attended at the sessions and in some matters the "Sessions" could only function on the jury's recommendation. Until 1865 the county grand juries appointed the town officers but a statute then enacted provided that the grand jury should only nominate such officers and the appointment should be by the Court of General Sessions of the Peace.

Under an Act of 1859 any county could obtain municipal government if one hundred freeholders so petitioned the sheriff, but no incorporations took place under this Act. In 1879,[53] however, the inhabitants of each county or district into which the province was divided were created a body corporate for purposes of municipal government. This latter Act might be said to be the origin of the existing municipal system. The government of these counties and districts was to be by a council composed of councillors elected by the people and a warden

[51] *New Brunswick Municipal Monthly*, vol. IV, no. 5.
[52] *Canada and Its Provinces*, vol. XIV, p. 478.
[53] 42 Vict., c. 1.

chosen by the council. Although individual towns had previously secured incorporation by special legislation it was not until The Towns' Incorporation Act of 1888 that machinery was provided whereby the ratepayers of any town could, by a vote, obtain incorporation as a town.

New Brunswick

Following the arrival of large numbers of Loyalists into Nova Scotia in 1782 and 1783, and as a result of demands of those who settled in the St. John River valley, New Brunswick was established as a separate colony distinct from Nova Scotia in 1784. As in the other Maritime Provinces, the municipal development in New Brunswick was slow until the present century, although Saint John was incorporated as a city in 1785, almost fifty years before any other city in what is now the Dominion of Canada.

The early local administration was divided between the justices of the peace in Quarter Sessions and the legislature. The justices in sessions made their decisions assisted by a grand jury. The functions of the jury, which represented the people, were to submit a statement of the expenses for the support of the poor, the maintenance of the jail, and payment of local officials and to present the names of persons for every office to which appointments were to be made by the Court of Sessions. The jury could also present petitions, but it was the justices who had the executive power.[54] Not until 1851 was there provision for establishing municipal institutions and this legislation was merely permissive. Under this provision Carleton County was incorporated in 1852, and York County and the town of Woodstock in 1856, but there was no further action until 1875 when the counties of Northumberland and Gloucester and the town of Moncton were incorporated. The Municipalities Act of 1877 established a municipal system in every county by a general law. Similar legislation in 1896[55] provided a uniform system of establishing towns.

The development of local self-government in Nova Scotia and New Brunswick has been a more recent development than in the two central provinces which are comparable in time of settlement. The people of the local communities in what is now Ontario persistently agitated for local control; on the other hand it was accepted at first with reluctance in Quebec. But the general attitude in the more easterly provinces in earlier years appears to have been one of indifference. One historian

[54]*New Brunswick Municipal Monthly*, vol. IV, no. 5.
[55]59 Vict., c. 44, 1896.

has commented: "That New Brunswick should have been so dilatory in the adoption of the municipal system may have been partly due to the desire of the magistrates to retain the honour and dignity of presiding over public affairs at the Quarter Sessions. Many of these gentlemen were men of probity and ability though rather antiquated in their ideas of civic administration and jealous of innovation. But the chief reasons why the province was tardy seem to have been the apathy of the people and the indifference of the legislature. It was not the fault of the Lieutenant-Governors, since several of them recommended the establishment of municipal government."[56] The indifference may have been due, in part, to the place of origin of the Loyalists who settled in the eastern provinces. To a much greater extent than in Upper Canada, the Loyalist group was made up of those from the southerly American colonies where they had been accustomed to local government by Quarter Sessions. Distance and the difficulties of overland travel barred the southern colonists from Upper Canada; as their exodus had to be by sea, the Maritime Provinces were their logical destination.

Two other factors which may have had an influence in retarding the development of local government institutions in the Maritimes were the greater compactness of the areas involved, which increased the possibilities of retaining centralized control even with communications and transportation as they then existed, and the fact that the provision of roads was not so pressing a problem in provinces where water borne transportation helped to solve what was for many years the major problem of the communities in the more westerly provinces.

Prince Edward Island

The province of Prince Edward Island, originally named St. John's Island, formed a part of Nova Scotia until 1769. In 1767 it was laid out into counties, parishes, and townships but these subdivisions were only used for judicial purposes and as the basis for representation in the legislature.

Charlottetown and Summerside were incorporated as municipalities in 1855 and 1875 respectively, but no general system of local government covering the whole of the territory in the Island has ever been established. An Act of 1870 provided that the residents of any town or village might petition the Lieutenant-Governor in Council for incorporation but only a few have done so, there being but eight incorporated municipalities in the province. In 1948 a general Towns Act

[56]*Canada and Its Provinces*, vol. XIV, p. 425.

was passed which provides local government for all the towns except Summerside and in 1950 the Village Service Act provided general legislation for the creation of municipal government in villages.

The provincial legislature continues to function for most local purposes for the greater part of the province. This is feasible in view of the limited territory and population; there are but 98,429 persons in a total area of 2,184 square miles, an area approximately equal to Halifax County in Nova Scotia or somewhat more than twice the area of the average Alberta municipal district. Local boards of school trustees, elected by the school ratepayers, however, have power to levy taxes for school purposes. Except in Charlottetown and the incorporated towns, these school boards are also the local boards of health for their respective school districts.

Newfoundland

St. John's was created a town in 1888 but it was not until 1938 that any further municipalities were formed. According to Powell,[57] the attitude of the people of Newfoundland toward municipal government has been founded on the firm conviction that the provincial government is responsible for local services and an almost fanatical dread of real property taxes.

The belief that the province should provide these services results from the fact that Newfoundland governments of the past have assumed full responsibility for them because there was no local government. The dread of property taxes is associated with Newfoundland's history. The policy of Great Britain for many years was opposition to permanent settlement on the island and it was only after a long and bitter struggle that the right to own real property was conceded in 1824. The ownership of land was essential in order to have a base of operation for fishing, the main occupation of the settlers; their livelihood thus depended on retaining their property. Municipal government would mean property taxes and with property taxation was associated the spectre of losing property through inability to meet the taxes. Consequently the people of Newfoundland were not merely indifferent to municipal institutions, they were definitely hostile.

The Local Government Act of 1933 permitted the incorporation of municipalities by proclamation and the Local Administration Act of 1937 authorized the creation of municipalities by order of the Governor in Commission. However, no municipalities were compelled to incor-

[57]C. W. Powell, "Problems Arising from Lack of Organized Municipalities in Newfoundland," *Proceedings of the First Annual Conference of the Institute of Public Administration of Canada*, 1949, p. 171.

porate under either Act and none requested incorporation. As an inducement to action by communities, the government instituted a policy of offering substantial general subsidies to those which incorporated but there was still no response.

A policy was next adopted of providing by special Act for any town desiring to incorporate; such Acts would provide for whatever form of taxation was preferred in each case. As a result one town was incorporated in each of the years 1938, 1942, and 1943. Subsequently a programme of publicity explaining the government's policy of financial assistance to muncipalities brought increased response and by 1948 twenty municipalities had been created, only five of which impose real property taxes. At its first session after Confederation the legislature, in 1949, passed a general Act to provide for the establishment and administration of local government under which the Lieutenant-Governor in Council may declare any area in the province, outside the city of St. John's, to be a municipality. This Act provides for the formation of municipal councils and determines their powers.

The Western Provinces

Manitoba

The territory which now forms the province of Manitoba was originally part of Rupert's land, granted in 1670 by royal charter to the Hudson's Bay Company. The Company in 1811 granted to Lord Selkirk the territory described as the District of Assiniboia in which the Red River colony was established in 1812. Subsequently, in 1836, the Company bought back Assiniboia and thereafter, except within the limits of the Red River colony, the Company exercised full judicial, legislative, and administrative authority.

The colony's affairs were managed by a council, known as the Council of Assiniboia, which had been constituted in 1835 with the consent of the Company. The council members were appointed by the Company's Governor in the colony. However, as the members were not representative of the interests of the people but rather of the Company there were, from the first, continuous demands by the settlers for the right to elect the members of the council. Pursuant to resolutions of the Dominion Parliament in 1867, the Company's rights were bought out in 1869, after which Rupert's Land and the Northwest Territories became part of the Dominion of Canada. The new province of Manitoba was created by the Manitoba Act of 1870.

Although the population of Manitoba in 1871 was only 12,000 in an area of 13,000 square miles, the first legislature was confronted with the necessity of providing for local organization. At its first session it passed a County Assessment Act and a Parish Assessment Act. The first of these Acts provided for the annual preparation of a general tax roll for the province by a meeting of the county assessors. The grand jury, at the Court of Sessions at Fort Garry, prepared a statement of the money required in the various districts for roads and bridges, etc. and the clerk of the peace, a court officer, apportioned this amount among the taxpayers on the basis of the general tax roll, the collection being left to the constables. Purely local improvements were provided for by the Parish Assessment Act under which the heads of families in the parishes in each of the five counties decided at a public meeting what work needed to be done and, pursuant to their resolutions, the clerk of the peace assessed the amounts required against the inhabitants of the parish.

The first general municipal Act, in 1873, provided that on petition of two-thirds of the male freeholders any district with not less than thirty freeholders could secure the issue of letters patent constituting a local municipality with power to raise revenue by taxation up to the amount of one per cent of the value of the real estate. In 1881 the municipalities were made responsible for the roads within their boundaries.

A municipal system based on that in Ontario was introduced in 1883. The province was divided into twenty-six counties, each with a county council. The counties were composed of local municipalities, which varied in number from one to eleven, including both rural municipalities and incorporated towns and cities. The county councils were composed of the reeves and mayors of these local municipalities but where the county council would have less than five members, additional representatives were appointed by the local councils from their own membership on a basis determined by the statute. The county councillors elected the warden from among themselves. The counties were grouped into three judicial districts and the court house and gaol costs for the district were allocated to the various municipalities by a board composed of the county wardens and the mayors of the incorporated cities and towns.

This county system, which had been found satisfactory in Ontario, proved "expensive and inefficient" and unsuited to conditions in Manitoba. The people objected to the double council or two-tier system, and it was difficult to get a quorum at county council meetings on account of the distances members had to travel. After three years' experience the county basis of local government was abandoned; the province was divided into smaller areas called "rural municipalities," the judicial districts boards were abolished, and their functions were transferred to the Attorney General's Department.

An Act passed in 1902 established the system which exists today, providing by general legislation for the incorporation of every city, town, village, or rural municipality. The city of Winnipeg, however, was provided for by a special charter in the same year.

Saskatchewan and Alberta

The territory which now forms the provinces of Saskatchewan and Alberta was part of the domain of the Hudson's Bay Company until it was purchased by the Dominion of Canada in 1869, and from that date until the two provinces were created, September 1, 1905, it formed part of the North West Territories.

The North West Territories Act of 1875[58] provided that the Territories were to be governed by ordinances of the Lieutenant-Governor and an appointed council of five members. Among the Council's powers was that of framing ordinances for establishing municipalities with full power of taxation for local purposes. Municipal affairs were administered by the territorial Department of Public Works. As the population increased, the settlers, many of whom came from Nova Scotia and Ontario, pressed for municipal government to which they were accustomed and also for some voice in the North West Territories Council. The Dominion government eventually conceded elective representation on the Council and the members so elected continued to urge the need for municipal self-government.

In 1883 the Council passed an ordinance providing for the creation of both rural and urban municipalities and established a Committee on Municipal Affairs to consider applications for municipal incorporation. Two rural municipalities, Indian Head and South Qu'Appelle, and the town of Regina were established under this ordinance. The next year a new municipal ordinance was adopted and two more rural municipalities, Wolseley and Qu'Appelle,[59] and the town of Moosejaw were created.

The provisions for municipal organization, however, did not prove popular in practice. To quote one authority, "it was soon found that this Ordinance provided for a system of local government for the rural areas which was too elaborate and too expensive for the stage of the country's development and no additional municipalities were

[58]This Act took effect October 7, 1876.

[59]These two municipalities were disorganized and ceased to function January 1, 1898.

organized."[60] Black points out that it was "another attempt to transplant Ontario institutions, at least in part, into a more sparsely settled territory where local conditions differed greatly from those in older Canada."[61]

Although experience had demonstrated that the system of local government provided for the rural areas was unsuitable, "the government recognized the necessity for some form of local organization to provide road improvement and to effect certain protective measures against the spread of prairie and forest fires."[62] Accordingly, an ordinance of 1887 provided for the establishment of "statute labour and fire districts" in areas not organized as rural municipalities. The affairs of these districts were in the charge of an overseer elected by the resident owners or occupants of land. The overseer was responsible for road improvements and in the early days was practically the entire local administration. Only 57 of these districts had been organized by 1896, at which time their organization was made compulsory. As a result, 181 were established in 1897 and 178 in 1898. In this latter year the name of the districts was changed to "local improvement districts."

After a prolonged struggle the people of the North West Territories in 1897 finally won from the Dominion the right of responsible government, a freely elected Assembly, and a responsible cabinet. The Assembly's provision for local jurisdiction consisted of elective committees to administer the local improvement districts. In 1903 the 304 local improvement districts, which until then had been one-township units,[63] were reorganized into four-township units. The residents of each township elected one councillor and these four councillors, who constituted the municipal district council, chose a chairman from among themselves.

In 1904 the Assembly provided funds for a study of the whole question of the organization, administration, and financing of municipal units in the area under its jurisdiction. Meanwhile, continuous immigration had increased the population in the prairie areas and in the same year the Dominion provided for the creation of two new provinces, Saskatchewan and Alberta, to take effect September 1,

[60]F. W. Pohlman, "Functions of Rural Municipal Government," *Western Municipal News*, vol. 41, No. 4, p. 101.

[61]N. F. Black, *History of Saskatchewan and the Old North West* (Regina, 1913), p. 237.

[62]Department of Municipal Affairs, *The Municipal System of Saskatchewan* (Regina, 1947), p. 19.

[63]In the Prairie Provinces a township is a land survey area, normally six miles square, and is not a municipal unit.

1905. Thus, the two provinces came into existence before the study of the municipal problem was completed.

Saskatchewan. The province of Saskatchewan in 1906 appointed a Commission to complete the study instituted in 1904. This Commission recommended the immediate establishment of a system of municipal institutions in the province comprising cities, towns, villages, and rural municipalities, and separate Acts for each class of municipality. The City Act, the Town Act, and the Village Act were enacted in 1908 and The Rural Municipalities Act in the following year. The Municipal Commissioners Act of 1908 created a government department under a Minister of the Crown to exercise general supervision over municipalities. This department, which came into being November 1, 1908, was the first provincial department established to deal with municipal matters.

At that date there were 4 cities, 43 towns, 97 villages, 2 rural municipalities, and 359 local improvement districts in the province. The local improvement districts were reorganized in 1909, and provision was made for erecting the districts into rural municipalities when conditions warranted. By 1912 the number of rural municipalities, which normally contained nine townships, had increased to 200 and the local improvement districts had been reduced to 90. Legislation in 1912 provided that, effective January 1, 1913, all local improvement districts having local organization would become rural municipalities.

Alberta. When Alberta was formed there were 47 organized municipalities within its area—2 cities, 15 towns, 30 villages[64]—and 72 local improvement districts. In 1912 a Minister of Municipal Affairs was appointed and a comprehensive system of municipal government was established. The rural portion of the province was divided into local improvement districts, each including approximately nine of the former townships. As these were six miles square, the district comprised an area of 324 square miles. These districts could be erected into "rural municipalities" (later called "municipal districts") when the population amounted to 324. The rural municipalities had their own elected councils but the local improvement districts were to be administered by the province. The existing cities, towns, and villages were confirmed and provision was made for creating new ones, subject to compliance with minimum qualifications. The cities, towns, and villages, however, did not form part

[64]J. W. Judge, "Some Aspects of Local Government in Alberta," *Municipal Finance,* vol. XXIV, no. 2 (Nov. 1951).

of the municipal districts for municipal purposes. The system thus established is essentially the system prevailing today although the province in 1942 adopted a policy of enlarging the municipal districts by amalgamation, reducing the total number from 133 in 1942 to 60 in 1944.

British Columbia

The development of municipal institutions in British Columbia has been more affected by the physical characteristics of the area than has been the case in any of the other provinces, except perhaps Newfoundland. As a great part of the province is mountainous, the early settlements were isolated from one another, large areas were very sparsely settled, and what local administration there was in the pre-Confederation period was handled by government agents who had to be allowed considerable discretion owing to the difficulties of communication.

The first municipalities, such as New Westminster (1860) and Victoria (1862), were incorporated under the provisions of "An Ordinance for the Formation and Regulation of Municipalities in British Columbia" applicable to the colony. This ordinance was supplanted in 1872 by an Act of the new provincial legislature respecting municipalities. Some nine additional municipalities were incorporated prior to the passing of The Municipal Clauses Act of 1892. This latter Act, which provided for an adaptation of the Ontario municipal system to the special conditions of British Columbia, was the forerunner of the existing municipal legislation.

In Manitoba and in the provinces farther west, there was no prolonged struggle over the right of the inhabitants to the powers of self-government. By the time the "West" was settled that issue had long been conceded and the settlers who went west from other portions of Canada assumed municipal institutions to be a natural part of community organization. This lack of a struggle between the provincial authorities and the local communities over self-government is reflected in the greater willingness of the municipalities in these provinces to accept provincial control than is the case in some of the central and eastern provinces. This may in part also be explained by the large numbers of people who came to the Prairie Provinces from European countries where they had not been accustomed to local self-government. The main problem in the development of local institutions in the western provinces was to devise the system which would give the best results under their special conditions. It was natural in the early stages to copy the Ontario system, for not only was it the nearest established system in Canada but great numbers of the early settlers came from Ontario and they assumed that the type of institutions they were accustomed to would be satisfactory. When experience proved that different conditions required different institutions, they adjusted the system to the special provincial needs.

Because community development in the western provinces came later in time than in the east, the generally accepted standards of community plant and service were higher and the demands upon government were most pressing in the early years of growth. Their problems were accentuated by the rapid expansion which forced local authorities to rely more upon provincial assistance than was the case in the more gradually developed eastern provinces. The general attitude of the provincial authorities in British Columbia toward the municipalities has been expressed as "a certain leniency toward them . . . in an earnest effort to stimulate their growth and to keep them solvent." There has been a greater tendency in the West for the province to assume responsibility for community services of various kinds than has been the case in the more easterly provinces.

CHAPTER III

LOCAL GOVERNMENTS

MUNICIPAL CORPORATIONS

THE LAW and the courts which administer the law recognize two types of persons, natural persons and artificial or corporate persons.[1] These latter are legal inventions created to enable groups of persons to carry on certain activities with a legal status as a group, and not as a number of separate individuals. Some of the characteristics common to these corporate bodies are a perpetual existence which does not terminate with the death of the individual members, the right to sue and be sued, the right to enter into contracts, and the possession of a seal. Corporate bodies are possessed of many additional powers which vary from one corporation to another according to the purposes for which they are created. The right to hold property is an example of such a power which is possessed by many corporations, but not by all.

All corporate bodies are the creations of some superior body which has the power to increase or decrease their powers or terminate their existence at will, and it is characteristic that their privileges and powers are defined by some written instrument. As with natural persons, an artificial person or corporation is limited in its capacity to the powers with which its creator has endowed it. These corporate powers are set out in words in some document, and it is important to remember that the legal competence of a corporation to act is limited to the powers given in its charter or other source of incorporation and conversely that powers which are not so expressly granted are beyond its legal capacity.

Corporate bodies are of many kinds. There are business corporations, such as the Canadian Pacific Railway Company or the T. Eaton Company, Limited, educational corporations, such as Queen's University,

[1]A corporation has been defined as follows: "A corporation or a body politic or body incorporate is a collection of many individuals united into one body under a special denomination, having perpetual succession under an artificial form, and vested by the policy of the law with the capacity of acting in several respects as an individual, particularly of taking and granting property, of contracting obligations, and of suing and being sued, of enjoying privileges and immunities in common, and of exercising a variety of political rights more or less extensive, according to the design of its institution or of the powers conferred upon it, either at the time of its creation or at any subsequent period of its existence."

and religious corporations, such as the United Church of Canada, and many others. Among this great variety is a class or type known as municipal corporations.

Most units of local government are corporate bodies. This device enables groups of persons to join together for the purposes of local government and to obtain the results desired through one medium, rather than by the sum total of their individual efforts and responsibilities. It has, moreover, the added advantage that as a corporation they may be endowed with additional powers which as individuals they would not possess. The origin of the municipal corporation is attributed to the Romans and it is the form of local government usually found today in England, in parts of Europe, throughout the British dominions, and in the United States of America.

A municipal corporation has been defined as "a body corporate constituted by the incorporation of the inhabitants, residing within a defined area upon whom the Legislature has, either directly or through some intermediate agency, conferred corporate status, rights and liabilities, including the right to administer through the agency of an elected council or other governing body such matters of local concern as are either expressly specified, or as are necessarily implied from the nature and extent of the authority conferred."[2] Canadian municipal corporations are composed of the inhabitants in the area comprising the municipality.[3] The body corporate under English law, however, is always a legal entity separate and distinct from the members composing it.

The powers which these municipal corporations have received from the authority which created them are not exercised by the inhabitants who constitute the members of the corporation, but by a council elected by that portion of the members who comprise the electorate. Thus, councils correspond in some respects to the elected boards of directors of other types of corporations.

The Source of Municipal Powers

The written basis of the Canadian constitution is The British North America Act, passed by the British Parliament on March 29, 1867, which took effect on July 1, 1867, as proclaimed by Her Majesty Queen Victoria. This Act, to which there have since been several amendments, provided, among other things, for the form of govern-

[2]*Canadian Encyclopaedic Digest* (Toronto, 1931), p. 682.

[3]Exceptions are the New Brunswick county where the ratepayers form the corporation and Alberta municipalities where it is comprised of the head of the council, the councillors, and the electors.

ment of the Dominion and of the four original provinces of Ontario, Quebec, Nova Scotia, and New Brunswick. It set out in detail the distribution of the legislative powers to be exercised by the Dominion and the various provinces.

Section 92 of the Act provided that the legislature of each province might exclusively make laws in relation to the matters coming within the classes of certain enumerated subjects. Five of these classes of subjects assigned to the legislatures of the provinces which are pertinent to a study of local government are as follows:

2. Direct Taxation within the Province in order to the Raising of a Revenue for Provincial Purposes.
7. The Establishment, Maintenance, and Management of Hospitals, Asylums, Charities, and Eleemosynary Institutions in and for the Provinces, other than Marine Hospitals.
8. Municipal Institutions in the Province.
9. Shop, Saloon, Tavern, Auctioneer, and other Licenses in order to the Raising of a Revenue for Provincial, Local or Municipal Purposes.
16. Generally all Matters of a merely local or private Nature in the Province.

Section 93 dealt with the matter of education which was also to be exclusively within the domain of the provinces, subject to certain provisions with respect to denominational schools.

Because the Act provided that the power to make laws respecting these matters was assigned exclusively to the provinces, legislation relating to municipal institutions is enacted by provincial legislatures only and not by the Dominion Parliament. The Canadian system is similar in this respect to that of the United States where local government comes under the jurisdiction of the states.[4] This is in contrast to the English system where, because there is a unitary and not a federal form of government, the omnipotent national Parliament enacts all legislation relating to local government.

Exercising their powers under the provisions of section 92, the ten provinces have enacted legislation to provide for the establishment of municipal institutions.[5] These institutions are not limited to what are usually referred to as municipalities (cities, towns, villages, counties, and rural municipalities) or municipal corporations, but include other municipal bodies such as school boards, health boards, and utility com-

[4]In the United States, however, this is not because the constitution so specifies but because it comes within the residue of powers not specifically assigned to the federal government.

[5]Previous to becoming part of the Dominion of Canada on April 1, 1949, the situation in Newfoundland was similar to that in England but is now the same as in the other provinces.

missions, some of which are corporate bodies and some of which are not, according to the provisions of the legislation which provides for their creation.

Extent of Municipal Powers

To what extent can a provincial legislature confer powers upon the municipal corporations and other municipal bodies which it creates? Both the extent and nature of the powers which the legislature can commit to a municipal body of its own creation depend upon the legislative authority which it possesses under the provisions of section 92. In other words, the provincial legislatures, in granting power to municipal bodies, are limited to those matters assigned to them by The British North America Act. Thus, they could not grant to a municipal corporation power to establish a bank or to issue money, for these are matters which, under the Act, are exclusively reserved to the Dominion Parliament.

In England no such limitations exist, for Parliament is all-powerful and subject to no restriction upon its power to legislate. In the United States, on the other hand, state legislatures are frequently restricted in municipal matters by the constitutional rights of the citizen under the national constitution and also by limitations imposed on the powers of the legislatures in some states by the state constitution. In Canada, however, the legal doctrine is that a province "having created the municipality is able to confer upon that body any or every power which the Province itself possesses under the Confederation Act."[6]

Each province has divided all or a portion of its territory into geographical areas, referred to generally as municipalities and more particularly as counties, cities, towns, villages, townships, rural municipalities, or municipal districts; has provided that the inhabitants of these municipalities shall be incorporated, and that the powers of such corporations are to be exercised by elected councils. The legislatures have also assigned to the various classes of municipalities the powers and responsibilities which they feel such municipalities should possess.

Provincial Legislation Respecting Municipalities

A variety of methods of legislating for municipalities is found in the several provinces. Ontario provides for the creation of all types of municipalities, from the smallest to the largest, and sets out their basic powers and responsibilities, by one general Municipal Act. In Mani-

[6]*Smith* v. *London*, (1909) 20 O.L.R. 133.

toba, while a few of the larger urban municipalities are provided for by special Acts applying only to them, the fundamental municipal law applying to all other municipalities, urban and rural alike, is contained in one Act. In contrast, most of the other provinces provide a general municipal Act for each of various classes of municipalities, as in Quebec with its Cities and Towns Act and the Municipal Code, the latter applying to all municipalities other than cities and towns, or as in Saskatchewan which has The City Act, The Town Act, The Village Act, and The Rural Municipality Act. Newfoundland municipalities which were created prior to 1949 were provided for by individual Acts but in that year a municipal Act of general application was passed.

In all the provinces such general municipal legislation is supplemented by two types of municipal legislation. The first type is legislation generally applying to all municipalities in the province but limited to a particular subject. Thus, in most provinces there are such Acts as an Assessment Act, a Public Health Act, or a Planning Act. The second type includes what are variously described as private, special or local Acts which apply only to individual municipalities and which provide for deviations from the general municipal law or which cover matters peculiar to one municipality and which are not dealt with by the general law.

These private Acts in turn are of two varieties. There are those which provide for the general municipal government of individual municipalities which do not come under the general municipal Act of the province. All of the provinces except Ontario, Saskatchewan, and Alberta deal with some of their larger cities by such special Acts which are sometimes referred to as their charters.[7] In some instances the individual city "charters" were enacted before there was a general municipal Act and in some provinces there are not enough cities to justify general legislation. Among the cities so provided for are all the provincial capitals except Toronto, Regina, and Edmonton and a varying number of other cities in the different provinces. The other variety of private Acts comes into effect when, at the instance of a municipality, the legislature passes a special Act to meet some need of an individual municipality which otherwise is governed by the general municipal legislation. A city such as Toronto, which comes under the general municipal legislation which applies to all Ontario municipalities, has a special City of Toronto Act passed by the legislature

[7]The provincial government of Alberta, which heretofore has provided for each city by special legislation, has passed a Cities Act which came into effect on January 1, 1952.

practically every year to deal with particular matters not otherwise provided for.

Opinions differ as to whether it is better to legislate for all types of municipalities by one general Act or to have a general Act for each class of municipality. To provide for all municipalities by one general Act introduces uniformity into the municipal system, but it is argued that it is not possible to devise legislation that will serve equally well the needs of a large city and of a rural municipality. Legislating for all by one Act has proved feasible because the special needs of individual municipalities have been met by special or local Acts. Where the provisions so enacted for one municipality have been found to work satisfactorily, they sometimes have been later included in the general municipal legislation. The method of providing for larger places by special legislation is useful in a province with only one or two cities but if followed in a province with twenty or thirty cities would produce confusing diversity.

It is asserted that where all municipalities are governed by one general Act the legislature is reluctant to make changes to meet needs which are peculiar to certain classes of municipalities but which are not of concern to others, and there is thus a brake on experimentation and progress. A municipality which desires special legislation to meet its peculiar needs must bear the expense of securing private legislation; but this normally does not amount to more than a few hundred dollars and is not prohibitive as in England.[8]

The Exercise of Municipal Powers

These municipal Acts of the provincial legislatures, whether of general or special application, determine the powers which the council of a municipal corporation may exercise and, by reason of the nature of corporate bodies, the council cannot legally exercise any powers other than those so conferred. When a council wants to deal with any local problem the first question which arises is that of the legal authority to take the proposed action. Frequently, however, the municipal electors want their council to do things for which no powers have been granted. A councillor then must choose between voting to do what is desired by his community or refusing to take action because there is no statutory authority. If the proposed action does not flagrantly violate some legal prohibition, the councillor is more likely to be

[8]"The average cost of unopposed Local Acts is about £3,000; if the Bill is opposed in one House of Parliament the cost averages about £4,500; if it is opposed in both Houses the cost averages more than £7,000." E. G. Hasluck, *Local Government in England* (Cambridge, 1948), p. 309.

swayed by the wishes of those who elect him, and who are providing the funds, than to be unduly concerned with legal niceties. Thus in 1939 many municipalities expended more upon the arrangements for the Royal Visit than was permitted for the reception of distinguished guests under the governing statute, but they relied on the public desire to have adequate preparations rather than on the strict wording of the law. Occasionally such action by a council will be questioned by an individual before the courts and the action of the council may be disallowed or set aside. More frequently, if what the council does is acceptable to the people, or if no one is sufficiently interested or personally damaged to undertake an appeal to the courts, the action stands unquestioned.

It is, of course, desirable to keep municipal operations within the law, but the law respecting local government, like the Sabbath, was made for man and not man for the law. The exercise by councils of powers which they do not possess may be classed as technically illegal although it might be more considerately described as without the law rather than contrary to the law. Such practices are inevitable where popularly elected bodies have the task of meeting the demands and problems of citizens and have at the same time to operate under statutes which grant limited powers in detail. The amending of statutes of this type is more frequently behind than in advance of public opinion and public needs. Councillors and citizens alike are frequently irritated by a sense of frustration when met with the constantly recurring argument of lack of legal authority, although councillors sometimes find this a convenient excuse for inaction.

One major function of municipal corporations is to perform duties which the legislature imposes upon them. Councils have no choice but to carry out these mandatory duties, although they may determine the manner in which they do so. An Ontario council is thus allowed no discretion about providing current funds for school boards; on the other hand, while the council must maintain the streets, it need only do so up to such a standard that the corporation will not be held liable for damages as a result of negligence.

The second group of functions are those which a council may or may not exercise as it sees fit. A council may or may not maintain a fire department, it may or may not license second-hand dealers, or it may or may not build sewers, according as the council deems expedient. Some of these optional functions, however, may only be exercised in accordance with regulations laid down by provincial authorities or subject to the supervision of some provincial authority.

Some Differences between the Local and the Senior Governments

Local governments differ in many respects from the senior governments. A municipal council is vastly different in its make-up and organization from a legislative assembly or the House of Commons, for in Canada it rarely operates on a party basis. Although council members may be elected with political party support they seldom run as party candidates in most Canadian municipalities nor do they openly or officially work together as party groups in council. There is no "Government" in power and no "Official Opposition" in a council, and there is nothing comparable to the executive and the cabinet of the senior governments. While the head of the council is nominally the chief executive, the actual power rests with the council. Because there is no party alignment, councils do not divide consistently on the various issues but usually each member votes on the issues before council as he feels inclined, or as he feels his personal political interests require. There are no government issues which take precedence because there is no "Government."

There are several reasons why councils are not organized on party lines. Most councils are too small to make a party basis of organization feasible. Canadian municipal electors generally object to admitting party politics openly into their municipal affairs. Experience in the United States has indicated that the organization of councils on party lines tends to make the local administration merely an appendage to the national parties and a convenient source of rewards for party workers and there has resulted an effort in many of their urban municipalities to get away from the party basis. In England, on the other hand, "in many of the local authorities there exist well organized party divisions. Elections are frequently run on party lines, and the usual party discipline is applied to the members by their political organizations."[9]

It is argued that municipal government is primarily concerned with administration and that the type of issues with which councils are normally concerned present no occasion for division along traditional party lines; that there is no Liberal or Conservative basis for division, for example, on the merits of a snow ploughing programme. However, it may be that as the social services extend to occupy a larger place in the municipal programme and if the national political parties tend

[9]W. Eric. Jackson, *Local Government in England and Wales* (Liverpool, 1945), p. 139.

to divide on the basis of greater or lesser degrees of socialism there may be more justification for the introduction of party at the municipal level. The increasing importance of long-range planning in municipal programmes also may encourage party organization as a means of securing greater continuity of policy and to avoid the hazard of frustrating such programme by individual changes in council personnel.

The lack of something corresponding to the Cabinet and to the Opposition imposes an obligation on each councillor to do his share in initiating action or in giving leadership. Unfortunately, what is everyone's business usually turns out to be no one's business. There is a recognized responsibility on the head of the council to give leadership but, as his power in council is no greater than that of any other member, he can hardly be held to account for action or inaction on the part of his council. Because he does not and cannot act as the head of a party in the council, he has no weapon, comparable to party discipline, to compel support of the measures he proposes. He is also handicapped in giving leadership to his council because some of the other members may be potential competitors for the mayoral chair and they may not be anxious to see his proposals succeed. Furthermore the absence of any one who can speak with authority on behalf of the council in the interim between meetings is a handicap in carrying on negotiations on behalf of the corporation.

The lack of an opposition means that there is no one person or group whose duty it is to look for the flaws in the proposals made to council and thereby to protect the citizens against ill-advised action. Here again, what is everyone's business is frequently that of none. The situation is complicated by the fact that a member may hesitate to call attention to the shortcomings in the proposals of a fellow member whose support he may subsequently require for one of his own proposals. Frequently proposals of dubious value are adopted by councils, not because the members approve of them, but for want of any one who will assume the thankless task of criticizing and opposing them.

At the same time, the absence of party in municipal government may be a factor contributing to its sensitivity to public opinion. Councils are notorious for their ability to change their minds and to reverse their decisions. Not infrequently a recommendation which receives wide support in committee may be killed with the compliance of members of the sponsoring committee when it appears in council, for in the interval between committee and council meetings the councillors have had an opportunity to learn what the public thinks about the proposals. Where, however, proposals have been advanced by party groups there may be hesitation to accept the loss of prestige involved in reversing a stand once taken, and much greater reluctance to retreat in the face of public opinion on less important issues. Undoubtedly the feeling that he is one of a continuing group gives a member much greater courage in supporting a policy in the face of adverse criticism than an individual feels when he must rely on his own judgment as to what is best.

It may be, however, that where a party group has to accept responsibility for such measures as they support they give a proposal more thorough consideration before committing their members to its support. McEvoy, in considering the early development of the Ontario township, was "convinced that if it were not that 'party Loyalty and party organization' are so much fostered here our local institutions would be much worse administered. . . . the party enthusiasm which spreads through our whole system of government is almost necessary; and while in the higher and fewer offices it may detract from our chances of securing good men, in the meaner and much more numerous offices it certainly calls out talent and ability which would not otherwise be reached." If councils are to be organized on party lines, the party group, to justify its appeal for electoral support, is compelled to sponsor a more positive and comprehensive programme than are members who run and function as individuals. It is less possible for a majority group to explain away inaction in carrying out their programme than for an individual member who can always plead that he was in the minority. While the generally held attitude in Canada is that the benefits of party participation in municipal affairs are bought at too high a price, this may result from over concentration on United States experience. A contrasting English view is that the growing complexity of municipal administration and the necessity for continuity in carrying through long-run programmes have outmoded government by a group of independent councillors and require the greater consistency of policy and the dividing of work among councillors which the party basis of organization makes possible.

Local governments also differ from the senior governments in that a council has a fixed term of office, and there can therefore be no threat of an election as a means of securing support for measures. In this regard councils are like the Houses of Congress in the United States. The term of office being generally short, however, the salutary effect of an imminent appeal to the electors is fairly constant, for most councils in Canada hold office for only one year.

The personnel of municipal councils, with a few exceptions, is smaller in number than that of the legislative bodies of the senior governments with correspondingly less oratory and more discussion. Their meetings, save for those of county councils, are usually only a few hours long and are held at frequent intervals, a marked contrast to legislative sessions which continue from day to day for a period of weeks or months.

Municipal councils combine within one body both legislative and executive functions which at the other levels of government are separated. In municipalities, the operating departments are not headed by elected representatives although this is partly compensated for by the greater frequency of council and committee meetings and the part played by the mayor and the chairmen of standing committees. It is thus possible for the elected representatives to give almost continuous supervision of administration.

Local governments are more restricted in their sources of revenue than the senior governments. Their basis of taxation is determined by the province and the municipalities are limited to one main source for almost 90 per cent of their tax income. As the costs of government have risen, the senior governments have found it necessary to extend the range of their own taxation, but the provinces, busily engaged in devising new sources for their own purposes, have shown no inclination to admit municipalities as competitors for tax revenues in additional fields.

There is an important difference in the relationship between the elected representatives and their constituents at the local level compared with that at the other two levels of government. Those who represent the provincial or Dominion electorates carry on their legislative duties at a distance from their home community. In doing so they are in constant contact with representatives from all parts of the province or Dominion, as the case may be, and they tend to develop a broader provincial or Dominion viewpoint which is desirable if they are to make their greatest contribution. But, to the extent that their viewpoint broadens and changes, it tends to depart from the thinking of the people whom they represent. The municipal representative, however, carries out his duties in the community and environment in which he was elected. He is in daily contact with his constituents and is subject to the influence of the same day-to-day community experiences as are the people he represents. While it may be argued that his outlook is narrow, as compared with legislators at the other levels, it cannot be denied that his thinking on the issues of the day is more likely to be in tune with that of his constituents than is the case with representatives in the larger spheres.

It is probable also that the close and continuous association of the councillor with his electors and the ease with which they can let him know their attitude toward what is being done by the council make him more responsive to public opinion than other representatives. He has not the protection of time and distance, for he must be prepared to answer on the street in the morning for council action of the previous night, before other events have diverted people's attention.

Fiscal Importance of Local Government

Local government expenditures in the pre-war years represented about 30 per cent of the total government expenditure in Canada; the total of municipal expenditures exceeded those of the provinces, but were less than those of the Dominion. The relative position of the three levels in the matter of expenditures is as shown in Table 4.

TABLE 4

Total Expenditures of Dominion, Provincial, and Local Governments for Selected Years 1913 to 1948[a]

	1913	1921	1926	1930	1934	1938	1942	1945	1948
	(Millions of dollars)								
Dominion	131	381	313	369	410	473	3714	4793	2100
Provincial	48	91	127	184	229	266	275	374	550
Local	100	204	240	284	282	287	286	335	440
Total	280	677	680	838	922	1027	4276	5502	3092
	(As percentages of combined total)								
Dominion	46.8	56.3	46.0	44.0	44.5	46.1	86.9	87.1	67.9
Provincial	17.4	13.5	18.7	22.0	24.9	25.9	6.4	6.8	17.8
Local	35.8	30.2	35.3	34.0	30.6	28.0	6.7	6.1	14.3
Total	100	100	100	100	100	100	100	100	100

[a]*Report of the Committee on Provincial-Municipal Relations, Saskatchewan,* 1950, p. 22.

While the smaller municipalities have relatively small expenditures the larger cities have annual budgets approaching and in some cases exceeding those of some of the provinces, as indicated in Table 5.

The figures for any single year, however, do not tell the whole story, for while the total of municipal expenditures increased gradually over the period from 1930 to 1948 by approximately 56 per cent, the increase in the provincial total in the same period was 198 per cent and that of the Dominion 469 per cent.

Municipal Organization

The provinces differ as to the extent to which their territory has been organized into municipalities. The entire area of Nova Scotia and New Brunswick lies within some municipality. In other provinces large areas are still unoccupied, owing to lack of settlers or the unsuitability of the land for settlement, and are without municipal organization and in Prince Edward Island the rural areas are administered by the province without any municipal organization except for school authorities as previously noted. Table 6 indicates the extent to

TABLE 5

ANNUAL GOVERNMENTAL EXPENDITURES, 1948[a]

Governmental unit	Total Expenditure
	(Millions of dollars)
Ontario	201.7
Quebec (province)	157.4
British Columbia	83.9
Montreal[b]	62.4
Toronto	48.7
Saskatchewan	47.5
Alberta	39.0
Manitoba	27.5
Nova Scotia	26.1
New Brunswick	24.0
Vancouver	22.0
Winnipeg	14.0
Hamilton	12.6
Ottawa	10.1
Quebec (city)[b]	7.4
Edmonton	7.1
Windsor	6.9
Calgary	5.6
London	5.4
Halifax	5.2
Saint John	3.6
Prince Edward Island	3.5

[a]The figures for provincial expenditures are taken from *Bank of Canada Statistical Summary, 1950 Supplement*.

[b]Fiscal year ended April 30, 1949.

TABLE 6

MUNICIPALLY ORGANIZED TERRITORY AND POPULATION IN CANADIAN PROVINCES

Province	Percentage of population within a municipality	Percentage of land area within a municipality
Newfoundland	24.5	a
Prince Edward Island	25.6	a
Nova Scotia	99.6	100
New Brunswick	99.6	100
Quebec	97.5	7
Ontario	96.5	10
Manitoba	91.3	12.3
Saskatchewan	91.9	41.5
Alberta	78.9	15
British Columbia	75.0	.4

[a]Estimated to be less than one per cent.

which the territory and population of each province is included within some organized municipality.

Canadian local government systems may be said to be non-hierarchical in that each municipality functions independently under the provincial law, and such provincial regulation as may be in effect, and is not subject to direction or control of a superior unit of local government. This is in contrast to the hierarchical system of French local government.

The various types of municipalities in Canada are shown in Table 7.[10]

TABLE 7
TYPES OF MUNICIPALITIES IN CANADIAN PROVINCES

	Urban			Rural	
				Basic unit	Second tier
Newfoundland	City	Town		Rural district	
Prince Edward Island	City	Town	Village		
Nova Scotia	City	Town	Village	County or district	
New Brunswick	City	Town	Village	County	
Quebec	City	Town	Village	Parish or township	County
Ontario	City	Town	Village	Township	County
Manitoba	City	Town	Village	Rural municipality	
Saskatchewan	City	Town	Village	Rural municipality	
Alberta	City	Town	Village	Municipal district	
British Columbia	City		Village	District municipality	
	10	9	9	9	2

All the provinces have cities which are urban centres with relatively large populations. Six provinces have established a minimum population qualification for city status: Ontario, 15,000; Manitoba, 10,000; Quebec, 6,000; Saskatchewan and Alberta, 5,000; and British Columbia, a male population of 100. Each province also provides for incorporating smaller urban communities either as towns or villages and most provide for both.

There is greater diversity, however, in the organization of the rural areas for municipal purposes. The Newfoundland rural districts consist of two or three contiguous communities which are amalgamated for municipal purposes. These districts have the same powers and duties as the towns. In addition there are four local government areas governed by councils appointed by the province. The rural areas of Prince Edward Island, except for school and health matters, as previ-

[10]For simplification certain limited forms of local government such as police villages, organized hamlets, improvement districts, etc. have been omitted.

ously noted, are governed directly by the province. In Nova Scotia and New Brunswick the county is the basic unit of rural government, and in Quebec and Ontario, each of which has a two-tier system, the county area is divided into rural municipalities called parishes or townships. The rural municipalities and municipal districts of the Prairie Provinces are much larger in area than the parishes and townships of the central provinces and the trend in recent years is toward the nature of the terrain permits widespread settlement, in contrast further enlargement of area. Some students believe that changing problems of municipal administration may yet result in the re-establishment of something comparable to the county system in the Prairie Provinces. District municipalities are the basic rural units of British Columbia. Their small number and limited total area reflect the nature of the terrain and the resulting limitations on rural settlement. The greater part of the rural portion of the province has no municipal organization.

Table 8 shows the average area of the basic unit of rural government in the various provinces for which such information is available.

The county unit of government which occurs in Nova Scotia and New Brunswick should be distinguished from the county as it occurs in Quebec and Ontario. In Nova Scotia and in New Brunswick all of the territory comprising the province is divided into geographical areas called counties. In Quebec and Ontario only the southerly portion of each province is divided into counties. In general, the areas so divided into counties take in those portions of these latter two provinces where with the portions where there are small pockets of settlement, isolated in many cases from other similar pockets, as in the mining areas. The greater part of the population lives within the county areas.

Each county area in Nova Scotia[11] and New Brunswick forms a municipality which is the basic rural unit of government. These county municipalities in Nova Scotia do not include the incorporated cities, towns, and villages which lie within the geographical area of the county but New Brunswick cities and towns other than Fredericton have representation on the county council and take part in county government.

In Quebec and Ontario all the area within the county limits, which is not included within some city, town, or village, is divided into parishes or townships.[12] Thus, the county of Champlain, in Quebec,

[11]Six of the Nova Scotia counties are divided into two districts each. Each of the districts is a "municipality."

[12]In Quebec, parishes or cantons or townships; in Ontario, townships.

TABLE 8

Basic Units of Rural Government in Canadian Provinces

	Unit	No.	Population			Area (in acres)		
			Range		Average	Range		Average
Newfoundland	Rural district	3						
Prince Edward Island	None							
Nova Scotia	Municipality[a]	24	3,698	41,321	12,934	140,800	1,398,669	551,214
New Brunswick	County	15	8,296	45,514	20,713	390,432	3,020,421	1,122,879
Quebec	Parish or township	1059	117	6,423	1,042	244	147,000	23,396
Ontario	Township	571	78	81,652	2,084	1,975	244,985	42,659
Manitoba	Rural municipality	115				4,759	493,000	175,365
Saskatchewan	Rural municipality[b]	302	500	6,083	1,359	115,088	511,040	199,699
Alberta	Municipal district	60	700	20,175	5,784	116,480	1,313,449	520,902
British Columbia	District municipality	28	404	30,328	6,460	390	85,000	34,767

[a]In Nova Scotia and New Brunswick the use of the term "municipality" is restricted to the county or district units of local government and when so used does not include cities, towns, or villages.

[b]The normal rural municipality consists of a 9-township unit (a township being six miles square) but in 1947 there were 23 with an area of 6 townships or less, and 15 with an area of 12 or more townships, the largest, No. 395, was established in 1944 with an area of 22½ townships.

is divided into twenty-one parishes and the county of Simcoe, in Ontario, into sixteen townships. These parishes or townships are not uniform in shape, size, or population. The parishes and townships are incorporated municipalities and form the basic units of rural government.[13] Within the sphere assigned to them by provincial statute they are not subject to direction or control by the county.

There are, however, in these two provinces, county municipalities which include all of the teritory within the county area except that within the limits of any city, or, in Ontario, of any separated town[14] lying within the county. These county municipalities have jurisdiction in certain matters, such as the upkeep of main roads or the maintenance of gaols, in the towns, villages, and townships within the county boundaries, but not within any city or separated town within the county area.

The county municipalities in Quebec and Ontario do not have a direct tax levying and collecting function as this work is performed on their behalf by the local municipalities comprising the municipal county. When the county council have determined the amount required to be raised for county purposes the county allocates the amount among the various component municipalities according to their equalized assessments. The county then forwards a demand to each local council for its share. Each local council is responsible for paying over to the county the amount of this requisition or precept, and to raise the amount the local council adds to the local levy a county levy. This county levy is at the rate which when applied to the local, not the equalized, assessment will produce the amount required by the county.

Alberta, in 1950, made provision for the creation of counties[15] in any area by the Lieutenant-Governor in Council on receipt of a resolution from a municipal council or the board of a school division comprising the major part of the area. The county council is to have complete jurisdiction within the area in the usual municipal matters and in addition is the school authority, under The School Act, and the hospital authority, under the Municipal Hospitals Act. The council is required to appoint three major committees, the municipal committee, the educational committee, and the hospital committee which

[13]In northern Ontario there are unincorporated townships which are not municipal units but merely territorial subdivisions laid out for land survey purposes.

[14]In Ontario there are eight towns which, by special legislation, are separated from the counties within which they are situated and which in their relationship to the county have the same status as a city.

[15]The first two counties came into being January 1, 1951, the County of Grand Prairie No. 1, comprising 55 townships, and the County of Vulcan No. 2, comprising 40 townships. Incorporated towns and villages in the area do not form part of the county.

have power to co-opt lay members, but the council retains the responsibility for all major decisions and complete financial and administrative responsibility. This type of council appears to be the most comprehensive of Canadian municipalities in its jurisdiction. As this county organization is an experiment the Act limits the number of counties which may be created to four, and further provides that after four years of operation a county council must conduct a plebiscite of the electors on the question of continuing the county or reverting to the previous form of government.

Table 9 indicates the number of municipalities of various types in the Canadian provinces but it does not include all the units of local government. In addition to the municipal corporation there are in most municipalities school boards and boards of health, and in the larger municipalities there is a wide variety of special purpose bodies such as utility commissions, parks boards, transportation commissions, hospital boards, etc. While many of these bodies are dependent upon the municipal council for their revenues or for meeting any deficiency between revenues and expenditures, they are in varying degrees independent of council control, financial or otherwise. The members of such bodies are in some cases elected, in some appointed, and in others the members are *ex officio*, that is, they are members of such bodies because they hold some other public office. The relationship between these bodies and municipal councils is more fully discussed in chapter VI.

It is a nice point to decide what degree of independence in policy or finance is necessary to justify the classification of a municipal body as a separate unit of government. Many of these various bodies other than councils have completely independent powers to make decisions in matters of policy. If they are dependent upon some other body for revenues, however, their independence may be more apparent than real, for without financial resources they can do little to implement their policies. There are municipal bodies engaged in trading operations which are independent in policy making and which can, by the sale of their services, raise revenues. Yet these would not be classified as units of government for they are merely agencies of the local government. The criterion of a unit of government would appear to be the possession of the legal power to raise revenue by compulsion or, in other words, either the power to tax or the power to require some taxing authority to raise and pay over the required revenues. There are many municipal units of government which have no power to levy taxes but which have the legal right to require revenues to be raised and paid over to them by the municipal councils.

TABLE 9

MUNICIPALITIES IN CANADIAN PROVINCES[a]

	Cities	Towns	Villages	Total urban	Rural	Total local municipalities	Counties	Total
Newfoundland	1	19		20		20		20
Prince Edward Island	1	7		8		8		8
Nova Scotia	2	41		43	24	67		67
New Brunswick	3	19	4	26	15	41		41
Quebec	32	129	328	489	1,097	1,586	76	1,662
Ontario	29	147	157	333	584	917	38	955
Manitoba	4	33	33	70	114	184		184
Saskatchewan	8	84	401	493	304	797		797
Alberta	7	62	138	207	57	264		264
British Columbia	35		39	74	27	101		101
	122	541	1,100	1,763	2,222	3,985	114	4,099

[a]Based on *Canada Year Book*, 1951, p. 102.

There is no accurate record of the number of local government bodies in Canada, but it far exceeds the number of municipal corporations. Goldenberg[16] estimated that in 1939 there were in Canada 24,126 school districts alone and a total of 28,090 local government bodies.

Creation and Erection or Change of Status of Municipalities

The creation of new municipalities is usually the result of one of two circumstances. In those provinces which are not completely organized into municipalities and where settlement is expanding into previously unsettled areas, as in parts of northern Quebec and Ontario, growth of population gives rise to a need for municipal institutions. Even in areas which have long been settled but which have not been organized municipally, as in Newfoundland, the occasion for creating new municipalities occurs. As the creation of municipalities is a provincial matter the conditions vary from province to province.

The changing of status of existing municipalities occurs when increasing population results in changing municipal problems which can best be solved by a change of status accompanied by extended or altered municipal powers. Thus, increasing population in a rural area develops needs which can better be met by a village corporation. A continuing population development usually results in demands for the erection of the village into a town, or of a town into a city.

Most provincial legislatures have established minimum population requirements, within a fixed area, for creating a municipality or changing its status. These requirements are set out in the Appendix to this chapter. Instances occur where municipalities do not measure up to these requirements. It may be that such a municipality was granted its status before minimum requirements were established, or it may have met the requirements when incorporated but subsequently lost population, or it may have been created by special legislation in which case the general rules do not apply, for a legislature can always make exceptions to its own general legislation.

In some provinces there are no statutory provisions relating to the creation of certain classes of municipalities, as with respect to cities in Nova Scotia and New Brunswick. This is usually because there are not enough municipalities in a class to justify the provision of general legislation. Such matters are dealt with by special Acts relating to individual municipalities.

[16]H. Carl Goldenberg, *Municipal Finance in Canada* (Ottawa, 1939), p. 12.

Area Adjustments

The problem of adjusting the area or boundaries of municipalities to changing conditions and population growth is a difficult one in which both rural and urban municipalities are involved. It has not been satisfactorily solved either in Canada, in England, or in the United States.

In purely rural municipalities it arises as municipal activities increase and their administration becomes more complex. As expensive mechanical equipment has become essential to provide for modern standards of road construction and maintenance, and the overhead cost of skilled administrators grows with expanding social services, it becomes necessary to spread the cost over wider areas to secure greater tax resources and to equalize the heavier burden as between communities with varying degrees of capacity to bear that burden. Some provincial authorities have made wholesale adjustments of boundaries in rural areas without local consent. This was done in Alberta in the years 1940–4, when the rural municipalities were increased in area and the number reduced by 100. Similar proposals have been under discussion for several years in Saskatchewan.

In urban and suburban municipalities the problem is to devise a method of orderly adjustment of boundaries in accordance with the over-spill of the urban population. A growing urban municipality may desire to extend its boundaries for a variety of reasons to bring within its limits adjacent territory which in many cases is suburban in character or which may be purely rural. The purpose may be to obtain room for expansion or sites for industrial development or housing, to control the development of the fringe area surrounding the urban centre, to increase the size and importance of the urban centre, or to permit more effective long-range planning.

Some provinces provide for this procedure by general legislation and others deal with individual cases by special legislation. Quebec provides that the council of a city or town which wishes to extend its municipal limits may pass a by-law setting forth the area to be annexed and the terms and conditions of annexation. The by-law, before being finally passed, must be approved by the council of the municipality from which territory is being taken, as well as by the electors, who are proprietors, in the area to be annexed. This latter approval may be given by vote at a properly called public meeting. Even if so approved, the by-law requires the further approval of the Lieutenant-Governor in Council.

The Ontario Municipal Board, on application of a council or of the Minister of Municipal Affairs authorized by the Lieutenant-Governor in Council, may annex the whole or any part of an applying municipality to any other municipality or the whole or any part of any other municipality to an applying municipality. The Board determines the terms and conditions of annexation and may make all adjustments of assets and liabilities as agreed upon by the municipalities or, failing agreement, as the Board considers equitable. The Board must hold a public hearing in the matter and if the Board considers it advisable it may require the applying council to obtain the assent of the electors entitled to vote on money by-laws. A council must submit a question respecting annexation to the electors if sufficient electors (in a town, village, or township, 150, and in a city, 500) petition that the municipality or a part of it be annexed to the adjacent municipality on the terms set out in the petition and, if the vote is favourable, must apply to the Board accordingly. No annexation order may be made by the Board when a municipality is in default nor does an annexation order take effect until twenty-eight days after being made. If within that period objection is filed by 10 per cent of the electors entitled to vote on money by-laws in the applying municipality, or in the territory being annexed, the order is not effective until the objection is withdrawn or the order is confirmed by special Act.

In Manitoba, on request by a two-thirds vote of the council of a city, other than Winnipeg or St. Boniface, for the addition of any part of an adjacent locality "which from the proximity of the streets or buildings thereon or the future exigencies of the city it seems desirable to add" the Lieutenant-Governor in Council may, by proclamation, add to the city any part of the adjacent territory. He may also add territory to a city if one-quarter of the resident ratepayers of the city petition for a redivision of wards.

Annexation in Saskatchewan cities and towns may result from action by persons wanting to be included in another municipality, by municipalities wanting to add territory, or by the Lieutenant-Governor in Council on his own initiative. Where two-thirds of the householders in territory adjacent to a city or town petition the council to annex the territory and the council agrees, the Lieutenant-Governor in Council may add the territory to the city or town and fix the terms and conditions. An unusual requirement is that there shall be no annexation under this provision unless the owners of land in the territory to be included contribute to the city or town an area, of at least 5 per cent of the addition, to be used for parks, open spaces, or other civic purposes as the council deems expedient. Failing agreement among the land owners as to the area to be contributed, the city may purchase the same amount of land and assess the cost against the land in the area to be annexed in proportion to their assessed value. The Lieutenant-Governor in Council, on request of a city or town, may add to it adjacent territory but no such request may be made until the owners of land in the proposed addition have been heard by the council; or the Lieutenant-Governor in Council, on his own motion and without request, but after consultation with the council, may alter the limits of a city or town and provide for the adjustment of matters arising from such alteration.

The Board of Public Utility Commissioners has jurisdiction in annexation matters in Alberta. On petition of resident landowners in territory adjacent to a town it may, with the consent of the town council, add the territory to the town. No area, however, may be annexed to a town unless a plan for its subdivision has been registered, nor unless there is at least one occupied dwelling or place of business for every five acres. The Board may annex adjacent territory to a town on request of its council; or the Board, without any request and on its own initiative, may add territory to a town. In all cases the Board fixes the terms and conditions of annexation. The Board also has wide powers respecting the addition of land to villages and the adjustment of boundaries between a village and adjacent villages or rural areas.

While provision may be made from time to time for annexing[17] territory to an urban centre, this action usually involves prolonged and often acrimonious inter-municipal negotiations respecting the areas to be annexed and the adjustments of assets and liabilities. At best it operates in a series of fits and starts and usually occurs, if at all, long after the need for adjustment has been urgent.

The solution of these problems is far from simple. Boundary changes run counter to many vested interests and arouse local patriotism of an unusually virulent kind. Civic organizations rally to defend local independence, resolutions are passed and petitions are presented, and it frequently becomes politically impossible to proceed. On occasion, if the municipalities involved are unable to arrive at an agreement, the province may take action as was done in Ontario in 1935 when the cities of Windsor and East Windsor and the towns of Walkerville and Sandwich were amalgamated by provincial statute. It is, of course, more difficult to secure agreement where more than two municipalities are concerned, as in the Toronto metropolitan area. In many areas

[17]Annexation consists of adding a part of one municipality, amalgamation consists of joining or merging the whole of two or more municipalities.

surrounding rapidly growing cities in Canada and the United States the battle for adjustment of boundaries has been carried on in vain for many years.

What then is the ideal size for a municipality? That is a question which can not be answered with exactness nor would any answer be universally applicable. With respect to a rural municipality, the Honourable J. H. Brockelbank, then Minister of Municipal Affairs of Saskatchewan, believed that

> a rural municipality should be large enough for the purpose of owning and operating to full capacity good road-building machinery. It should also be a natural community. People who work together, who play together, who go to the same central town, are the people who can best work together in any organization, whether it is a Municipal Council or some other voluntary organization. There should be a logical centre in the municipality. . . . Municipal Councils should be close to the people and should be on a basis where that personal touch will not be lost and it should not be lost. The ideal municipality which is large enough, but not too large, which is a natural community, should be something else than most of our municipalities have been in the past. You see, beyond the Municipal Councils actually it is the people within the boundaries of that municipality working together to give those services which they could not give on an individual basis.[18]

The ideal size for an urban municipality is even more difficult to determine.[19] Size in this case is measured by population rather than by area. The optimum size is to some extent dependent on the industrial development which the community exists to serve. Some of those who have studied the matter believe that to afford its inhabitants the maximum advantages of the services of an urban community a population between 100,000 and 250,000 is desirable. Major factors to be considered from the viewpoint of municipal government are representation, administration, and the population required to support or justify the various services. As a municipality becomes to an increasing extent primarily a service organization, the administrative functions become of more importance in determining the ideal size for a municipality.

[18] *Western Municipal News*, vol. 40, no. 5, p. 124.

[19] *Report of the Local Government Boundary Commission for the year 1947 (England)*. "It is not possible by any process of arithmetic or logic to arrive at exact figures for an optimum size of a local government unit either in relation to local government as a whole or to any one function or group of functions. At best one can, to use an engineering term, arrive at a reasonable tolerance, and it is fairly certain that even in regard to that there will be special cases demanding exceptional treatment. Moreover, the process is largely one of weighing conflicting aims and deciding where on balance the advantage lies. Opinions on these matters differ and will continue to differ."

Disorganization, Dissolution, and Disincorporation

Several provinces provide for dissolving certain types of municipal corporations. These are usually the smaller municipalities as it is not likely that dissolution would be feasible where a large population is involved. The main points of interest in connection with dissolution are the dissolving authority, the conditions prerequisite to such action, and the disposition of the assets and liabilities of the corporation being dissolved. The dissolving authorities, where provided for, and prerequisites are shown in the accompanying summary.

The adjustment of assets and liabilities of a dissolved municipality may be made by a referee or adjuster appointed by the Minister of Municipal Affairs,[20] or may be made by a provincial administrative board, as by the Ontario Municipal Board. The municipality which absorbs the dissolved corporation makes the adjustment in Manitoba, and British Columbia simplifies the problem by vesting the assets of a disincorporated municipality in the province.

Any excess of assets over liabilities is shared pro rata among the electors of dissolved villages in New Brunswick; is disposed of as directed by the Minister, in Saskatchewan; and in Alberta, the Minister may require that it be expended within the area of the dissolved municipality. If, however, the liabilities exceed the assets the referee, in Nova Scotia, Saskatchewan, and Alberta, may levy a rate on the area of the dissolved municipality to make up the deficiency, but in Nova Scotia the extent to which the liabilities are to be discharged by such a rate is subject to the Minister's approval.

Reduction of Status

Alberta provides for reducing the status of cities and towns. If a city council passes a resolution in favour of reducing the status of the city to that of a town, or if the majority of the electors voting on the question favour the change, the Lieutenant-Governor in Council may reduce it. Under similar conditions, and also if a town fails to elect a council, the Minister may reduce a town to village status. The Lieutenant-Governor in Council in Saskatchewan may also reduce a town to village status on the recommendation of the Minister.

[20]This applies in Nova Scotia towns, New Brunswick villages, Saskatchewan villages and rural municipalities, and Alberta villages and municipal districts.

Province	*Dissolving authority*	*Conditions precedent to dissolution*
Nova Scotia		
Towns	Minister of Municipal Affairs with approval of Lieutenant-Governor in Council	Minister may require ratepayers' approval at public meeting or by plebiscite and of council of municipality to which area is to be added
New Brunswick		
Village	Minister	
Quebec		
Township or parish	Lieutenant-Governor in Council	Request of Minister of Municipal Affairs or of council or resident ratepayers and only if population has fallen below minimum required for incorporation
Ontario		
Any	Ontario Municipal Board	Application of council or of Minister of Municipal Affairs on authorization of Lieutenant-Governor in Council; a public hearing; if required by the Board, the assent of the electors
Manitoba		
Village or town	Lieutenant-Governor in Council	Two-thirds vote of council and three-fifths vote of ratepayers voting; or if population below minimum for incorporation
Saskatchewan		
Rural municipality	Lieutenant-Governor in Council	
Village	Minister of Municipal Affairs	
Alberta		
Municipal district or village	Lieutenant-Governor in Council	
British Columbia*		
Any		Petition of majority of electors representing more than half value of land and improvements in the municipality; and provision, to satisfaction of the Lieutenant-Governor in Council, for discharge of all obligations of the municipality

*In British Columbia dissolution is effected by annulling the letters patent incorporating the municipality and is described as disincorporation.

APPENDIX

Statutory Requirements for:

A. The Creation of New Rural Municipalities[a]

Province	Authority	Conditions	Municipality created
Newfoundland	Lieutenant-Governor in Council		Rural district or Local Government Area
Quebec	Lieutenant-Governor in Council	300 population in a township; on petition of interested parties	Township
Ontario	Ontario Municipal Board	Petition of 75 male inhabitants in locality in unorganized part of province, if has population of 1,000 people	Township
Manitoba	Lieutenant-Governor in Council	Petition of residents	Municipal District
Saskatchewan	Lieutenant-Governor in Council	On own motion or on petition of 100 ratepayers, area 18 miles square or 324 square miles	Rural Municipality
Alberta	Minister of Municipal Affairs	On own motion or on petition	Municipal District
British Columbia	Lieutenant-Governor in Council	On petition of 30 males, British subjects, 21 years of age, who own over one half of the total land value in the area	District Municipality

[a]No provision in Prince Edward Island, Nova Scotia, or New Brunswick.

APPENDIX—*Continued*

B. The Creation of Villages

Province	Authority	Population conditions	Area (in acres)	Other conditions
Prince Edward Island[b]	Lieutenant-Governor in Council	100		Vote of ratepayers
Nova Scotia[b]	Governor in Council	100		Vote of electors
New Brunswick	Minister of Municipal Affairs	300	1,500	Petition of residents
Quebec	Lieutenant-Governor in Council	40 inhabited houses	60 arpents, $50,000 assess	Petition of majority of owners
Ontario	County Council	750	500[c]	Petition of residents
Manitoba	Lieutenant-Governor in Council	400[d]	640	Petition of 75 householders
Saskatchewan	Minister	100	240	On petition or on own motion
Alberta	Minister	35 dwellings		
British Columbia	Lieutenant-Governor in Council			On petition

[b]The body created is a corporate body composed of the village commissioners and derives its powers under the Village Service Act.

[c]Not over 500 acres for first 1,000 population and 200 acres for each additional 1,000 or fraction thereof and in unorganized territory not over 750 acres for first 500 population and 300 acres for each additional 500 population.

[d]The residences of such inhabitants must have a taxable assessment of not less than $150,000.

APPENDIX—*Continued*

C. The Creation of Towns and Cities[e]

	Conditions for the erection of villages to towns			Conditions for the erection of towns to cities		
Province	Population	Area in acres	Other conditions	Population	Area in acres	Other conditions
Nova Scotia	1,500	640	On petition: sheriff takes a vote	No provision		
New Brunswick	1,000		do	No provision		
Quebec	2,000		Petition of village council	6,000		Petition of town and village
Ontario	2,000[f]	Same as villages		15,000 (town)[g] 25,000 (township)		
	1,500[h]	Same as villages	Petition of 75 male inhabitants			
Manitoba	1,500	640	Petition of village	10,000		Petition of town
Saskatchewan	500		Petition of village approved by 2/3 vote of electors	5,000		Petition of town
Alberta	700		do	5,000		
British Columbia				100 males		Petition of individuals

[e]The Lieutenant-Governor in Council is the authority which erects villages to town status and towns to city status in all the provinces indicated here, except Ontario. In Ontario the Ontario Municipal Board is the authority.

[f]If in the organized portion of the province.

[g]If town is erected to status of city the population requirement is 15,000 but if a township is raised to a city there must be a population of 25,000.

[h]If in the unorganized (northerly) portion of the province.

CHAPTER IV

MUNICIPAL COUNCILS

PROVINCIAL LEGISLATURES have provided that the powers of the municipal corporation[1] which they create are to be exercised by elected municipal councils. The council is the governing body of the corporation. Councils in the several provinces, and in different types of municipalities within the same province, vary in size, in the basis of their election, in term of office, and in their powers. Yet there are many characteristics which are common to all.

COUNCIL PERSONNEL

Municipal councils are composed of the head of the council and other members, called councillors, commissioners, or, in cities, aldermen.[2] Ontario cities over 100,000 in population and British Columbia cities and district municipalities have an additional class of members called controllers.[3] All members of councils are elected by the municipal electors,[4] although county councillors in Quebec and Ontario are elected by indirect election for they are first elected to a local municipal council and by virtue of that office they sit in the county council.

The head of a council is not always elected directly as such. County wardens[5] are elected by the county councillors from among themselves. The head of the council in most other municipalities is directly elected

[1]The word "municipality" should in most cases be used only to designate a locality or area the inhabitants of which are incorporated and the "municipal corporation" to designate the legal entity composed of all the inhabitants. In actual usage the word "municipality" includes both and in addition has a special meaning in Nova Scotia where it is equivalent to the term "county" or "district."

[2]The members of the Charlottetown city council, other than the mayor, are called councillors; members of town councils in New Brunswick are called aldermen.

[3]Controllers are mandatory in Ontario cities of 100,000 or over and are optional in cities of lesser population.

[4]There are some exceptions to this general statement. In Quebec and in some of the western provinces members of council, under some circumstances, may be appointed by provincial authorities. In some circumstances councils appoint persons to fill the unexpired portion of the term of office when a vacancy occurs in a council. Thirty-three members of the Montreal city council are appointed by thirteen semi-public bodies, such as the Montreal Board of Trade, Montreal University, the Property Owners League of Montreal, etc. The Minister in Prince Edward Island may fill vacancies still remaining on a town council after a deferred election.

[5]In Nova Scotia counties and districts and New Brunswick, Quebec, and Ontario, counties.

to that office by the electors although in some cases[6] he is selected by the council from their own membership or by either method as the council may decide.[7] The head of the council is designated as warden in counties, as mayor or maire in cities and towns,[8] and in villages and townships as reeve, chairman, or overseer.[9]

The number of council members depends somewhat on the basis of election. The smaller councils usually occur in the smaller municipalities. In villages in Prince Edward Island, New Brunswick, and British Columbia the number is fixed at three; in villages and townships in Ontario, at five; and in Prince Edward Island towns and in Quebec villages, parishes, and townships at seven. The members of these councils are elected by general vote. The number is usually larger where councils are elected by wards or districts, as are Nova Scotia and New Brunswick county councils and Manitoba and Saskatchewan rural municipalities councils, as well as those in many cities, or where the council is composed of representatives of municipalities making up a county, as in Quebec and Ontario county councils.

Most city councils have from seven to fifteen members although there are some larger councils, usually in the larger cities as in Montreal, one hundred, Toronto, twenty-three, Winnipeg, nineteen, Hamilton, twenty-one, and Ottawa, thirty-three. Not all the larger cities, however, have large councils, for the Vancouver and London councils have only nine members. A few smaller places also have large councils: such as Kingston with twenty-two members, Hull and Belleville with fifteen, and Cornwall with thirteen. In forty-nine Canadian cities having over 10,000 population the council personnel is as follows:

Cities	1	1	1	1	1	1	2	3	1	13	5	8	3	7	1
Council members	100	33	23	22	21	19	15	13	12	11	10	9	8	7	6

Twenty-nine of these forty-nine councils are composed of an odd number of members and twenty of an even number. An advantage of

[6]Village mayors and reeves of municipal districts in Alberta, chairmen of village commissions in British Columbia, and village councils in New Brunswick, overseers of Saskatchewan villages, chairmen of Newfoundland municipal councils, and the mayor of Lethbridge, Alberta.

[7]The mayors of Quebec cities and towns coming under The Cities and Towns Act may either be elected directly by the electors or by the members of the council from among themselves.

[8]The head of a council of a village, township, or parish in Quebec is a *maire* and in Manitoba and Alberta villages is also a mayor.

[9]A reeve, in Ontario villages and townships, in rural municipalities in Manitoba and Saskatchewan, in Alberta districts, and British Columbia district municipalities; a chairman, in Newfoundland towns and rural districts, in New Brunswick and British Columbia villages; and an overseer in Saskatchewan villages.

an odd-numbered council is that it reduces the problem of tie votes although this difficulty may not arise in an even-numbered council if it is not the local practice for the head of the council to vote, except in the case of a tie vote.

Subject to a few exceptions, the general rule in Canadian urban municipalities is that the smaller the population the greater the number of representatives in proportion to the population. Thus, Toronto and Vancouver have one council member for every 30,000 inhabitants; in cities from 50,000 to 100,000 there is a member for approximately every 7,000–8,000 people; in cities from 20,000 to 50,000, a member for every 2,500–3,500; and in cities under 20,000, one for every 2,000 and in many cases for as small a number as 1,000 or 1,100. Similarly in rural municipalities where the council personnel is usually fixed by a general law, the representation per thousand of population decreases as population increases. Two extremes in the province of Ontario are the Township of Dalton with a population of 193 with a council of five members, compared with the same number for the Township of Brantford with a population of over 13,000.

Quebec and Ontario county councils vary in size according to the number and population of the local municipalities in the county. In Quebec, the most commonly recurring number is twenty-nine, which occurs in six of the seventy-six counties, and fifteen, which occurs in five. The range is from three to thirty-seven members. In Ontario, the members vary from ten to fifty-one. Here the most commonly recurring number is eighteen, which is the number in five of the thirty-eight counties, and the range is from nine to fifty-one members.

Nova Scotia and New Brunswick county councils are composed of representatives elected directly by electoral subdivisions of the county. In Nova Scotia one councillor is elected for each of these polling districts.[10] The general rule in New Brunswick is that two councillors are elected to the county council from each parish but there are numerous exceptions, especially in the urban parishes. In Nova Scotia the most frequently recurring number of members of a county council is eight, which occurs in five of the twenty-four county councils.

Quebec and Ontario county councillors are elected by indirect election. In Quebec the electors of each local municipality[11] elect a council composed of a mayor and six councillors, the mayor being

[10]There are thirty-one districts in the province which elect two councillors to their county council, and two districts which elect three.

[11]A local municipality in Quebec is one coming under the Municipal Code, which excludes cities and towns. In Ontario the term local municipality includes all municipalities other than counties.

TABLE 10

COUNTY COUNCIL PERSONNEL

Councils having	Nova Scotia	New Brunswick	Quebec	Ontario
Less than 10 members	7	0	12	1
10–20 members	11	7	38	18
21–30 members	6	4	21	10
31–40 members	0	4	5	7
over 40 members	0	0	0	2
	24	15	76	38

One reason for the larger county councils in Ontario is that local municipalities with more than 1,000 municipal electors have two representatives on the county council.

elected as such. The county council is then composed of the mayors of all local municipalities within the county area. In Ontario, township and village electors elect a council composed of a reeve and four councillors or, if the number of municipal electors exceeds 1,000, a reeve, a deputy reeve, and three councillors. The town councils are composed of a mayor, a reeve, a deputy reeve, and a varying number of councillors.[12] The reeves and deputy reeves of the townships, villages, and towns sit as members of the county council but as cities and separated towns do not form part of the county for municipal purposes they are not represented on the county council.

TERM OF OFFICE

The term of office of council members varies from province to province.[13] In New Brunswick, Ontario, and in Saskatchewan cities the term is usually one year, although New Brunswick county council elections may be on a biennial basis if the council so decides.[14] While Ontario councils, with the approval of the electors, may extend the term to two years the general practice is the one-year term.[15] In Nova Scotia towns, in all types of Quebec and Manitoba municipalities,

[12]Towns in the "unorganized" portions of the province where there is no county organization do not have reeves or deputy reeves nor do villages and townships in unorganized territory have deputy reeves.

[13]See Appendix to this chapter.

[14]Special legislation in New Brunswick respecting four counties provides for a two-year term, and for two counties a four-year term.

[15]Terms of office of Ontario municipality councils, 1948:

	One-year term	Two-year term
Cities	19	10
Towns	126	18
Villages	152	0
Townships	552	10
Total	859	38

Saskatchewan towns and rural municipalities and in British Columbia cities and district municipalities the term is usually two years.[16] The three-year term applies in Nova Scotia counties, in Saskatchewan villages, to councillors in all Alberta municipalities, and in British Columbia villages. Newfoundland provides for a four-year term with half the council being elected every two years.

In Saskatchewan and Alberta, where the term of councillors may be two or three years, the term of office for the head of the council is frequently shorter, being one or two years. In the three Prairie Provinces and in Quebec local municipalities, if the term is longer than one year, staggered or overlapping terms are the general rule; if the term is two years, one-half of the total number is elected each year and if the term is three years, one-third is elected annually. The two- or three-year term does not usually eliminate an annual election.

The merits of the long and the short term of office are constantly under discussion. Under the short term the electors can maintain closer control over their representatives because of the frequency of elections, for an unsatisfactory council can be promptly turned out of office. Nothing makes elected representatives more ardent in attending to their duties than the imminent prospect of an appeal to the electors.

Advocates of the longer term point out that it takes a new man in office three or four months to learn the procedure and the method of municipal work and the last three months of his term to prepare for election, so there remain only a few months in the middle of the year (usually the slack months in council activity) in which to accomplish anything. A major deficiency of councils has been the lack of long-range planning and the failure to take long views owing to the prospect that they may not remain in office long enough to carry such plans through. With a longer term, councillors need not think so constantly of their re-election nor are they under compulsion to produce some evident accomplishment, within the year, as justification for their re-election. Frequent elections may serve to keep council members on their job but they may be expensive for the taxpayers as councils like other elected bodies tend, on the eve of an election, to incur ill-advised expenditures which they would not make under other circumstances. The more frequent the elections, the greater will be the total of such expenditures.

W. B. Munro[17] observes that the Canadian one-year term developed

[16]British Columbia, in 1947, made the two-year term mandatory except that municipalities divided into wards which had a one-year term at the date of the legislation could continue the one-year term.

[17]William Bennett Munro, *American Influences on Canadian Government*, p. 123.

in imitation of the practice which prevailed in the United States in the nineteenth century but that it had been found to work badly in American cities and had been replaced in most of them by longer terms, up to four years, with a partial renewal of the council each year. Dr. H. L. Brittain in the annual report of the Bureau of Municipal Research, 1945, referring to the one-year term in effect in the city of Toronto, stated:

> Both elected and electors are victims of an outmoded system. The one year term, adopted originally because it was regarded as more democratic, long ago was found to be unworkable in the country of its origin, the United States, while the three year "overlapping term" or "staggered term" found in Britain, politically the most democratic country in the world, was ignored by all large Canadian cities except one. . . .
>
> This one year term is probably the most effective method ever devised for preventing the adoption of bad measures, but is equally effective in preventing or delaying good measures. It grows out of lack of faith in representatives and electors, and if we are to go anywhere but backwards it must be abandoned.

Basis of Election

Mayors and reeves, except where the mayor is elected by council, are elected by general vote, for there is only one to be elected in each municipality. The other members of council may be elected either on a general vote or a ward vote basis. Where the general vote plan applies, all the electors of the municipality have a choice from the same list of candidates and the whole municipality is the candidate's constituency. Under the ward or district plan the municipality is divided into a number of areas known as wards, in urban municipalities, and parishes, divisions, or districts in rural municipalities. From each of these areas a number, usually but not always an equal number,[18] of members are elected to the council. The elector in a ward or district has a choice limited to the candidates who are running in his ward and the candidate's constituency is only a portion of the whole municipality.[19]

The Appendix to this chapter shows the basis of election under the general laws of the various provinces; 24 out of 45 urban municipali-

[18]An exception is Charlottetown which has five wards with one councillor for each of three wards, two for one ward, and three for one ward. Also in Nova Scotia counties (municipalities) some districts elect two councillors and some, three, although the usual number is one.

[19]There are some cases, such as Moncton, where the two plans are combined; a portion of the council being elected by wards and a portion by general vote. The same effect is obtained in cities with boards of control, where the controllers are elected at large and the councillors by wards.

ties with a population of 10,000 and over elect on the general vote basis, in one the council is elected partly by general vote and partly by wards, three have aldermen elected by wards and controllers by general vote, and seventeen elect on the ward basis. In the twenty-one using a ward basis the number of wards range from three to eleven, and the representatives per ward range from one to six, as follows:

MUNICIPAL DIVISION INTO WARDS

Cities	6	4	3	3	2	1	1	1
Wards	3	4	5	6	7	8	9	11

REPRESENTATIVES PER WARD

Cities	2	14	4	1
Representatives per ward	1	2	3	6

Whether the general vote or the ward vote plan shall apply in a municipality may be determined by statute, it may be optional with the local council, or it may be determined by the council subject to the approval of the municipal electors. Speaking generally, in Quebec towns and in rural municipalities where the rural unit is large in area the ward or district voting plan is mandatory, and the general vote plan is mandatory in the smaller urban municipalities and in rural municipalities which are small in area; a choice is allowed in the larger urban centres and in the rural municipalities in the Prairie Provinces. There are, of course, exceptions to this general statement. Table 11 shows the basis of election under the general municipal law of the various provinces.

TABLE 11
BASIS OF ELECTION OF COUNCILLORS
(under general provincial statutes)

	General vote mandatory	Ward or district vote mandatory	Basis optional with municipality
Nova Scotia		Counties	Cities, towns
New Brunswick	Towns, villages	Counties	
Quebec	Villages, parishes, townships	Cities, towns	
Ontario	Villages, townships[a]		Cities, towns
Manitoba	Villages		Cities, towns, rural municipalities
Saskatchewan	Villages, towns		Cities, rural municipalities
Alberta	Villages, towns		Cities, municipal districts
British Columbia	Villages	District municipalities	

[a]There are some exceptions to this provision.

Opinions differ as to which basis of election is the better, particularly in urban municipalities. Because the ward is a small area with fewer electors than the whole municipality, a ward representative is close to his people, knows their needs and problems better, and is likely to be more responsive to their wishes than in the larger constituency. As the area is smaller and the electors less numerous the cost of election campaigns is less and there is greater opportunity for the man of limited means to get elected. Under the ward plan a man can be elected who is well and favourably known in his section of the community who could not get elected by general vote because he is not well known throughout the whole municipality. It is claimed that as groups or classes with common interests tend to locate in the same section of the community, such as the "working man's district" or the "foreign section," the ward system permits such groups to obtain representation of their special interests to an extent not possible if their votes are merged with the votes of the whole community. It is also asserted that under the general vote an unrepresented section may suffer from lack of service and attention. Moreover, because the support of a ward representative is based to a greater extent on personal relationship between electors and representative, there is less likelihood of a complete change of councillors than where members are elected at large; the complete elimination of experienced councillors and the substitution of an entirely new personnel destroys continuity in the governing body and considerable time must elapse for the new council to learn the methods of municipal operation and the background of the established policies. Finally, supporters of the ward system claim that it is the more democratic of the two alternatives.

The advocates of the general vote claim that better and more capable representatives, often described as "bigger men," can be induced to run for office in the larger constituency who would not expose themselves to the rough and tumble of a ward election; that a substantial man in the community who has no strong personal following in any one section may draw enough support from citizens of all sections to assure his election, because of widespread public appreciation of his achievements or abilities. Men elected on a ward basis are under the necessity of getting something for their ward to justify their re-election. Under the general vote system, however, much of the "log-rolling" or "back scratching," by which a representative undertakes to support action to benefit another ward, in return for expressed or implied promises of support for something for his own ward, is eliminated. Those elected at large can afford to take a community rather than a sectional view, for they are compelled, by the nature of their constituency, to support measures designed to benefit the greatest number rather than one section. The claim is also advanced that dividing the community into sections, with sectional representation, is detrimental to the best community spirit and may serve to perpetuate and intensify objectionable racial or class feelings. Experience shows that many of those who can retain office under the ward system fail to return to council when a change is made to the general vote basis.

Even those who advocate election at large, however, agree that there comes a point in the growth of population beyond which it is advisable to have councillors elected on a ward basis. Beyond this undetermined point it is impossible for the mass of the voters to have an adequate knowledge of the candidates, and election costs exceed the resources of many citizens. Ontario provides that cities over 100,000 population must have both a board of control elected by general vote and aldermen elected by wards. The result is that to a great extent the board of control becomes the dominating body concentrating on administration and the council devotes itself largely to representing the sectional views of the inhabitants.

It is difficult to see the logic of splitting a municipality into a number of wards with two or three representatives from each ward.[20] If there is merit in sectional representation it would appear more reasonable to divide a municipality into three times as many wards with one representative from each. Another question which arises is what constitutes a proper grouping of population or areas into wards. Toronto is divided into wards one of which has a population of 115,000. If the need for sectional representation is met in this case by electing three aldermen in such a ward why, in another city with a population of 115,000, should it be necessary to divide into wards at all?

The representation on the council under the ward system may not be equitable because, while the number of representatives from the

TABLE 12

WARD POPULATION IN SELECTED CITIES

City	Largest ward	Smallest ward
Toronto	115,914	48,011
Winnipeg	79,317	75,309
London	30,452	14,035
Verdun	23,135	14,871
Hull	8,487	2,971
Kingston	6,084	3,779

[20]There may, however, be sound political justification for such an arrangement.

various wards is the same, the population of the wards may be far from equal. This situation occurs because the population of wards which may have been approximately equal when they were established has not increased uniformly. The same reasons that make it difficult to change municipal boundaries or redistribute provincial or Dominion ridings prevent the readjustment of ward boundaries.[21] Sitting councillors know from experience that they can be elected in a ward and are, therefore, reluctant to run the risk of a change. Many municipal records, also, are tied to the wards as a basis of subdivision, and any change involves tedious administrative problems.

It would be difficult to justify the claim that the one basis of representation is more democratic than the other. To a degree such a decision depends on the interpretation of what constitutes democracy.[22] In practice, the standard of performance appears to be higher under a general vote system. But more efficient administration and better government may not be what the electorate want. The democratic principle implies that the majority of the people are entitled to less efficiency and poor government if they want it. If, however, an elected representative is to survive politically he must work in the interests of those he represents and it is obvious that if he represents the whole municipality he must support policies which appeal to or benefit the greatest number and alternatively, if he is elected on a sectional basis, he is forced to think first of the part and only secondly of the whole.

Head of the Council

The head of the council is the chief executive officer of the corporation and in all Canadian municipalities he is the presiding officer at council meetings. Although the powers of the corporation are exercised by the council as a whole, most provinces place upon the head of the council, as an individual, responsibilities which are distinct from those which he shares with the other members as a part of the whole council. In some provinces he is given specific powers as well as responsibilities.

The duties imposed upon the head of the council by statute, as expressed in the Ontario Act, are as follows:

[21]District municipal councils in British Columbia are required to redivide the wards on the basis of assessed valuation whenever the amount of assessed property in any ward exceeds, in proportion to its representation in council, by more than 40 per cent the assessed property in any other ward in proportion to its representation.

[22]The opinions of elected representatives in this regard are scarcely entitled to the weight ordinarily afforded to those with practical experience for, not unnaturally, they tend to favour the basis which reflects the better judgment of the electorate as evidenced by their own election.

(a) to be vigilant and active in causing the laws for the government of the municipality to be duly executed and obeyed;

(b) to oversee the conduct of all subordinate officers in the government of it, and, as far as practicable, cause all negligence, carelessness and violation of duty to be prosecuted and punished; and

(c) to communicate from time to time to the council such information and recommend to it such measures as may tend to the improvement of the finances, health, security, cleanliness, comfort and ornament of the municipality.

Similarly stated duties in almost identical language are imposed upon the heads of councils in Nova Scotia towns and on mayors and reeves in the four western provinces. A Quebec mayor, by statute, has the right of superintendence, investigation, and control over all the affairs, departments, and officers of the municipality and "especially shall see that the revenue of the municipality is collected and expended according to the law and that the provisions of the law and all by-laws, rules and regulations of the council are faithfully and impartially enforced." The mayors and reeves of British Columbia cities and districts are given somewhat more direct control of corporation employees expressed as "unrestricted authority and power to inspect and order the conduct of all officers and employees of the municipality and to direct the method of management of the municipality's business and affairs."

Appointments

The heads of municipalities have very limited powers of appointment to office. Mayors of Ontario cities have the right to appoint one of the three members of the Court of Revision; the heads of Saskatchewan and Alberta municipalities have power to appoint special constables for short periods, but in Alberta these appointments require confirmation of council. In general Canadian mayors are not vested with a power of appointment comparable to that exercised by mayors in many United States cities, in appointments either to civic boards or to senior paid municipal offices. It is a common practice, however, for councils to authorize the mayor to appoint the personnel of unofficial bodies or of special committees of council.

Suspensions

Some provinces give the head of the municipality a statutory right to suspend employees. Mayors and reeves in British Columbia and mayors of Alberta towns and villages may suspend the officers and employees of the municipality subject to review by the council or board of control. The same statutory power exists in Saskatchewan except that the mayor may not suspend a city commissioner. Mayors in Quebec cities and towns may suspend an officer or employee but must report thereon immediately to council. The warden of a Nova Scotia municipality, with consent in writing of three councillors, may suspend an officer appointed by council who is guilty of malfeasance, misfeasance, or non-feasance and may appoint someone to perform his duties until the council or the warden, with the consent of five councillors, reinstates him, or the council appoints a successor. Some councils by by-law give the head of the municipality certain powers of suspension subject, as a rule, to confirmation by council.

Veto Power

The heads of municipalities have a limited or qualified veto over certain actions of the council in some cases. In Halifax no resolution of council authorizing expenditures or any contract involving expenditures is effective if, in the opinion of the mayor, it is not authorized by law, if the amount is not fixed by law or is only fixed by a maximum limit, or if the making of the expenditure is permissive only and in the mayor's opinion is not expedient. The mayor's disapproval must be submitted in writing within one week but the council by a two-thirds vote of the whole council can override the veto.

Every by-law, resolution, obligation, or contract approved by the council of a Quebec city or town must be presented to the mayor for his approval and signature within forty-eight hours after approval by council. If the mayor refuses to sign he must return such by-law, etc., together with his objections in writing, and the clerk in turn submits the mayor's objections for consideration of the council at its next meeting. If an absolute majority of the aldermen reaffirm the action, the mayor must sign and approve the action. If the mayor of a local municipality in Quebec refuses to sign by-laws, etc., passed by the corporation when presented to him for signature, the secretary-treasurer submits them again to council at its next meeting, when a majority approval makes them as valid as if signed by the mayor.

The head of every Manitoba council may veto any by-law, resolution, or measure authorizing the expenditure of money, within twenty-four hours of its being passed by council, by written notice to the clerk. This veto may be overruled if a majority of the whole council, other than the head, is present and a majority of those present vote in favour of overruling the veto. For the purpose of voting on the matter the head of the council is not counted as a member of the council.

A British Columbia mayor or reeve at any time within one month from the adoption of any by-law, resolution, or proceeding may intervene and return it to council for consideration, provided the matter has not been affirmed by a vote of the ratepayers. He must state his objections, suggestions, or amendments, which are to be entered in the minutes, and the council may accept or reject them. If on such consideration by council the by-law, resolution, or proceeding does not pass council in either its original or its amended form it is considered to be absolutely vetoed and may not again be introduced during council's then term, except with the unanimous consent of council including the mayor or reeve. At the first reconsideration after being returned by the mayor or reeve a matter only requires a majority to pass and it is then as valid as it was prior to the intervention of the mayor or reeve.

Mayor's or Reeve's Vote

The statutes in some provinces specifically provide that the head of the council has the same right to vote on matters in council as any other member.[23] Others only permit him to vote if there is an equality of votes on an issue in which case he gives the casting vote.[24] Mayors of Saskatchewan towns are required by statute to vote unless otherwise disqualified, and the chairman of a Newfoundland council not only has the right to vote but in case of an equality of votes, including his own, he has an additional casting vote. Even in those councils where the head of the municipality has the same right to vote as the other members, local rules or custom in some councils provide that the head votes on all issues and, in other, that he refrains from voting except where there is a tie vote.

If the head of the council is considered in his capacity as presiding officer at council meetings there is something to be said for his abstaining from voting and attempting to maintain his impartial position as chairman, but if the head is to be regarded as the one to give leadership and direction to the council it would seem hard to justify the practice of not voting. From the viewpoint of the mayor or reeve it is often convenient, politically, not to be obliged to commit himself on an issue on which there may be sharp difference of opinion among the electorate.

Status of Head of Council

The head of a municipal council in Canada does not have the

[23]In Nova Scotia "municipalities," New Brunswick counties, all Ontario municipalities, Saskatchewan cities and rural municipalities, and all Alberta municipalities.

[24]In New Brunswick towns, all Quebec municipalities, and all Manitoba municipalities.

executive powers possessed by the "strong mayors"[25] in some United States urban municipalities. His position lies somewhere between that of the United States strong mayor and the English mayor. Such power and influence as he may appear to have is based more upon prestige and personality than upon legal authority. The public generally credits the head of a council with greater powers, and consequently holds him individually responsible for the results of municipal administration to a greater extent than his legal authority justifies.

The office of mayor, reeve, or warden is one of great antiquity among Anglo-Saxon peoples and has associated with it, in the minds of the people, the position of headship. It is to such community leader that the people as a whole look for the solution of their problems, for it is he who epitomizes the civic administration. As the head of the council, he personifies the whole local government in the minds of the electorate in a manner similar to that in which, at other levels, governments are thought of as the Bennett or the King Government, or the Churchill Government or the Roosevelt Administration. The individual catches the imagination; the group has little popular appeal. The people cannot or will not bother to follow the activities of the individual members of the group comprising the government be it local, provincial, or national.

The social status which the mayor attains as first citizen of his community, his appearances on public occasions as the ceremonial head of the municipality, the fact that in an emergency he has to make final decisions in circumstances not provided for by the normal routine procedures, all serve to emphasize his position. It is further enhanced in municipalities which operate on the ward basis, for there he is the only council member who can claim to represent the people of the whole area.

This pre-eminence has its drawbacks as well as its advantages. The mayor becomes the official to whom all citizens turn when in need of assistance. The deficiencies of the local administration and its inequitable results in particular cases, the problems of the erring husband, the insistent bailiff, and the elusive landlord—all are laid upon the mayor's doorstep. Many of these problems are not his responsibility nor within municipal jurisdiction, and often he is powerless to

[25]Some of the larger cities in the United States have adopted what is known as a strong mayor type of city government. Under this plan the mayor has wide executive powers which vary from city to city, but which include such powers as a veto over council actions, the right to appoint and discharge department heads without council approval, exclusive jurisdiction over the administration, and, in extreme cases, the sole right to initiate budgets appropriations.

assist, but citizens, desperate to find a solution, come to him for help because he is the nominal official head of the community. As a result much of the time of the head of a council in urban communities is taken up with matters which are not municipal nor of major importance to the community as a whole but which are of paramount concern to individuals. In many instances the mayor is able to modify the rigid application of general rules even in fields far removed from municipal jurisdiction.

The prestige which a mayor is accorded by the public is reflected in the attitude of his council. His weight and influence in their deliberations is out of proportion to his voting strength as a member of the group. In general, of course, mayors are of a higher average calibre than the members of their councils for advancement from councillor to mayor or reeve is a selective process. Electors may retain for many years as councillor a representative who would not stand a chance in a contest for head of the council. The public has no hesitation in expressing through the ballot box its opinion that a man is stepping out of his class in running for top position.

Ex officio Duties

The head of the council, by virtue of his office, is a member of various statutory civic boards and committees. He is also asked to act on numerous non-governmental civic bodies and to head varied community activities. Thus he serves as a connecting link between the many groups in the local government and the community organization. More than any other citizen he is in a position to know what is going on in all sectors of community activity and is able to keep each of these various bodies and his council in touch with developments elsewhere in the municipality. By reason of this knowledge he can work effectively to bring the policies of all closer to a common aim and to prevent the different bodies from working at cross purposes.

Opinions differ among elected representatives as to the position of the head of the municipality when acting as an *ex officio* member of other civic boards. Some feel that he is answerable to the council and when acting on such boards should support policies approved by the majority of the council. Others take the position that as he sits on these other boards by virtue of his office as mayor or reeve, he is responsible only to those who put him there, namely, the electors, rather than to the council. This issue most commonly arises in connection with the spending policies of such boards or with respect to police administration in municipalities where the police are not under council control.

Deputy Mayor

A council may appoint one of its members to take the place of the head of the council in the event of his absence, illness, or inability to act, or if the office is vacant. The member so appointed has all the powers and responsibilities of the office, subject to a few minor exceptions, and is variously known as an acting mayor or reeve, deputy mayor or reeve, or pro-mayor. In some instances the power to make such appointments is permissive and may be exercised from time to time as occasion requires.[26] In other cases, however, councils are required to make such appointments at regular intervals. Such compulsory appointments must be made every three months in Nova Scotia and Alberta towns (deputy mayor) and every six months in Alberta municipal districts (deputy reeve).

Mayor's Term of Office

The term of office for the head of a council varies from one to two years except for wardens in Nova Scotia and New Brunswick. The trend in the United States toward longer terms for mayors has not as yet been followed extensively in Canada. Some United States cities with the long term provide that a mayor may not succeed himself but this restriction is rare in Canada.[27] While most Canadian municipalities have a one-year term, it is an unwritten law in many urban municipalities that unless the mayor has proved to be clearly incompetent he will be allowed a second term, either by acclamation or without serious opposition. More frequently in the smaller than in the larger municipalities a man may be retained as mayor or reeve for many years. In county councils, the wardenship is usually considered as an honour for the municipality represented as well as for the man selected and in many counties it is an accepted understanding that "a man can only be warden once." At the other extreme are found cases such as that of the late Mayor Joseph Beaubien of Outremont who was mayor for over thirty-five years. Normally a mayor has a tenure of office of from two to five years and it is not uncommon for a mayor who has been defeated to have a subsequent term or terms.

THE COUNCIL

The council, which is the governing body of the municipal corporation, is composed of the head of the council and other elected

[26]This is the case in Nova Scotia "municipalities" (deputy warden), in Quebec municipalities under the Municipal Code (pro-mayor), in Ontario (acting mayor), in Manitoba (deputy mayor), in Alberta villages (deputy mayor), and in British Columbia cities and districts (acting mayor or reeve).

[27]The Halifax Charter provides that no person who has filled the office of mayor for three successive years may be elected mayor until eleven months after the termination of his last occupancy.

members. It is upon the council as a whole that responsibility rests for carrying out the duties and for exercising the powers of the corporation. A council can exercise its powers only by action in the proper form, as explained below, taken at a regularly constituted meeting at which a quorum is present and when the majority of those present vote in favour of such action.

Meetings

Council meetings may be regular or special meetings. The time and frequency of meeting may be regulated by statute or may be left to the decision of the council. The frequency of meetings is optional with all councils in Newfoundland, Ontario, Manitoba,[28] Saskatchewan, and British Columbia, and with special classes of councils in other provinces.[29] A minimum number of meetings is required in some provinces, as shown in the accompanying summary.

Province	*Statutory meeting requirements*
Nova Scotia	
"Municipalities"	Annual and semi-annual meetings*
New Brunswick	
Counties	Annual and semi-annual meetings*
Towns	Quarterly meetings
Quebec	
Counties	Quarterly meetings unless council limits meetings to two
Local municipalities	Meeting first Monday of each month unless council decides otherwise
Cities and towns	Monthly meetings
Alberta	
Towns and villages	At least six meetings annually

*The council may dispense with the semi-annual meeting.

The date for the first meeting of a council is usually fixed by statute. This may be a definite date, as for New Brunswick counties, the third Tuesday in January, or a date on or before which the meeting must be held, as for Ontario local municipalities, not later than the second Monday in January. It may also be related to the election proceedings, as in British Columbia where the date is the second Thursday following nominations.

As a rule the frequency of regular meetings varies according to the population of the municipality, for the greater quantity of business in larger places requires more meetings. County councils, which usually meet from two to four times a year, continue their sessions for three or four or more days until their work is completed. The trend, however, is towards shorter sessions and more frequent meetings of county

[28]In rural municipalities regular meetings are limited to thirteen annually.
[29]Nova Scotia towns, and Alberta municipal districts.

councils. Other councils usually complete their work at one meeting and then adjourn till the next regular meeting date.[80] Councils of smaller municipalities ordinarily meet monthly, while most city councils meet at least twice a month. Boards of control in large cities meet several times a week. Most councils have fixed dates for regular meetings with provision for calling special meetings as required.

Special meetings of a council may be called by the head of the council and must be called if a specified number of council members so request in writing.[81] Notice of a special meeting must be given all the members, stating the business to be dealt with at the meeting, and usually must be delivered to the members by a fixed time preceding the time of meeting. This time varies from twenty-four hours in Saskatchewan cities to five days in Nova Scotia counties. Local councils make their own rules in this regard where it is not provided for by statute. In some provinces special meetings may be held at any time if all members are present and are prepared to waive notice.

County council sessions are held throughout the day and in the evening but most other councils meet regularly in the evenings, for if their meetings of council and committees were held in the day-time it would be difficult for any but self-employed individuals to serve as councillors.

Before a council can legally transact business there must be a quorum present at the meeting. A quorum usually consists of a majority of the whole membership of the council. In New Brunswick towns a quorum consists of the mayor and four councillors, while in Quebec counties, if the council has twelve or more members, seven constitute a quorum.[82] It is the duty of the head of the council to preside at all meetings of council although provision is usually made for the council to elect one of its members to take the chair if the head of the council is absent.

Some provinces require that all meetings of council be open to the

[80]An exception is noted in W. R. Plewman's account of the discussion of the Toronto "Waterfront Grab": "The debate in the Toronto City Council over the Beck radial entrance agreement began on August 29, 1922 and continued daily, with several night sessions, until seven o'clock in the morning of September 6th. It was a meeting without parallel in the history of Toronto." W. R. Plewman, *Adam Beck and the Ontario Hydro* (Toronto, 1947), p. 315. Such endurance contests, however, are rare in municipal councils.

[81]This number may be (*a*) a majority of council, as in Ontario and in Saskatchewan cities and towns, (*b*) one-third of the council in Nova Scotia "municipalities," (*c*) one-quarter of the council in Manitoba, (*d*) a stated number of members, three in Nova Scotia towns, Quebec cities and towns, and Saskatchewan rural municipalities, and in Alberta and British Columbia; two in Quebec municipalities under the Municipal Code and in Saskatchewan villages.

[82]Charlottetown, with a council of eight councillors and a mayor, requires five councillors and the mayor, or acting mayor, to constitute a quorum.

public[33] while others only require that ordinary meetings be open.[34] A majority of council in Quebec cities and towns can order a meeting with closed doors and in Ontario a special meeting may be closed to the public by special resolution. The fact that a meeting is open to the public does not mean, of course, that citizens have any right to speak in council.

Majority Vote

Matters before a council are decided by a majority vote of those present unless, as happens in a few cases, the statutes require a greater or permit a lesser number.[35] The usual alternatives are a two-thirds' vote, a three-quarters' vote, or a unanimous vote of council. In five-member councils in Ontario the concurrent votes of three members are required to adopt any measure. A general statutory rule is that where there is a tie vote the decision is in the negative, except in British Columbia councils when voting on the question "Shall the chair be sustained?"

In several provinces[36] all members of council who are present at a meeting and who are not disqualified or excused from voting must vote on all matters before council. In others, where there is no statutory requirement in this matter, a similar rule is often found in local councils' procedure rules.

Disqualification from Voting

Members of council are prohibited by statute from voting on issues before the council under some circumstances. These provisions vary in the different provinces. The Ontario provision, for example, is that a member shall not vote (1) on any by-law appointing him to any office in the gift of the council, (2) to fix his pay for any services to the corporation, except for attendance at meetings, (3) if a shareholder in an incorporated company having dealings or a contract with the corporation, on any question affecting the company, (4) if a lessee of the corporation for a term of twenty-one years or upwards, on any question affecting his lease, (5) if the proprietor of or otherwise interested in a newspaper, on any question affecting its dealings with the corporation, or (6) if the owner of land wholly or partially exempt, on any question affecting such exempt property.

[33]All councils in Nova Scotia, New Brunswick, and Manitoba, and councils of municipalities under the Municipal Code in Quebec.

[34]Ontario, Saskatchewan, Alberta, and British Columbia.

[35]In New Brunswick counties in voting on the question of making a valuation, it is sufficient to obtain the assent of two-fifths of the councillors, which is as valid and effectual as a majority vote of the council.

[36]In Manitoba and Alberta, in villages in New Brunswick, and in Saskatchewan rural municipalities.

The purpose of such disqualification is to avoid a situation where a member may find his personal interest in conflict with his duty as a representative. It is sometimes difficult to know just where the line should be drawn but "there is a consensus of opinion that where the personal or pecuniary interest of the member is that of a ratepayer, in common with other ratepayers or 'where, though he is personally interested, his interest is not different from that of the community in general,' the member is not disqualified."[37] In councils where rules of procedure require all members to vote, those who wish to avoid embarrassment can request to be excused from voting and may be so excused by a formal motion. Some provinces provide penalties for members who vote on matters on which they are disqualified.[38]

Council Action

The actions of a council take the form of by-laws or resolutions. The statutes require that action be by by-law in some cases; in others no particular form of action is specified. A municipal by-law[39] is a law passed by a municipal council.[40] It must comply with statutory requirements as well as with any rules established by the local council. A resolution is an expression of the decision or wishes of a council which has been submitted to council in the form of a motion and which has been adopted by majority vote.

In general, a council's powers are exercised by by-law in the more important matters and where the action taken affects members of the public directly. Resolutions usually deal with "the smaller acts of administration" and matters of internal management within the municipal organization or are used to place on record an expression of council opinion which may have no binding effect. It is difficult to draw the correct line between the areas covered by these two forms of council action.[41]

Some limitations, however, are imposed upon a council in exercising its powers. Subject to exceptions, the jurisdiction of a council is limited

[37]See H. A. Robson and J. B. Hugg, *Municipal Manual* (Toronto, 1920), p. 278 *et seq.*

[38]If a member of an English local authority has any pecuniary interest, direct or indirect, in any contract or matter being considered at a meeting at which he is present, he is required to disclose his interest, under penalty of a fine not exceeding £50 if he fails to do so.

[39]The term "by-law" was originally used to designate a law made for the government of a *bye*, which was the name given by the Danes to the old English *tun* or township. The word is still frequently spelled bye-law.

[40]Municipal bodies other than council also have statutory power to pass by-laws.

[41]The British Columbia Municipal Act is more specific than that of any of the other provinces as to matters which may be dealt with by resolution.

to the municipality which it represents.[42] Exceptions to this general rule are provided for by statute to permit municipalities to maintain parks, airports, disposal plants, hospitals, public housing, and other projects in adjacent municipalities. Such exceptions usually concern cities which establish such facilities in adjacent rural or suburban areas.

Councils must be certain that they have the powers they desire to exercise, for, if they exceed their authority, persons who are injured thereby or who object to the action taken may appeal to the courts and the corporation or the councillors may be required to pay damages or their action may be voided. Councils must act in good faith and without discrimination as between citizens or their action may be upset by the courts. They must also comply with any conditions or formalities which the statutes set out as a condition of exercising specific powers.

It follows that a municipal government in all its actions must constantly consult its legal advisors as to its rights and powers and it must be meticulous in its observance of legal requirements and restrictions. This does not mean, however, that municipalities always do keep within the law. Councils are created by provincial authority to serve certain stated purposes, and it is hardly to be expected that general legislation can cover all the problems that will arise in the operations of a community. As we have already seen, councils are constantly being asked to take actions for which they have no legal authority, and the local electors are not always satisfied with the answer that their council has not the authority to deal with a particular matter. Moreover, situations may arise which need to be dealt with, and if no other person or body can or will deal with them, then the council does. Consequently councils frequently do things for which they have no authority. Such actions are classed as *ultra vires* or beyond the legal competence of the council. Councillors, being laymen, draw a distinction between an action which is illegal because it is prohibited by law and one that is illegal because it is not specifically authorized.

Actions which are *ultra vires* are allowed to stand unquestioned in many cases because the people of the community are satisfied that the council should act regardless of its lack of jurisdiction. A council in

[42]Thus, a municipality which requires all owners of bicycles in the municipality to take out a licence can not penalize a resident of an adjacent municipality who travelled its streets on an unlicensed bicycle, nor can a city take any action against a grocer on the non-city side of a boundary street for staying open after the hours when the city grocers are required by a city by-law to close.

such cases is exposed to the possibility that some person may take action to upset what has been done. The council's protection lies in the expediency of its action and in the general preoccupation of the public with their private affairs. Where a council exercises powers beyond its legal competence it may consider it wise to protect itself against the possibility of litigation by obtaining from the provincial government an unofficial assurance that at the next session of the legislature retroactive authorization will be introduced to validate the action in question.

There are several means of keeping a council within its proper sphere. One is the power of the electorate to replace the members of the council though, in practice, this is not very effective, for citizens are not inclined to condemn their representative for actions which are *ultra vires*, if they have community approval and do not offend the moral standards of the community. The courts are the main protection. A person damaged, or likely to be damaged, by illegal acts of council may sue to obtain damages or to restrain the council from proceeding and the courts will determine the matter; or a citizen may apply to the courts to quash a by-law or declare it to be *ultra vires*. One common method of questioning certain types of *ultra vires* legislation is to allow a case under the by-law to come before a magistrate. He will refuse to convict if he is satisfied that a council acted beyond its powers, and thereafter it is pointless to attempt to continue to enforce the by-law. Many by-laws, however, which are in excess of a council's powers, are successfully and often beneficially enforced, because no one has questioned their validity.

Council's Powers

The powers granted to municipal corporations vary from province to province and from one type of municipality to another within a province. The legal source of every power which a council exercises is found in some provincial statutory enactment. The statutes may set out in considerable detail the manner in which a council shall exercise certain of its powers or may grant a power in general terms leaving councils free to adopt what they consider the expedient method of accomplishing the desired end. Thus the statutes governing municipal elections provide for minute detail of procedure, whereas in providing for the maintenance of roads councils are left ample discretion as to methods and standards.

In recent years there has been developed a volume of supplementary legislation in the form of regulations. As the business of the legislatures has increased and provincial supervision and regulation has been extended, the legislatures have developed a practice of enacting laws in general terms and authorizing a minister, a department, or some provincial officer or board to supplement this legislation with rules and regulations which have the same force and effect as statutory enactments. To obtain a complete knowledge of the powers of councils it is necessary therefore to look both at the statutes and at the regulations issued under authority of the statutes. These regulations are produced in a continuous and ever increasing flow.

Councils' powers may be either mandatory or optional. Mandatory powers are those which are granted to a corporation but which the statute requires the council to exercise, although considerable discretion may be left with the council as to the manner of doing so. There are several incentives for a council to exercise its mandatory powers: if it fails to carry out its duty a council may be liable for damages incurred as a result of such failure, provincial grants may be withheld, the power may be exercised by some provincial authority and the cost charged to the corporation, action may be compelled by writ of mandamus, or in some types of municipalities the Minister may dismiss a council. In general, the mandatory powers relate to functions which are of wider than local concern or which deal with matters of such fundamental importance in community living that the legislatures have felt the local citizens should be protected against inaction by their representatives.

The optional powers which are granted may be exercised or not by councils as they see fit, but in many instances if councils do choose to exercise a power they may only do so subject to conditions and regulations provided by statute or by some authority authorized by statute.

The usual powers of councils might be classified[48] as follows:

1. powers to take positive action to do certain things, e.g. to maintain fire brigades, parks, or playgrounds, to lay sewers, to maintain streets, etc.;
2. powers to make grants, e.g. for charitable or patriotic purpose, to encourage athletics, to provide scholarships;
3. powers to prohibit certain actions, e.g. the making of loud and disturbing noises in the streets, prolonged emission of dense smoke, the keeping of explosives within the municipality;
4. powers to regulate, e.g. parking, building construction, plumbing installation;
5. powers to license activities or businesses, e.g. pedlars, laundries, bicycles, taxi cabs, restaurants, butcher shops;
6. powers to enter into agreements or contracts, e.g. for franchises

[48]This classification should not be considered as all-inclusive.

such as bus or street railway franchises, for supplying municipal services to adjacent municipalities, for the construction of watermains;
7. powers to conduct its own business, e.g. appoint and pay officers and employees, or to regulate the procedure of council meetings;
8. powers to acquire, hold, or dispose of real property;
9. powers to raise money by taxation or by borrowing, e.g. to provide for making assessments, to levy taxes, or to issue debentures.

Even though municipal councils are authorized to exercise numerous powers, they are subject to control in many cases in doing so, even where the action taken is clearly within their legal competence. Such control may be broad in its nature or may be limited in its scope. An example of the broad type of provincial control occurs in Nova Scotia where every council by-law is subject to the approval of the Minister. Even when a by-law is approved, the Minister may subsequently revoke his approval, after which the by-law ceases to have any force or effect. In Quebec cities and towns also, except in the case of a loan by-law already approved by the proper Minister, the Lieutenant-Governor in Council may disallow any by-law within a period of six months. It is a general practice in some provinces to require that the exercise of certain types of powers, the passing of certain by-laws such as traffic by-laws, or provisions of certain by-laws, such as the amount to be charged by way of a licence fee, shall require the approval of some provincial authority.

As previously noted, the exercise of certain powers is, in all provinces, made subject to the consent and approval of a vote of the electors entitled to vote on the matter involved. This provision for control of council action by the electorate is carried to the extreme in the city of Medicine Hat, the Charter of which provides that no by-law[44] shall go into effect before the expiration of ten days from the date of its final passage. If during the ten days a petition with sufficient signatures[45] protesting against the by-law is presented, the by-law is suspended from going into effect. If the council does not entirely repeal the by-law it must submit it to a vote of the persons qualified to vote on it and unless a majority of the persons voting on the by-law vote in favour the by-law is of no effect. A similar provision applying to Saint John requires repeal, or submission of the issue to a vote of the electors, if a petition from 10 per cent of the electors is submitted within twenty days.

[44]Except where otherwise provided or, except for a by-law for the immediate preservation of the public peace, health, or safety, which contains a statement of its urgency and is passed by a two-thirds' vote of council.

[45]Signed by electors equal in number to 25 per cent of the entire vote for all candidates for mayor at the last general municipal election.

Although the corporation to which these powers are granted is a continuing body, the personnel of the council which exercises the powers changes from time to time. Consequently it is a general rule that the acts of one council cannot bind a succeeding council so that if a council is not satisfied with an action taken or a by-law passed by its predecessors, it may alter the action or repeal or amend the by-law to which it objects. There are, however, exceptions to this general rule. Thus, where a franchise has been granted for a term of years with the assent of the electors, succeeding councils are bound by the terms of the franchise for the duration of the period. The same condition prevails where, by statute, a council is specifically authorized to make an agreement which is binding over a period of years. Similarly, if a council issues and sells debentures to finance a project of which a succeeding council does not approve, the latter cannot repeal the authorizing by-law and thus deny the purchasers of the securities the fulfilment of the terms of sale. There are also some actions, such as those which involve zoning by-laws in some provinces, which a council may not alter without first having obtained the assent of some designated provincial authority.

Although councils may not be legally bound by acts and undertakings of their predecessors, whether formalized or not, in most instances they do carry them out provided there is no suggestion of improper dealings. Thus, if an industry is induced to come to a municipality on an unwritten understanding that there will be some concession on assessment, or if an employee on appointment is promised adjustments in pay after a period of service, subsequent councils will usually implement the promises given.

Payment of Council Members

In most provinces the payment of council members for their services is authorized by statute, but in a few cases[46] such payment is prohibited. Payment of councillors in "municipalities" in Nova Scotia and of aldermen in Saskatchewan cities is compulsory. The decision as to payment usually rests with the council, subject to statutory limitations and in some cases subject to a vote of the electors.[47]

The more common basis of payment is a fixed amount per day for

[46]Nova Scotia and New Brunswick towns, British Columbia villages, and Quebec local municipalities under the Municipal Code.

[47]In Quebec cities and towns the decision to pay members requires a two-thirds vote of council and also must be approved by a vote of the proprietors; in Alberta towns and villages the council must give public notice of the intention to pass a by-law authorizing payment and if within twenty days twenty electors register objection the question must be submitted to the proprietory electors for their approval.

attendance at meetings. The other method is a fixed annual sum with a deduction for any meetings missed. Under the first method the maximum rates payable are fixed by statute and they vary from $2.00 per day for Saskatchewan villages and Alberta towns and villages, to $10.00 per day for Nova Scotia and New Brunswick county councillors.[48] The most frequently recurring maximum rate is $5.00 per day.[49] In addition to payment for council meetings, members of county councils in Nova Scotia and members of all Ontario councils may be paid for attendance at committee meetings. The Prairie Provinces place a limit on the total amount council members may receive: either by fixing the total amount, e.g. in Manitoba towns, $100 a year; or by limiting the total number of meetings for which pay may be received, e.g. Saskatchewan towns, fifteen, and Alberta municipal districts, twelve. Rural municipalities in some cases may pay a mileage allowance for attendance at meetings.[50]

Under the plan of paying an annual sum to council members, which is frequently provided as an alternative basis of payment, the statute usually fixes the maximum annual amount payable. This plan is applicable to Nova Scotia towns and counties, Ontario municipalities, Manitoba cities and suburban municipalities, and British Columbia cities and districts. The amount ranges from $50 per year in Nova Scotia counties to $1,800 for aldermen in Ontario cities over 300,000 population. In Ontario cities under 200,000 population, the amount is not specified but must be approved in each case by the provincial Department of Municipal Affairs. The maximum rates for controllers in Ontario are similarly fixed by statute and vary from $2,500 in cities between 100,000 and 150,000 population to $7,500 in cities over 300,000. It is a common practice to pay the chairmen of standing committees a slightly larger amount than is paid to the other councillors.

The head of the council may be paid on a higher per day basis than councillors, as in Saskatchewan municipalities other than cities, or he may be paid the same per day rate with an additional annual lump sum, as in Manitoba.[51] The council is free to fix the annual remunera-

[48]Alternatively New Brunswick county councils may provide for an allowance not exceeding $100 per annum in lieu of all other allowances and compensation for attendance at meetings, except mileage.

[49]This rate applies in Nova Scotia "municipalities," in most Ontario municipalities, to city aldermen and reeves of rural municipalities in Saskatchewan, and in Alberta municipalities.

[50]In Nova Scotia, New Brunswick, and Ontario counties and townships, Manitoba and Saskatchewan rural municipalities, and Alberta municipal districts. The rate in most cases is ten cents per mile. In Ontario the mileage is only allowed one way, but in the other cases is allowed both ways.

[51]In towns $300, in rural municipalities $100.

TABLE 13

REMUNERATION OF MEMBERS OF COUNCIL IN CERTAIN CITIES

Municipality	Head of council	Other members
Brantford	$2,500	$ 5 per meeting
Belleville	750[a]	5 per meeting
Calgary	6,000[b]	750 per year
Charlottetown	325	None
Fredericton	1,000	300 per year
Halifax	3,000–5,000[c]	600 per year
Kingston	2,200[d]	None
London	5,000	700 per year
Moncton	1,000	250 per year
Montreal	10,000	600 per year[e]
Peterborough	1,500	5 per meeting
Quebec	8,000[f]	2,000 per year[g]
Sherbrooke	None	None
Toronto	15,000	7,500 per year (controllers) 1,800 per year[h] (aldermen)
Vancouver	7,500[i]	1,800 per year
Winnipeg	8,000	1,800 per year

[a]$300 additional as member of the Public Utilities Commission.

[b]In addition receives $50 a month for car and general expenses and $25 a month for special out-of-pocket expenses.

[c]Council determines mayor's indemnity annually within the range shown; deputy mayor between $200–$1,200; aldermen have $6.00 deducted for each council or committee meeting missed.

[d]In addition receives $500 as a member of the Public Utilities Commission and $400 as a member of the Police Commission.

[e]Chairman of Executive Committee, $10,000 plus $600 as councillor; other members of Executive Committee (five), $7,000 plus $600 as councillors; leader of Council, $2,400 plus $600 as councillor; each councillor $600.

[f]$5,000 salary and $3,000 car allowance.

[g]$1,500 salary and $500 car allowance.

[h]Chairmen of Standing Committees receive an additional allowance of $100.

[i]Reduced to $1.00 in 1951.

tion of the head of the council in Nova Scotia towns and counties, in all Ontario municipalities, and in Saskatchewan cities, while in British Columbia the statutes fix a maximum amount which varies according to the population. Some urban municipalities which do not pay the mayor a salary allow a fixed amount for expenses of office or pay for certain expenses incurred by reason of his position. The stated salary frequently is supplemented by payments for acting on other boards.[52]

Table 13 shows the rates of pay for council members in some urban municipalities.

Such pay as the ordinary member receives helps him to meet elec-

[52]In Welland the stated salary is $900 but in addition there is a $300 car allowance, $200 for acting as a water commissioner, $300 for acting as a police commissioner, and $5.00 per meeting as a member of the Hydro commission.

tion expenses and the many requests for charitable and other donations to which those in public office are particularly exposed. It is claimed by the advocates of pay for councillors that it makes it possible for men to serve who could not otherwise afford to lose the required time from their work. One of the objections to such payments is that they may be an inducement to persons who have little to contribute, but who are primarily interested in the added income. The type of representative who is most needed is not likely to be influenced to seek office by the pay involved. Some representatives prefer not to be paid as it frees them from the suggestion that they seek the position for the remuneration. Those opposed to paying councillors point out that it is hardly reasonable for men who use every possible inducement to persuade the electors to vote for them, to expect to be paid to perform the duties they are so anxious to assume. Whatever may be the justification for paying Dominion and provincial legislators, the cases are not comparable, for in these latter cases the prolonged absence from the home municipality involves considerable additional expense for living costs and is much more likely to result in a reduction in the member's private earnings. If councillors are to be paid, the lump sum annual basis, with deductions for meetings missed, appears to be much the better plan as it removes any suggestion that councils are meeting with unnecessary frequency and councils feel free to meet as the occasion requires.

The Lindsay Committee, studying this question in England in 1947 reported, in part, "The health of this democracy depends upon the fact that large numbers of men and women give their time and trouble to all sorts of voluntary work, and it is from such public spirited people that the members of public authorities should be recruited. Such voluntary work must involve sacrifice, and indeed, would lose its savour if it did not." The practice of paying councillors is on the increase in Canada and any loss of savour is apparently offset by the soothing effect of increased income. Many councillors feel that if members of other civic boards and other governments are to be paid, the councillors have an equal right to remuneration.

The position of the head of the council is somewhat different from that of other council members, for he is called upon to devote so much of his time to civic affairs that his business will inevitably suffer or, if he is an employee, his employer can not be expected to maintain his full rate of pay. To a much greater extent than other members, he is called upon to contribute to a wide variety of worthy causes and is at considerable expense for transportation, hospitality, and the innumerable incidental expenses that cannot be covered in an expense account. In general, the salaries paid Canadian mayors are not as high as those paid in comparable cities in the United States but, on the other hand, the responsibility for the municipal administration does not rest so directly on the mayor in a Canadian municipality. As a consequence, except in very large cities, the office does not occupy his full time.[58]

[58]*Municipal Wage Survey, September, 1947*, made by the Department of Municipal Affairs of British Columbia in conjunction with the Bureau of Economics and Statistics, Department of Trade and Industry, showed the extent of the practice of paying heads of municipalities in British Columbia, as follows:

Municipalities	Total number	Number paid	Range per annum	Average
Under 1,000 pop.	39	14	$ 12–$ 300	$ 126
1,000– 4,000 pop.	28	21	96– 2,000	459
4,000–37,000 pop.	27	25	360– 3,000	1,259
Over 37,000 pop.	2	2	4,000– 7,500	
Total	96	62		

Comparable statistics are not available for other provinces.

APPENDIX

Basis of Election and Composition of Municipal Councils under General Legislation

Province and municipality	Head of Council		Councillors			
	E or C[a]	Term[b]	Number	Term[b]	Number elected[c]	Vote basis[d]
Newfoundland						
Municipalities	C		5–10	4	½ total	
Prince Edward Island						
Towns	E	2	6	2	all	W or G
Villages	C	1	3	3	1	G
Nova Scotia						
Towns	E	2	6[e]	2	½ total	W or G
Counties	C	3	1–3[f]	3	all	W
New Brunswick						
Towns	E	1	2 per ward	1	all	G
Villages	C	1	3	1	all	G
Counties	C	1, 2, 4	2 per parish	1, 2, 4	all	W
Quebec						
Cities and towns	E or C	2	Fixed by charter	2	all	W
Parishes, townships, and villages	E	2[g]	6	2	½ total	G
Ontario[h]						
Cities	E	1 or 2	2 or 3 per ward[i]	1 or 2	all or ½	W or G
Towns (U.T.)[j]	E	1 or 2	4, 6, 7 or 9	1 or 2	all or ½	G[k]
Other towns 5000 and over	E	1 or 2	2 or 3 per ward[l]	1 or 2	all or ½	W
under 5000	E	1 or 2	4 or 6[m]	1 or 2	all or ½	G
Villages and townships	E	1 or 2	4[n]	1 or 2	all or ½	W or G
Manitoba						
Cities and towns	E	2	2 per ward[o]	2	all	W
Villages	E	2	4	2	½ total	G
Rural municipalities	E	2	4 to 6[p]	2	½ total	W or G
Saskatchewan						
Cities	E	1	6–20[q]	1 or 2	all or ½[r]	W or G
Towns	E	1	6	2	½ total	G
Villages	C	1	3	3	1	G
Rural municipalities	E	1	6[s]	2	½ total	W[t]
Alberta						
Cities	E	2	6–20	2	½ total	G
Towns	E	2	6	3	⅓ total	G
Villages	C	1	3	3	⅓ total	G
Municipal districts	C	1	6	3	⅓ total	W or G[u]
British Columbia						
Cities	E	2	5–10	2[v]	½ total	G
Villages	C	1	3	3	1	G
District municipalities	E	2	4–7	2[v]	½ total	G

[a]E—elected by electors; C—chosen by council.
[b]Term in years.
[c]The number or proportion of councillors elected at each election.
[d]W—ward or polling or electoral division basis; G—general vote basis.
[e]At least 6.
[f]One for each polling district with statutory provision that in 31 polling districts in the province there shall be 2 councillors and in 2 cases, 3 councillors.

[g]Elected in the "odd" year.

[h]Reference to reeves and deputy reeves in towns and deputy reeves in villages and townships has been omitted as their terms and bases of election are the same as for mayors. A deputy reeve is elected only where there are more than 1,000 municipal electors in the municipality. In villages and townships the total council personnel is five. If there is a deputy reeve there are only 3 councillors.

[i]Or the same total number if by general vote.

[j]In "unorganized territory" i.e. in territory not organized into counties.

[k]Council may provide that one councillor be elected from each ward and the balance to make up 4, 6, 7, or 9 be elected by general vote.

[l]If less than 5 wards, 3 per ward; or council may provide for 2 per ward, or 6 or 4 to be elected by general vote; where there are 5 or more wards council may provide for 2 or 1 per ward.

[m]Council may provide that one councillor be elected from each ward and the balance to complete 4 or 6 be elected by general vote.

[n]This number may be increased in the limited number of cases where village and township elections are on a ward basis.

[o]In towns may be 1 per ward.

[p]Or 1 per ward.

[q]Always an even number—the total number determined by council subject to vote of electors.

[r]If by general vote, half the total elected each year; if by wards, council may provide that a part retire each year or all retire each year or all retire every two years.

[s]One for each division; normally there are 6 electoral divisions.

[t]Councillors in odd numbered divisions one year, in even numbered divisions in alternate year.

[u]Where electoral districts have been established elections are by districts; otherwise by general vote.

[v]Municipalities which in 1947 were divided into wards may continue to elect on a one-year term basis.

CHAPTER V

COUNCIL ORGANIZATION AND OPERATION

Committees

Much of the work of municipal councils, particularly those with a large membership, is done by committees. Committees are usually composed of a portion of the members of council and are selected by the council, although in British Columbia the members of standing committees are selected by the mayor or reeve. In a few cases, such as Vancouver and London, all members of council sit on all the standing committees. It is a general, but not universal, practice that the mayor is an *ex officio* member of all committees.[1] Except on special committees and subcommittees, the practice of having non-council members act on committees is not widespread in Canada as it is in England,[2] perhaps because so many functions, such as education and the operation of parks, libraries, utilities, etc., which in England are under council jurisdiction, are in most Canadian municipalities controlled by special purpose bodies; the members of these bodies, which are discussed in chapter vi, are not members of council and many are appointed rather than elected. Whether or not a council operates on a committee basis rests in most cases with the council.

Committees fall into two classes, standing committees and special or select committees. Standing committees are chosen early in a council's term of office, usually at its first meeting, and continue to function throughout the council's year. Each standing committee has jurisdiction over a section of council operations either designated by by-law or established by custom. Ordinarily a committee has supervision over one or more departments, such as the fire department or the parks department, or over one or more functions of a department. Thus the activities of a works department may come in part under the Works Committee, in part under the Streets and Traffic Committee, and in part under the Town Planning Committee. In a general way the scope of a committee is indicated by its title, but differences in local practice may mean that the duties of committees with identical names in two municipalities show a wide variation of responsibilities. The com-

[1]In Quebec cities and towns the mayor is an *ex officio* member of all committees by statutory enactment.

[2]Councils are required to have co-opted members on certain committees in England.

mittees exercise a general supervision over the work and the staff under their jurisdiction, consult with and advise the officials responsible for such work, and make reports and recommendations to council on matters within their sphere.

Special committees are established by council from time to time, as occasion requires, to study and report upon, and in some cases to deal with, some special matters assigned to them. The personnel of special committees may be selected by the head of the council, under the authority of council, or may be named by resolution of council. They may be composed entirely of councillors or may include other citizens whose experience and advice will be of assistance. Occasionally the citizen members may be in the majority with sufficient council representation to keep the council in touch with the progress being made, to interpret the council viewpoint to the committee, and to serve as spokesmen for the committee when its recommendations are submitted. Special committees are able to give that extended study to problems which preoccupation with the mass of current detail makes impossible for council or its standing committees, and they enable a council to use the special knowledge and skills of citizens who are not council members. When a special committee has made its final report to council it is discharged and the committee ceases to exist.

Many advantages are gained by referring matters to committees. To assign problems to smaller groups speeds up the work and eliminates much speech making in council. Committees sift out the detail and bring matters before council in the form of a positive recommendation based on their study. Where issues come to council without any recommended solution, endless time is lost in arriving at a concensus of opinion of the members but a positive proposal will usually be accepted without further discussion. Moreover, committee members become acquainted with the work under their jurisdiction in a more intimate way than is possible if they try to cover the whole field of municipal activity, and their recommendations are correspondingly more valuable. Committee meetings are informal and the discussion is less restricted than in council where the rules of procedure and the more formal atmosphere discourage hesitant members from taking part in debate. Another useful result of the committee system is that, in the interval between the committee meeting and consideration of its report by the council, public opinion has an opportunity to develop and make itself felt regarding the recommendations. This interval of time for reflection and the opportunity to ascertain the public's views provide an insurance against hasty and ill-considered action. It is much easier to get a committee to take back its proposals for further consideration than it is to get a council to reverse its decisions once they have been made. For a council to reconsider its actions under the pressure of public opinion involves a loss of prestige.

A common complaint against the committee system is that it tends to slow down the process of arriving at decisions. Citizens whose patience is sorely tried by the reference of issues from committee to subcommittee or officials and the return trip of reports through various committees to council for final determination are often loud in condemning the cumbersome machinery. This slow process, however, is a protection for the citizens as a whole against ill-advised decisions based on incomplete information, or the "railroading" of measures under pressure from self-interested groups. Public bodies deal with other people's monies and rights, and their decisions, which may vitally affect far more citizens than those whose requests are immediately under discussion, should only be made after adequate deliberation. The "snap judgment" decisions attributed to master minds in the business world are out of place for those acting as trustees on behalf of the whole community. While it is essential that local government should endeavour to increase the tempo of its operations, if it is to play its part in the whole machine of governments, that end should not be attained by reducing the consideration which councils give to the matters under study but rather by eliminating the quantity of inconsequential matters with which they become absorbed and by concentrating on the more important issues.

The proper scope of committees is to study matters referred to them and to report thereon to council. They normally have no power to act except on the specific authority of council, although there are exceptions to this general rule. The council may adopt a committee's report, reject it, or send it back for further study, but is not in any way bound by its committees' recommendations. In most provinces the committees have no legal status but in some they are given the right to summon witnesses for examination on oath and to enforce such summons.[3] The statutes in several provinces are specific in providing that no report or order of a committee shall have any effect unless authorized by by-law or resolution of council.

The general rule is that a council cannot delegate its powers to a committee but there are several exceptions,[4] and even those councils

[3]Quebec municipalities under the Municipal Code and British Columbia cities and districts.

[4]If a New Brunswick county council dispenses with the semi-annual meeting it may appoint a committee to examine, pay, or withhold payment of accounts; in

which do not have a legal right to delegate their powers to committees do so in practice. Where power is delegated to a committee it is with the tacit understanding that the majority of council, when in council, will sustain the committee's action. This procedure is often necessary in dealing with matters which require prompt decision and yet which do not justify calling council into special session. It is also frequently adopted where council discussion has indicated the acceptable policy but the details remain to be worked out. Councils as a rule do not leave to their committees final decision on matters of major importance or on those in which the legality of any action taken is likely to be called in question.

Councils differ greatly in the number of their standing committees and in the number of committee members. This variation does not appear to depend on the amount of business to be done for while Vancouver has eight standing committees, Fredericton has fourteen, and while London has only two, Sherbrooke has ten. The number of committees may be a result of long established practice or the desire to provide chairmanships for as many members as possible. Three or five members, together with the head of the municipality as an *ex officio* member, is the most frequently occurring membership of standing committees. The committees usually provided for are finance, fire, industrial, works, market, reception, transportation, police, parks, property, health, administration, and welfare. The number of special committees and of their personnel vary even more than those of standing committees as they are determined by local circumstances. It is not possible to specify the ideal number of standing committees but it is more likely that there will tend to be too many committees, rather than too few. When there are too many committees, it becomes impossible for one person to keep the work of all in view and this usually results in a lack of co-ordination. Experience suggests also that if committees have too little work to do, they do not even do that work well. Up to a point, a heavier load induces better results.

The chairmen of standing committees may be selected by the council or they may be chosen by the members of the committees from among their number. The chairmen have considerable influence both in arriving at committee decisions and also in the conduct of council meetings. In the same way that the mayor's position brings him in closer contact with the operations of the municipality than is the case

Saskatchewan rural municipalities and in Alberta municipal districts the council may delegate to any of its committees, which may be composed of one or more members, any of the duties or powers conferred or imposed on the council by statute except the power to borrow money, pass a by-law, or enter into a contract.

with the other members, so the committee chairman is usually better informed on issues coming before the committee than are the other members. The other members tend to rely on the chairman to give study to matters on the agenda and to give leadership in coming to conclusions. Again, when the committee's recommendations come before the council it is normally the chairman who is expected to present the case for the committe if there is any difference of opinion in council. The extent to which a chairman dominates his committee or is dominated by them is to a considerable extent dependent upon his capacity and personality. Where decisions have to be made by the mayor in the intervals between council meetings, the committee chairmen can be of great assistance. As a result of their close contact with their committees the chairmen can pretty well predict what will be the reaction of their committees to any proposal. If, then, the mayor wants to get the reaction of council to a proposal his committee chairmen can fairly accurately advise as to its acceptability to their groups. The chairman's position in this respect is strengthened by the loyalty which normally develops within a committee, for it is not unusual for a committee member to take the attitude that, while he may not wholeheartedly favour a particular course, he will support his chairman if he has made some commitment on behalf of the committee. A committee chairman, however, cannot expect to carry his committee with him in such matters unless he has some real justification for having spoken for the committee without consulting the members.

Committee of the Whole

The committees referred to should not be confused with the "Committee of the Whole" in council, a term which is used to describe what is a council meeting procedure. When in the course of a council meeting a matter arises which it is desired to discuss without the restraint of the usual rules of procedure, a motion may be made for the council to resolve itself into Committee of the Whole to discuss the matter. The council then resolves itself into a committee composed of all the members of the council. The mayor as a rule will leave the chair and some councillor is appointed by council to act as chairman. The discussion then proceeds under the much more flexible and informal procedure of the Committee of the Whole. When the discussion is finished, and a motion that the committee rise and report has been adopted, the mayor resumes the chair, the chairman of the Committee of the Whole reports its decision, and the report is dealt with by the council. The council then proceeds to the next order of business.

Caucus

A caucus also should not be confused with a council committee. It is merely an unofficial meeting of council. A caucus meeting has no power to make legally binding decisions and is not recognized by law. It permits the members to discuss freely amongst themselves a matter which is, or will be, before the council. Because it is unofficial, the public and the press can be excluded and members may therefore express themselves freely without danger of being reported. A secret ballot, something which is forbidden by law in council, is frequently used in arriving at decisions in caucus.

The caucus is a device used to deal with matters which it may not be expedient to discuss publicly, or to avoid embarrassment to individuals, as when a choice has to be made from among a number of persons in making an appointment. It is a common practice to hold a caucus of the members of a new council prior to its first meeting to discuss organization, appointments, and committee personnel. There is usually a gentlemen's agreement[5] that those present will not reveal publicly the discussion which takes place in caucus, but such information has a way of leaking out. It is also sometimes agreed in advance that all members will support in open council decisions arrived at in caucus.

In principle the public's business should be open to public scrutiny. Too much secret discussion by councils is bound to raise suspicion. Yet there are times when the public interest or an individual's rights require that public business be conducted in private. The caucus has certain advantages even over a closed special meeting of council in dealing with these matters.

Procedure

Councils are authorized by statute to pass by-laws governing their own proceedings in matters not governed by provincial legislation. Many councils, particularly those in urban municipalities, have enacted detailed "procedure" by-laws comparable to the English Standing Orders, regulating the conduct of, and the procedure to be followed in, council meetings. Where no local rules have been adopted, or in matters not covered by local rules, the assumption is that parliamentary procedure applies as far as it is applicable.

Even though the membership of most councils is relatively small it

[5]A gentleman's agreement to be effective requires that the parties to the agreement carry out their undertakings like gentlemen.

is important to have rules of procedure and to adhere to them. Such rules eliminate much unnecessary repetition and tedious argument as to how the business shall be conducted and assist in keeping councils from becoming hopelessly confused and lost in a maze of motions, amendments, and amendments to amendments. The formalizing of established procedures into written rules also helps new members of councils to understand how the council operates. A council is both a legislative and an administrative body and while a reasonable amount of discussion, sufficient to present fully the merits and demerits of any proposal, must be allowed and encouraged yet discussion cannot be permitted to extend to the point where the day-to-day business of running the municipality is held up and becomes impossible. Public bodies have worked out rules of procedure as a result of many years of experience in attempting to reconcile the right of free debate and the necessity of getting the public's business done. The purpose of council meetings is to arrive at decisions agreed upon by the majority and the rules of procedure are designed to assist in attaining that end. Members may at time find the restrictions of procedure irksome, but rules are necessary for the greater good of the whole membership and the orderly, effective handling of the public's affairs. Not infrequently, when councils disregard their rules of procedure the debate becomes bogged down in a confusion of motions and amendments and, being unable to follow the proceedings clearly, the council finally makes a decision quite different from that which the members intend.

This brings up one of the important problems of council organization. Councils have the twofold function of determining policy and of applying it in particular cases. They are limited in their power to delegate discretionary power to their officials and most councils in any case are reluctant to leave the application of policies to officials. The constant flow of practical problems to council for its decision keeps a council in touch with the needs of the community and with shortcomings in its policies and in their administration. However, so great is the flow of detail, and so clamorous are the parties concerned, that individual cases absorb practically all of the council's time and the larger issues, which are not being pressed by interested persons, tend to be overlooked or sidetracked.

Most council members must earn their living and so have only limited time and energy to devote to public business. When too much of their time and effort is absorbed in dealing with individual cases no opportunity remains for the more deliberate consideration of larger matters of policy.[6] As a result the larger issues are repeatedly postponed and eventually buried for want of time or opportunity to consider them. Because of these conditions, councils are content to deal with problems as they become urgent, and often long after they should have been tackled, rather than to plan a long-term programme of community development. A council has two alternatives, either to leave more of the detail to the paid officials and to give more time to the larger problems, or to retain within its control the handling of small matters and to let the larger matters wait indefinitely. It is not suggested that the decisions of the officials would be wiser or fairer than those of the elected representatives, and certainly the officials would not be as flexible in applying policies, but the greater flexibility and protection against bureaucratic errors of judgment comes at too high a price. The citizen with a problem will protest that it is not democratic to deny him an appeal to the elected body. He feels entitled to his day in court. But it is not in the interests of the majority that councils be so preoccupied with the minor problems of the few that the larger problems of the many are ignored or overlooked.

Unwritten Rules or Conventions

In addition to statutory rules and regulations and local procedures there are many local unwritten rules which have behind them the weight of tradition and established practice. Some of these are understandings to which the public is a party, as in Sherbrooke where it is generally accepted that the office of mayor is to be held alternately by a French Canadian and an English Canadian,[7] or as in Charlottetown and Regina, that a mayor only hold office for two terms. Some are applicable only within the council organization, such as the understanding that the wardenship in Ontario counties shall be passed from municipality to municipality, or that no warden hold office for more than one term, or that the warden is alternately a Liberal and a Con-

[6] "The Council is literally immersed in a labyrinth of trifling affairs that ought never to come to its attention. Seemingly it can not learn that its part in administration should be limited to broad supervision." Austin F. Macdonald, *American City Government and Administration* (New York, 1941), p. 176.

[7] In Coaticook, Quebec (88 per cent French Canadian population) there has been an unwritten understanding since 1928 that the office of mayor would be occupied by a French Canadian during two consecutive terms while the third would be accorded to a representative of the English Canadian minority. The English Canadian mayor elected in 1948 over a French Canadian candidate who maintained that it was time to change the practice of alternating mayors stated, "The election was carried out on a principle of considerable significance because the French Canadians of my town have stood by an agreement which dates back to 1928."

servative. In some municipalities certain racial, religious, or other groups are conceded the right to a proportion of appointments in the gift of the council. These unwritten rules vary from place to place and except for those who are intimately involved in municipal life may be quite unknown to the general public. They are effective, however, in their operation and the individual who fails to observe them may be penalized by a variety of methods. The existence of such unwritten rules may serve to throw light on some actions that might otherwise be inexplicable.

There is also an unwritten code of ethics among the members of councils which is not immediately apparent to nor appreciated by non-members. Council members become relatively intimate through long hours of working together in council and committee meetings. Hence there frequently develops an unexpressed, but none the less effective, understanding as to how far a member may go in attacking the policies or views of another and to what extent opinion expressed in the confidence of a committee meeting can be publicized or used as ammunition in inter-councillor contests. There is no exact line to mark these limits, yet with few exceptions they are observed. Just as there is reputed to be honour among thieves, so must elected representatives realize that there is a limit to mutual exposure and recrimination, and that unless they stand together in many matters, all may fall in the public esteem. On the whole, this attitude probably results in better government than would otherwise be possible. While it may serve to protect minor shortcomings from exposure it enables the members to express themselves with a candour which would otherwise be impossible, and retains competent men in public office who might otherwise be eliminated on grounds which have campaign value but have no bearing on the member's capacity for public service.

Precedent

Many observers of municipal government are at first unfavourably impressed by the constant reference to precedent and the harking back to established practices, when new methods of dealing with problems are proposed. Although councils are not bound by the actions of previous councils they have a healthy regard for precedent. Councillors like most human beings are conservative and, to a degree, lazy. They dislike changing their methods of doing things and are usually content to follow the methods established by their predecessors and, if there is experimenting to be done, to let someone else do it. So much of municipal action is based on written law that if a practice has been established which is consonant with the law, as interpreted by the courts, councils and their officials are hesitant to try new methods lest in the process they run foul of some legal technicalities they have not foreseen. The known way is the safest, if not necessarily the shortest.[8] Perhaps the most compelling reason for the considerable weight which councils accord to precedent may be the bitter experience which has resulted from ill-considered departures from practices which years of trial and error have developed and have proven to be safe and satisfactory.

One difficulty in public business, as compared with private business, is that it is public and every citizen is entitled to be treated the same. To change a policy or method of handling some problem immediately raises a protest from those who may have received less beneficial treatment under the earlier policy. If, for example, a council decides to change from a local improvement to a general tax basis for paying for pavements, all those who have already paid for pavements on the frontage basis are up in arms because they feel it is unjust that they should pay again for some other person's pavement. To experiment and adopt new methods may have its appeal but it may also result in expensive legal or political costs. "When in doubt, don't" is often the cautious approach to proposals for change.

The Council Meeting

It must appear to a citizen who attends a meeting of his municipal council, if it operates on the committee system, that the matters coming before council are given very perfunctory consideration and that there is almost a conspiracy among the members to avoid discussion. The impression he receives is that of a meeting run by the presiding officer and the clerk, faced by councillors whose sole contribution appears to be an occasional mumbled "Carried" or a half-hearted raising of right hands.

Where the committee system is used all matters to be dealt with by the council, except in cases of urgency, are automatically referred to the appropriate committee for study and report. This assures a more careful study of the issue than would be possible in council and is a protection against some matter being "sprung" on a council and rushed through without due consideration. It is in the committee that

[8]An example of this may perhaps be seen in the use of the two systems of collecting arrears of taxes in Ontario. The old and long established system of tax sale may be cumbersome, protracted, and expensive, and may involve much detailed work, but numerous cases before the courts over many years have established a precise procedure and many treasurers have been hesitant to adopt the more modern and simpler registration system because there may be pitfalls not yet clearly marked out by case law.

most of the discussion takes place. When the committee arrives at a conclusion its recommendation goes forward to the council as a committee report.

The greater part of the proceedings at a council meeting consists of the consideration of the various committee reports. As these recommendations have had the consideration outlined above, the council member realizes that they are the agreed-upon opinion of the majority of a committee specializing in the matters being dealt with. Usually he will agree with the recommendation, but even if he does not do so he appreciates the improbability of persuading his fellow councillors that his views are correct and the majority of the committee are wrong. There is normally sufficient solidarity among committee members that the best an objector can hope for is to get the particular portion of the report referred back for further consideration.[9] He can express his objection to the item in the report for the purpose of showing his constituents that he did what he could to change the decision. If he raises objections too frequently on unimportant matters, however, his fellow councillors come to look upon him as a consistent objector, and when he takes issue on matters of real importance to him, his influence has been discounted by his record. Council members, therefore, in council usually assent to the clauses in the various report without comment or discussion, and if the members have had advance copies of the reports, the clauses may not even be read, but are merely called by number.

A considerable part of a meeting is taken up with passing by-laws, most of which are merely a formalizing of decisions already made by council, so that little discussion is called for. Thus, except on rare occasions when a major issue is debated on the floor of the council, a council meeting is an unimpressive performance. It is little wonder that the citizen who attends one and who does not understand the background is often belittling in his comments and is discouraged by the impression he receives of the manner in which the public's business is handled.

Minutes

A written record or minutes of the proceedings of each council meeting is made and kept by the clerk.[10] In this record are the names of the members present, the decisions of council, and a record of the

[9]It is one of the unwritten rules of many committees that a member is expected to support and argue for his committee's recommendations even though he may have opposed them in committee, unless in committee he warned his fellow members that he would oppose the report when it came to council.

[10]Citizens have a statutory right to examine such minutes and other municipal records in the custody of the clerk.

votes, where there is a recorded vote. Similarly minutes of committee meetings also are kept. The statutes require the clerk to record the proceedings of council "without note or comment." Consequently proper minutes merely record what council has done and do not record debate or the reasons offered by members for their individual votes on various questions.

In some councils each matter is voted upon by each member indicating orally, or by holding up his hand, whether he votes for or against the adoption of a motion or by-law. In other councils the matters are presented to council by the presiding officer and their adoption is declared if no objection is raised. Any member has the right to demand a recorded vote on any matter before council and in such cases the members individually state their vote, "Yea," if in favour of adoption, and "Nay," if opposed, and the clerk records in the minutes the name of each member and how he voted. In Quebec municipalities under the Municipal Code and in Ontario and Manitoba voting in council must be by open vote as distinct from a ballot vote.

The minutes of each meeting are presented at a subsequent meeting of council and corrected or confirmed by motion in council. In larger municipalities the council members are supplied with a copy of the minutes of the previous meeting prior to the meeting at which they are to be confirmed but in many smaller municipalities the minutes of the previous meeting are read by the clerk. The minutes are an essential record in the conduct of the corporation's affairs for they constitute the sole authority for any action by or on behalf of the council and for the expenditure of municipal funds.

Council Activities

A council's main activities fall into two groups, legislative and administrative. The legislative activities consist of passing by-laws for the benefit or protection of the people of the municipality, or by-laws necessary to the conduct of the corporation's affairs. The administrative activities include the carrying out of the responsibilities and duties of the corporation, and the control and direction of the operation of public services.

Municipal legislation covers a wide range of subjects. They vary from restrictions on parking to regulation of the details of building construction. One class of legislation is that which affects the general public; such are zoning or licensing by-laws. Another class is largely internal and does not affect the public directly; such, for example, are by-laws to appoint officials or to authorize the signing of contracts.

The first class of legislation referred to usually provides for a penalty to be imposed upon those who do not comply, and such legislation, to a degree, restricts the citizen's freedom of action. It is the duty of the police or other specially appointed enforcement officers, such as building or sanitary inspectors, to see that these by-laws are complied with but, failing compliance, the final enforcement rests with the courts. The citizen is not usually affected directly by legislation of the internal type and, by reason of its nature, penalties for non-observance are not called for, nor is there a problem of enforcement.

Municipal administrative activities include the operation of the machinery of government—assessing, financing, tax collecting, auditing, etc.—as well as the performing of such services as the corporation maintains for the inhabitants. Usually the larger the population of the municipality, the greater the variety of such services; they range from the maintenance of roads and the provision for surface drainage, which are common to all municipalities, to the provision of parks, refuse disposal, band concerts, or day nurseries in the larger urban centres.

The council in most cases determines what services are to be provided, as well as their quality and extent. The work of carrying on the services is left to paid officers or employees who are responsible to council, usually through a standing committee, for the manner in which the council's policies are carried out.

Intangibles

A knowledge of the machinery of local government and the statutory duties and responsibilities involved does not provide a complete understanding of the subject. What makes it work? Why do men compete for public office when the visible rewards, if any, are so small and the price to be paid in interference with their private pursuits and in criticism and abuse is so high? These questions are somewhat difficult to answer.

Men and women seek public office for a variety of reasons. They may desire to serve their community, or want to promote a pet project. Some like to be in the limelight or to feel that they are a power in their community. Some see in municipal office the first rung in the political ladder, and with others municipal service is a family tradition. Some run for office to keep someone else out, or because they have been persuaded, often against their better judgment, that they are the man or woman for the job. Once having committed themselves and having been elected, they react as do most people who have contested for something and won; they set out to do the job which they feel will assure them of re-election.

Some feel that the surest way to be re-elected is to do nothing, for thus they make no enemies; others believe that the way to re-election is to be exceedingly vocal and active. Regardless of the method which they adopt, the first thought of most of those in office, aside from moral issues which may raise a man above practical considerations, is to secure re-election, not because of any fruits of office, but because human vanity abhors the reflection implied by a public defeat. It can be said without exaggeration that most of those in municipal office do not have a programme of community or municipal development which they wish to promote, but rather that they desire to contribute of their ability and judgment to the solution of the problems which arise.

The politician is not necessarily to be condemned if his first consideration is his re-election. If he did not believe, rightly or wrongly, that he had something to offer or some justifiable reason for being in the office he would not have run in the first place. It is natural for a man to believe that the public's interests will be better looked after by him than by anyone else. It is an easy step to reason, therefore, that his first duty, not to himself but to his constituents, is to secure his own re-election. The result is that the conduct of local affairs is particularly sensitive to effective public opinion for it is only by adjusting his activities to effective public opinion that a representative can hope to remain in office. Whether or not he personally believes in that which he advocates may often be quite another question. Up to a point, he is where he is to do what the people want done. Beyond that point he will do what he feels he must do, and will accept the consequences.

By effective public opinion is meant the opinion of that portion of the public that is sufficiently interested in the conduct of the local government to have opinions, and to do something about it. In few communities are the people completely satisfied with the conduct of their local affairs, but the dissatisfaction is not effective so long as they merely grumble and do nothing more. Public opinion becomes effective when the people who have opinions let their representatives know what those opinions are; when they let councillors know that they are watching the conduct of municipal affairs; and when they prove their interest by actively supporting and voting for those whose policies, rather than personalities or affiliations, meet with their approval. The salvation of politicians, local as well as others, lies in the inertia and indifference of the mass of the electorate. The people they must consider are those who will go to the polls. They know from bitter experience that many people do not go out to vote for, but rather against someone or something. More than one municipal politician has discovered that those for whom he has done the most are too busy or too tired to go to the polls on election day. If the majority are reasonably satisfied, or at least not sufficiently dissatisfied, with the conduct of local affairs, and if there is no apparent danger that the obviously better man will be defeated by an obviously inferior one, they will not take the trouble to exercise their franchise. There is probably less danger in the long run from the misguided voter than from the non-voter.

It is impossible to understand the working of local government unless one realizes the real importance of apparently insignificant matters and of the personal element. Councils are small in membership and the members are thrown in close and continuous contact with one another. Coming as they do from the same community, they bring with them personal prejudices based on previous social, business, or political contacts; nor is there any unifying organization, comparable to the party in the province or Dominion, to bring them together. Every man is on his own and his fellow members from the ward or, if election is by general vote, all his fellow members are potential competitors at the next election. In some cases this close association produces warm personal friendships which result in consistent alliances in council matters, but on the other hand it may result in bitter enmities which reflect themselves in unreasoning opposition and the blocking of worthwhile proposals, merely to satisfy personal dislikes. On rare occasions the whole programme of a council may be bedevilled by personal feuds.

Even such an apparently minor matter as the seating arrangements of a council may build up an attitude of hostility to the point where those on one side of the chamber, by reason of their location, unconsciously constitute themselves into an opposition and consistently oppose proposals coming from the other side. The importance of such apparently trivial matters was emphasized in the remarks of Mr. Churchill in 1943, in discussing the rebuilding of the Commons' chamber destroyed in the blitz, when he said in part:

> The semi-circular assembly which appeals to political theorists, enables every individual or every group to move round the centre, adopting various shades of pink, according as the weather changes. . . . The party system is much favoured by the oblong form of Chamber. It is easy for an individual to move through these insensible graduations from Left to Right but the act of crossing the Floor is one which requires serious consideration. . . . Logic which has created in so many countries semi-circular assemblies which have buildings which give to every member, not only a seat to sit in but often a desk to write at, with a lid to bang, has proved fatal to Parliamentary Government as we know it.

Why do municipal councils show so little positive leadership in community progress? In part, as has already been pointed out, the answer lies in their preoccupation with the mass of small matters with which they have to deal. Another contributing factor is the natural inertia of human beings, who hesitate to tackle a new and difficult task unless they are forced to do so. Some individuals, possessed of an excess of energy, are always willing to pioneer on behalf of new causes, but the majority prefer to meet their troubles as they arise, rather than to go looking for them, hoping in vain that if the problems are ignored they will disappear. There is also political danger for the man who devotes himself to the larger long-run issues for he may find he is too far ahead of public opinion or that he can not produce tangible results in his short term of office to justify his re-election.

This lack of positive leadership may be explained, too, by the changing type of municipal problems and the conditions under which councils are compelled to operate. Most Canadian municipalities are young in years, few having had a century of existence. In the relatively short period since they were agricultural lands or virgin territory, extensive systems of streets, sewers, and other physical structures have been constructed, systems of transportation, parks, etc., created, and numerous protective and regulatory services established.

Necessarily in a growing country the emphasis has been on building the physical plant of the community. More recently, however, with the pressing tasks of construction completed or well under way, and in response to the problems of increasing urbanization, attention has turned to the social services such as community planning, recreation, health, housing, and welfare programmes. The method of approach to these latter problems, the administrative techniques required, and the conflict of opinions to be resolved in arriving at satisfactory policies are entirely different from those to which the people and their elected representatives have been accustomed in the past. Probably not until citizen opinion has crystallized regarding municipal responsibility for such activities will councils make very definite moves. There has been little difference of opinion in the past as to municipal responsibility for physical services. Any differences of opinion have been as to the degree or quality of service to be supplied, and the cost which taxpayers could afford. But there are sharp differences of opinion as to municipal responsibility for the social services.

The situation is complicated by the facts of municipal finance. Most major municipal expenditures of the past, except those for education, have been associated with servicing real property. As real property was supplying the tax revenues, differences of opinion centred around the question of how much the taxpayers wanted to pay. The social services, however, benefit many who are not taxpayers, yet thus far there has been no adequate compensating extension of the sources of revenue. To the question of how much the taxpayer is prepared to pay is added the question of who should pay for these services which are provided for all.

Consequently councillors are in doubt as to the extent to which it is equitable to provide facilities for the use of all at the expense of the limited group. There are serious differences of opinion not so much as to the desirability of many of the suggested lines of activity but rather as to the justification for undertaking them as a municipal activity, so long as real property pays the bulk of the municipal taxes. In this dilemma the safe thing for the elected representatives is to fight a delaying action and to undertake no more of such activities than they are forced to by circumstances, pending an adjustment in the basis of municipal finance. This situation is likely to continue until the citizens become sufficiently conscious of the possibilities for improved living conditions which lie in community action that they will do something about it. When they do so, self-interest should drive them to take sufficient part in local affairs to compel their local representative to take action and at the same time, in their capacity as provincial electors, to compel a change in the basis of municipal financing. The secret of getting results lies in an awakened and sustained public interest.

Public interest is the source of effective public opinion and the mainspring of action in a democratic form of government, but with so many counter attractions, interest in public affairs can only be aroused by a continuous programme of education. Such a programme could start in the schools with the teaching of the principles and methods of our form of government and the responsibility of the individual in its successful operation. This might be followed by a well-planned publicity programme regarding local affairs for adult consumption. It is difficult, however, to keep such publicity from becoming propaganda designed to justify current policies. There may be unpredictable dangers in programmes of propaganda paid for out of tax revenues and inspired by governments at any level. It should be carefully considered whether the dangers of using the schools as a medium of such an educational programme may not outweigh the possible advantages.

Some headway in developing greater public interest could be made if municipal reports were made more intelligible to the general reader, were issued more promptly, and were attractively set up, and if interest were actively encouraged and the fullest co-operation afforded to the press. It is not always the case, however, that those in office encourage publicity and public interest, for public interest once aroused may be difficult to control. Frequently both elected and appointed officials are content to carry on with things as they are, rather than take the risks of arousing active citizen participation.

CHAPTER VI

SPECIAL PURPOSE BODIES

Local Boards and Commissions

Not all the activities of local government come under the control of municipal councils. The provincial legislatures have created numerous other local governing bodies, sometimes referred to as *ad hoc* or special purpose bodies, and have given them jurisdiction over limited spheres such as education, town planning, utilities, or health. Many of these boards or commissions are corporate bodies. Some of them are entirely independent of the municipal council, while others have varying lesser degrees of independence. The personnel of these bodies may be composed (1) entirely of persons elected by the electors,[1] (2) of elected members and *ex officio* members, (3) of appointees of one or more municipal councils, (4) partly of appointees of council and partly of *ex officio* members, (5) of appointees of a number of municipal bodies, with or without *ex officio* members, or (6) entirely of *ex officio* members. Many of these statutory bodies are created under general Acts applicable to all municipalities within a province; others are established by special legislation which applies only to one municipality.

The extent to which local functions are assigned to special purpose bodies varies from province to province. The extent to which such bodies are used is the result of provincial policy. Where an active provincial department has a programme to promote it may find it expedient to provide that the function in which it is interested be removed from council control and placed under a special purpose body which is more likely to be amenable to provincial guidance than is a municipal council. In part, the use of special purpose bodies is the result of the vogue at the time when the particular function became a matter of local concern. Thus, in imitation of Great Britain and the United States, such special bodies were frequently provided for in Canadian municipal systems which were developing at the time when British and United States practice favoured decentralization within the municipal structure. It may depend also on the degree of urban-

[1]These electors are not always identical with the municipal electors; public school electors are those of the municipal electors who are public school supporters.

ization in a province for, with the exception of education, the functions which in the past have been assigned to special purpose bodies have been those peculiar to urban municipalities.

There are usually more of such boards and commissions in the larger urban municipalities than in the smaller ones, for many of the activities which are handled by these special purpose bodies are not carried on in smaller places or, if carried on, are of such minor importance that they do not justify the establishment of a special body to handle them. In any case, the councils in smaller communities, having fewer problems to deal with, have more time to devote to such activities.

The activities which more commonly are assigned to special purpose bodies are education, police, health, libraries, parks, hospitals, cemeteries, planning, and utilities such as transportation and gas, electricity and waterworks. The following tabulation sets out the civic boards of Winnipeg and the composition of their personnel as an example of the many kinds of local boards and commissions whose work supplements that of the municipal council:

1. Board of Police Commissioners: The mayor, a senior county court judge, a police magistrate, and two members of the city council appointed by the city council.
2. Public Parks Board: The mayor, seven aldermen, and ten citizen members appointed by city council.
3. Playgrounds Commission: The same personnel as the Public Parks Board.
4. Sinking Fund Trustees: A member of council appointed by council and three citizen members appointed by the Court of King's Bench, or any judge thereof, on application of the city council.
5. Winnipeg and St. Boniface Harbour Commissioners and River Control Board: Three members appointed by the council of the city of Winnipeg, two appointed by the council of the city of St. Boniface, one by the council of the municipality of West Kildonan, and one by the council of the municipality of East Kildonan. Appointees may be either members of council or citizen members.
6. Municipal Hospital Commission of the City of Winnipeg: Three members of council and two citizen members, all appointed by city council.
7. Administration Board, Greater Winnipeg Water District: The mayor and four aldermen of the city of Winnipeg, the mayor and one alderman of the city of St. Boniface, and the heads of seven other municipalities.
8. Administration Board, Greater Winnipeg Sanitary District: The

mayor and four aldermen of the city of Winnipeg, the mayor and one alderman of the city of St. Boniface, the mayor and one councillor of Transcona, the heads of three additional municipalities, one representative of the provincial government, and one representative of the Dominion government.

9. The Board of Revision: Three citizen members appointed by the council.

10. Building Commission: The Commissioner of Building, and six other members appointed by council, three of whom must be members of council.

11. Winnipeg Auditorium Commission: Five members of council and four citizen members appointed by council.

12. The Dwelling Rehabilitation Commission: Three aldermen and three citizen members appointed by council.

13. The Winnipeg Town Planning Commission: The mayor, three aldermen, and seven citizen members appointed by council.

14. St. James–Winnipeg Airport Commission: Two members of Winnipeg city council, two members of St. James city council, and one citizen member appointed by each of the two municipalities and one citizen member appointed alternately by each of the two municipalities on the recommendation of the Aviation League of Manitoba.

15. Public School Board: Fifteen members elected by the electors.

This example of the complicated machinery of local government, which is typical of cities of any considerable size, explains the perplexity of the citizen in trying to understand the operation of his municipal government. It is little wonder that he finds it a problem to place the responsibility for any lack of efficiency in the over-all operation of his city.

The assignment of certain activities to these special bodies is sometimes compulsory, as is the general practice in dealing with educational matters. In other cases the council may decide whether it will continue to carry on certain activities under its own jurisdiction or assign them to a special purpose body. If, however, a council wishes to transfer functions to another body it may do so only on the basis provided for by statute[2] and may transfer only such activities as the law permits. The boards established by special or private legislation to manage particular local activities, such as transportation in Toronto or the civic hospital in Ottawa, are created as a rule at the request of the local authorities.

[2]Thus, in Ontario, if a council wishes to divest itself of the responsibility for the public parks it may transfer that responsibility to a Parks Board but only in accordance with the provisions of The Public Parks Act of the province.

In addition to these statutory bodies, urban councils frequently set up special purpose boards on their own initiative. These have no legal status but are virtually committees, with power only to consider, study, and report upon matters referred to them by council. They are different from the usual council committees in that a portion or all of the membership may be non-members of council. Councils in practice allow some of these boards a considerable amount of discretion to make decisions within the field assigned to them and permit them to carry on their work without reporting for approval by council.[3]

The control which a council has over other statutory bodies in the local government structure varies greatly from one board to another. In some cases, as with school boards in Ontario, the control may be negligible. In others the council has jurisdiction in financial matters varying from complete control to control only of the expenditures in excess of a fixed minimum amount. In yet other cases, while there is no control or only a limited control over current expenditures, there is a control over capital expenditures.

Where a council appoints all or a majority of the personnel of a board it can control the policy in a general way by its selection of appointees or by asking for resignations of appointees if policies are adopted which council does not approve. If, however, council appointees are in the minority the effectiveness of this control is restricted. In the case of an elective board, a council has little control, for the board members, not unreasonably, take the attitude that they are responsible to the electors in the same way as is the council and it is for their electors, rather than for the council, to decide if their policies are acceptable.

Conflicts of opinion occur between councils and special purpose boards over which the former have little or no control. Perhaps the more frequent are with educational and with police authorities. Disputes with educational bodies are usually on financial grounds, and with police authorities on matters of finance and on law enforcement. The usual attitude of the special purpose bodies with respect to finances is that their first consideration is to accomplish the special purpose for which they are established, even if the cost exceeds that which the council, the money raising body, feel is justified. Councils are usually the levying and tax collecting authority for all of the various boards and commissions in the local government organization.

[3]In the thirties many councils established welfare boards to supervise and direct the granting of relief. They were allowed wide discretion both in determination of policy and in its application subject to an appeal to council in certain circumstances.

Council members believe that they constitute the only body which has a comprehensive view of all the varied activities of the local government and which can weigh the relative justification for the financial requirements of all the boards. They further believe that as the levying and collecting authority they are in a better position than any other body to judge the equity of the tax burden and the taxpayers' ability to carry the ever growing load. In fact the taxpayers do hold the members of council politically responsible for the tax burden regardless of how great a portion of the load may be attributable to bodies over which council has little or no control.

Where a council has some control over the expenditures of a board they may reduce the requested appropriation, with or without consultation with the board concerned, although the usual practice is to consult such a board to explain the council's reasons for a reduction. Even though a council may have no financial control over a board it may refer requests for appropriations back to the originating board for reconsideration, accompanied by council's reasons for seeking reductions. If this fails, the council has an appeal to public opinion by publicity measures or it may appeal to provincial authorities to exert pressure on a board to comply with the council's proposals.[4] It is not unknown for a council to refuse to provide the monies requested even though the board involved have a clear legal right to obtain what they have asked. Such refusal may be plain obstinacy, or it may be that the council feel it is the only way to bring the situation forcefully to public attention. A council is not always deterred from such refusal by the prospect that the courts will inevitably maintain the board's demand, for it is the taxpayer who ultimately meets the cost of the litigation.

The practice of establishing special purpose bodies to handle particular local functions was followed in England to a considerable extent throughout the greater part of the nineteenth century because of the inefficiency of the existing municipal corporations and the lack of a complete system of local authorities. The results over half a century have been described as "a chaos as regards authorities, a chaos as regards rates, and a worse chaos than all as regards areas." Following the reorganization of local government in the period between 1871

[4]The Halifax Charter provides that if the council reduce the estimates of the board of school commissioners the board may appeal to the Governor in Council who may order the council to provide an additional sum not exceeding the amount of the reduction. If school boards in British Columbia refuse a council request to reduce their estimates, the council and board may agree to arbitrate the matter or either party may demand arbitration, the resulting award being binding on both parties. The Ontario Municipal Association in 1950 requested the province to enact legislation which would authorize the Ontario Municipal Board to arbitrate as between councils and local police authorities on budgetary matters.

and 1888, a policy of consolidating local authorities was followed. As a result there evolved the "compendious" or all-purpose municipal corporation with jurisdiction over the whole range of local government activities, including education, health, planning, utilities, parks, and trading operations. In more recent years there has come a new trend toward *ad hoc* or special purpose bodies to handle problems which extend beyond the limits of one municipality. In the United States the practice of setting up special boards during the last century is generally attributed to an extension of the prevailing theory of checks and balances in government and in part to the desire to remove particular activities from the influence of party-dominated councils. In more recent years it has continued in an attempt to circumvent rigid tax and debt limitations.

This practice in Canada, more extensive in Ontario and the Prairie Provinces than in the rest of the Dominion, was in part an imitation of the United States and in part an effort to remove from the sometimes penny-pinching control of councils those services which a council might be disposed to sacrifice in preference to expenditures which would give more immediate and tangible results. Education, of course, would present special difficulty if it were under council control in provinces having separate school systems. To a limited extent councils themselves have been responsible for the transfer of powers to other bodies, for when faced with a difficult problem they sometimes have been willing to transfer functions voluntarily to some other body to avoid the effort required to deal with the matter as well as the political consequences of making a decision.

There are both advantages and disadvantages in this diffusion of authority. A function which is placed under a special board receives the undivided attention of the members of that board and thus receives the benefits of specialization. To a great extent it removes the function from the political field and reduces the chances of it becoming a "political football." It is probably true that, if the aim is to promote some activity regardless of all else, the best results can be obtained by removing it from council control and placing it under a specially constituted body. On the other hand special purpose bodies have all the shortcomings of the specialist. Local government should be viewed as a whole. The importance of the various activities and the burden which they impose upon the taxpayers must be looked at with a proper perspective and the financial requirements for each must be considered in relation to the whole. This can be done only by a body which has the entire field of municipal activity within its purview. The special purpose bodies are likely to lack this perspective.

The claim that it is an advantage to remove issues from the political field hardly seems justifiable in a democracy, for the essence of democracy is that the ultimate control should rest with the governed. It is a fact, even in the case of special purpose boards which are entirely elected, that actions by these boards are not as exposed to public pressure as they would be if performed by councils, for unquestionably the citizen interest concentrates on the council. To hail this freedom from the more direct influence of public opinion as an advantage is a denial of the whole democratic principle. If the claim be that such activities would not be as effectively administered if under council control, the answer would appear to be to raise the calibre of those elected to council, rather than to shelter the particular function from the effects of public opinion. Few things have done more to reduce the willingness of able men and women to stand for election to councils than the constant whittling away of council powers and their transfer to other bodies. Probably nowhere has municipal administration been on a higher level than in England where practically all local powers have rested with the council. Experience demonstrates that men and women tend to measure up to their responsibilities and the converse is probably true, that the less the responsibilities, the lower the calibre will tend to be.

Inevitably, where the responsibility for various municipal activities is distributed among independent bodies there is overlapping, shifting of responsibility, duplication of staffs, lack of co-ordination, and often lack of co-operation. Jealousies and bickering develop at both the elective and the appointive levels and the lack of any over-all control results in policies and programmes which work at cross purposes or, at best, are carried out in ignorance of the aims and purposes of the other bodies, with loss to the citizens both in money and service. These disadvantages are intensified as the municipality grows in size and the personal relationships between the executive officers become less intimate.

Inter-Municipal Bodies

No municipality lives to itself alone. Except for a few isolated municipalities in mining areas or in the newly developed portions of Canada, and a few island municipalities, most municipalities have boundaries in common with one or more others. The ebb and flow of business and population between adjacent municipalities sometimes makes it difficult even to distinguish one from the other. Such is the relationship between the larger urban centres and their suburban neighbours. The problems associated with inter-municipal relations, and particularly the metropolitan area problem, are acute in twelve of the principal cities[5] and are present to a lesser degree in many others. Some provisions have been made to deal with these problems which affect more than one municipality.

Nova Scotia councils are required to appoint annually an arbitration committee not exceeding three members. These committees have power to adjust the objects of municipal expenditure which are for the joint benefit of the municipality and the cities and towns within the county area and the proportion of such expenditure to be borne by each. If the arbitration committees of the councils fail to agree, each council appoints an arbitrator and the two arbitrators choose a third. These three arbitrators determine the difference by their award, which is final. The results of these provisions have not been entirely satisfactory.[6] In Quebec and Ontario the county council serves as a meeting place for representatives of the various local municipalities within the county area, other than the cities and the towns which may not come under county jurisdiction. In New Brunswick even the cities and incorporated towns are represented on the county council. The basis of such representation throughout that province, however, is not uniform.[7] The counties are responsible for a number of functions which, but for their existence, would be matters of joint concern for local municipalities. In Quebec inter-county matters are dealt with by a board of delegates. This board consists of three delegates, the warden and two county councillors, from each county interested or affected by the matter under consideration.

The range of activities carried on by larger urban municipalities and the concentration of population in the adjacent suburban areas give rise to many inter-municipal problems. In Ontario provision has been made, under The Suburban Development Act, for establishing a suburban service board (five residents elected by the municipal electors in the suburban area) which may enter into agreements with the urban municipality for the extension of urban services in the suburban

[5]Halifax, Saint John, Quebec, Montreal, Ottawa, Toronto, Hamilton, London, Windsor, Winnipeg, Vancouver, and Victoria.

[6]See Donald C. Rowat, *The Reorganization of Provincial-Municipal Relations in Nova Scotia* (Halifax, 1949), vol. I, p. 9 *et seq.*

[7]The city of Saint John is represented on the council of the municipality of the city and county of Saint John by the mayor and four commissioners, each of whom has three votes; the council of the city of Moncton selects six of its members to act as *ex officio* county councillors; the councils of the towns of St. Stephen and Milltown each select one of their members to sit on the county council; the ratepayers in each of the towns of Woodstock and Newcastle elect three county councillors to sit on the county council; and the councils of incorporated towns for which special provision is not made elect one of their own members to sit on the county council as an *ex officio* member.

area and for their management by the board or by a joint body composed of representatives of the board and of the urban corporation. This provision has not been utilized. More recently[8] Ontario has attempted to deal with the problem by providing for the creation of an inter-urban area by the Ontario Municipal Board, on application of a municipality, the area to include parts of two or more adjoining municipalities. The legislation contemplates that such areas will operate under an elected board of management, which would in substance be another municipal council, and which would have exclusive jurisdiction over the functions assigned to it by the Municipal Board. The funds needed are required to be raised by the councils of the municipalities whose territory is within the area, the share being allocated on the basis of the equalized assessment. Only one such inter-urban area has yet been established.

General legislation for establishing machinery or bodies for joint action by municipalities is usually confined to single purpose bodies on which the various interested municipalities are represented, such as the town planning bodies in Nova Scotia, New Brunswick, Ontario, Manitoba, Saskatchewan, and Alberta, or the suburban road commissions in Ontario, or the district hospital boards in Alberta.

In addition to these bodies provided for by general legislation, special bodies have been set up by statute to deal with special problems affecting a number of adjacent municipalities. Such are the Montreal Metropolitan Commission, the Greater Winnipeg Water District, the Greater Vancouver Water District, and the Grand River Conservation Commission. Three of these are briefly described below as illustrations.

Montreal Metropolitan Commission[9]

The Montreal Metropolitan Commission was established in 1921 to provide a system of financial control by one central authority representative of the municipalities of the Island of Montreal. It has fifteen voting members representing the fifteen municipalities and the provincial government.[10] Its creation resulted from recurring instances of over expansion and extravagant real estate development in suburban municipalities, followed by financial difficulties which were

[8]1946.

[9]Based on *The Borough System of Government for Greater Montreal*, edited by Frederick Wright (Montreal, 1947).

[10]The commission consists of eight members representing the city of Montreal, one representative each for Verdun, Outremont, Westmount, and Lachine, one representing the municipalities of Mount Royal, Hampstead, St. Laurent, Montreal West, St. Pierre, and LaSalle, one representing the province, and one non-voting representative of Montreal East.

solved by annexation to Montreal with resulting increases in that city's burden of debt. When in 1921 Montreal was faced with the prospect of demands for annexation by four more municipalities deeply in debt,[11] the Metropolitan Commission was established, primarily to put the delinquent municipalities on a sound financial basis.

The Commission has power to control and supervise financially involved municipalities and to borrow on the credit of the whole metropolitan district to meet their debts. The annual debt charges for the amounts borrowed are levied on each of the member municipalities in proportion to their assessed real estate values, the assessment being under the control of the Commission. The portion raised from the solvent municipalities is to be repaid, at least in part, by the delinquent municipalities as their finances permit. The Commission can borrow not only on behalf of the delinquent municipalities but also for any of its member municipalities, other than the city of Montreal. This power to borrow and loan is accompanied by the further power of supervision of the finances of the member municipalities.

The work of the Commission has been extended beyond that of financial control to the undertaking of works outside the limits of Montreal such as a master plan for the Island, the opening of a boulevard crossing the Island from end to end, and the opening and planning of traffic arteries to co-ordinate with those of the city of Montreal.

Greater Winnipeg Water District[12]

As the population of Winnipeg increased the city outgrew the available water supply and in 1912 it was decided to obtain water from Shoal Lake, the western arm of the Lake of the Woods, some eighty miles distant. The Greater Winnipeg Water District was incorporated by provincial legislation in 1913 to supply both the city of Winnipeg and the contiguous territory.

The area comprising the Greater Winnipeg Water District includes all of the city of Winnipeg (area 24.9 square miles) and parts of the city of St. Boniface, of the towns of Transcona and Tuxedo, and of the municipalities of Fort Garry, St. Vital, St. James, West Kildonan, and East Kildonan, a total area of 54.54 square miles.

[11]". . . after having annexed 23 suburban municipalities in 27 years Montrealers had had enough of this doubtfully desirable and very expensive method of enlarging its territory.

"The long procession of annexations had added more than $30 millions of debt to the already heavily burdened debt structure of Montreal without any corresponding additional revenue." J. O. Asselin, "Government of Metropolitan Montreal," *Municipal Review of Canada*, vol. XLVII, no. 5–6, p. 9.

[12]City of Winnipeg, *Municipal Manual, 1947.*

The powers and function of the Corporation of the Greater Winnipeg Water District are exercised by an Administration Board composed of the mayor and four aldermen of the city of Winnipeg, the mayor and one councillor of the city of St. Boniface, and the mayor or reeve of the other municipalities. The undertakings of the Corporation are under the management of a two-man Board of Commissioners.

The Grand River Conservation Commission

This commission, provided for by Ontario provincial statute in 1938, was created to conserve the waters of the Grand River valley, to afford a sufficient supply of water for the municipal, domestic, and manufacturing purposes of the participating municipalities during periods of water shortage, and to control flood waters. The Commission is made up of three members appointed by the city of Brantford, two each by the cities of Galt and Kitchener, and one each by the towns of Paris and Preston, the villages of Elora and Fergus, and the city of Waterloo.

The commission appoints its own employees and has authority to investigate the problem of conservation, to erect works, to create reservoirs by constructing dams, to acquire land and other property, and to apportion the benefit received by the participating municipalities. Any council dissatisfied with the apportionment may appeal to the Ontario Municipal Board. The costs of maintenance and for capital expenditures are levied on the participating municipalities in proportion to the benefit received.[18]

There are thus two trends in municipal organization which are steadily reducing the functions and scope of municipal councils and which are piling upon councils financial responsibility for activities over which they have little or no control. The earlier trend was towards establishing within the municipality special purpose bodies to which were assigned functions previously under the jurisdiction of the council. The councils continued to have the responsibility for providing the funds for current operations or to meet deficits, as well as the funds required for capital construction. The later trend, which appears likely to continue as those problems which transcend municipal boundaries increase, is towards establishing inter-municipal bodies or joint-municipal bodies composed of appointees of the participating municipalities, to which are assigned limited activities of concern to all the participating municipalities. Again the particular

[18]In 1951 there were thirteen such conservation authorities in the province involving 271 municipalities.

function is removed from the jurisdiction of the local councils, who severally remain responsible for financing current or capital expenditures but with no control of the amounts of money to be provided.

More and more, as these trends continue, the system of local government, in the interests of efficiency and faced with the necessity of getting the job done, is departing from the basic principle that the spending power should be accompanied by responsibility for the tax levy. It would appear that provincial authorities, while they may delay the issue by grants and subsidies, will inevitably be forced to tackle the difficult and politically unpalatable task of reorganizing their municipal systems to re-establish the relationship between the power to determine the burden of taxation and direct political responsibility to the electorate.

CHAPTER VII

ELECTIONS, BY-LAWS, AND "QUESTIONS"

Elections

Members of municipal councils are elected by the municipal voters although, as noted previously, election to some county councils is indirect. Election to the office of mayor, warden, or chairman may be by council, yet it is always from among those already elected to council by the electors. There is no such thing in Canadian municipal government as the election of private citizens to office by council, as may be done when councils in England elect a mayor or alderman.[1]

In most municipalities there is an annual election. This is necessary where the term of office is one year, but even where there is a two or three year term, the terms may be staggered so that a portion of the council is elected each year. Election is usually by ballot, although there are some exceptions as in the case of municipalities governed by the Municipal Code in Quebec where the council, with the approval of the electors, may provide for oral voting.

The date of the regular election is fixed by the statutes, which also provide for special elections to fill vacancies and for special votes for the purpose of submitting by-laws or questions to the electors at times other than the regular election. Provincial statutes regulate in detail the conduct of municipal elections. If free elections are to mean anything the voter must be assured that the election machinery is under strict control and free from manipulation, and that his franchise is really secret. To assure freedom from local "skul-duggery" the provinces have imposed rigid and detailed statutory regulation. A minimum of discretion remains with the local authorities to adjust special cases or to rectify errors or omissions on election day, but this is one instance where the local power to adjust must be sacrificed to the greater need of rigid rules for the protection of the majority.

The main points of interest in elections are the candidates, the electorate, and the electoral process.

Candidates

The qualifications required of municipal candidates vary from province to province. One universal qualification is that the candidate

[1]An exception to this general statement is the election of a private citizen by a council when filling a vacancy in council.

be a British subject and in most cases he or she must be twenty-one years of age. It is customary also to require that the candidate be an elector whose name is on the list of municipal voters and that he or she be a resident of the municipality. However, in Ontario he is only required to live in or within five miles of the municipality and in Saskatchewan cities, in or within two miles of the municipality. In Saskatchewan rural municipalities, residence within the province is sufficient.

There is a literacy requirement in some provinces. Candidates in Quebec cities and towns must be able to read and write "fluently," in Manitoba and Saskatchewan, to read and write, and in Alberta municipalities, to read and write "in the English language." The other provinces either assume these qualifications to be universal or else not sufficiently important to be required, either of which assumptions is erroneous.

Most provinces[2] require that a candidate must have paid all taxes owing to the municipality which were due prior to a date fixed by statute. In some cases, as in Newfoundland and in Nova Scotia towns,[3] this requirement covers all taxes, while in Ontario it only applies to taxes of years prior to that in which nomination takes place and only to the property on which the candidate qualifies.[4] In other provinces the requirement that taxes be paid applies only to certain classes of municipalities.[5]

The qualifications for candidates for the office of head of the municipality are more restrictive than those for other council members in some cases. Thus, in Nova Scotia towns a candidate for councillor must have been a ratepayer for one year and a resident or have had his principal place of business in the town for one year, whereas to qualify as mayor a candidate must have been a resident and a taxpayer for at least three years and be assessed for real property at not less than five hundred dollars or personal property at not less than one thousand dollars. Similar differences of qualifications also apply in New Brunswick towns and in British Columbia municipalities. Such varying qualifications are not the usual practice although they have existed in some of the other provinces in the past.

In addition to requiring that candidates possess certain qualifications, all the provinces have established grounds for disqualification

[2]Newfoundland, Nova Scotia, Quebec, Ontario, Manitoba, and Saskatchewan.
[3]Also in Fredericton.
[4]The taxes referred to are real property taxes. In Ontario all business taxes of a candidate must have been paid prior to his nomination.
[5]As in New Brunswick, to towns; in Alberta, to towns and villages.

and persons to whom they apply may not be candidates nor hold municipal office. Two bases for disqualification in all provinces are employment by the municipality or a contractual connection with the municipality. In four provinces, Quebec, Manitoba, Saskatchewan, and Alberta, persons who are sureties for municipal employees also are disqualified.

Many provinces disqualify persons in specified official positions, although the offices involved vary from province to province. It is usual, for example, to disqualify sheriffs and bailiffs; in some provinces, gaolers and magistrates; and in others, members of Parliament and senators. Some provinces disqualify persons on an occupational basis. Thus in Nova Scotia, New Brunswick towns, and Quebec, members of the clergy are disqualified; in Nova Scotia towns and New Brunswick municipalities persons engaged in selling intoxicating liquor; in Quebec, full-pay army and navy officers and in Quebec cities and towns, hotel, tavern, and restaurant keepers. There are numerous other grounds for disqualification, some of which are related to the status or characteristics of the individual.

Basis of disqualification	*Where applicable*
Persons under interdiction of habitual drunkenness	Nova Scotia towns
Persons who have made an assignment	Nova Scotia towns, Saskatchewan
Undischarged bankrupts	Nova Scotia towns, Ontario, Manitoba, Saskatchewan, Alberta
Persons convicted of certain criminal offences	Nova Scotia "municipalities," Quebec, Saskatchewan, Alberta, British Columbia
Relief recipients	New Brunswick
Persons with an unsatisfied claim against the municipality	Ontario, British Columbia
Mental incapacity	Newfoundland

In Ontario, except for the head of the municipality who is an *ex officio* member of many outside boards, any person who is a member of a school board or of a board or commission appointed or elected to operate a steam, electric, or street railway owned, leased, or controlled by the municipality or to operate a public utility belonging to the corporation is disqualified as a council member.

There appear to be three main bases for disqualifying candidates: (1) that by reason of his relationship to the municipality as an employee or by having a contract with or claim against the municipality there might develop a conflict of interests, in which the candidate, if elected, could not be expected to deal impartially with matters involving his personal interests, (2) that by reason of his occupation, whether as a public official or by reason of the peculiar nature of his private occupation, it is inexpedient that he should be in elective municipal office, and (3) that owing to his personal shortcomings, as indicated by habitual drunkenness, financial incapacity, or criminal record, he is not suitable for public office.

Some provinces exempt certain classes of persons from municipal office. At one time it was obligatory that those elected should serve or be subject to a penalty. Certain groups, however, were exempt from the obligation to serve. Penalties are still imposed upon those who are elected and who refuse to serve in Nova Scotia and Quebec. In Nova Scotia towns, for example, any qualified person who is elected and who refuses to serve is subject to a penalty of forty dollars, unless he has served on the council within the three preceding years, but judges, senators, members of Parliament or the Legislature, teachers, and persons over sixty years of age are exempt. In Quebec municipalities under the Municipal Code the same persons are exempt and in addition, pilots, gaolers, and railway employees, but service in municipal office provides exemption only for a period of two years thereafter. In Quebec, the obligation to accept office extends even to certain appointive offices. The penalties for non-acceptance, without cause, vary from twenty-five dollars for those elected or appointed as councillor, assessor, road inspector, auditor, or pound keeper to thirty dollars for mayors or county councillors, and forty dollars for wardens.

The Electorate

The electorate consists of those persons who have the right to vote for the election of candidates to municipal office. All the inhabitants of the municipality are members of the municipal corporation, but not all have the right to participate in selecting the members of its governing body. That right depends upon whether the members can meet certain requirements established by provincial statute. In some cases additional persons, who are not inhabitants of the municipality, and therefore by definition not members of the corporation, have a right to vote.

There are qualifications which are common to most of the provinces while others are peculiar to individual provinces, and there is some variation even within a province, as shown in Appendix A to this chapter. An elector must be twenty-one years of age in all cases except in Saskatchewan where eighteen is the age requirement. In most cases, except in New Brunswick towns and in Saskatchewan and Alberta municipalities other than cities, electors are required to be British subjects or Canadian citizens. It is a usual condition that the name of the elector must be included in the municipal voters' list and that he or she be assessed, although in several cases provision is made for adding to the list names which have been omitted in error. In New Brunswick towns and, if the council so determines, in Ontario municipalities the payment of all taxes due is a condition of exercising the franchise.[6]

As will be seen from Appendix A, a property qualification is required of some classes of voters in most of the provinces; a property or tax qualification is required of all classes of voters in seven of the provinces. The property qualification, however, is usually so low as to permit practically all owners or tenants of real property and their wives or husbands to qualify as electors. In Nova Scotia, in Saskatchewan cities and towns, and in Alberta there are no property qualifications for residents, the only requirements being age, residence and, in some cases, citizenship.

Voters' Lists

Three methods of preparing municipal voters' lists are used in Canada. Under the registration system, used in Nova Scotia, the onus is on the citizen to apply to be registered as a voter to the revisal officers, three of whom are appointed by the council for each town and for each revisal section of "a municipality." These revisal officers[7] are supplied by the assessor with a copy of the assessment roll and from the roll and the applications they prepare the list of voters. After publication of the list, the revisers decide upon any complaints of errors or omissions in the list, subject to an appeal from their decisions to the sheriff, and a further appeal to a county court judge.

A registration plan is also in effect in Saskatchewan cities and towns.[8] Any person eighteen years of age, a British subject, and with five months' residence in the municipality may register with the assessor prior to August first. From these registrations, from duplicates of the hospital services cards issued under the provincial hospitalization plan, and from the last revised assessment roll the assessor prepares the voters' list.

In the other provinces, except in Alberta, the list is prepared without action being required on the part of the voter, other than to check the list for errors. The general procedure is that the clerk of the municipality[9] annually, prior to a date fixed by statute, prepares a list of

[6]In Quebec municipalities under the Municipal Code the franchise is limited to males, widows, and unmarried females.

[7]There is only one in the city of Halifax, known as the Registrar of Voters.

[8]A registration system also occurs in Drumheller and Lethbridge in Alberta.

[9]In Charlottetown the clerk of the Stipendiary Magistrate is the "Electoral Officer" for the city and he prepares the voters' list with the assistance of the city clerk. The list is prepared by the parish assessors in New Brunswick counties and by the assessor in Manitoba.

voters based on information contained in the assessment or valuation roll. The posting of the list for public scrutiny is advertised and within the time allowed by statute complaints as to errors or omissions may be filed with a designated official.

Alberta municipal councils appoint enumerators who by actual visits to residences ascertain the names of the persons qualified to be listed as electors. These lists are then filed by the enumerators with the assessor or secretary-treasurer who from them and from the assessment roll information makes up the voters' list.[10]

No voters' list is prepared in New Brunswick villages nor in Quebec municipalities under the Municipal Code, for the assessment or valuation roll itself is used as the list of qualified voters.

There is a variety of methods for dealing with complaints. The clerk or secretary-treasurer who prepares the list deals with the complaints in some cases[11] and there is no appeal from his decision. Quite frequently[12] the council, sitting as a court of revision, revises the list. In the Saskatchewan cities which have "commissioners," the commissioners act as the court of revision, while in British Columbia the court consists of the head of the council and two councillors. There is no further appeal in Saskatchewan and Alberta but in Quebec there is a final appeal to a superior or county court judge and in British Columbia, to a magistrate or a supreme or county court judge. In Ontario and Manitoba complaints about the voters' lists are dealt with in the first instance by a county court judge and his decision is final.

Electoral Process

The electoral process is a difficult one to outline briefly because of the variations in the different provinces and the complexities even within any one province. The main stages in the process are nomination, qualification, polling, declaration of the result, and sometimes the recount. These stages are not always separate and distinct nor do all occur in every election. An election, which is popularly considered to take place on the polling day, is a continuing process which starts with the nomination and extends until the result is finally determined.[13]

The conduct of an election is the responsibility of the returning officer. The municipal clerk is *ex officio* the returning officer in many

[10]A similar enumeration plan was abandoned in Saskatchewan cities and towns in 1949.

[11]In New Brunswick towns, in Saskatchewan villages and rural municipalities, and in Alberta municipal districts.

[12]In Quebec cities and towns, in Saskatchewan cities and towns, and in Alberta towns and villages.

[13]The election in Fredericton runs from the publication of notice of the election to the making of the return by the city clerk.

municipalities[14] and in others the council appoints the returning officer.[15] In most municipalities of any considerable size, either in population or in area, the council[16] divides the municipality or its wards into polling divisions for the convenience of the voters.[17] A deputy returning officer or presiding officer and a poll clerk are appointed by council for each polling division to conduct the actual polling.[18] When a municipality is not so subdivided, the returning officer, assisted by a poll clerk, usually conducts the poll.

Nomination. Provincial statutes require public notice of the time for nominating of candidates for election. Nominations are usually made at a nomination meeting but in the provinces of Prince Edward Island, Nova Scotia, and New Brunswick nomination papers merely have to be filed with the returning officer on or before the date and time specified.[19] Nomination meetings are held at a time and place determined by the council and usually last for one or two hours.[20]

The date of the nomination meeting may be: (*a*) a date fixed by statute, as in Quebec cities and towns, January 25; or (*b*) a day fixed by statute as in British Columbia cities, the second Monday in January; or (*c*) optional with the local council within statutory limits—as in Ontario, any day between November 15 and December 23, excluding Sundays, provided it is at least seven days prior to polling day.

Saskatchewan and Alberta councils are required to call a public meeting of the electors approximately a week before the nomination date to receive the auditor's interim statement and reports of council committee chairman and, in Alberta, the report of the secretary-treasurer of the municipality. In Alberta municipal districts the public meeting and the nomination meeting are held on the same day, the former being at 1 P.M. and the latter from 3:00 to 4:00 P.M.

Where a nomination meeting is part of the election procedure, a candidate is nominated when a nomination paper signed by the required number of electors is filed with and accepted by the presiding

[14]In Nova Scotia towns, Quebec cities and towns, in Ontario, and in Manitoba.

[15]The mayor of Charlottetown appoints the returning officer.

[16]In Charlottetown the mayor designates the polling subdivisions.

[17]An exception to this general rule is the city of Victoria which has only one polling place.

[18]In Saskatchewan cities the city clerk has statutory authority to make these appointments. In many other municipalities in practice the election officers are selected by the clerk and the appointment by council is a formality.

[19]In British Columbia the nomination papers may be filed with the returning officer at any time between the date of the public notice of the meeting and the close of the nomination meeting.

[20]In Quebec cities and towns and in Saskatchewan and British Columbia cities nomination meetings last for two hours.

officer for the meeting. Where there is no meeting, a similar formal nomination paper must be given to the clerk or other designated official within the time provided by statute. Usually the nomination paper must be signed by two qualified municipal electors[21] and in some cases, if the elections are by wards, the nominators must be electors in the ward affected. Six electors are required as nominators in Nova Scotia municipalities, ten in Quebec cities and towns,[22] and five in Alberta municipalities where the election is by general vote. In a few cases the number of nominators varies for different classes of candidates, as in Halifax, ten for mayoral candidates and two for aldermen, or as in Saskatchewan rural municipalities, five for reeves and two for councillors. Nominators are not usually limited as to the number of candidates they may nominate. In some provinces a person cannot be nominated for more than one office.

There would appear to be considerable merit in the Maritime practice of permitting a prospective candidate to file any necessary qualification papers without the formality of a nomination by other electors. The original purpose of requiring nominators presumably was to give some evidence of public demand for the particular candidate but as it has developed this requirement only adds to the work of a candidate who must line up his nominators and shepherd them to the nomination meeting lest they forget the appointed time. Except in a few rare instances the idea that his fellow citizens voluntarily and without prompting attend and nominate a candidate is largely a myth. But it is a poor candidate indeed who cannot find at least two people who will not refuse a direct request to nominate him.

An exception to the general practice occurs in Charlottetown where no nominators are required, but a person who wishes to be a candidate merely files the necessary declarations with the municipal clerk between 12:00 P.M. and 4:00 P.M. on the seventh day before the election.

If no more candidates are nominated or qualify than there are vacancies to be filled, either at the time of the close of nominations or, in Ontario, by the end of the time for qualification, the candidates are declared to be elected by acclamation. Otherwise the election proceedings are adjourned until the day of polling.

Qualification. Nomination papers usually must be accompanied by a statement or declaration by the candidate that he is qualified or eligible for election to office, and in New Brunswick villages and in all municipalities in Manitoba, Saskatchewan, and Alberta, by a written

[21]In Ontario the nominators must be present at the nomination meeting.
[22]Ten or more also in Fredericton.

statement by the candidate that if elected he is willing to serve. In Fredericton and in Quebec cities and towns the candidate's consent to the nomination must be filed, and in Ontario there must be satisfactory evidence of consent if the nominee is not present at the nomination meeting.

Some provinces require a supplementary report, certified by a municipal official,[23] respecting the candidates's property qualifications and as to whether or not the candidate's taxes have been paid. Statements of qualification in Ontario are not filed with the nomination papers but candidates who wish their names on the ballot must file a declaration of qualification, an oath of allegiance, and, in cities, towns, and townships adjacent to cities over 100,000, a certificate of the treasurer or collector that the taxes are paid on the property on which they qualify for election. These supporting documents, in Ontario, must be filed with the returning officer by 9:00 P.M. of the day following nomination and failure to do so constitutes a withdrawal.

An election deposit is required of candidates in a limited number of municipalities; the practice, however is not general.

Municipality	*Candidates' deposits*		*Returnable if elected or if candidate obtains:*
	Mayor	Councillor	
Charlottetown	$100	$50	1/3 number of votes of a successful candidate
P.E.I. towns	10	10	1/2 number of votes of a successful candidate
Quebec cities and towns	50	50	1/3 number of votes of a successful candidate
Winnipeg	100	25	15% of the quota at time of being counted out

Several provinces provide for the withdrawal of candidates after nomination, as shown in the accompanying chart. No provision is made for withdrawal in those provinces in which the attitude is that it is a citizen's obligation to take his share of public service. The candidate's consent is required for a nomination only if he has served as mayor or councillor within three years. Provision is made in some instances for disposing of cases where a candidate is nominated for more than one office and fails to decide for which one he will stand. In Saskatchewan and Alberta, however, no person may be nominated for more than one office.

Polling. In the interim between nomination and the polling day it is the responsibility of the municipal clerk, in most cases, to see that

[23]In Nova Scotia towns and in Manitoba, the treasurer; in Quebec cities and towns, the clerk or the collector.

Province	*Time for withdrawal of candidates*
Prince Edward Island (Charlottetown only)	Any time before the close of the poll[a]
Nova Scotia	No provision
New Brunswick	
villages	Within forty-eight hours of nomination
other municipalities	No provision
Quebec cities & towns	At any time up till the close of the poll
Ontario	Automatic if candidate fails to qualify by 9:00 P.M. of day following nomination; if he has qualified, may withdraw up till 9:00 P.M. of day following nomination
Manitoba	Until 2:00 P.M. of day following nomination
Saskatchewan	Within twenty-four hours of nomination
Alberta	
cities	Within twenty-four hours of nomination
other municipalities	Within forty-eight hours of nomination
British Columbia	Before the day preceding the opening of the poll

[a]Any votes cast for a withdrawn candidate are null and void. Candidate forfeits his election deposit.

ballot boxes, ballots, voters' lists, poll books, and other necessary election supplies are furnished to each deputy returning officer. The election is by ballot[24] in all cases except as previously noted. The ballot is usually a printed one, although in some cases it may be typewritten or partly printed and partly typed. The form of the ballot in most provinces is determined by statute and the candidates' names appear on the ballot in alphabetical order of their surnames.

There are exceptions to the general outline contained in the above paragraph. In New Brunswick counties the clerk is required to supply to the chairmen at the various polling places sufficient uniform envelopes to provide one for each voter; the candidates are permitted to place ballots in the polling booth with the name or names of candidates on them and the voter chooses which of the prepared ballots he prefers and inserts it in the envelope which he hands to the deputy returning officer or chairman. Saskatchewan and Alberta cities may adopt the "rotating ballot" in which case the ballots are printed in as many lots as there are candidates. The first lot is printed with the surnames in alphabetical order, on the second lot the first name is moved to the bottom and the original second name becomes the first, and so on. The ballots are then made up in pads for each polling place, with the ballots from each of the different lots, arranged so that no two successive voters receive ballots from the same lot. This plan aims to offset the advantage which accrues to candidates whose name otherwise would appear in such favoured positions as the first or the last place on the ballot.

[24]The ballot is alleged to have been introduced in British North America in 1856 when New Brunswick used it for municipal elections.

Municipal elections are held in the different provinces in January, February, March, April, October, November, and December, and on every day of the week except Sunday, and, as will be seen from Appendix B to this chapter, the interval between nomination day and the polling day varies from three to twenty days. There is somewhat more uniformity in the number of polling hours, although the minimum period during which the polls are open varies from six to twelve hours. It is standard practice that all the polling in a municipality normally takes place on one day. Some provinces, however, permit a council to hold an advance poll, varying from one to three days immediately preceding the regular day of polling, at which voters who do not expect to be in the municipality on polling day may vote. In Ontario and in Saskatchewan cities, the advance poll is restricted to occupational groups, such as railway or postal employees or commercial travellers, whose occupation necessitates their absence on the regular polling day, but all electors who have reason to believe they will necessarily be absent on election day may vote at the advance poll in Manitoba, in Saskatchewan towns, and in British Columbia. The ballots cast at an advance poll are not counted until after the close of the polls on the regular polling day.

Declaration of Result. Except as noted below, the candidates who receive the highest number of votes are declared to be elected. Manitoba, however, provides that on petition of 25 per cent of the electors a council must provide for elections on the basis of proportional representation.[25] The by-law to authorize this plan must be approved by the provincial Municipal Commissioner and by a majority vote of the electors voting at an annual election. Similar procedure—petition, ministerial and electoral approval—is required to repeal such a by-law once adopted. This method of election has been adopted by Winnipeg, St. James, and St. Vital, and has not been abandoned in any Manitoba municipality where it has been adopted.

Under this form of proportional representation the elector, in marking his ballot, does not make the usual "X" opposite the name of the candidate for whom he votes, but places figures opposite the names of the candidates indicating by the figures 1, 2, 3, 4, etc., his order of preference among the candidates listed on the ballot. After the close of the poll the ballots are all delivered to the returning officer for the municipality. A quota is then arrived at by dividing the total number of valid ballots polled in the whole electoral division by the number

[25]Calgary also uses proportional representation under the provisions of its special charter.

which exceeds by one the number to be elected, and then adding one to the result.[26] Any candidate for whom the ballots marked "1" are equal in number to the quota is declared elected. Any additional ballots on which he is marked as first choice are transferred to the remaining candidates in order of the preferences marked on the ballots. If at any time in the counting no candidate has a surplus and vacancies still remain unfilled the candidate with the lowest number of votes is dropped and his ballots are transferred according to the preferences indicated. When the number of remaining candidates is reduced to the number of vacancies unfilled the remaining candidates are declared elected even though they have not received votes equal in number to the quota.

The accompanying example of the count for aldermen in Ward Three in Winnipeg for 1949 illustrates the manner in which the result is determined.

Ward Three, Winnipeg[a]

	1st count	2nd count	3rd count	4th count
Beckford, George H.	2,384	3,269	3,923	4,395
Blumburg, J.	7,358E	5,686E	5,686E	5,686E
Forkin, M. J.	4,434	4,840	4,982	5,185E
Rebchuk, S.	3,580	3,648	4,505	5,599E
Stepnuck, J.	2,655	2,779	3,105	
Ward, F.	2,332	2,521		

[a]E—Elected; quota 5,686.

Counting votes under this system is complicated; it was adopted in many countries prior to the last war[27] but its use in municipal elections in Canada has been limited. The main criticisms against it have been that the complicated count delays the issue of the final results, that because it is complicated people do not understand it and are suspicious of it, that the extra clerical work required makes it expensive to count.

The advocates of this system of voting claim that it makes representation of groups of like-minded voters in the municipality more possible than the usual system. While proportional representation has the disadvantage in the national field that it frequently fails to give a clear party majority this is not so valid an objection in the muni-

[26]Thus, with three members of council to be elected and 26,355 votes cast, the quota would be: $\frac{26,355}{4} = 6588 + 1 = 6589$, which is the smallest number which will go three times into 26,355 and yet will not go four times.

[27]Austria, Belgium, Czecho-Slovakia, Denmark, Esthonia, Finland, France, Holland, Jugo-Slavia, Poland, Sweden, Switzerland, and a few cities in the United States including New York in which city the plan has now been abandoned.

cipal field. It is subject, however, to the same criticism in the municipal field as the ward system, for it may serve to perpetuate community division by providing representation of common-interest groups as such.

The voting procedure is basically the same in all provinces, with minor exceptions. The voter applies to the deputy returning officer[28] for the ballot or ballots; the D.R.O., having ascertained that the elector's name is on the voters' list, gives the elector the ballots to which he is entitled and which have been initialled by the D.R.O. on the back[29] so that when they are returned to him by the voter, folded, he can identify them as ballots which he issued.[30] The name of the voter and the ballots he receives are noted in a poll book. The voter then enters a screened compartment, marks the ballots with an "X" opposite the name of the candidate or candidates for whom he wishes to vote, folds the ballots so that no one may see how he voted, and hands them to the D.R.O. who verifies his initials and then deposits the ballots in the ballot box. A voter can vote for as many candidates as there are offices to be filled or for a lesser number. If a ballot is marked for more than that number or otherwise than with an "X" it is void. In New Brunswick villages and in Saskatchewan towns and villages, however, the ballot is void if the voter marks a ballot for a less number than the number to be elected.[31] Such is also the case in some municipalities under the provisions of special legislation.[32] This provision is designed to prevent the practice known as "plumping."[33]

After the close of the poll the ballots are counted by the D.R.O. and the poll clerk, and the ballots and other election records are delivered to the clerk of the municipality who keeps them for periods varying from three weeks to two months and then destroys them. The returning officer, when he has totalled the returns made by the D.R.O.'s, declares the candidate or candidates who have received the highest number of votes to be elected.

If two candidates have the same number of votes, it is the respon-

[28]In practice referred to as D.R.O.

[29]In the 1949 election in Eston, Sask., on a recount, 372 of a total of 377 ballots were ruled invalid as they were not initialled. The council was declared elected on the basis of the five ballots which were initialled.

[30]In Charlottetown and in Quebec cities and towns counterfoil ballots are used.

[31]This provision applied to Saskatchewan cities until 1951.

[32]In Peterborough, with five aldermen to be elected, electors must vote for at least four or their ballot is void. 8 Geo. V, c. 75.

[33]A "plumper" is a ballot on which the voter votes only for one candidate although there may be a larger number to be elected. Plumpers are much sought after by candidates and much deplored by academic advocates of good government who are less vitally affected. From a candidate's viewpoint a voter who votes for him and also for two of his competitors adds to the total vote of all three, giving him no advantage over the others. But the plumper helps only the one candidate and gives no assistance to his competitors.

sibility of the clerk or the returning officer to give a casting vote, except in Saskatchewan where a tie is broken by a draw, and in Ontario where, in the event of a tie vote, there is a recount of the votes by a county or district judge; if there is still a tie after the recount, the clerk is required to give a deciding vote.[34]

Recount. Any candidate who is not satisfied with the count may apply for a recount of the ballots within a specified time, varying from three to fifteen days. In most instances a recount of votes is conducted by a county judge, although in Nova Scotia it is conducted by the clerk of the municipality. In British Columbia a recount may be had only if the difference in the totals for two candidates is less than fifty. The costs of such recounts are in the discretion of the judge. A recount does not necessarily involve counting all of the ballots cast. The usual practice at a recount is to count the ballots of the candidate asking for the recount and those of the candidate receiving the next highest count.[35]

Vacancies in Councils

All provinces provide for filling vacancies which occur in the interval between regular elections. Vacancies may arise because the electors fail to nominate sufficient candidates or because the number of candidates who run may not be enough to fill all the seats on a council; candidates who are elected may fail to take the necessary oath of office; a sitting member may be unseated by judicial proceedings; a member's seat may become vacant because he is absent from more meetings than is permitted; members may resign or die or, during their term of office, they may cease to hold the required qualifications.[36]

Under some circumstances a member's seat may be automatically vacated. The usual reasons are that the member has been convicted of a criminal offence, has been declared bankrupt or has made an assignment for the benefit of his creditors, or is absent from council meetings without authorization of council for a stated period, usually three consecutive months. In a few instances a councillor loses his seat if he ceases to reside in the municipality and the same result occurs

[34]In Nova Scotia towns if the mayoral candidates are tied, the retiring mayor breaks the tie, or, if he is also a candidate, the town council decides; if the town council vote is a tie then the clerk casts the deciding vote.

[35]In Newmarket, Ont., in 1950, with six candidates to be elected the seventh candidate applied for a recount. The ballots of candidates six and seven were recounted. Both gained votes on the recount so that candidate six moved to fourth place. Candidate seven then had more votes than candidate five but could not supplant him as his votes had not been subject to recount.

[36]The Fredericton council by a two-thirds vote of all members may expel a member who, after his election, has been guilty of immoral or disgraceful conduct, of which the council is the judge.

in Manitoba if he applies for relief from the corporation as an indigent. Council members may resign in New Brunswick counties, Quebec cities and towns, and Ontario municipalities only if the council accepts the resignation. In British Columbia a person who fails to complete his term of office, except because of illness or for cause satisfactory to council, is subject to a penalty of fifty dollars.

Where a vacancy occurs in an office which was originally filled by election from council, as in the case of a warden, the council fills the vacancy by appointing another of its members. There is diversity of practice in filling other vacancies. Many types of vacancies are filled by special elections, although if the vacancy occurs within periods varying from one to three months of the date of the next regular election the vacancy may be left unfilled. Vacancies in Quebec municipalities under the Municipal Code are filled by appointment by council. In Ontario and Alberta, if the office of mayor is vacant, the council appoints one of its own members to fill the vacancy. In Ontario cities vacancies in the office of alderman are filled in two ways: if the election is by general vote the runner-up is appointed, and if by wards the council appoints a qualified elector to fill the position. Where the council has the responsibility for filling a vacancy it is a common practice to appoint the runner-up at the previous election. Councils sometimes hesitate to choose among the would-be councillors and so leave a vacancy unfilled for a considerable period.

Several provinces have provided for the situation which arises when a council lacks a quorum, either because the majority of the members have resigned or because there have not been sufficient members elected to form a quorum. If a city or town council in Quebec cannot function for want of a quorum due to resignations, the Lieutenant-Governor in Council orders an election to fill the vacancies and may appoint sufficient members to form a quorum pending the election. In Ontario, if less than a majority of a new council are elected the old council continues in office until another election is held to fill the vacancies, and sufficient are elected to form a majority of council. In Manitoba and British Columbia the new councillors, if a majority, appoint enough persons to fill the vacancies. Where the electors fail to elect candidates in Saskatchewan rural municipalities the Minister of Municipal Affairs may fill the vacancies. This is also the case in Alberta both in the event of failure to elect and where resignations reduce council personnel to less than a quorum.

Recall

Provision for recalling those in municipal office in Canada is rare but does occur under the Medicine Hat Charter which has had a provision since 1916 that the holder of any elective office—mayor, alderman, or school trustee—may be removed at any time after three months from his election, on petition of the electors entitled to vote for a successor to the office. The petition must be signed by a number equal to 25 per cent of the entire vote for all candidates for the office at the last general municipal election. It must also state the reasons for the removal and be filed with the city clerk who must certify as to its sufficiency within ten days. A further ten days is allowed for amendment and if it then is sufficiently signed, the council must fix a date for an election not earlier than thirty days or more than forty days after the clerk's certification. The name of the person whose removal is sought is placed on the ballot without nomination, unless he requests otherwise. The candidate who receives the highest number of votes at such election fills the unexpired term of the office involved. The members of Saint John council also are subject to recall on petition of 10 per cent of the number of electors who voted at the preceding election.

Most provinces provide that an elector, within a fixed period after an election, may institute proceedings to question the validity of the election of a candidate. The usual grounds for such actions are that essential formalities have not been observed, that the candidate who was declared elected was not elected, that the candidate was not qualified, or that the election was invalid by reason of corrupt practices.

The court which determines the issue may declare the election to have been valid or may declare that a candidate was not duly elected and that another candidate was elected. Where no other candidate is declared to have been elected a new election is usually ordered.

Action may be instituted by an elector in some provinces to unseat a member of council where the member, although duly elected, has subsequently forfeited his seat or has ceased to be qualified.

Questions and By-Laws

The electors may be asked by their council from time to time to vote on other matters than the election of candidates. In practically all cases, except counties other than in Quebec, a council may, and under some circumstances must, submit certain by-laws or questions to the electors or limited classes of electors for their approval or for an expression of their opinion.[87]

[87]The authority to submit questions is not unlimited but in general is restricted to questions which would come within the limits of the term "municipal questions."

These by-laws and questions fall into three classes. There are by-laws such as money by-laws (those to authorize a council to incur a debt) which require approval by vote of the appropriate electors before the council can finally pass the by-law. Whether or not the council is to take the action proposed in the by-law is optional with the council but if it desires to take such action, it must first submit the by-law for approval by the electors. With respect to other by-laws and some questions, the council may be obliged to submit them to a vote of the electors, provided specified preliminary conditions have been met, such as the submission of a petition from the requisite number of electors, and the council must take action in accordance with the expressed wishes of the electors. There is yet a third group of by-laws or questions which the council is not required to submit to a vote, and which deal with matters entirely within the competence of the council, but upon which a council may wish to obtain the guidance of the electorate or with respect to which they may wish to shift the responsibility for decision.

Unless otherwise provided by statute or by the authority under which a vote on a by-law or question is held, all the electors are entitled to vote on by-laws and questions. In some cases, however, and invariably on money by-laws, the vote is restricted to the electors known as "ratepayers" in Nova Scotia, New Brunswick, and Manitoba, "proprietors" in Quebec, "electors entitled to vote on money by-laws" in Ontario and British Columbia, "burgesses" in Saskatchewan, and "proprietary electors" in Alberta. These persons, in general, are those who are electors by virtue of the ownership of assessed property and not by reason of being the wife or husband of an owner or of being an elector as a tenant or a farmer's son, or by reason of a mere residence qualification. In voting on money by-laws, an additional class of voters is introduced in Ontario, Saskatchewan, Alberta, and British Columbia. In these provinces any corporation assessed as the owner of real property, which if held by an individual would entitle him to vote, is entitled to one vote by its nominee, provided, in the case of Alberta, that the nominee is not otherwise entitled to vote.

Matters which are referred to a vote of the electors may be submitted either in the form of by-laws or questions. When the voting is on a by-law, the by-law in its final form is approved or given one or two readings by the council. The by-law, or the substance of it, is then advertised for the information of the electors. The ballot merely refers to the by-law by its title. The voter marks his ballot with an "X" in the space "For the by-law" or in the space "Against the by-law." When a question is submitted, as for example, "Are you in favour of the adoption of daylight saving time in the City of . . . . during the months of July and August?" the actual question is printed on the ballot and the voter places his "X" in the space "Yes" or "No" as the case may be.

The council usually may decide when the vote is to be taken although in some cases, as in voting on granting a franchise in Ontario,[38] the vote may only be taken at the time of the regular municipal election. The procedure respecting the appointment of election officers, the conduct of the poll, and the completion of the returns is, except as noted below, essentially the same as in voting for candidates. In the case of a tie vote, however, there is no casting vote, except in Quebec municipalities where the mayor has a deciding vote. In some matters the statutes require the approval of three-fifths or two-thirds or three-quarters of those voting.

Special features in two provinces should be noted. When a Nova Scotia town proposes to apply to the legislature for authority to borrow money by debenture issue or for certain other powers, it is a condition that the application must have the approval of the ratepayers. The council may obtain this approval either by calling a public meeting of the ratepayers for the purpose, or by holding a plebiscite of the ratepayers by a poll similar to that used for the election of candidates.

In Quebec, the electors' approval of certain types of by-laws is conditional upon (*a*) a minimum fraction of the voters having voted;[39] and (*b*) approval by the majority both in number and in real-property value of all the owners who have voted. These conditions have resulted in two features which are unique in Canadian municipal voting. When a by-law is submitted for approval of the electors, the polls are open for two days. If at the end of the second day the required proportion of the electorate has not voted, the poll, on application of the mayor, an alderman, or three electors, is continued for a third day. Where the approval of a by-law requires a majority both of the number voting and of the value of the property which they represent, two sets of ballots are prepared and each voter is given two ballots. One ballot is similar to that used in other provinces, but the ballots of the second set have on them the words "Valeur-Value" followed by one

[38]The term "franchise" as used here refers to the right which may be granted to private parties to use the streets for business purposes and not in the sense of the right to vote.

[39]This minimum varies from one-eighth where the electors number less than 1,000, to one-twentieth where they exceed 2,000.

of the numbers, $100, $500, $1,000, $5,000, $10,000 or $50,000, to indicate in round figures the assessed value of the elector's property. The voter is given the second ballot according to the figures which apply in his case and he marks the ballot with an "X." In the final count the ballots are sorted into two lots, those representing persons and those representing assessed values and the total "for" and "against" are then totalled on both bases.

A county council in Quebec may submit a by-law under the provision of the Municipal Code. In such case, the warden convenes in each local municipality a meeting of the electors, presided over by the local mayor, to vote on the by-law. If, however, the tax to be imposed as a result of the passing of the proposed by-law is to be borne by the ratepayers of only one or more of the local municipalities, and not by all, the by-law is submitted only to the electors of the municipalities concerned.

Any question to be submitted to the electors should be stated in the clearest possible terms, if the voters are to vote on it intelligently and if the council are to know what are their wishes. Any ambiguity in the wording which permits two or more interpretations of the question, and subsequently of the result, defeats the purpose of the vote, unless it is intentionally so worded. Thus, when the following question, "Are you in favour of the supervision and administration of the ——— Department by a ——— Board appointed by the Council, the actions of the Board to be subject to the approval of the Council?" was submitted to the electors of an Ontario city, it was supported both by those who wanted the particular department removed from council control and by those who wanted its actions to be subject to council approval; and the council, after the vote had been taken, were no further ahead in knowing what the electors really approved. If a clear indication of the electors' wishes is to be obtained any question submitted to them must be short, simple, and clearly expressed.[40]

What has been said above is applicable only where the aim is to get a clear understanding of what the voters want. There are, however, other reasons for submitting questions. A council may be genuinely perplexed as to the desirable solution to a problem and wish the advice of the citizens, but sometimes when councillors are faced with the necessity for taking some action they try to shift the responsibility

[40]In Ottawa in 1933 the electors were asked to vote on whether they favoured having a council composed of a mayor and six councillors, having a council composed of a mayor, four controllers, and eleven aldermen, or retaining the then existing system. The electors carried all three choices and as a result the council took no action.

for the decision.[41] If, then, the citizens vote to take the proposed action they can not subsequently hold the council responsible for doing so or, alternatively, if they reject the proposal, they can not blame the council for inaction. Such procedure may not be quite fair to the electors for, although it is always difficult to justify objection to a demand to consult the people, it is not to be expected that the citizens can have as intimate knowledge of the facts of the case, upon which to base their decision, as the councillors should have.

The appeal to the electorate may be used as a device to defeat or at least to delay a decision of Council or to gain public support. When a councillor finds he can not secure sufficient votes in council to defeat or to carry a proposal, he may move that the people be consulted. As suggested above, this is a very difficult request to oppose in a popularly elected body. The member who proposes the appeal to the electors may do so in the hope that the electors will vote for the action for which he could not secure sufficient support in council. If his purpose is to defeat the proposal, particularly where it involves the expenditure of money, he may attain that end by having several other money expending issues submitted at the same election so that the voters, confused and frightened by the grand total, will vote against all of them.

Opinions differ among elected representatives as to their personal responsibility where matters are referred to the electorate. Some hold that it is their duty to support or oppose the proposals publicly and to give leadership to the voters, while others take the attitude that the electors should be left to make their own decision. Some take the position that, where the matters involved will result in expenditures or the granting of franchises, etc., the representatives should strive in council to work out the best plan possible and then allow the people to decide. Others believe that in such cases, unless the proposal is a sound one in their opinion, the representatives should not approve of its submission to the electors, on the ground that the electors are entitled to assume that it would not be placed before them for approval if it were not satisfactory to the council.

In submitting issues to a vote of the people the council are limited in their means of presenting the case to the electors. Councils have only one avenue of paid publicity, the official advertisement of the by-law or question. In practice, this "legal advertising" is usually set up in very fine type because newspapers charge for it at the highest rates, and

[41] In Halifax if a plebiscite is to be submitted to the electors the question must first be voted on by the council and the result of the vote in council must be advertised at the same time as the question.

in any case the technical phraseology of a by-law frequently makes it unintelligible to a layman. Interested groups, in contrast, may promote or oppose the proposals by the use of display advertising, radio, and any other form of publicity to the extent of their resources. If the voters are to obtain both sides of the story and to understand the full implications of a proposal, they would appear to be justified in expecting their representatives, as individuals, to supply the information required and to give leadership by taking a public stand on the issue under consideration.

Initiative

Alberta provides for the expression of the opinion of the electorate on municipal matters on the initiative of the citizens. In cities, if 10 per cent of the resident proprietary electors petition for the submission of a by-law dealing with any matter within the legislative jurisdiction of the council, the by-law must be submitted to a vote. If the majority of the votes polled, or in the case of a money by-law if a two-thirds majority of the votes of the proprietary electors, are in favour of the by-law it must be passed by the council within four weeks of the vote. In Saint John also, if an ordinance or by-law is submitted to the council, supported by a petition of 10 per cent of the number of electors who voted at the last election, the council must either adopt the by-law or submit it to a vote of the electors. If the vote is favourable the by-law becomes a valid by-law and may not be repealed or amended except on a vote of the electors.

Several provinces require that councils submit specified matters to the electorate on receipt of a sufficiently signed petition of electors or at the request of a special purpose body. The council in such cases must abide by the result of the vote. Such is the case, for example, in Ontario where on petition of sixty municipal electors in a town or city the council must submit a question on the establishment of a public library, or where a school board requests a council to submit to a vote of the electors a question on borrowing money for capital expenditures. Where, however, councils submit a by-law or question to a popular vote and the by-law or question is not one which the council are required by law to submit, they are not legally bound by the decision of the electors.

APPENDIX A

Property and Residence Qualifications Required of Municipal Electors Under General Provincial Legislation (Excluding Corporations)

Province	Property qualifications	Residence requirement
Newfoundland	liable to taxation under Local Government Act	one year
Prince Edward Island		
Charlottetown	owner of land assessed for $500, and spouse of such: males or females, at yearly rent of $100; or any one one who has paid poll tax	one year
	non-resident occupant of business premises	none
towns	assessed for $100, real or personal, and spouse of such	none
	males who pay poll tax or are exempt from poll tax	one year
Nova Scotia	residents—none	6 months
	non-residents—real property assessment of $300	none
New Brunswick		
towns	ratepayer on real property to any amount; on poll tax, or on personal property assessment of $100	none
villages	ratepayer	none
counties	same as town[a]	in parish
Quebec		
cities & towns	owner or tenant of real property of $200 value or $20 annual value	none
other municipalities	assessed in own or wife's name for real property—if resident for $50, if non-resident for $200; resident farmer or lessee at annual value of $20; owner's son if assessment sufficient to qualify both	none
Ontario	owner or tenant of real property and resident spouse of such assessed in cities for $400, towns of 3,000 or over, $300, other towns $200, villages and townships $100	none
	assessed farmer's son, daughter, sister, or son's wife	one year
Manitoba	owner of real property assessed for $100	none
	actual residents	6 months
Saskatchewan		
cities & towns	person who is assessed, or who pays licence fee of at least $10, a service tax, or rental tax, and spouse of such who resides with such person	6 months
villages	person assessed and resident spouse	in province
	tenants, if annual rental of $60, and resident spouse	6 months

APPENDIX A—*Continued*

Property and Residence Qualifications Required of Municipal Electors Under General Provincial Legislation (Excluding Corporations)

Province	Property qualifications	Residence requirement
rural municipalities	person assessed and resident spouse	in province
	shareholder of incorporated co-operative association engaged in farming and assessed and not exempt from taxation	in municipality
	tenant of 80 acres of land or $60 annual rental, and resident spouse	6 months
Alberta		
cities, towns, and villages	owners of real property and persons liable to business tax	none
	other persons	6 months
municipal districts	persons assessed	none
	other persons	6 months
British Columbia	owners, or persons paying municipal trade licence fee of $5.00, or householders	none

[a]In Gloucester County electors may be rated on poll or personal property to the amount of $50; in York County every person qualified to vote for candidates for the Legislature may vote in county elections.

APPENDIX B

Municipal Elections Schedule

Municipalities	Nominators required	Polling day	Interval between nomination and polling	Minimum polling hours
Prince Edward Island				
Charlottetown	1	February—2nd Wednesday	6 days	9:00 A.M to 5:00 P.M.
towns	2	February—1st Tuesday[a]	13 days	9:00 5:00
Nova Scotia				
towns	2	December—1st Tuesday[b]	6 days	9:00 5:00[c]
counties	6	October—3rd Tuesday[d]	13 days	8:30 6:00
New Brunswick				
towns	2	April—3rd Tuesday	3 days	9:00 5:00
villages	2	December—2nd Monday	6 days	1:00 P.M. to 8:00
municipalities	1	see below[e]	7 days	9:00 A.M. to 4:00

APPENDIX B—*Continued*

Municipal Elections Schedule

Municipalities	Nominators required	Polling day	Interval between nomination and polling	Minimum polling hours		
Quebec						
cities & towns	10	February—1st juridical day	6 days		7:00	5:00[c]
code municipalities	2	January—Monday following 2nd Wednesday[f]	4 days		8:00	6:00[c]
Ontario	2	January—1st Monday[g]	6 days		9:00	5:00[c]
Manitoba	2	October—10 days after 2nd Tuesday	9 days[h]	cities	9:00	8:00
				others	9:00	5:00[c]
Saskatchewan						
cities	2	October—Wednesday of the week following that in which 4th Monday falls	8 days		9:00	8:00
towns	2	"	8 days		9:00	5:00
villages	2	"	8 days		10:00	4:00
rural municipalities	5/2[i]	"	8 days		9:00	5:00
Alberta						
cities	2	October—3rd Wednesday following the 4th Wednesday in September	20 days		8:00	8:00
towns & villages	2	March—2nd Monday after 3rd Monday in February	13 days		10:00	7:00
municipal districts	2/5[j]	March—4th Saturday after 3rd Saturday In February	27 days		9:00	5:00
British Columbia						
cities	2	December—2nd Thursday	6 days		8:00	8:00
districts	2	December—Saturday following 2nd Thursday	8 days		8:00	8:00

[a]Every second year.

[b]Councils could provide for elections in February if by-law to that effect was passed not later than September 30, 1951.

[c]Council may extend these hours.

[d]Every third year after 1940.

[e]The date varies from county to county: three counties, 1st Tuesday in September, one county, 2nd Tuesday; one county, 1st Monday in October, five counties, 1st Tuesday, two counties, 2nd Tuesday, one county, 3rd Tuesday, and one county, last Tuesday. In four counties the elections are biennial and in eleven, quadriennial.

[f]With approval of Lieutenant-Governor in Council, may be changed to May or July.

[g]Council may fix the polling date at any day between November 22 and January 2 except a Sunday or December 24, 25, or 31 and the nomination day not less than seven days prior to polling day.

[h]Council may extend up to three weeks if necessary for obtaining ballots.

[i]Five nominators required for candidates for reeve; two for councillors.

[j]Two nominators required where election is on electoral division basis; five where on general vote basis.

CHAPTER VIII

MUNICIPAL ADMINISTRATION

A MUNICIPAL COUNCIL has both legislative and administrative functions and combines in one body the activities which at the other levels of government are divided between Parliament or the legislature and the executive or cabinet.[1] The legislative activities of a council are important but in time a framework of legislation is built up to cover the range of problems requiring major legislative action. While this basic municipal legislation is not, or at least should not be, static, the bulk of current legislation of most municipal councils deals with the amendment or revision of existing by-laws or the passing of by-laws relating to administrative matters. After a municipality has enacted legislation covering traffic, streets, public health, licensing, fire prevention and control, the regulation of building, zoning, and similar matters, most of its legislative activity is of a routine nature arising out of its administrative function.

The administrative activities of councils vary according to the area and population under their jurisdiction and the extent to which functions have been transferred to special purpose bodies. Obviously the activities under a rural or village council will be much fewer than those for which the council of a city must provide. Not only do the powers granted to the more populous municipalities permit more extensive activities, but the need and demand for public services increases as the population concentration increases. This demand has been intensified in recent years by the change in viewpoint of the citizens as to the purpose and function of governments. Hence the legislative function of local government is relatively less important than the administrative function in so far as the day-to-day operations are concerned, and in the extent to which it absorbs the attention of councils. Macdonald, referring to the cities of the United States, states: "It is safe to say that nine-tenths of the work of our cities is administration. Only at rare intervals does a vital issue make its appearance."[2]

The policies arrived at by a council are carried out by paid perma-

[1]This statement should be modified as applied to councils which have a Board of Control or an Executive Committee of the type found in Montreal.

[2]Austin F. Macdonald, *American City Government and Administration* (New York, 1941), p. 207.

nent officials, who may be either full-time or part-time employees, a matter which chiefly depends on the size of the municipality. In total number, considering all the smaller and rural municipalities, the part-time officials probably exceed those on a full-time basis. Council members may personally supervise the carrying out of council policies in the smaller municipalities, but this is impossible in a community of any considerable size to the extent that was possible before skilled techniques and scientific knowledge were such important factors in the operation of municipal services.

Councils in larger municipalities usually assign to each of their standing committees the supervision of one or more of the departments or services. These committees make reports and recommendations to council on the work under their jurisdiction. Usually the responsible official attends the committee meeting to be available for consultation, and he can obtain the committee's advice on his problems, and explain his reasons for any recommendations he may make. As a rule officials in charge of what might be called service departments such as Works, Fire, Parks, and Welfare, do not deal directly with council, unless specifically instructed to do so, but rather work through and with the committees. More frequently those in charge of internal departments, such as the treasurer or clerk, deal directly with council, although in most instances their recommendations go to council through a committee.

It is the council which makes the major decisions as to policy, to build a bridge, to pave a street, or to put the fire department on a three-shift basis. The council is the ultimate authority on all matters, large or small, that may come before it or with which it may choose to deal. To a considerable extent, however, the task of supervising the carrying out of policy and many final decisions in minor matters are left to the committees. The task of actually doing the job as well as many of the detailed decisions are left with the officials.

The chairmen of standing committees play an important part also in administration. While committees as a rule do not specifically confer on their chairmen any power other than to preside at committee meetings, it is the accepted practice that, if an official requires instruction or advice on matters of urgency in the intervals between committee meetings, he should confer with and be guided by the committee chairman. The same thing is true of the great bulk of minor issues which it is not practicable to take up with the committee and which have not been covered by precedents or established policy. The result is that committee chairmen are continuously in contact with the officials and have considerable influence in the administrative decisions.

If decisions have to be made and the official has neither precedent nor established policy to guide him, he has to decide whether to take the responsibility for making a decision and stand by the consequences or to consult his chairman. The chairman, after hearing the official's report and advice, may accept responsibility for a decision or may decide to refer the matter to the committee where, in turn, the committee may consider the matter sufficiently important to ask council for an official ruling. Council's ultimate control is effective because the person responsible for making the decision at each of these stages knows that any citizen who is sufficiently interested, and who does not like the decision that has been made, can usually find a member of council who will raise the matter in council and the person responsible for the decision must be prepared to justify the decision made. Thus, while council is the body ultimately responsible for exercising the powers of the corporation, the great bulk of the detail is dealt with by its paid employees. The protection for the citizen lies in his right of appeal to council and in the willingness of elected representatives to follow up complaints and their effectiveness in doing so.

In larger municipalities a considerable portion of what are really policy decisions are neither made by council nor even known to council. To operate otherwise would be impossible. The justification for such a system is that it works. It works because the rules, regulations, and precedents which have developed permit an employee who is actually dealing with the public to know how far he can go in making decisions, keep the discretion involved in those decisions within proper limits, and establish a definite and traceable line of responsibility for action extending from the minor official at the lowest level to the ultimate governing body. The sum total of these rules and regulations is frequently condemned as red tape. Red tape is irritating to the public because they do not understand its purpose and because individuals often want the very thing that red tape is designed to prevent, namely, partiality and special favours in dealing with an individual case.

Council or committee decisions are recorded in the minutes of their meetings and it is the duty of the clerk to notify the persons concerned of these decisions. Such notice in larger municipalities is usually in writing, although in minor matters or where the official involved has been at the meeting, the notice may be oral or the official may be assumed to have been notified. An official's authority for taking action under council direction lies in the resolution or by-law of council as recorded in the minutes, and as formally certified to him by the clerk of the council.

The statutory officers of a municipality, those whom by statute a council is required to appoint, have a dual responsibility. They are appointed and paid by the council and are, within limits, subject to its direction, but they also are assigned duties and responsibilities by the statutes and are therefore answerable through the courts for any failure to carry out their statutory duties. These particular officers find themselves responsible to two different authorities or subject to two separate sources of direction. They are in a difficult situation when directions from these two sources are in conflict, in other words, when a council may not wish the officer to carry out his duties in accordance with the statute. In such an event there is no question as to the proper course for the officer to follow—it is to carry out his statutory duty. He would be exceptional, however, if he could overlook the fact that as a rule both his tenure of office and his rate of pay rest with his council. As a result there has been a gradual extension by the provinces of the security of tenure of office for municipal officers and, in some cases, even a protection against reductions in pay.

The ultimate authority for an official appointed by council is the council itself, except for his statutory obligations. But a council can speak only through resolutions adopted at a council meeting. Frequently it is a nice question for an officer to decide to what extent he will act under the direction of the head of the council, a committee chairman, or even a standing committee in matters not decided by council. This is not a serious matter when there is a fair degree of unanimity in council and when relationships in council are harmonious; but when there are sharp differences of opinion, or when various factions in council are at loggerheads, the officer must be somewhat of a diplomat to parry the various pressures to which he may be subjected.

There is an inherent and often unrealized conflict underlying the relationships between a council and its permanent officials which is based upon the different viewpoints with which they approach the execution of policy. Because local governments function in the community where their decisions are made effective, the members of council are constantly being approached by individuals who feel they are unfairly dealt with under the general application of policies and regulations. They consider that their case merits special consideration and exceptional treatment and they seek the assistance of their representatives to that end. Because he is elected to represent the people and under the system of popular election his political life depends on keeping his people satisfied, and because the individual's claim is usually plausible, the representative tends to be more concerned with the exceptions than with the rule. The permanent officials, who in most cases have been long in office and expect to continue there, are more conscious of the difficulties which result from making exceptions to general rules and, in the interests of equity to all, tend to resist requests for special treatment. Thus, on the one hand, the representatives are constantly seeking a relaxation of the general rules in particular cases and, on the other hand, the permanent officials stress the necessity for adhering to the general rule.

Obviously there must be general rules and regulations in the conduct of public business. The alternative would be chaos, for too constant a flow of exceptions and special dispensations renders a general rule of no effect. Yet too rigid an adherence to general rules does not allow for the incalculable variety of situations to which a general rule will apply and the unfairness which it may involve in some cases. Either view if carried to the extreme is undesirable. In practice this conflict of viewpoints brings a compromise that is usually beneficial to the community. A by-product of the conflict, however, is that the elected representative sometimes gains the impression that the officials desire to run the show and are not co-operative. The official for his part may come to regard himself as the guardian and protector of the corporation, and conceive that it is his duty to protect the mass of the citizens against the constant barrage of special interests on whose behalf the members of council are constantly appealing, and against what to him appear to be the shortcomings of the elected representatives.

Council Organization

To understand how a council functions it may be well to examine the organization of particular councils. There are great variations between municipalities and therefore it is not possible to say that the organization of any one is typical. The four examples noted below show marked differences but do not cover all the variations which do occur.

1. Welland, population 15,972, has a council composed of a mayor and eight aldermen. There are two standing committees, Finance Committee and Works Committee. Each committee is composed of the mayor and four aldermen and each committee member, other than the mayor, is assigned to the supervision of a particular portion of the activities coming under the jurisdiction of the committee.

2. London, population 95,612, has a council composed of a mayor and eight aldermen. There are two standing committees, No. 1 Committee (Finance) and No. 2 Committee (Works). Each committee is composed of all the members of the council including the mayor.

3. Moncton, population 22,763, has a council composed of a mayor and eight aldermen. There are sixteen standing committees, thirteen of which are composed of three aldermen each, one of four aldermen, one of the mayor and three aldermen, and one of the mayor and five aldermen.

4. Kingston, population 41,056, has a council composed of a mayor and twenty-one aldermen. There are five standing committees. Three of the committees are composed of seven aldermen each, and one, Social Welfare, is composed of the mayor, four aldermen, and five citizens. The Finance Committee is composed of the mayor, the chairman of the Social Welfare Committee, and the chairmen and vice-chairmen of the three other standing committees.

DEPARTMENTALIZATION

The number of separate departments into which the administrative staff is divided varies. The number tends to be larger in larger cities where there is greater variety of functions and where functions which in a small municipality do not justify a separate department are sufficiently important to require a full-time directing head. Differences also depend on what functions have been assigned to independent boards. What are listed as separate departments may in some cases be subject to some direction from another department rather than directly responsible to council or its committees.

The organization of three of the larger cities provides for the following departments in each case: Legal, Clerk's, Finance, Assessment, Works, Health, Welfare, Fire, Planning. They also have the following departments which are peculiar to the individual organizations:

Montreal	*Toronto*	*Winnipeg*
Purchases & Stores	Property	Audit
Police	Street Cleaning	Hydro-Electric
	Building	Libraries
	Parks	Signals
	Abattoir	
	Audit	

In part the differences result from varying practice in transferring activities to special purpose bodies. Thus, in Toronto and Winnipeg the police departments are not under the council but come under the jurisdiction of police commissions. Moreover, many departments in larger cities are broken down into sub-departments, bureaus, or branches. For example, the Winnipeg Engineering Department has the following branches: Waterworks and Sewerage Branch, Roads and Streets Branch, Inspections Branch, Design Branch, Shops Branch, Clerical and Accounting Branch, and Maintenance of Civic Buildings Branch. Some of the activities which in Winnipeg are under a branch within the Engineering Department have departmental status in the Toronto organization. In any municipal organization there is a continuous pressure from within to expand the number of departments, for the elevation of a branch or division to departmental status enhances the prestige and the remuneration of the head of the branch and, as a result of its direct access to council and its committees, improves the prospect of greater budgetary appropriations.

While the departments provided for in different municipalities vary according to local conditions and needs, the following departments occur in almost all urban municipalities: Clerk's, Treasury, Assessment, Fire, Health, Welfare, Works, and Audit. There may be no Audit Department where the auditing is done by an outside auditor.

Most civic departments are responsible through the department head to council or its committees, a fact which gives rise to one of the major problems of civic administration, the lack of interdepartmental co-ordination and of effective over-all direction. While all departments are responsible to one head, the council, it is impossible for a body of laymen, functioning in their spare time, to give close direction and control to a large number of operating departments. Councillors, by reason of their lack of intimate knowledge of the workings of the various departments, are not in a position to trace the responsibility for any lack of co-operation between departments or any working at cross purposes. Mayors are not usually elected on the basis of their executive ability, and even a mayor who happens to be an able administrator can hardly be expected in his short term of office and in the limited time he can give to administration to keep abreast of the operations and developments of the wide variety of activities carried on by numerous civic departments.

It is not intended to suggest that department heads are scheming individuals whose aim is to "put something over" on their councils, but department heads are human, and it is a universal tendency for departments to attempt to build up their own importance and to develop as water-tight compartments, pursuing their own ends with little regard to the programme of other departments. One would sometimes think it was the intended policy for a water department to delay the laying or repairing of mains until streets have been newly paved. This tendency towards lack of co-operation is modified or intensified by the personal relationships which exist between the department heads, but these relationships may be marred by competition for personal or departmental prestige in dealing with council.

The task of co-ordination and over-all direction is, to a degree, exercised by the clerk of the council because, not being the head of one of the service departments, he is in a somewhat impartial position and because he has continuous contact with and access to council. His status as first among the officers of the council is a tradition of the office developed through long years of English experience. As municipalities grow and their activities expand, however, the need for some formally recognized co-ordinating control and direction becomes more imperative. It is in response to this need that Canadian urban municipalities are tending to concentrate more over-all administrative direction in the hands of one of the senior officials. The manager plan is a popular method of dealing with this problem in the United States. Two other devices, that have been developed in Canadian municipalities in an attempt to solve the problem of improving the executive direction of the municipal organization, are the board of control, which is found in Ontario and British Columbia, and the commissioners or city commissions of Saskatchewan and Alberta.

The City Manager

The manager plan is an importation from the United States where it has been adopted in over 1,000 municipalities. It was first introduced in Canada in 1913 in Westmount, Quebec, and has spread gradually so that it is now the form of municipal administration in thirty-five Canadian urban municipalities in six provinces:[3] Nova Scotia (1), New Brunswick (2), Quebec (28), Ontario (3), Alberta (1), and British Columbia (1). The extent to which the plan as adopted in Canadian municipalities departs from the United States standard varies from place to place.

The main features of the council-manager plan are described by the International City Managers' Association,[4] in part, as follows:

[3]Halifax, Saint John, Woodstock, N.B., Arvida, Baie-Comeau, Cap de la-Madeleine, Chicoutimi, Grand'Mère, Hampstead, Isle-Maligne, Lachine, Lac Mégantic, La Tuque, Louiseville, Malartic, Montreal-East, Mont-Royal, Outremont, Quebec City, Rimouski, Roùyn, Ste-Agathe-des-Monts, St-Lambert, St-Laurent, Shawinigan Falls, Temiskaming, Trois-Rivières, Val-d'Or, Valleyfield, Verdun, Westmount, Chatham, Niagara Falls, Sarnia, Lethbridge, and Victoria.

[4]International City Managers' Association, *Recent Council Manager Developments and Directory of Council-Manager Cities (1947).*

A small council elected at large on a nonpartisan ballot determines all municipal policies which are not set forth in the charter itself, adopts ordinances, votes appropriations, and is required to appoint a chief executive officer called a city manager. The council is the governing body of the city, and the city manager is its agent in carrying out the policies which it determines. The mayor, who is usually elected by the council from its own number, does not interfere with the administrative functions of the manager, nor do individual members of the council. It is definitely understood that the council deals with administration only in a formal manner through the city manager, and that administrative functions are at no time delegated to committees or individual members of the council.

The city manager, the head of the administrative branch, is appointed by the council as a whole. The theory is, and the charter usually provides, that he be selected on the basis of his training, ability, and experience. The exercise of administrative authority is concentrated in this appointive executive who is accountable to the council. He provides the council with information which enables it to determine municipal policies, advises the council in matters of policy if the council so desires, and executes the policies determined by the council. He introduces the best principles of advanced administrative organization and practice, and is held responsible for the proper co-ordination of all administrative activities under his direction.

The duties of the city manager as set forth in most council-manager charters, broadly stated, generally include: (1) To see that all laws and ordinances are enforced. (2) To exercise control over all departments and in accordance with civil service regulations, appoint, supervise, and remove department heads and subordinate employees of the city. (3) To make such recommendations to the council concerning the affairs of the city as may seem to him desirable. (4) To keep the council advised of the financial condition and future needs of the city. (5) To prepare and submit to the council the annual budget. (6) To prepare and submit to the council such reports as may be required by that body. (7) To keep the public informed, through reports to the council, regarding the operations of the city government. In addition the charter generally states that the manager is to perform such other duties as may be prescribed by the charter or required of him by ordinance or by resolution of the council.

Five provinces, Quebec, Manitoba, Saskatchewan, Alberta, and British Columbia, have made statutory provision for the office of manager or city manager. In Quebec cities and towns, in British Columbia municipalities, in Saskatchewan cities, and in Alberta towns the initiative in this matter rests with the council but in Manitoba action is conditional on a petition signed by 25 per cent of the resident electors. A British Columbia council can be forced to submit the question of the appointment of a manager to a vote of the electors on petition signed by 5 per cent of the electors and if approved the plan must be put into effect.

In all of these provinces, except British Columbia, a by-law to provide for a manager must be approved by the municipal electors and in Manitoba can be voted on only at the regular election. Additional approval by the Lieutenant-Governor in Council is required in Quebec and by the Minister in Manitoba and Alberta. A British Columbia council can take final action if the by-law is approved by three-fourths of the members of council. If it is passed by a mere majority of council it may be submitted to the voters and if approved by them it must then be passed by council and a manager appointed.

The manager in Quebec cities and towns is appointed for a period of four years but may be reappointed. His salary is determined by the council. Manitoba and Saskatchewan require that when the by-law proposing the manager plan is submitted to a vote of the electors it shall provide for a minimum and maximum salary and the council when making an appointment is required to keep within those limits. A manager in Quebec may be dismissed by a resolution supported by an absolute majority of the council; but on application of the manager, or an alderman, or ten electors the resolution must be submitted for the approval of the voters, and if the majority vote against the dismissal of the manager he resumes his duties. In the interval, pending the vote, the council takes over the administration. In the other provinces the manager, like most other officials, is employed at the pleasure of the council. The dismissal of a manager, however, does not necessarily terminate the operation of the system for in both Quebec and British Columbia the legislation requires that if a manager is dismissed the council must proceed to appoint another. Manitoba provides that once established the manager plan may not be abandoned without the approval of the Minister, who may require that the repealing by-law be submitted to a vote of the electors. Any repealing by-law in Saskatchewan must be approved by a vote of the electors, and in British Columbia the plan can only be abandoned or amended by a three-quarter majority of council or a vote of the electors, according to the original basis of its approval.

Manitoba and Saskatchewan require that the duties of the manager be set out in the by-law to be approved by the electors. Alberta councils are free to determine the powers they will delegate to the manager while British Columbia, by its Act entitled An Act to provide for the Delegation of Duties and Powers to a Municipal Official, permits a council to delegate to an official any of the powers given to the municipal council by any statute, except the power to pass by-laws and resolutions. The Quebec legislation sets out in detail the powers of the manager, who is declared to be the executive officer to supervise and direct, under the control of the mayor and council, the affairs of the municipality and the work the council orders to be carried out. This places on him responsibility not only for routine matters such as the approval of pay rolls and accounts, the preparation of the annual estimates, and the preparation of contract specifications, but also to give his views to council on proposed by-laws, to advise council on steps to be taken to carry out by-laws and enforce their observance, to investigate and report on complaints and claims, and to attend council and committee meetings, where, with the permission of the chairman, he may give his opinion and make suggestions on the subjects under discussion but without the right to vote. It is also his duty to study the needs of the municipality, to suggest whatever steps may be expedient for an efficacious and economical administration, and to promote the progress of the municipality and the welfare of the citizens. The manager has control and direction of all officers and employees of the municipality except the clerk and the treasurer and may suspend any of them, reporting such suspension immediately to the council for final decision. He may also call a special meeting of a committee whenever he thinks it necessary, after consulting the chairman.

Elected representatives come and go and in the normal course of events their political life is short. Hence there is little inducement for them to take long-range views. Most of the permanent department heads are immersed in the day-to-day details of their work. They are inclined to limit their range of vision to their own sphere of activity and to avoid appearing to have opinions on the activities of other departments. The appointment of a manager, whether or not he is designated as such, places on one whose tenure of office is relatively permanent a definite responsibility to plan for the long term rather than the short run and places that responsibility on an official whose more elevated position gives him a perspective which is not confined to the needs or interests of one limited section of municipal activity. A manager, or an officer in a comparable position, can only accomplish this much needed end if he can avoid becoming too absorbed in the details of current administration.

Boards of Control

Every city in Ontario with a population of 100,000 or over is required to have a board of control, composed of the mayor and four controllers, who are elected by general vote. Smaller cities may have a board of control with the assent of the electors, but if it is under

45,000 in population the board of control is composed of the mayor and two controllers. The members of the board of control function in two capacities. When meeting by themselves they constitute the board of control, but they also sit with the aldermen as a part of the city council.

A board of control is really an executive committee of the council. Its duties are assigned to it by statute and include, among others, the preparation of the annual estimates, the calling of tenders and awarding of contracts, the nomination of all heads and subheads of departments and other permanent employees, and the suspension or dismissal of department heads. The council is not permitted to appropriate any sum not provided for by the estimates, as certified by the board to the council, without a two-thirds vote of the council, nor may it vary the action of the board with respect to tenders except by a like vote. The council may not make appointments to the permanent staff in the absence of a nomination from the board nor reinstate a department head dismissed by the board except on a two-thirds' vote. The council may assign such additional duties to the board as it deems expedient.

The council of any British Columbia municipality with a population of 15,000 may, by a three-quarters' vote, provide for a board of control composed of the mayor or reeve and two controllers to be elected at large. The controllers, other than the mayor or reeve, hold office for two years and, as in Ontario, the controllers are members of the council for all purposes.

The duties and powers of a British Columbia board of control are almost identical with those of an Ontario board, with the addition of a general provision that the board has full authority over all the executive work of the municipality subject to the power of the council, by a two-thirds' vote, to set aside, alter, or refer back for reconsideration any order, action, report, or matter initiated by the board, to the end that legislative duties, as distinguished from administrative duties, are to be exercised by the council. As yet no British Columbia municipality has used this legislation.

The Executive Committee of the Montreal city council has somewhat similar powers except that it may award contracts without council authorization if the amount does not exceed the amount placed at its disposal for the purpose. This committee, which the council is required by statute to appoint at its first meeting, consists of six councillors selected by the council. The Montreal council members are of three categories: one-third are elected by all the city voters in the eleven electoral districts, one-third are elected by the property owners in each of the electoral districts, and one-third are appointed by public bodies designated by law. The Executive Committee must consist of two councillors from each of these three categories. The chairman is selected by the council.

Opinions differ as to the value of boards of control in smaller municipalities but they would appear to be necessary in larger cities which have large councils. The amount of day-to-day business requiring attention in a large municipality requires more time and constant attention than most councillors can devote to public service. It also requires a greater despatch in handling business than is possible in a large group. Where there are boards of control, however, there frequently is bickering between council and board for councillors are jealous of their position in the eyes of their public. In a large municipality, however, where it is difficult for a councillor to become known throughout the whole community, service on the board of control provides an opportunity for a representative to demonstrate to the electors his capacities as an executive and as a potential mayor. Public interest and attention concentrates on the limited group in the board of control rather than on the larger group of councillors. Thus the board serves a useful purpose in the process of elimination of less capable men as aspirants to the chief office.

City Commissioners

Saskatchewan city councils may appoint one or more commissioners, who hold office at the pleasure of the council, and in addition the mayor is *ex officio* a commissioner. Subject to the legislative jurisdiction of the council, the commissioners may be vested with such powers and duties as the council decides, including executive duties of the council which require the exercise of a discretion or are judicial or quasi-judicial in character. The commissioners are paid officials whose annual salary is fixed by the council.

Such commissioners have been appointed in Regina, Saskatoon, and Moose Jaw. In Regina there are two appointed commissioners but only one in each of Saskatoon and Moose Jaw. Their duties vary according to the provisions of the local by-laws. The Regina by-law provides that the duties of the commissioners are, in part, (1) to carry out and enforce all orders, resolutions, and by-laws of the council, (2) to have general supervision, administration, and control of all departments of the city, (3) to recommend the appointment of all department heads and subheads, (4) to report monthly on all work being carried on by city departments, (5) to attend all council and committee meetings in an advisory capacity, (6) to be responsible for the preparation of all specifications, to call for tenders and recommend the awarding of contracts, and to award contracts or to purchase material or equipment to an amount not exceeding $500, and (7) to settle claims against the city where the amount involved does not exceed $1,000. The powers and duties of the commissioners in Saskatoon are similar to those in Regina, with the added provision that no permanent employees except the city solicitor or the medical health officer shall be appointed by the council in the absence of a nomination from the commissioners, but they do not have the responsibility for settling claims against the city. In Saskatoon and in Moose Jaw the commissioners are responsible for preparing and submitting the estimates to council.

There are several provisions with respect to the commissioners of Moose Jaw which do not apply in the other two cities. They are to nominate for approval all department heads and other officers and are authorized to make other staff appointments and to recommend the salaries for all officials and employees; they are authorized also to consider all communications and petitions before they are submitted to council or its committees and make recommendations as to their disposition, and generally to perform all executive and ministerial functions vested in the council. The appointed commissioners are required to devote their full time to the business of the city and are entitled to be paid $5.00 for attendance at each meeting of the council or its special committees, in addition to their regular remuneration.

The Edmonton charter, enacted in 1913, provided that the council appoint one or two commissioners and that the mayor be an *ex officio* commissioner. At present there are two appointed commissioners who hold office at the pleasure of the council and who can be dismissed only on a two-thirds' vote of the council. The commissioners, by statute, are given a general executive jurisdiction over the affairs of the city including the care, management, and control of the police force, fire brigade and other public services, public works and utilities of the city, and of all property, works, improvements, roads, streets, and public places owned or controlled by the city, together with such other powers and duties as the council may delegate to them. The Cities Act of 1950 permits any Alberta city to appoint a commissioner.

The commissioners' authority is subject to the legislative jurisdiction of the council. Although it is the responsibility of the commissioners to prepare and submit the budget, the council retains full authority with respect to the funds to be provided. The council has the right to demand information from the commissioners and to direct and control their administrative policy.

The city commissioner plan is similar to the manager plan, but there are significant differences. Instead of a single executive officer, this plan usually provides for a group executive, for even where there is only one appointed commissioner the mayor may also be a commissioner. Another important difference is that one of the members of the executive is an elected representative, whereas under the manager plan the sole executive officer is a permanent paid official.

CHAPTER IX

MUNICIPAL OFFICERS AND EMPLOYEES

TYPES OF EMPLOYEES

THE PERSONS EMPLOYED by municipal councils may be classified in a number of ways. For our purposes we will consider their classification on several bases.

Compulsory and Optional Appointments

There are certain officers which all municipal councils are required by law to appoint, such as a clerk, a treasurer, or an auditor. The number of such compulsory appointments varies from province to province and, to some extent, as between different types of municipalities within the same province. In Ontario, for example, while local municipalities[1] are required to appoint assessors and tax collectors, the counties are not required to do so, inasmuch as counties do not have an original assessing function and but little of the tax collecting function. Except for these compulsory appointments, councils are left fairly free to appoint such officers and employees as they feel are required to carry out the activities which the council may legally perform. The number of these other employees and the range of their activities varies according to the size of the municipality and the scope of municipal activities.

Officers and Servants

Another basis of division of municipal employees is into two groups designated as officers and servants. The term "officers" as used here "includes such persons as occupy offices of an executive or administrative nature established by the Legislature, who exercise powers conferred by the Legislature in relation to the affairs of a particular municipality and who are appointed by and subject to the control of the council of such municipality and also such persons as are appointed by a municipal council to discharge the duties attendant upon an office established by it."[2] The difficulty of drawing the dividing line between officers and servants is stated by Mr. Justice Middleton in giving judgment in the case *re Board of Education for the City of Toronto*

[1]Cities, towns, villages, and townships.
[2]Frank B. Proctor, *The Law of Municipal Corporations in Ontario* (Toronto, 1931), p. 974.

and Doughty et al in which he quotes as follows: "The position of an officer appears to involve some discretionary authority and it is to be distinguished from that of a mere servant whose only duty is to obey orders, though it is not always easy to draw the line," and further states: "It is easy, dealing with those holding positions of importance, to say that they are officers within the meaning of the enactment. As one descends the scale and approaches the position of a subordinate employee whose duty it is to obey, yet where there is some element of discretion, it is hard to say upon which side of the line the particular case falls. . . . Every officer of the municipal corporation is in one sense a servant of the corporation, but the converse is not true; every servant is not an officer but only those who have real responsibility to perform the vital duties of the corporation."[3]

Statutory and Non-Statutory Officers

Provincial legislation places upon certain municipal officers statutory responsibilities and duties regardless of what may be the instruction or direction of the council which appoint them. Thus, a treasurer may be required by statute to pay out funds for some purposes as directed by law even though the council may have provided for some other disposition of the money involved. In most cases the officers who have statutory duties are those which a council is required to appoint, but the personnel of these two classes of employees is not identical.

Part-time and Full-time Employees

In the several thousand smaller and rural municipalities in Canada most of the employees are on a part-time basis, for the work involved is not sufficient to require full-time occupation. As the population of a municipality increases the proportion of full-time employees increases so that in most cities all employees are on a full-time basis. But as the range of municipal activities grows and the administration becomes more complex, the need for full-time employees increases even in smaller municipalities. As a result there is a trend in the smaller municipalities towards combining two or more municipal offices and appointing one man to several offices. This enables a council to pay the employee sufficient to permit him to devote all his time to municipal work. Frequently as many as three and even more offices are so combined. The positions that lend themselves to such combination are those of clerk and treasurer, or treasurer and tax collector, and there are cases where the office of clerk, treasurer, assessor, and welfare officer are filled by one man. It is not ordinarily feasible to com-

[3]*Ontario Weekly Notes*, 1935, p. 33.

bine positions requiring professional qualifications, such as medical officer of health or engineer, with other positions, and for obvious reasons it is usually forbidden by law that the office of auditor be combined with that of any other office.

This combination of duties of clerk and treasurer in one officer is contemplated by statute in some provinces, as in New Brunswick counties, Quebec counties and rural municipalities, and in municipalities other than cities in the four western provinces where the office of secretary-treasurer is provided for. In Ontario, although the statute contemplates, but no longer requires, separate and distinct offices, the positions of clerk and treasurer are held by one individual in one of the 29 cities, 117 of the 141 towns, 115 of the 156 villages, 280 of the 571 townships, and 15 of the 38 counties.

Permanent and Casual Employees

While there is considerable difference among local practices a great many councils, formally or informally, divide their employees into two groups, permanent and casual or temporary. The permanent group is usually composed of salaried employees and the casual employees are those who are paid by the hour, day, or week and as a rule are taken on the staff and let out by the head of the department rather than by the council. The use of the term "temporary employees" is frequently used to distinguish this group from the permanent employees but is a misleading term for, as in other civil services, a "temporary employee" may have been on the staff full time for twenty or thirty years. Frequently the conditions of employment of the two groups such as working hours, holidays, pensions, and sick leave show marked differences.

Range of Employees

The range of employees is wide. Certain types such as clerks, treasurers, assessors, auditors, medical officers of health, office clerks, labourers, and truck driver are common to all municipalities. In the larger municipalities, some of which are engaged in many activities other than those classed as strictly governmental, we find police, firemen, mechanics of various types, nurses, chemists, engineers, lawyers, social workers, publicity experts, playground attendants, landscape gardeners, architects, veterinary surgeons, plumbing, building, sanitary, and other inspectors, radio operators, harbour masters, transportation experts, traffic engineers, two planners, photographers. Naturally, the total number of employees shows a wide range from the few in the small rural municipality, most of whom may be part-time employees, to the 7,572 full-time employees, exclusive of some 3,500 school employees, in a city such as Toronto.

The employees of a municipality may be roughly divided into six classifications as shown in the accompanying chart.

Classification	*Examples*
Administrative officers	Clerk, fire chief, assessor
Professionally trained employees	Health nurses, architects
Clerical employees	Stenographers, cashiers
Uniformed forces	Policemen, firemen
Skilled mechanics	Electricians, carpenters
Labourers	Common labourers, street sweepers, refuse collectors

Appointment and Dismissal of Employees

Municipal officers and employees in Canada are all appointed. The appointments are made either by the council or by its authority, or by such other boards or commissions as may employ them. There is no election of municipal officers such as occurs in many states in the United States. The usual practice is that senior or important officers, uniformed employees, and, as a rule, clerical or inside staff employees, are actually appointed by council, but in larger places the employment of what are described as outside workers, such as street workers, mechanics, construction workers, garbage collectors, labourers, and parks employees, is left to the head of the department under which they operate.

Councils are free to appoint who they will to most municipal positions although in some cases the provinces have imposed requirements as to qualifications or require provincial approval of the appointee. Thus, in Alberta municipalities other than cities, appointments to the office of secretary-treasurer, assessor, or auditor are subject to the approval of the Minister of Municipal Affairs. In Ontario, only a "legally qualified medical practitioner" may be appointed as a medical officer of health, only a person who is licensed by the Department of Municipal Affairs may be appointed as a municipal auditor, and only a graduate in civil engineering or an Ontario land surveyor may be appointed as a county road superintendent. The approval of the appropriate provincial department in Ontario is required for appointments to the offices of county road superintendent, medical officer of health, or sanitary inspector. Similar provisions are found in other provinces.

Some provinces require evidence of qualification even for non-professional personnel. Manitoba has established a provincial Civil Service Board of five members which has power to prescribe qualifications, hold examinations and prescribe periods of probation for candidates appointed by municipalities as clerks, treasurer, or secretary-treasurers. Saskatchewan clerk-treasurers must be approved by the chairman of the Provincial Board of Examiners and can only obtain the necessary certificate after written and oral examinations by provincial authorities.[4] In Alberta not only are all appointments to the office of secretary-treasurer in a town, village, or municipal district subject to the approval of the Minister of Municipal Affairs but the appointee must meet the established minimum qualifications with respect to education, experience, age, citizenship, and character, and the appointment is only on a temporary basis until the appointee has had two satisfactory annual audits and two satisfactory annual inspections by a provincial department inspector. British Columbia provides for a Board of Examiners of three members with power to establish standards of proficiency for municipal administrative officers, to hold examinations, and to grant certificates of qualification. Nova Scotia, New Brunswick, Quebec, Ontario, and Saskatchewan all provide for the licensing of municipal auditors by a provincial authority. It is a growing practice on the part of the provinces to establish standards of qualification and thereby to assure at least a minimum of competence in certain classes of municipal employees. Subject to these limitations, however, municipal councils may appoint whom they will to paid municipal office.

In most cases appointments to municipal employment are "at pleasure of the council" which means that the council may at any time dispense with the service of the employee, "without cause assigned and without recourse."[5]

Some exceptions to this general rule are as follows:

Nova Scotia: Clerks and treasurers of "municipalities" and clerks and solicitors of towns hold office during good behaviour but may be dismissed by council for cause.

New Brunswick: In Fredericton the clerk, assistant clerk, treasurer, assistant treasurer, city engineer, assessor, receiver of taxes, and building inspector may only be dismissed on a two-thirds' vote of council for cause.

Quebec: Secretary-treasurers of rural municipalities may only be dismissed on a two-thirds' vote of council.

Ontario: Medical officers of health hold office during good behaviour and residence in the municipality, or in an adjoining municipality, and may be removed from office only on a two-thirds' vote of the

[4]This provision was not enforced during the war years.
[5]Proctor, *The Law of Municipal Corporations in Ontario*, p. 978.

whole council and with the consent and approval of the Minister of Health, who may require cause to be shown for the dismissal.

County road superintendent's appointing by-law may not be repealed or amended without the consent of the Minister of Highways.

Auditors hold office during good behaviour and are removable for cause on vote of two-thirds of members of the council.

Unemployment relief administrators or assistants may not be removed from office without approval of the Minister of Public Welfare.

Manitoba: Clerks, treasurers, and secretary-treasurers appointed prior to January 1934 or, if subsequently appointed, who have been confirmed in office by the provincial Civic Service Board may only be dismissed for cause.

Saskatchewan: Treasurers and secretary-treasurers of rural municipalities may not be dismissed until thirty days after the reeve has given written notice to the Local Government Board stating the reasons for dismissal.

British Columbia: Appointees to municipal positions hold them during good behaviour and efficiency but council may terminate an appointment after one month's notice.

Method of Appointment

The procedure in appointing municipal employees varies according to the importance or character of the position to be filled. Appointments to the senior or statutory positions are usually made by by-law, whereas the less important appointments are frequently effected by a resolution. Manual labourers are usually taken on and laid off by the head of the department within which they work. The extent to which the department head is left free to decide who shall be employed in such cases varies from place to place and from time to time and according to the temperament of the department head and his committee members. A department head may be content to appoint those who are recommended to him by members of council or he may take the attitude that, if he is to be held responsible for results, he must have the decision as to who is to be appointed. The pressure upon a department head in this regard depends in large measure upon the rise and fall in economic prosperity.

Where appointments are made by council, the actual decision as to the appointee may be made by the members of council or, as is frequently the practice with the lower ranks, the council may merely approve the recommendations made by the head of the department involved. The appearance of non-interference with department heads in making appointments may be illusory, for while the council may adopt the recommendation of the department head without question, it may the more readily do so if he has arrived at his recommendation in response to unofficial pressure behind the scenes.

Politics in Appointments

Canadian municipalities have never had the problem of party politics in the appointments of either permanent or casual employees to the extent that it has existed in some United States cities. Unquestionably political affiliations do influence many municipal appointments, but the practice has not developed that members of the paid staff go out of office as the political complexion of a council changes in order to provide room for other appointees. One reason why party politics and the spoils system have not obtained the hold on municipal government in this country that they have in some others, is the general observance of the rule that once appointed to municipal office appointees withdraw from open political activity. Rarely, if at all, are Canadian municipal employees required to contribute any percentage of their pay to "the party."

Recruitment

When a staff vacancy occurs in a larger municipality it may be filled either by promotion from within the organization, or by appointing some person from outside who has not had previous experience. It is a common practice in rural and smaller urban municipalities to appoint persons who are or have been members of the municipal council. This practice is not as common in the larger municipalities where the complex duties of the senior officers make previous experience almost indispensable. Many urban municipalities advertise for applicants for positions and in more recent years there has been increased willingness on the part of the councils to appoint to administrative positions applicants who have had successful municipal experience elsewhere. For many years Canadian municipalities adhered to the "local son" rule in making appointments other than to the teaching staff. As more officers were required to have professional qualifications, as with engineers, nurses, and social workers, there developed a greater readiness to appoint non-residents. This trend has been reinforced by the manpower shortage throughout the forties and is perhaps most marked in the appointment of trained social workers who have been in short supply throughout the Dominion.

The practice of establishing provincial standards of qualifications for appointment to municipal office, previously noted, is the result of the increasing complexity of municipal problems and the provincial regulations relating to municipalities, the development of more positive provincial policies, and the expansion of provincial financial contributions to municipalities. If the municipalities are to serve adequately in carrying out provincial policies and the provinces are to be assured that their contributions are being effectively expended, the provinces are concerned with the quality of the key members of the municipal administrative staff. This practice is likely to continue and increase in extent.

Merit Systems

Few Canadian cities have adopted extensive merit systems or "civil service" plans such as have developed in recent years in many cities in the United States where 28.5 per cent of the cities of 10,000 or over have all their permanent employees under a formal merit system. This perhaps is accounted for by the smaller size of the Canadian cities, by the fact that the conditions which such a system is primarily designed to offset have not been as acute, and by the greater hesitancy to experiment in the field of local government. In fairness it should be noted that these programmes in United States cities are now not so much protective and preventive measures as positive plans for raising standards of performance through improved organization and personnel administration.

Montreal and Toronto are two Canadian cities which have a merit system. The Montreal Civil Service Commission, established in 1945, is composed of three members who are appointed by the city council on the recommendation of its Executive Committee and who may be dismissed by the council. The president of the commission is the director of personnel for the city. The commission has jurisdiction over all employees who are in continuous occupations and who are required to devote their full time to such employment. Excluded from its jurisdiction are the Director of Civic Departments and his assistant, the directors of the various departments and their assistants, the members of the Board of Revision of Valuations, and the members of the commission itself.

The commission may prescribe the qualifications required for any office, classify the various offices and decide the duties of each office and rank, determine which offices shall be filled only after examination, prescribe and hold the examinations, and draw up lists of those eligible for appointments based on the examination results. The commission, on request of the Executive Committee, may make studies and submit recommendations respecting the organization or administration of departments and the establishment of new departments or divisions. Where a vacancy is to be filled, the department director must notify the commission, which supplies him with the list of eligible persons. The directors of the departments, however, select, appoint, and replace their subordinate employees with the approval of the Executive Committee and it is the director's selection which is submitted to the Executive Committee.

The Toronto merit system, which has been in effect for only a few years, applies to all positions in the permanent service, covering some 5,000 employees, other than department heads and their deputies. All vacancies in the permanent service must be advertised by bulletins to employees and any employee may apply irrespective of the department in which he is employed. The system has progressed to the point where all clerical, supervisory, and junior executive positions are filled only after examination and the area covered by examination is being continuously extended.

Where an examination is not conducted the department head is supplied with a list of applicants in order of seniority. He may select and recommend, after interview, the senior employee who, in his opinion, is qualified for the position, and he must give adequate reasons if he does not recommend any of the senior applicants. Where there is an examination, it may be a written, oral, or practical examination or a combination. In practice there is always an oral examination. Written examinations are used as an eliminating process; to qualify for an oral examination applicants must obtain 50 per cent on each subject and 70 per cent of the total marks for all subjects. Members of an oral examination board are chosen by the Director of Personnel. Such a board usually consists of three to five members and, except where purely clerical positions are involved, one or two of them are qualified men from outside the civic service. Usually the Personnel Supervisor or other senior member of the Personnel Office is also a member. An applicant must be considered to be 70 per cent efficient by the oral board to be qualified.

The marks of applicants declared eligible by the oral board are added to the marks obtained on the written or practical examination together with seniority marks of ½ mark for each year of service over one year, to a maximum of 15 marks. The applicants are then entered in an "eligible list" in order of their total marks. All lists are maintained for six months and on recommendation of the Director of Personnel may be extended for a further six months. A department head is entitled to have referred to him the first three persons eligible for any one vacancy, and one additional for each additional vacancy in his department. He may recommend for appointment to a vacancy without question any name referred to him from the list.

Duties of Municipal Employees

The greater number of municipal employees work under the direction of department heads and have little direct contact with the council or its committees. Their duties are assigned to them by their department heads. A limited group is in frequent and direct contact with the council and work under its supervision.

As previously noted some of the officers have statutory duties but, in addition, they and the other officers are required to perform such other duties as the council may assign to them. In the larger municipalities there are usually formal by-laws designating some of the responsibilities and duties of the various senior officers of a council, supplemented by an even wider range of duties and responsibilities which, while not officially listed, have developed out of practice and custom. The acquisition of these added duties may be the result of council action referring a particular matter to the official, of instruction of a committee, or of direction by the head of the municipality, or they may be assumed by the official because something needs to be done and, as no one else is dealing with the matter, he takes on the responsibility more or less by default.

With respect to most municipalities it would be safe to say that in no one place can a complete record be found of the various duties and responsibilities of each of the senior officers of the council. While it would probably be advisable that a more definite allocation of responsibilities be on record, such record could never be complete because of the constant succession of new problems which arise from the continuous expansion of governmental activities and the infinite variety of citizens' problems which must be dealt with at the municipal level.

Working Conditions

As no extensive nation-wide surveys of working conditions of municipal employees are available, the generalizations respecting working conditions set out below are based on limited sources of information. In some cases it has been possible to obtain information only with respect to one province.

Pay

It has long been an accepted generalization that in the public service in normal times the lower grades of employees receive higher pay, and the higher grades of employees receive lower pay, than those of comparable quality in private employment. In some respects this is true of municipal employment, but there are exceptions. One difficulty in making comparisons is that with respect to so many types of municipal employees there is no comparable work in the sphere of private business and the only possible comparison is with similar employment in another community where the whole wage scale of the community may be on a different basis. Thus, while the position of clerk or clerk-treasurer of a municipality may appear at first glance to be comparable to the secretary-treasurer of a commercial corporation, there is, in fact, little basis of comparison in so far as the duties and the responsibilities are concerned; private employment in most communities supplies no comparative standard by which to measure the rates of pay of such employees as firemen, policemen, utility managers, or librarians.

Where the employee has skills or training which are in demand by private employers, a municipality, except in times of depression, is forced to keep its rates of pay fairly well in line with those paid for comparable services by private employers. This applies to professionally trained and clerical employees, skilled mechanics, and labourers. For the administrative officers and the uniformed forces, the rates of pay are determined by a number of factors such as established practice, comparisons with other employees in the service of the same employer, comparisons with other municipalities, and political expediency. As a rule, the skilled mechanic receives the going union rate of pay or slightly less where his employment on a year-round basis protects him against any loss of time. Because all types of employees work for the same employer and information respecting rates is public information, there is a tendency to keep all types in the same relative position in any adjustment upward or downward. Councils argue that municipal rates of pay should not respond to the upward swing in rates in private employment because there is never any unemployment for the permanent municipal employee and he does not suffer as drastic reductions in a time of depression as do privately employed persons. This attitude, however, has had to give way to the upward pressure in the post-war period and municipal wage and salary rates have shown substantial increases in recent years.

The accompanying chart gives samples of the rates paid some administrative officers, professionally trained employees, and uniformed forces taken from a survey made in forty-eight Ontario municipalities of over 7,500 population in December, 1951.

Generally speaking the rates of pay of municipal employees are

Position	*Salary range*	
	Low	High
Clerk	$2,900	$ 9,000
Assessment Commissioner	2,600	10,000
Treasurer	2,400	11,300
Senior Nurse	1,900	3,756
Municipal Engineer	3,700	9,000
Fire Chief	2,400	7,000
Fireman, 1st class	1,900	3,522
Police Chief	2,800	9,690
Constable, 1st class	2,340	3,453

fixed by the council or other civic body under which the employee works and such body has the power to increase or decrease those rates as it deems expedient. There are exceptions to this generalization, however. Any officer of a Nova Scotia town whose tenure of office is on a good behaviour basis may apply to a county or a Supreme Court judge if he is removed from office or if his salary is reduced. The judge may order him reinstated or, if he determines that the salary before reduction was excessive, he decides what is adequate compensation. If, however, he decides that the reduction was not a *bona fide* exercise of discretion on the part of the council or was to compel or induce the resignation of the officer, he is required to void the reduction. In Ontario a medical officer of health can apply to a county judge who has the power to fix his salary.

Ontario, in 1948, provided that, where the members of a fire or police department were unable to come to an agreement with their employing council or police commission, as the case might be, respecting working conditions, they could ask for an arbitration board. This board consists of one member appointed by the employees, one by the employer, and a third to be chosen by these two arbitrators. The award of the arbitrators is binding on the employers for the year to which the award applies and thereafter until a new agreement or award has been made. The members of a number of fire and police departments have utilized this legislation to obtain adjustments in rates of pay and other working conditions such as holidays, reduction of hours, and perquisites, which under all the awards to date have been upward.

Pensions[6]

It is only in the last quarter century that Canadian municipalities have made provision for pensioning municipal employees on a systematic basis. Previously the general practice, which still prevails in many municipalities, was to provide for retiring employees on an indi-

[6]The information dealing with pensions is based largely on *Canadian Municipal Pension Plans* (The Institute of Local Government, Queen's University, 1946).

vidual basis varying according to the individual circumstances. In more recent years there has been a rapid increase in the number of municipalities adopting pension plans. At first these were limited to the larger urban centres but now are established in many of the smaller urban communities as well as rural municipalities. Table 14 indicates the development of municipal pension plans in the period 1924 to 1945.

TABLE 14
CANADIAN URBAN MUNICIPALITIES IN WHICH FORMAL PENSION PLANS EXIST

Period in which present plan instituted	Number of cities with plans, by population					Total
	over 100,000	50,000–100,000	25,000–50,000	10,000–25,000	5,000–10,000	
1921–25	0	0	0	1	0	1
1926–30	2	0	1	1	7	11
1931–35	1	2	0	0	0	3
1936–40	3	1	3	0	1	8
1941–45	2	1	2	11	0	16
Total	8	4	6	13	8	39
Percentage of possible number[a]	100	57	31	30	11	26

[a]The possible number is the total number of all Canadian urban municipalities in the population class indicated.

The pension plans in effect are of four types: (1) those handled by an insurance company, (2) those provided for by the establishment of a local pension fund, (3) those provided for by arrangement with the Annuities Branch of the Department of Labour, and (4) those provided for by a provincially established and operated fund, as in the case of Saskatchewan urban municipalities and of British Columbia. The funds established in recent years are predominantly of the Dominion annuity type, a trend accounted for in part by the simplicity of operation for the local authorities and the elimination of the hazard of losses which accompanies a locally operated fund.

In 1946 the distribution of municipal pension plans in urban municipalities of 5,000 or over was as follows:

	P.E.I.	*N.S.*	*N.B.*	*Que.*	*Ont.*	*Man.*	*Sask.*	*Alta.*	*B.C.*	*Total*
Number of plans	0	0	4	4	14	1	3	3	10	39
Percentage of possible	0	0	80	10	22	20	43	75	90	26

Participation by the employees in the pension plan is usually compulsory for employees entering the service after the plan has been established. In somewhat more than half the plans, retirement at normal retiring age is compulsory; retiring age is usually either sixty or sixty-five years for men and five years earlier for police and firemen and female employees. All of the plans are maintained by contributions from both the employer and the employee, although the basis of sharing varies. Under most plans the two parties contribute on an equal basis but in two the employer's share is the larger and in thirteen, the employee's. The amount of pension varies from one municipality to another due to variations in the basis of contribution.

In 1945 in twenty-eight Canadian urban municipalities with 30,879 employees, 86 per cent or 26,617 were included under the provisions of a municipal pension plan. The number of municipalities providing pensions has increased rapidly in the period since 1945, the increase having taken place largely in the smaller municipalities.[7] By 1950, pension plans were in effect in over fifty Ontario municipalities in contrast to fourteen in 1945.

[7]Saskatchewan in 1951 provided for a province-wide compulsory plan for retirement for employees of villages, towns, and cities.

CHAPTER X

MUNICIPAL FINANCE: EXPENDITURES

FINANCIAL PROBLEMS are basic problems of municipal government, for the activities and services which a municipality is able to carry on depend ultimately on the money available to pay for them. There is almost no limit to the possible demand for municipal services and the natural attitude of elected representatives is to give the people the services they want, subject to the restraining spectre of the resulting taxation. Almost every proposal for expenditures made to civic bodies has some merit. The problem of the elected representatives is to select from among the many requests either those which are relatively more essential or more meritorious or, as sometimes occurs, those which are supported by the most effective vocal group. One reason why councils appear to show little initiative may be that their resources are exhausted in providing for the existing services without undertaking new commitments.

The major portion of local taxes is raised by taxation of real property. Accordingly councils, in determining their expenditure programmes, must keep in mind the probable limit of the tax burden which real property can be made to carry. There is no accepted fixed point at which it can be said that the limit of taxation has been reached, but it is evidence that such limit has been passed when any considerable number of property owners prefer to let their properties be sold for arrears of taxes rather than to pay the taxes and retain their properties.

The position of councillors is made more difficult by the fact that, in most urban communities at least, the majority of the electorate is composed of those who are not directly municipal taxpayers. If councillors are to retain office, their programme, which finally means their expenditures, must meet with the approval of the majority of those who are sufficiently interested to vote. If, however, the burden of cost of those expenditures is unduly onerous, it may so arouse the resentment of the taxpaying group that, although they constitute a minority, they may outvote the less active majority who have not the same incentive. Hence, the councillor must maintain a nice balance between the demands for expenditures and the limit of the taxpayers' passive endurance.

In one respect public financing is the reverse of private financing, for in local as in other governments the normal procedure is to determine first what is to be the expenditure programme for the year and then to adjust the income accordingly, whereas in private financing the individual attempts to adjust his expenditure programme to a predetermined income. There have been instances in which councils have determined that the tax levy shall be at a stated rate and the year's programme required to come within that limit. This practice is not a sound one, however, as it is probable either that needed services will be neglected, or that there will be a substantial deficit at the end of the year for the taxpayers of later years to meet.

The total expenditures of the municipalities in the pre-war years were slightly greater than those of the provinces and about one-half those of the Dominion. In 1939 they represented approximately 26 per cent of the combined Dominion-provincial-municipal expenditures. Over a long period municipal expenditures have shown a steady increase, subject to temporary interruptions in the upward trend during periods of war and depression. In more recent years, however, the rate of increase in municipal expenditures has fallen far behind that of both the Dominion and the provinces so that by 1948 municipal expenditures represented but 14.3 per cent[1] of the total government expenditure.

The expenditures for which a municipal council provides may be divided into four groups: (1) debt charges, provision for which is obligatory; (2) funds to finance other municipal bodies whose requirements may be of two types, those for which council, the tax levying body, is required to raise the amount demanded by the other civic body, and those with respect to which the council has discretion as to the amount to be provided; (3) expenditures to provide for services which, under the law, the council must pay for; and (4) expenditures for services which are discretionary with the council.

Debt charges. When a council incurs a debt repayable over a period of years, succeeding councils are required to levy taxes in each subsequent year during the lifetime of the securities issued, in order to provide for payment of the interest falling due each year and for the repayment, into a sinking fund or otherwise, of a predetermined portion of the principal sum borrowed. As an inducement to subsequent councils to make this annual provision, penalties in the form of disbarment from office or personal liability for any amount not provided

[1]This figure was as low as 5.7 per cent in 1944 when Dominion war expenditures distorted the picture. See page 59.

for are enforceable in some provinces. In others, provincial authorities may take legal action to compel the council to raise the required amount. The importance of this expenditure depends upon the borrowing policies of previous councils and the load of debt which they have built up. At the present time debt charges do not represent as large a proportion of the expenditures as was the case prior to the thirties, for municipalities restricted their capital expenditures during the war years and, in many instances, during the preceding depression. A considerable portion of these charges in some municipalities does not actually become a part of the tax burden for it may be offset by revenues derived from utilities, such as water and electrical works, to pay the charges on the debt incurred for their construction. The significance of this expenditure is suggested by the fact that in Ontario cities 17 per cent of the current expenditure is to meet debt charges.

Funds to finance other municipal bodies. The usual practice is that the taxes required to finance all civic boards are levied and collected by the council as it is undesirable to duplicate the assessing and tax collecting function. The other municipal bodies which require funds advise the council, prior to the time for fixing the tax levy each year, of the amount of money they require or desire for the year.

These requirements or requests are of several types. Some bodies, as with most school boards, have the right to requisition annually from the council whatever amount they require for current expenditures for the year, and the council must provide the sum demanded, levying therefor upon the persons liable to taxation. In other cases, as with library or parks boards in Ontario, the board is entitled to demand from council for current expenditures an amount up to a limit fixed by statute, in the case of library boards, fifty cents per capita, and in the case of parks boards, the amount produced by a one-mill tax levy. These boards may request larger amounts but the provision of any amount in excess of that fixed by statute lies within the discretion of council. A third type includes those boards or commissions which submit their requirements to council but with respect to which the council has complete discretion either to grant the request or to reduce or amend the amount requested.

Expenditures to provide for statutory obligations. Several provinces provide that services which are rendered by a number of agencies, including provincial departments, shall be paid for by that municipality which, under the legislation, is determined to be liable. The basis of such payment may be fixed by statute or in the manner provided by statute. Such services include those of providing hospitalization for indigents, in which the hospital authorities submit a bill to the responsible municipality based on a statutory per diem rate, or the cost of maintaining wards of Children's Aid Societies, which is also chargeable to the responsible municipality at a fixed per diem rate. There are other services which a municipality may be required to supply but over which it has little or no control such as providing after-care for tuberculous patients following discharge from sanatoria in Ontario, the erection and maintenance of court houses, or provision for the administration of justice.

Another group of expenditures are incurred to cover the cost of statutory obligations imposed upon the municipal corporation in which the performance of the service is under local control. These would include the maintenance of streets and walks in a safe condition or, in Ontario, the relief of the unemployed. In some provinces, also, services performed by provincial authorities are, in whole or in part, charged back to the municipalities and must be provided for, as in the provision for the administration of justice in Manitoba.

Expenditures for optional services. There is a wide range of services which municipal corporations are authorized to perform but which are not mandatory. These include such services as street lighting, the collection and disposal of refuse, or the maintenance of a fire brigade. While the council have full authority to decide whether or not such services are to be provided, in fact once a service has been established a council's discretion is largely limited to deciding whether or not these services are to be improved or extended, for public demand will not permit their elimination or reduction. A council may have the legal right to close the fire halls, or to reduce the frequency of garbage collections, but obviously it is not politically feasible to do so.[2] The citizens, in spite of their demands for economy, will not tolerate a reduction in services to which they have become accustomed.

There remain some expenditures over which councils retain full discretion, both legally and in practice, but they are limited and of minor financial importance. Such items as special grants, the maintainance of the physical plant of the corporation, expenditures on publicity, travelling expenses, etc., can be reduced or eliminated as council see fit without raising any general outcry from the citizens. The accompanying analysis of the expenditure of the city of Kingston for the year 1951 illustrates the significance of the uncontrollable expenditures in the civic expenditure programme of the council of that year.

[2]During the depression years of the thirties some municipalities having a number of fire stations closed some as an economy measure. They did not long remain closed, owing to public protests.

Group I	Expenditures		
	Debt charges	$351,647	18.5%
Group II	Expenditures		
	Education	550,474	
	Library	16,462	
	Board of Health	26,064	
	Juvenile Court	5,643	
	Police Commission	130,379	
	Suburban Roads Commission	8,500	
		$737,522	39.0%
Group III	Expenditures		
	Administration of justice	27,137	
	Hospitalization	74,387	
	Children's Aid maintenance	37,839	
	Training Schools maintenance	1,307	
		$140,670	7.4%
Group IV	Expenditures		
	All other expenditures	652,482	34.9%
		$1,890,709	100. %

In one sense a council has more actual control over expenditures than the above outline might suggest, for a great part of the expenditure is represented by wages and salaries which, in so far as they apply to council employees, are largely under its control. Here again council's discretion is limited by the prevailing rates in private employment in the community. Not only are there political hazards in a policy of pay reduction but, if councils are to have any but the dregs of the labour supply, their rates of pay must be within reasonable distance of those in private employment, with due allowance for any advantages which may be peculiar to municipal employment.

There has been a long-run continuous increase in municipal expenditures due to public demands. Increased services have accompanied greater concentrations of population and standards of service have been progressively raised. The municipalities have been increasingly used as a medium of community service because they have demonstrated their capacity to perform a wide range of services with reasonable efficiency and economy and because the public has awakened to the possibilities for better living conditions through positive community programmes. In some cases also the provincial authorities have required municipalities to undertake additional functions. All of these factors have combined to produce an ever growing demand for greater expenditures.

If it is not feasible to control expenditures by reducing or lowering the standards of existing services, any effort to control expansion must be concentrated on proposed new activities and new avenues of expenditure. These proposals arise from a variety of causes. Interested groups concerned with promoting a special project may arouse sufficient public support to induce a council to undertake a service, such as the provision of supervised playgrounds or traffic guards for school children. Individuals or groups may start a project, the supplying of milk to needy school children, for example, and support it with funds privately subscribed. In the course of time the service may outgrow the resources of private charity or the original promoters go to their reward or grow weary in their well doing and the municipality is asked to take over the service which, by its very growth, has proven its value to the community. Such organizations or individuals perform a valuable community service in demonstrating the need and the possibilities of meeting it.

Because the local unit of government in many respects is in fact, though not constitutionally, the residual unit of government, councils frequently assume responsibilities which are not legally theirs. If some need arises which requires action, it is much more difficult for the local government on the spot to hide behind the question of constitutional responsibility and do nothing than it is for the more remote governments located at Ottawa or the provincial capital. In urgent matters, where there is no clearly established rule or practice as to which level of government is responsible, as in providing emergency housing, the senior governments by taking ample time to consider the situation can virtually force the municipalities to take action and thus assume responsibility. The municipality, to borrow a rugby term, is at the end of the line and, as there is no one to whom it can pass, it must carry the ball itself. It is not always the unwilling victim of circumstance in these matters, however. Councillors are often prepared, for their own advantage, to involve the corporation by assuming services which are not its legal responsibility and which, if the councils were not so prompt to assume the load, might well be provided by the senior governments.

In addition to these self-imposed new expenditures, there are others which are imposed by the provincial authorities. Over the years during which the municipal systems have developed, a considerable number of such services have been built up and from time to time additional services are being added. In some provinces, however, of late years the municipalities have been relieved of their share of some costs, as was the case in Ontario where the municipalities were relieved of their share of mothers' allowances and old age pensions in 1937, and of sanatorium care for indigents in 1938. Although the new services from time to time being imposed do not involve large costs, there has been a progressive increase in the statutory per diem rates chargeable against the municipalities for some services charged to them.[8]

The Trend in Expenditures

Large expenditures are involved in the new demands arising from technical and social changes and increased scientific knowledge. A conspicuous example is the expenditure in which municipalities have been involved as a result of the widespread use of automotive transportation, which has been accompanied by the need for better roads and paved streets, parking regulation and traffic control, street widening, improved lighting, snow removal, grade separation, etc. The large-scale transfer of population to the suburbs made possible by this medium of transportation has in turn produced a host of additional difficulties included under the general term of the metropolitan area problem.

If the continuous upward movement in municipal spending is to be slowed down the expansion into new activities must be continuously resisted. But the upward movement is not necessarily undesirable, for it can reasonably be argued that if the citizen gets more value for his dollar when he expends it through his municipal taxes than when he expended it privately, then the more of his dollars he spends through the municipal medium for things he otherwise would purchase privately the better off he is. The important condition is that such municipal service be more efficient or more economically performed than if it were being performed privately. On the other hand, very often the individual citizen is compelled to purchase services through municipal taxes which he would not purchase if he were spending his money privately, as is the case of the bachelor property owner who is compelled to purchase educational facilities, unless his school tax can be regarded as a stand-by charge.

There is no reason to suppose that the upward trend will not continue. As the wants of the people expand and they realize the extent to which these wants can be supplied by community action, there is likely to be a sustained demand for expanded local government activity. In the social services, there is almost no limit to the possibility of expansion, other than the limit of revenue. Other types of services

[8]In Ontario, for example, the statutory per diem charge to the municipalities for hospitalization of indigents has developed as follows: 1912—$1.00 per day, 1917—$1.25, 1926—$1.50, 1928—$1.75, 1945—$2.25, 1948—according to the class of hospital. $3.00, $2.50, $2.25.

are likely to increase also if they can meet the requirements that they can be more efficiently, effectively, acceptably, or economically supplied by the municipality than by arrangements between private parties, that the product or service is a reasonably standardized one in which the factors of style or personal taste are not important, and that the service is in fairly wide demand.

When faced with a request to undertake a new service, a council must keep in mind that new avenues of expenditure tend to become perpetual once a service has been established. Thus, if snow removal from the streets is undertaken as an emergency measure in one winter, it is almost inevitable that the motorists will demand that it be done every winter and that the number of streets from which it is removed be continuously extended. It is also the lesson of bitter experience that frequently the first cost is not the last or total cost. Many municipalities have been the beneficiaries of private benevolence in the form of gifts or bequests for purposes such as a swimming pool or an art gallery or other community amenities only to find that the structure once erected involved an expenditure for maintenance and operation which was not adequately appreciated in advance. Yet a third point to be remembered is that once the precedent for a certain type of service, be it a traffic light or branch library, is established in one section of the municipality there will soon be demands for similar provision in other sections of the community which can not easily be denied.

Extensions of municipal service may be beneficial to the inhabitants, and councils may be criticized for their reluctance in responding to demands that they be undertaken but, so long as the existing basis of municipal taxation remains, councils are compelled to keep in mind the limits of the burden which a restricted source of revenue can be expected to bear. Considering the natural inclination of elected representatives to comply with any demands for expenditures, it is probably in the financial interests of the taxpayers as a whole that councils should be hesitant about extending municipal services, rather than that they should be too ready to take on new responsibilities. The onus is upon those who propose new activities to justify the right to require the taxpayer to provide the funds. It is a healthy attitude, from the financial point of view, that a municipal council should look askance at all demands for extended service, unless such service is self-supporting or the social benefit can clearly justify its cost, keeping in mind the limits of the burden that can be borne by that portion of the community which directly pays the cost of local government.

The Budget

The fiscal year of most Canadian municipalities is the calendar year, although there are exceptions.[4] The expenditures for the year are determined to a great extent when the council make up their budget. The budget, or "the estimates," constitutes the programme of municipal operations which in most municipalities is worked out in the early months of the year,[5] primarily to determine the taxes to be imposed for the current year. In some provinces councils are required to prepare an annual estimate of all sums required during the year for the purposes of the municipality.[6]

To determine the amount to be raised by taxation the council must first know how much money is required, and this in turn depends upon the spending programme. The procedure usually followed is that the department heads under the jurisdiction of the council and the special purpose bodies for which the council raises funds prepare estimates of their proposed operations for the year and the money needed to finance such activities. These estimates are reviewed in detail by the various committees of council and by the finance committee or, where such occur, by the board of control. If the committees see fit, they may, with or without consultation with the department concerned, amend, increase, or reduce any estimates of expenditures over which council have control, but usually such changes are made in consultation with the department head. Where they have no power to alter the estimates, the committees may confer with the other boards concerned and endeavour to arrange for reductions by persuasion. The estimates as approved by the committees are then submitted to, and dealt with by, council. When the estimates have been considered and adopted by council the general lines of the spending programme of the municipality for the year have been determined.

In practice the actual spending may not always correspond with the budget programme. In some municipalities, once the budget is passed it is promptly forgotten, but it is considered to be the best

[4]The fiscal year of Montreal, Quebec City, and Hull ends on April 30, of Shawinigan Falls on June 30, and of Newfoundland municipalities on March 31.

[5]Exceptions are the county of Grey, Ontario, and the municipalities within the county including the city of Owen Sound. Special statutory provision permits the councils to prepare and adopt estimates for the expenditures of the following year; such councils may in each year make a levy sufficient to pay all the expenditures and debts of the municipality falling due in the then next ensuing year and such taxes may be made payable partly in the current year and partly in the next ensuing year. Geo. VI, c. 90, s. 1 (1937).

[6]The Fredericton Act requires that the estimates be approved on or before April 10.

practice to maintain a reasonably close adherence to the provisions of the budget and to require that where funds provided for one purpose are to be diverted to some other purpose it must be specifically authorized by council. This practice is being followed by an increasing number of councils. The budget may thus become a controlling instrument which serves to keep municipal finances within reasonable control. It is of course impossible to foresee all the contingencies which may arise in the course of the year, for numerous expenditures have to be met which could not have been anticipated when the budget was being prepared, and there will inevitably have to be some transferring of appropriations during the year.

The law in most provinces requires that the council in each year provide for all debts coming due within the year, so that theoretically a municipality can not have an unbalanced budget or, in other words, can not plan on incurring an overdraft. As an added precaution against such an event, councils are required to provide an allowance in their budgets to cover the probable loss occasioned by inability to collect a portion of the taxes levied. Nevertheless overdrafts or deficits do occur. These may result from minor over-expenditures in a number of activities, or from some major increase in a particular item, as would be the case in a winter of excessive snowfall, or from a deliberate failure to provide for a known expenditure. Under certain circumstances it may be impossible to forecast with any reasonable degree of exactness expenditures which are beyond the control of council. Thus, in a period of economic depression it is impossible to estimate how many unemployed persons are likely to become charges on the municipality and the same is true where large expenditures are incurred by reason of disasters such as floods, tornados, or conflagrations. Changes in provincial legislation which impose greater financial obligations on the municipalities, or changes in provincial policy which result in reduced grants, may contribute to building up an overdraft if such changes occur, as they frequently do, after the municipal budget has been adopted.[7]

Some provinces have established a procedure to enable municipalities to expend funds not provided for in the annual budget. In

[7]In Ontario, councils may be required to pay large sums in retroactive wages under awards made by arbitration boards months after their budgets have been adopted. In the thirties, when the Dominion and provincial bases of assistance toward unemployment relief were determined annually at the time of dealing with governmental budgets, the municipalities were constantly in difficulties for as the municipal financial year starts three months earlier than the other governments' financial year, municipal budgets could not be delayed until after the Dominion and provincial budgets had been brought down. Changes in the basis of sharing the relief costs would substantially affect the municipal finances.

Ontario, for example, a council which proposes to do anything involving the expenditure of money which is to be raised in a subsequent year must first obtain the approval of the Ontario Municipal Board. In any event the council of each year are expected to allow in their budget for any deficit or surplus of the previous year. Councils, however, sometimes fail to provide for overdrafts of previous councils and where such a policy is followed a floating indebtedness of accumulated overdrafts may build up to the point where some future council, often under pressure from the banks, are forced to take action to deal with it.

Controls over Expenditures

There are several controls over the expenditures of councils. One is the control exercised by the courts. Municipal corporations are not unlimited in the scope of their operations, for their councils may exercise only the powers granted to the corporation. Frequently councils expend funds for purposes for which they have no authority. If no one objects the expenditure will stand, but it may be questioned before the courts by action of a ratepayer.[8] In practice this is not a very effective method of control as few ratepayers are sufficiently interested to go to the necessary trouble and expense involved, nor do they desire the notoriety which such an action brings.

A somewhat more effective control is that of having the financial affairs of the municipality subject to regular periodic examination and inspection by provincial authorities. In the provinces of Quebec, Saskatchewan, and Alberta there are regular inspections by provincial inspectors. The fact that their records are to be subjected to scrutiny by outside inspectors tends to keep councils within bounds. In no province, however, has the inspector the power to surcharge or charge back illegal expenditures to the members of council personally, as is the practice in certain types of English municipalities.

A limit is placed indirectly upon the total expenditures by the overall limit imposed by some provinces on the rate of taxation. A further limitation to the total of expenditures on council activities is imposed by the requirements of other civic bodies which have the right to demand definite amounts of money, for, as their demands increase, the leeway remaining before the tax limit, either legal or practical, is reached becomes progressively narrowed.

[8]An individual ratepayer may bring an action in a representative capacity to prevent an illegal expenditure of municipal funds by the council or, if a municipality neglects or refuses to sue for the recovery of corporation money illegally expended or diverted, may sue such members of the council as have concurred in the expenditure or have benefited thereby. Frank G. Proctor, *Municipal Corporations* (Toronto, 1931), p. 688.

Considerable influence over expenditures is exercised by the senior municipal officials who are in a position to take the long view and to advise councils as to the financial problems which unwittingly they may be developing. Particularly are the clerks, treasurers, and auditors qualified to advise and warn the elected representatives in the matter of illegal or unauthorized expenditures.

The ultimate control rests with the electors. If they are satisfied with the spending programme of their representatives, they will re-elect them. If they are dissatisfied, whether because the programme is too restricted or too extensive, they will indicate it at the polls. The electors themselves, however, frequently exhibit contradictory tendencies. Two common criticisms of councils are that they are reckless spendthrifts and that they are penny-pinchers and frequently both criticisms are aimed at the same council. The elector may be critical of council extravagance in general but he protests any curbing of expenditure on the matters which concern him or his interests. He may bemoan the cost of educational frills, but as a motorist is loud in his demands that the snow removal programme be extended. Whether the electorate's control is normally very effective is doubtful but when the burden becomes sufficiently onerous, as in the years of depression, such control unquestionably becomes very real. Its effectiveness is greater in the small communities where the proportion of the population who are taxpayers is greater and where, as a rule, the people are more aware of what their civic administration is doing or failing to do.

Comparisons of Expenditures

The range of expenditures, both in amount and variety of objects, is much greater in the larger municipalities than in the smaller ones, because the needs are greater. Comparisons, even among municipalities of comparable population, may be deceptive unless the expenditures are carefully analysed to establish a common basis for comparison. Thus, if the expenditure data of a number of municipalities are to be used as a basis for appraisal of policies and results, it is necessary to know something of the factors which go to determine those expenditures. Among these would be the area of the municipality, population density, topography, terrain, geography, climate, the services supplied, the quality of such services, wage rates, accounting practices, the general financial policy as to how much of past, present, or future costs is provided for in current expenditures, and whether provision for community development is on a hand-to-mouth or on a long-view basis. In short, it is necessary to know what are the conditions under which the expenditures are made and what the citizens get for their money. The amount expended or not expended is not the measure of efficient government, but the actual return in relation to the amount expended, with due allowance for the conditions under which a government operates.

Variations in some of the factors mentioned above may cause great differences in costs for the same quantity or quality of service, for instance in the construction of sewers and watermains in cities located on rock formation with only a thin overburden of soil as compared with others where rock is not a matter of concern. The location of the municipality may involve added costs for a particular service, such as the provision of special fire fighting service in port cities; in some, climatic conditions may involve heavy expenditures for the control of winter conditions on the streets, yet involve little expense for others. On the other hand, services which are called by the same title may vary greatly in quality between municipalities, as with refuse collection, depending on what is collected, how it is collected, how frequently it is collected, and how disposed of, or they may not mean the same things, as where accounting practices in one municipality classify school health services as a health cost and in others as an educational cost. It is also quite possible to keep expenses down by poor municipal housekeeping, by not properly maintaining the physical plant, yet such policies may give a false impression of economical operation.

In making comparisons it is also important to keep in mind the extent to which practice varies in the matter of placing certain functions under specially appointed bodies. Where a function is under a council the total expenditure for that purpose is included in the financial statements but where it has been transferred to a special purpose body, only the net deficit or surplus will form part of the corporation's financial picture.

Classification of Expenditures

There are numerous bases used for classifying municipal expenditures, but an increasing number of municipalities are using the basis recommended by the Dominion Bureau of Statistics.[9] Under this classification expenditures are grouped as follows:

1. General government
2. Protection to persons and property: fire protection, police protec-

[9]This basis of classification is the result of studies of the Continuing Committee appointed by the Dominion-Provincial Conference on Municipal Statistics in 1937, and is published in the *Manual of Instructions*.

tion, law enforcement, corrections, protective inspection, street lighting, destruction of pests

3. Public works
4. Sanitation and waste removal
5. Health: public health, medical, dental, and allied services, hospital care
6. Social Welfare: aid to aged persons, blind persons, unemployed employables, unemployables, mothers' allowances, child welfare
7. Education
8. Recreation and community services
9. Debt charges
10. Utilities and other municipal enterprises
11. Provision for reserves
12. Capital expenditures provided out of revenue
13. Joint or special expenditures, not otherwise provided for
14. Miscellaneous
15. Deficit from previous years

Table 15 gives some impression of the relative importance of the various objects of expenditure in the municipal programme in a number of urban municipalities.

TABLE 15

Distribution of Major Municipal Expenditures in Certain Cities, 1949, as a Percentage of Total Expenditure[a]

Objects of expenditure	Saint John (pop. 50,023)	Peterborough (pop. 35,065)	Winnipeg (pop. 234,561)	Edmonton (pop. 137,469)	Vancouver (pop. 385,500)
Education	27.9	29.2	32.1	33.9	30.1
Debt charges[b]	10.8	13.7	5.5	14.6	13.1
General government	7.9	7.3	4.9	7.7	5.3
Fire protection	6.8	5.8	10.4	6.2	9.0
Police	5.5	4.8	8.5	5.3	10.9
Welfare	.2[c]	7.1[d]	8.8	4.1[d]	4.0
Street maintenance, etc.	3.3	4.7	3.7	6.7	5.3
Garbage and refuse	1.3	4.3	4.0	4.8	2.6
Recreation and community service	2.0	6.9	3.7	7.0	3.9
Snow control	2.1	1.8	2.0	1.0	
Street lighting	1.5	1.4	1.0	1.1	1.4
Street cleaning	1.3	1.3	1.1	1.1	1.3
Health	0.0[c]	1.8	4.8[e]	.8	5.0[e]
Sewer maintenance, etc.	1.0	2.1	.8	1.9	.5
County assessment	16.0[f]				
Sewage Bd. Ass't[g]					2.1
Other	12.4	7.8	8.7	3.8	5.5
	100	100	100	100	100

[a]This table is designed to present a rough picture of the relative financial significance of the more important objects of expenditure which are common to all municipalities. Important expenditures which are not common to all are included under the heading "Other."

[b]Excluding educational debt.

[c]Much of the expenditure which in other cities is a city expenditure is a county expenditure in the case of Saint John and is included in the County Assessment.

[d]Includes hospital costs which in other cities is classed as health expenditure.

[e]Includes hospital costs.

[f]Includes among other items expenditures for health, welfare, and hospitalization.

[g]Vancouver District Joint Sewage Board assessment.

CHAPTER XI

MUNICIPAL FINANCE: TAX REVENUES

ONCE THE EXPENDITURES have been decided upon, the council is met with the problem of providing the revenues required to meet them. This involves the major problems of municipal finance—to obtain sufficient revenues to maintain the standard of services the community expects or which the municipal corporation is required to supply, and to find revenues which have both the stability to maintain essential services under adverse economic conditions and the flexibility to make possible the adjustment of revenues to changing demands and varying economic conditions. Municipal expenditures are of two types; one type is for the normal day-to-day services which do not vary greatly from year to year, and the other type is for extraordinary expenditures, such as those for the relief of unemployment, which may show sharp increases in times of economic depression, at the very time when the revenues of most municipalities are shrinking rapidly.[1]

The four main sources of municipal revenues are (1) taxation, current or deferred, (2) grants, subsidies, and shared taxes, (3) earnings from municipal enterprises, and (4) miscellaneous revenues. The third source noted above, however, may produce deficits rather than net revenues for the municipality. The extent to which municipalities derive their revenues from these different sources varies considerably. A rough analysis of the revenues of twenty Canadian urban municipalities of over 15,000 population (see Table 16) shows that municipal taxation provides approximately 74 per cent of the total revenues. There are wide variations from a low of 56.2 per cent to a high of 94.6 per cent. Grants and subsidies are a factor in only fourteen of the twenty municipalities studied as some provinces do not make grants to municipalities.[2] Neither do the percentages shown indicate the real importance of such grants where they occur, as in many cases govern-

[1]In 1934 Saskatchewan municipalities were able to collect in cash only the following percentages of the total arrears and current taxes: villages 31.92 per cent, towns 20.93 per cent, and cities 28.89 per cent.

[2]This source of revenue is changing rapidly; in New Brunswick in the first full year of provincial subsidy to municipalities, 1948, the total paid was $2,055,665; in Ontario total provincial grants to municipalities, including education grants, increased from $27,668,448 in 1940 to $86,412,500 in 1951. Provincial grants to Newfoundland municipalities excluding St. John's were about two and one-half times the local tax revenues in 1949–50.

ment grants are given direct to special purpose bodies such as school boards, and do not show in the municipal revenue statements. In the municipalities where grants do occur, as shown in the financial statements, they account for an average of 6 per cent of the total revenues, varying from .3 per cent to 16.6 per cent. The revenues derived from municipally operated enterprises vary according to the range of such activities, the range being usually more extensive in larger communities, and according as the practice is to show as municipal revenue the gross or the net revenue of such operations. The average share of the total revenues derived from such sources in the cities where enter-

TABLE 16
PERCENTAGE OF GROSS REVENUES DERIVED FROM VARIOUS SOURCES IN TWENTY CANADIAN CITIES (1949)

City	Taxes[a]	Grants & subsidies[b]	Enterprise earnings[c]	Miscellaneous
Montreal	68.3		16.4	15.1
Toronto	72.1	6.7	14.3	6.7
Vancouver	65.7	17.6	9.4	7.1
Winnipeg	79.7	1.0	7.8	11.2
Quebec	72.6		21.7	5.5
Edmonton	70.6	.3	11.5	17.4
Calgary	77.0	.4	15.7	6.7
London	86.4	5.0	1.1	7.3
Halifax	74.7	2.9	6.1	16.2
Verdun	76.4		18.7	4.7
Regina	67.7		21.1	11.1
St. John	56.8	16.6	16.1	10.3
Victoria	56.2	10.5	19.2	14.1
Hull	94.6			5.4
Westmount	75.1		10.8	10.8
Peterborough	86.0	5.0	4.3	4.5
Moosejaw	76.7	3.8	3.0	16.3
St. Boniface	65.7	1.1	26.8	6.1
Niagara Falls	69.2	9.4	12.5	8.7
Owen Sound	88.0	4.5	3.4	2.8
Average[d]	73.97	6.5	12.6	9.4

[a]The percentages of gross revenue supplied by tax revenues are not comparable in some cases because of differences in practice in making up financial statements. In some cases taxes for education are not considerd as municipal tax revenues; in some, charges for water supplied are treated as taxes, while in others such revenues do not appear in the city's statement at all. Adjustments have been made as far as possible to bring all to a common basis.

[b]The percentages shown do not necessarily reflect the true extent of provincial grants for municipal purposes as such grants in some cases, e.g. education grants, are made directly to independent boards and do not enter into the revenues of the municipal corporations.

[c]In some cases the enterprise earnings shown in the various statements are net earnings and in others gross earnings.

[d]The averages are the averages of the municipalities where there are revenues under the particular headings involved, e.g. under "Grants and subsidies" the average is of the 14 municipalities receiving such grants and subsidies.

prises were operated is 12.6 per cent, varying from 1.1 per cent to 26.8 per cent. This source of revenue is almost entirely lacking in most smaller and rural municipalities. Miscellaneous revenues represented an average of 9.4 per cent, varying from 2.8 per cent to 17.4 per cent.

The figures referred to above should be used with caution for they are based on the financial reports of various municipalities which show wide variations in their accounting practices, and are subject to great possibilities of misinterpretation.

Current Taxation

Municipal taxation is the major source of municipal revenue and therefore requires extensive examination. The power of a council or other municipal body to levy taxes is derived from some enactment of the legislature of the province in which it is located. Under section 92 of the British North America Act the legislature of each province was granted the exclusive power to make laws relating to "Direct Taxation within the Province in order to the raising of a Revenue for Provincial Purposes" and relating to "Shop, Saloon, Tavern, Auctioneer, and other Licenses in order to the raising of a Revenue for Provincial, Local or Municipal Purposes." Under these provisions the legislatures have granted powers of taxation to municipal corporations and some other municipal bodies which they have created, but because of their own constitutional limitations have passed on to municipalities only the power to impose some form of direct taxation.[3]

One of the difficulties of municipal taxation is the limited number of tax sources which are available. At the time when expanding services have required increased municipal revenues, the services and needs of the other levels of government have also been increasing with the result that the provinces have not substantially extended the range of municipal taxation but in some cases have even withdrawn sources previously available for the use of the municipalities. The field of real property taxation, with minor exceptions,[4] has been left exclusively to the municipalities. The almost total dependence of the munici-

[3]A direct tax as defined by John Stuart Mill is one "which is demanded from the very persons whom it is intended or desired should pay it" as contrasted with indirect taxes, "those which are demanded from one person in the expectation and intention that he shall indemnify himself at the expense of another."

[4]Several provinces levy real property taxes in the "unorganized" portions of the province. As at 1952, Saskatchewan levied a public revenue tax on real property which is collected by the municipalities and remitted to the province and in Nova Scotia the province requires the "municipalities" to levy a municipalities' Highway Tax at three-fifths of one per cent on all rated property, the proceeds of the tax being paid over to the province. This latter tax has not applied to cities and towns since 1948.

palities on the taxation of real property has not only limited their revenues, it has also deprived them of any great degree of flexibility. The result is that when real property fails to provide the required tax revenue, the municipalities have no other place to turn. Table 17 gives an indication of the limited scope of taxation of the municipalities as compared with the other levels of government. It shows not only that a relatively small number of tax sources are available to municipalities but also that while the largest single tax source of the Dominion provided only 26 per cent of the total tax revenue, and of the provinces, 31 per cent, the largest single source of municipal taxation provided 85 per cent of the total tax revenue. In times of financial stress the Dominion is free to look for tax revenues where it will and the provinces, within the limits of direct taxation, can invent new taxes but the municipalities can only expand their taxing powers with provincial approval. Most provinces have been reluctant to give the municipalities any new tax sources and thus admit a competitor in the desperate search for funds.

Tax Base and Tax Rate

Two factors in raising taxes are a tax base and a tax rate. Apart from fixing maximum limits, the provincial legislatures have left the determination of the rates of taxation to the local authorities but have themselves determined in all cases the permissible objects of taxation, that is the persons, objects, or activities which are to constitute the tax base. The tax base consists of the aggregate of the units upon which the tax rate is levied or applied to raise the desired tax revenue. The ascertaining of the tax base is known as the process of assessment and is dealt with in chapter XIII.

The bases on which municipal taxes are levied vary according to the type of tax and there may be several types in effect within one municipality. They include, among others, taxes levied at: (1) a flat rate per unit, as in the poll tax or telephone tax; (2) a flat rate, varying according to classifications, as in the taxation of dogs, with different rates for males and females; (3) a progressive rate, as in the case of chain stores, with the rate for additional stores in the same ownership being higher than for the first; (4) a uniform rate applied to an assessment which varies according to the value of the object assessed, as in the case of real property; (5) a uniform rate applied to an assessment which varies according to capacity, area, or classification, as in certain business taxes; (6) a uniform rate applied to the lineal measurement of frontage of real property, as in the case of local im-

TABLE 17

SOURCES OF GOVERNMENT TAX REVENUES, 1948[a]
(000,000's omitted)

Dominion	$	%	Provinces	$	%	Municipalities	$	%
Personal income	659	26	Personal income			Real property	334	85
Corporation income	364	14	Corporation profits	86	21	Sales	14	3
Withholding tax on			Other corporation taxes	19	4	Other taxes	41	10
dividends and interest	35	1	Succession duties	29	7			
Succession duties	30	1	Tobacco	8	2			
Excise on liquor	98	3	Amusement	17	4			
Excise on tobacco	176	7	Gas	124	31			
Sundry excises, etc.	194	7	Motor vehicles	51	12			
Customs duties	293	11	Real property	6	1			
Sales	372	15	Retail sales	48	12			
Excess profits	227	9	Miscellaneous taxes	7	1			
	2,451	100		399	100		390	100

[a]Based on *Bank of Canada Statistical Summary, 1950 Supplement.*

provement charges. Table 18 indicates the municipal tax bases which most frequently occur in municipalities in the various provinces.

Ordinary municipal taxes, as distinct from non-property types of local taxes, may be classified as (*a*) general rates, (*b*) special rates, and (*c*) local improvement or frontage rates.[5] The general tax or rate is that levied annually by a municipal council on that part of the tax base which includes real property and personal property or business assessments, for the purpose of raising the funds to finance the general expenditures of the municipality not otherwise provided for. It is a balancing rate varying from year to year to produce the revenue required to make up the difference between the total expenditures and the total of all other sources of revenue. It is normally a uniform rate applied to two of the three major bases of assessment just mentioned[6] and the proceeds of this rate are not earmarked for any specific purpose.

Special rates are of several kinds. Some are uniform and applicable to all the taxable assessment[7] but the proceeds of the tax may be applied only to a specified purpose, as in the case of a park rate or a library rate. Others may be uniform for one group of taxpayers with a different uniform rate applying to another group; thus, within one municipality where there are two school systems, the public school rate, which is uniform for all public school supporters, may be different from the separate school rate, which applies to all separate school supporters; or, where there are a number of school sections within one municipality, there may be different rates applicable for school purposes in the various school sections. Another type is a uniform rate applicable only to the ratepayers of a section of the municipality in which certain services are provided, as in the case of a fire rate in a partly urbanized municipality where fire protection service is provided only in the built-up portion of the municipality. All of the rates mentioned above are levied on the assessed value of the objects taxed.

Local improvement or frontage rates[8] are levied on a different basis.

[5]The terms "tax" and "rate" are used interchangeably in municipal practice in Canada, in contrast to the English practice where the term "taxes" denotes levies by the national government and "rates" denotes levies by the local authorities.

[6]As will be seen later the rate on the business assessment is not always the same as on real property assessment. Prince Edward Island towns may fix different rates of taxation to be levied on real property and on personal property.

[7]The "assessment" of a municipality includes the total of the assessed value of real property, and of the personal property or the business assessment. It does not include the various other bases on which special taxes such as rental, sales, or amusement taxes are levied. The "taxable assessment" is the total assessment less any portion which is exempt from taxation.

[8]Sometimes referred to as "special assessments."

TABLE 18

The More Common Types of Municipal Taxation in Canada[a]

Tax	Nfld.	P.E.I.	N.S.	N.B.	Que.	Ont.	Man.	Sask.	Alta.	B.C.	Total
Real Property	x	x	x	x	x	x	x	x	x	x	10
Business	x	x	x[b]	x	x	x	x	x	x	x[c]	10
Poll	x	x	x	x	x	x	x		x	x	9
Personal Property	x[d]	x	x	x	x[d]		x		x		7
Dogs[e]				x	x	x	x	x		x	6
Rentals				x	x			x			3
Amusement	x				x			x			3
Occupancy			x	x							2
Animals (except dogs)		x			x						2
Sales					x		x[f]				2
Telephone equipment	x				x						2

[a]Water rates or taxes are not included, where such occur, as they are considered a form of payment for services supplied.
[b]Halifax.
[c]Vancouver and New Westminster.
[d]Limited to a stock-in-trade tax.
[e]In several provinces dogs may be licensed rather than taxed.
[f]Winnipeg utility sales tax.

These rates are designed to meet the cost of constructing works or of carrying on services which are not charged to the general funds of the corporation but rather to the owners of the properties directly benefited. The basis of sharing the cost, however, is not determined by the assessed value of the real property benefited, but by the number of feet frontage of such property. Thus, in paying for a sidewalk, the individual property owner's share of the cost is determined by dividing the total cost of the walk by its total length in feet to arrive at a cost per foot, and the owners of the abutting properties are charged at this rate per foot frontage of their property. The rate is normally uniform but in some cases, where there are different degrees of benefit derived by non-abutting properties, as in the case of the construction of a trunk sewer or the construction of a bridge, there may be different rates varying according to the varying degrees of benefit, but with a uniform rate per foot for all properties receiving the same degree of benefit.

Services such as street flushing, sweeping, or road oiling are commonly paid for on a local improvement basis. Where this is the practice the cost is levied against the abutting properties at a uniform rate per foot frontage according to the service supplied. Thus, the rate for street sweeping would be the same per foot frontage in all areas where the service consisted of sweeping once a week, but would be a different but uniform rate for all in an area in which the streets were swept daily. It is not possible here to deal in detail with the numerous variations in the basis of levy for these special services.

The less important classes of taxes, such as poll taxes and dog taxes, will be dealt with under the heading of "Miscellaneous Revenues." While they are properly classed as taxes many municipalities do not include them as part of their tax revenues. Quite frequently municipal financial statements refer also to water rates, but these for our purpose will be considered as enterprise earnings, except in those municipalities in which the water consumers' charges are collected as a water tax.

Major Municipal Tax Sources

Real property tax. As real property taxation is of such relatively great importance in municipal finance, it is extensively discussed in chapters XIV and XVI which deal with real property assessment and taxation. A tax upon real estate for municipal purposes occurs in all the provinces and, except in Newfoundland, is not optional with the municipality.[9] Subject to the exceptions noted above and apart from Newfoundland, real property taxes are levied at a uniform rate upon the taxable assessed value of real property as determined by the assessors under the provisions of provincial legislation. They are levied annually, the rate of taxation being fixed annually by the municipal council, and the rates are usually expressed in mills on the dollar of assessment.[10]

Business tax. Some type of municipal business tax is in effect in all the provinces. In Manitoba, however, it is optional with a council whether to use a business tax or a personal property tax,[11] and in Alberta, if a business tax is levied, there is no tax on the stock-in-trade or other personal property used in a business. In Ontario and Saskatchewan the use of the business tax by a municipality is mandatory.

There is little uniformity in the basis of the business tax in the various provinces, except that it is not usually related to the volume of business done. The rate of taxation may be the same as the rate levied upon real estate, and must be so in Ontario and Saskatchewan, or it may be in the discretion of council with a maximum rate being fixed by statute, as in Manitoba where the maximum rate is fixed at 15 per cent. In Alberta, the maximum rate to be levied on one type of business assessment is 15 per cent and the maximum rate on other types is the real property rate.

Personal property tax. A municipal personal property tax occurs in Prince Edward Island, Nova Scotia, New Brunswick, Manitoba, and Alberta but there is considerable variation in the type of personal property taxed. The rate of taxation levied on personal property assessment is the same as that levied upon real property assessment except in Prince Edward Island towns.

The relative importance of the three major sources of municipal taxation is shown by Table 19, which tabulates the taxable assessments upon which municipal taxes are levied in nine of the provinces.

[9]In Newfoundland the tax on real property may be levied on one or more of the following classes of real property, viz: land, buildings, and machinery, or structures on highways or public communications. In 1950 only four municipalities including St. John's imposed real property taxes.

[10]A mill is one-tenth of a cent. Tax rates are variously expressed as a mill rate on the dollar of assessment, e.g. 42 mills. The same rate may also be expressed as a percentage rate on the dollar of assessment, e.g. 4.2 per cent, or as a dollar rate per $100 of assessment, e.g. $4.20. The more common practice in Canada is to use the mill rate basis.

[11]In 1950 business assessments in lieu of personal property assessments were used in all four cities, nineteen towns, fourteen villages, and twelve rural municipalities in Manitoba.

TABLE 19

TAXABLE MUNICIPAL ASSESSMENTS, 1948

(000's omitted)

Province	Real property assessment	Personal property assessment	Business assessment	Other
Prince Edward Island	$ 12,272	$ 5,353	$	$
Nova Scotia	172,646	32,901	10,866	3,934
New Brunswick	216,747	39,148	24,838	
Quebec	2,870,933		56,624[a]	
Ontario	3,097,590		337,253	
Manitoba	497,463	6,444	18,689	
Saskatchewan	828,407		44,521	224
Alberta	589,099	18,205	16,859	2,484
British Columbia	528,714			
	93.3%	1.0%	5.4%	

[a]This figure for Quebec is for 1942, the latest published.

Other Tax Sources

In addition to real property, business, and personal property taxes, other types of municipal taxes occur in a limited number of municipalities. Some of these are of relatively little significance while others, although not important in the whole municipal system, are of considerable importance in the municipalities where they are in effect.

Animals and vehicle tax. In Quebec cities and towns an animal tax may be levied on horses over three years of age, horned cattle over two years of age, dogs, certain animals kept for breeding purposes, and on every vehicle kept within the municipality. A similar tax may be levied on horses kept for pleasure purposes in Charlottetown. British Columbia municipalities may levy a tax not exceeding $2.00 on bicycles and other vehicles used within the municipality. These taxes are hardly distinguishable from a permit or licence fee although legally they constitute taxes. They are not of great fiscal importance.

Stock-in-trade tax. All Quebec municipalities, other than counties, may levy an annual tax on the stock-in-trade or goods kept by merchants and dealers and exposed for sale in shops or kept in vaults, warehouses, or storehouses, on all yards or depots for rough, sawn, or manufactured wood or lumber and on all yards or depots for coal or other articles of commerce kept for sale. The tax is levied on the estimated average value of the stock-in-trade but may not exceed one per cent in cities and towns, or one-tenth of one per cent in other municipalities.

Councils in Newfoundland may levy a tax on the occupiers of shops, warehouses and factories at not less than twenty cents nor more than one dollar for every one hundred dollars of the value of their stock-in-trade.[12] This tax is known as the stock tax.

A tax on the stock-in-trade of merchandise occurs as part of the personal property tax in the provinces where such is in effect.

Tenants and occupiers tax. There are several variations of these taxes and the instances referred to do not cover all the cases where such taxes occur.

Halifax has had a household tax since 1921. The tax is levied on the occupant of residential real property and is imposed on 10 per cent of the value of the premises occupied. Where there is more than one occupant, as in the case of apartments, the rental is used as the basis of assessment with reductions from the assessment of 25 and 5 per cent respectively for heat and light or janitor service if these are included in the rent. There is no household tax payable on property valued under $2,500. This household tax is levied at the same rate as the general city tax on residential real property, viz 3½ per cent.

Fredericton levies an occupancy tax on all occupants of residential real property. The tax, which is at the real property tax rate, is levied on 10 per cent of the assessed value of the premises or portion of the premises occupied, where the property is owner occupied. If the property is occupied by a tenant, the assessment is based on the actual annual rent or 10 per cent of the assessment, whichever is the greater. The tax is payable by both owner and tenant occupiers and is payable also by occupiers of otherwise exempt property. This tax replaced a tax on household personal property. Moncton also has a rentals tax levied at the regular tax rate on 10 per cent of the assessed value in the case of an owner occupied residence, and based on the gross rental in the case of tenant occupied residential property.

Quebec municipalities, other than counties, have power to levy an annual tax on tenants who pay rent and this tax is used in some municipalities. In cities and towns the tax may not exceed eight cents in the dollar on the amount of the rent or annual value of the property and in other municipalities may not exceed five cents in the dollar on the amount of rent. Cities and towns in Saskatchewan also have the power to levy a tax up to 10 per cent of the annual rental value of premises occupied by a householder, but this power has not been used by the municipalities. Medicine Hat, Alberta, did impose a tax on tenants of residential property at a rate of 10 per cent on the rental value prior to 1946, but was the only municipality in that province levying such a tax.

[12]The rates in effect (1951) varied from 30¢ to $1.00.

While business taxes might be classified as occupiers taxes, they will be separately dealt with elsewhere at greater length because of their relatively greater importance.

Sales tax. A general municipal sales tax occurs only in the province of Quebec.[13] Levied first in 1935 in the Montreal Metropolitan Area, it has now been authorized for some additional areas. It is in effect in the Montreal area, including Montreal, Westmount, Verdun, Outremont, and Lachine; in the Quebec area, including Quebec City and Levis; in the Three Rivers area, including Three Rivers and Cap-de-la-Madeleine; in Valleyfield; in the Chicoutimi area, including the cities of Chicoutimi and Arvida, six towns, three villages, and five rural areas; and in the Sorel area, including Sorel, one town, and one rural area. Two other villages outside these areas also have the right to impose a sales tax.

The tax is levied on the retail sale of any moveable or merchandise or article of trade subject to exceptions such as, among others, articles sold for delivery out of the area, securities, soft drinks and beer, gasoline, foodstuffs, the produce of the farm when sold by the farmer, transportation, tickets to amusements, and sales at a price of ten cents or less. The rate of the tax is 2 per cent. The tax is collected by the merchants or vendors who receive a commission of 2 per cent for collection.[14] They, in turn, remit the proceeds to the province together with the proceeds of the provincial sales tax of like amount. The city pays the province 1¾ per cent of the amount collected for the service of supervision which is performed by the province. The province pays to each municipality in the taxing area its share of the municipal sales

TABLE 20

SALES TAX REVENUE IN SOME QUEBEC CITIES

City	Year	Amount of sales tax revenue	Sales tax revenue as a percentage of total tax revenue[a]
Montreal	1949–50	$10,454,421	20.1
Quebec	1949–50	1,352,989	27.3
Verdun	1949	639,578	28.1
Westmount	1950	228,538	10.6

[a]Tax revenue used here does not include water taxes.

[13]The British Columbia sales tax is a provincial tax which is shared with the municipalities.

[14]The Montreal Catholic School Commission was authorized in 1949 to impose an additional one per cent sales tax for a period not exceeding three years, the proceeds of the tax to be shared by the various school authorities in the territories subject to the tax. Similar provision was extended to school authorities in a number of other Quebec municipalities.

tax, the division between the municipalities within each area being based on population. Table 20 indicates the importance of the sales tax in the tax revenue of some of the Quebec cities.

Amusement tax. Quebec municipalities levy a tax on the price of admission to all places of amusement, except race tracks, at a rate of 10 per cent plus a surtax of 25 per cent. The tax is collected by the municipality which is entitled to retain one-half of the 10 per cent, and 2 per cent of the surtax to compensate for the cost of collection. The balance of the proceeds is paid to the province.

Saskatchewan municipalities[15] also have statutory authority to impose a tax on admission to places of amusement, the maximum rate not to exceed 10 per cent. The rate may be varied according to the admission charged, or the council may make an arrangement with the owner of a place of amusement to accept a lump sum payment, in lieu of the tax, for an agreed period. Such a tax is imposed by the four largest cities in the province. Table 21 indicates the relative importance of the amusement tax in some of the cities where it occurs.

TABLE 21

MUNICIPAL AMUSEMENT TAX REVENUES

City	Year	Amusement tax revenue	Percentage of total tax revenue represented by amusement tax
Montreal	1949–50	$ 923,619	1.8
Quebec	1949–50	125,000	2.5
Verdun	1949	34,943	1.4
Hull	1949–50	22,223	2.1
Westmount	1949	13,351	3.6
Saskatoon	1949	69,708	2.9
Regina	1949	84,822	2.9
Moose Jaw	1949	29,376	2.5

Telephone apparatus tax. Montreal levies a monthly tax on any person subscribing to a telephone. The tax is at the rate of twenty-five cents per set connected directly with a central exchange and ten cents for each extension set. The telephone company collects the tax with the monthly bill and receives 5 per cent as a collection commission. Effective since 1940, this tax in the year 1949–50 yielded $707,226.

Newfoundland municipalities may levy an annual tax on telephone subscribers at one dollar for each main line telephone supplied within the municipality. The owner of the telephone service is designated the council's agent to collect the tax.

[15]Extended to rural municipalities in 1951.

Electricity and gas tax. In 1935 the city of Winnipeg was authorized to levy a sales tax on purchases of electricity and gas, the rates being 10 per cent on domestic sales. The rate was cut in half by legislative action in 1941. The tax in 1949 produced $260,896 representing 1.9 per cent of the city's total tax revenue.

Electricity and gas bills are subject to the general sales tax in Quebec if the combined bills for the month exceed $2.50.

Franchise taxes. The sums which franchise holders may be required to pay under their agreements with municipalities are in some cases treated as fees and in others as taxes. In Winnipeg they are classed as taxes and are derived from three privately owned utilities. The Winnipeg Electric Company is required to pay an annual tax of $20 for each car operated and 5 per cent of the gross earnings. The Winnipeg Heating Company and the Northern Public Service Corporation are each required to pay annually an amount equal to 3 per cent of their gross earnings. These franchise taxes in 1949 amounted to $345,811 or 2.6 per cent of the city's total tax revenue.

Under general legislation in British Columbia, in lieu of real property and business tax, telephone companies pay a municipal tax of 2 per cent on gross rentals from subscribers in the municipality and gas and electric companies pay the same rate on their revenues from sales in the municipality, other than for re-sale, and street railways pay the tax on the fares received. In Vancouver the rate of taxation on the same utility receipts is 1½ per cent.

Another form of franchise tax which occurs in Saskatchewan and Alberta is discussed in chapter XV under the heading "Business Assessment."

Turnover tax. Saint John, N.B., since 1947 has levied an annual tax at the general tax rate on a percentage of the gross sales or turnover of retail and wholesale merchants and traders. The sales used as the basis are those of the previous year. The percentages for retailers vary according to the type of business and are 10, 12½, 17, 20, 23, and 25. Persons selling food stuffs, automobiles, lumber, etc. are assessed at 10 per cent; those selling clothing, general stores, paint, plumbing, etc., at 17 per cent; and those not specifically classified, at 20 per cent. The percentages applicable to wholesalers are 7, 10, and 12½ with the provision that the tax only applies to the gross sales sold for resale within Saint John and with the further provision that if the gross sales are less than 75 per cent of the assessed value of the premises occupied by the business, the percentage shall be applied to 75 per cent of such assessed value. The percentages stated are maximum and may be reduced by the Board of Assessors with the approval of the Court of Revision. The tax is a personal liability of the persons assessed and does not constitute a charge upon the real estate.

Insurance premium tax. St. John's, Nfld., levies a tax of 2 per cent on fire insurance premiums, which is collected by the insurance companies as agents for the municipality at the time of the purchase of the insurance. Montreal similarly levies a tax of one per cent on fire insurance premiums.

Water taxes. Most municipalities finance their waterworks department by charging the water consumers, whether owners or tenants, on the basis of the service supplied. Where the water is metered the consumer is charged on the basis of the actual consumption, and where the water is not metered a wide variety of bases is used to determine the individual charge. The above practices occur both in cases where the waterworks operate under a special purpose body or commission and in cases where they constitute a department under the municipal council.

In some cities, however, the water service is largely financed from a special water tax. This is a common practice in Quebec cities and towns but in only a few cases, such as Vancouver, is it followed in the other provinces. In Montreal the water tax is 7.5 per cent on the assessed rental value except in the case of hotels, restaurants, and taverns for which the rate is 12 per cent. These taxes are subject to a surtax of 8 per cent. Where the water is metered the charge is $1.15 per thousand cubic feet with a minimum equal to 7.5 per cent on the assessed rental value plus a surtax of 8 per cent. Other municipalities such as Quebec, Hull, and Three Rivers levy the water tax upon the assessed value of the real property.

Municipal Taxes Peculiar to Newfoundland

Processing tax. This tax may be imposed annually by a council subject to the approval of the Lieutenant-Governor in Council at a rate of one-quarter of one per centum on the value of all commodities of any kind manufactured or processed within the municipality; the manufacturer may be required to submit a statement of the gross volume of business done. Such a tax is imposed in the town of Curling.

Non-residents' agents tax. This tax, not exceeding $10.00, may be levied not more than once a year on every commercial agent soliciting business in the municipality but not upon an agent who is a resident of the province and who does or solicits business for Newfoundland firms and companies only.

Motor vehicle tax. This tax of not less than $5.00 nor more than $10.00 may be levied annually on every motor vehicle ordinarily operated as a bus, truck, or passenger car from within the limits of the municipality for hire or reward. A similar annual tax not exceeding $1.00 may be levied on motorcycles and an annual tax not less than $2.50 nor more than $5.00 on every other motor vehicle ordinarily operated from within the municipality.

Motor boat tax. A tax of not less than $5.00 nor more than $100.00 may be levied not more frequently than once a year on every motor boat operated as a passenger boat from within the limits of the municipality for hire or gain.

Coal tax. This is a tax, not exceeding $1.00, which may be levied on each ton of coal delivered to the municipality. Two municipalities for which information is available levy this tax at 50 cents a ton.

Bowling alley and billard table, and slot machine tax. Municipalities may levy an annual tax on each bowling alley and billiard or pool table kept for the purpose of hire or gain. The tax for bowling alleys must be not less than $25.00 nor more than $50.00, and for billiard or pool tables not less than $20.00 nor more than $50.00.

The municipalities may also levy an annual tax, not less than $25.00 nor more than $50.00, on every juke box, or automatic or slot machine used for hire or reward except automatic scales, telephone apparatus, and gas or electric meters.

Payments in Lieu of Taxes

Section 125 of the British North America Act provides that "No Lands or Property belonging to Canada or any Province, shall be liable to Taxation," with the result that municipalities are unable to collect taxes on lands owned by the Dominion or the provinces. This is so obviously unjust in certain cases where there are large holdings of property by the governments, e.g. Ottawa, that payments have been made for some years to some municipalities by the senior governments, which payments were actually in lieu of taxes, even if not so designated.

In more recent years with the rapid extension of Crown companies during the war and also in cases where houses have been built by government agencies, numerous agreements have been entered into between such companies and municipalities for payments toward the cost of providing services or toward the cost of education of children of occupants of such houses.[16]

[16]*Dominion Public Accounts* (1948) records grants by the Penitentiaries Branch in lieu of school taxes in four municipalities. Wartime Housing Ltd. in 1946 paid $526,121 to forty-eight municipalities for municipal services rendered.

In the agreements entered into between Central Mortgage and Housing Corporation, a Dominion agency, and individual municipalities in recent years the Corporation has agreed to pay the various municipalities stated amounts annually in lieu of taxes. These amounts vary according to the number of housing units owned by Central Mortgage and Housing Corporation in the respective municipalities and according to the type of unit, and in some cases the agreements have provided that such payments shall be the equivalent of what the taxes would be if the properties were owned by a non-exempt person.

While these payments have not been of great importance in total amount, they are significant as a breach in the wall of the long-standing Dominion attitude of resistance to admitting any responsibility on the part of Crown, as a property owner, to bear its share of the cost of local government. In 1949 the Dominion adopted a formal policy dealing with payments in lieu of municipal taxes as also did Ontario in 1952 with respect to provincial property. This is more fully discussed in chapter XIV.

CHAPTER XII

MUNICIPAL FINANCE: BORROWINGS AND NON-TAX REVENUE

Borrowing or Deferred Taxation

Municipal borrowing includes both short-term and long-term borrowing. Short-term borrowing is to provide funds to finance municipal operations pending the annual collection of taxes or to provide money for capital expenditures pending the sale of the municipality's debentures.

Temporary Borrowing Pending Receipt of Taxes

Councils coming into office require considerable time to organize their work, to prepare and adopt their budgets, and to determine the tax rates for the year. Several additional weeks are needed to perform the clerical work of calculating the individuals' tax levies, to prepare and deliver the tax notices, and to allow the taxpayers a reasonable period between receipt of the demand and the due date for payment of the taxes. The expenditures of the municipalities, however, are continuous and suppliers of goods and services must be paid in the interval between the start of the fiscal year, which is usually the same as the political year, and the time when taxes are received. To finance these expenditures, pending receipt of taxes, many municipalities must borrow money because most provinces do not permit a municipality to build up a fund of working capital. Various devices are used to reduce the amounts which it is necessary to borrow. In some instances taxpayers are encouraged to make payments on account of taxes before they are due by allowing interest on such payments on account. Many councils have made effective efforts to so arrange their budget work that the date for payment of taxes can be advanced to a time earlier in the year.

Short-term borrowing pending receipt of taxes is usually effected by promissory note or by selling treasury notes which may be secured by being made a charge against the tax revenues as they are received. Municipalities are not entirely free to use their discretion in the amount of such temporary borrowing, but are subject to restrictions imposed by legislation as set out in Table 22. Five different bases for establishing such limitations are used in eight of the provinces. They are: (1)

a fixed limit stated in dollars, (2) a stated percentage of the total taxes *levied* in the previous year (50%, 75%), (3) a stated percentage of the revenue *collected* in the previous year (25%, 100%), (4) a stated percentage of the *estimated* revenue (70%), and (5) a stated percentage of the *taxes levied or to be levied* for the current year (50%, 60%, 75%, 100%).[1] The limitations which do apply are not always the same for all classes of municipalities within one province.

Temporary Borrowing Pending the Issue of or in Lieu of Selling Debentures

In some municipalities, when capital expenditures are to be financed by the issue of debentures or bonds,[2] it is the practice to finance the cost of construction by temporary borrowing and to issue debentures when the work has been completed and the actual cost is known. When the debentures are issued and sold, the proceeds of the sale are used to pay off the temporary loan. Such borrowing is referred to as borrowing pending the issue and sale of debentures. The advantage of this procedure is that it enables the issuing authority to know the exact amount required before fixing the amount of a debenture issue. Where the debentures are issued and sold before the work is done, the final cost may be either more or less than the amount actually raised and the municipality may have a deficiency to make up or an unexpended surplus to account for.

It is not always desirable, however, to sell debentures at the time when they are issued. The bond market conditions may not be favourable; it may be too short a time since the last issue of the municipality was sold to the public; it may be hoped that the full amount of the issue will not be required; or for other reasons it may not be expedient to offer them to the public immediately. If the work they are designed to finance is to proceed, however, the money must be secured by some other method of borrowing. To meet the situation the municipality may issue the debentures and transfer them to a lending institution as security for a loan, rather than sell them. This transaction is sometimes referred to as hypothecating the securities. The proceeds of such a loan must, of course, be applied only to the purpose for which the debentures were originally issued. The loan is secured by the debentures so hypothecated which constitute the same charge against the municipality as if they had been sold in the usual way.

[1]In Ontario the statutory limit may be exceeded with the approval of the Ontario Municipal Board, and in Manitoba, with the approval of the Minister.

[2]In Canadian public financing there is no real difference between bonds and debentures but in practice the long-term securities of municipal governments are usually referred to as debentures. British Columbia municipalities may issue stock which, however, is substantially the same as a debenture issue.

TABLE 22

LIMITATIONS ON TEMPORARY MUNICIPAL BORROWINGS FOR CURRENT EXPENDITURES

Province	Type of municipality	Provincial limitation on borrowing for current expenditures
Prince Edward Island	Towns	50% of total tax revenue of current or previous year
Nova Scotia	Municipalities	50% of tax levied in previous year or $40,000
	Towns	50% of tax levied in previous year or $15,000
New Brunswick (*a*)	Municipalities	No stated limit
	Towns	$7,000
	Villages	$1,000
Quebec	Cities and towns	25% of revenue collected previous year; requires approval of the Quebec Municipal Commission
	Parishes, etc.	No stated limit
Ontario	All municipalities	70% of estimated revenues of the year or of the previous year, excluding revenues from arrears of taxes
Manitoba	Cities, towns, villages	100% of tax collections of previous year
	Rural municipalities	75% of tax collections of previous year
Saskatchewan	Cities and towns	100% of estimated taxes for the year
	Villages & rural municipalities	60% of estimated taxes for the year
Alberta	Cities	Estimated amount of the taxes for the current year
	Towns and villages	75% of total levy of previous year
	Municipal Districts	100% of taxes levied
British Columbia	All municipalities	85% of levy of the preceding year

(*a*) Fredericton limit is fixed at two-thirds the amount of the previous year's assessment (levy) and arrears of taxes.

Long-Term Borrowing

Long-term borrowing, or borrowing money with provision for repayment over a period of years, is normally used by municipalities for financing the cost of capital construction or works or equipment of a permanent nature. Included under this heading would be expenditures which produce an asset of lasting value, such as a pavement or a fire truck, in contrast to objects of municipal expenditure which produce no permanent asset as in payment of salaries of stenographers or for the removal of snow. Frequently such capital expenditures are so large that they can not be paid for out of the current revenues without imposing an intolerable burden on the taxpayers of the year in which they are made. Long-term borrowing, however, is not entirely confined to financing assets of enduring value but is on occasion used to raise money to meet accumulated current deficits or to meet disaster costs. It was also quite widely used to finance relief costs in the depression years when some councils felt such expenditures were in excess of the burden which the current taxpayer should be expected to bear.

Long-term borrowing is effected by the issue and sale of securities known as debentures, bonds, or stocks, although the usual term applied to municipal securities is debentures. A debenture is a written promise by the municipal corporation to repay the stated principal sum at a fixed date and place, and to pay interest thereon at a stated rate and at fixed times and places in the interim, all payments to be made in the currency specified.

Each issue of debentures must be authorized by a by-law of the issuing authority and usually must be approved by a vote of the taxpayers of the municipality and/or by some provincial administrative authority. It must be for a specified purpose for which there is statutory authority. The ultimate security behind the debentures is the taxing power of the municipal authority, which means that, as the municipality has the right to sell the lands of the taxpayers for non-payment of taxes, the theoretical security for municipal debentures consists of all the real property within the municipality which is not exempt from taxation. This is described as the theoretical security because experience has shown that it is not politically feasible to attempt to realize on this security to the point where any considerable portion of the real property in the municipality is sold to raise the taxes required to service the outstanding debt.

Canadian municipal debentures usually are general security debentures. Only in British Columbia may municipalities issue revenue debentures which are secured by a claim against the revenues of the utility or service which they are designed to finance. In some cases, however, the statutes do specify that the assets provided from the proceeds of the debenture issue shall be the security behind an issue,[8] but they do not at the same time specifically restrict the security to such assets.

[8]The Ontario Public Parks Act provides that debentures issued to purchase park lands shall be a lien and charge upon all the land under the control of a Parks Board. The Public Utilities Act of Ontario provides that public utility works, lands, and property are specially charged with the repayment of any sum borrowed by the corporation for their purposes and for any debentures issued therefor and the holders of the debentures have a preferential charge on such works, lands, and property for securing the payment of the debentures and the interest thereon.

Except for a limited number of school authorities, the municipal council is the authority which issues the debentures to provide funds both for its own purposes and also to meet the needs of any special purpose bodies in the municipal organization.

Provincial Restrictions on Long-Term Borrowing

The power of the municipalities to incur debts and the conditions under which they may be incurred are restricted in many respects by the various provinces.

Restrictions on interest rates. The extent to which the provinces limit the interest rates payable on municipal debentures varies. Ontario provides no such limit by statute but as all debenture issues must be approved by the Ontario Municipal Board, it has an opportunity to exercise control. Other provinces have established such limits, though in some cases only for the smaller municipalities. The limits provided are not of great significance at the present time in view of the prevailing low interest rates but they are as set out in Table 23.

TABLE 23

STATUTORY LIMITATION ON INTEREST RATES PAYABLE ON MUNICIPAL DEBENTURES

Province	Municipalities	Maximum rates permitted
Nova Scotia	All (ex. Halifax)	6 per cent
New Brunswick	Villages	7 per cent
Quebec	All (ex. Montreal and Quebec)	6 per cent
Manitoba	All municipalities	6 per cent
Saskatchewan	Villages and rural municipalities	8 per cent
Alberta	Municipal districts	6 per cent
British Columbia	All municipalities	5 per cent

Restrictions on the term or period within which the debt is to be repaid. The general principle governing the allowable term or period for repayment of a loan is that it should be repaid within the lifetime of the asset financed by it. One method of control is to provide by statute an over-all time limit for all municipal debts, another is to provide terms varying according to the purpose of the loan. The application of these two methods in the various provinces is shown in Table 24.

Restrictions on the total amount of debt which may be incurred. These limits are established by general legislation supplemented by special legislation applying to individual municipalities. They are fixed on five different bases and may vary within one province for different

TABLE 24

STATUTORY LIMITATION OF DEBENTURE TERMS

(*a*) Over-all limit for term of municipal debts

Province	Municipalities	Maximum term (in years)
Prince Edward Island	Towns	25
Nova Scotia	All	40
New Brunswick	All	30
Manitoba	All	30
Saskatchewan	Cities and towns	40
	Villages	15
	Rural	20
Alberta	Cities	40
	Towns and villages	40
British Columbia	All	30

(*b*) Varying terms according to purpose, statutory maxima

Term in years	Quebec	Ontario[a]	Alberta municipal districts
40	Sewers, waterworks parks, playgrounds		
30	Pavements, buildings, land, bridges	Railways, harbours, sewers, waterworks, parks, schools, hospital land	Steel bridges, concrete culverts
20	Asphalt pavements, wooden structures	Other purposes	Other purposes
10	Walks, non-durable pavements, department equipment	Garbage collection and disposal systems, fire fighting equipment	
5		Road making machinery	

[a]The Ontario Municipal Board policy is that the maximum terms which will be approved by the Board are: sidewalks, curbs and gutters, and pavements—10 years; watermains and sanitary sewers—15 years; trunk sewers and buildings, including schools—20 years. *Forty-fifth Annual Report of the Ontario Municipal Board to December 31st*, 1950, p. 12. It will be noted that the limit permitted by the administrative board is considerably more restrictive than the statutory limit.

classes of municipalities. Limits may be: (1) a stated percentage of the assessed value of the assessable real property in the municipality, (2) established indirectly by providing for a maximum tax levy, (3) a stated amount per capita of the inhabitants, (4) a stated amount per acre of the land in the municipality, and (5) related to tax receipts. Table 25 indicates the various methods as provided for in Canadian municipalities by general legislation.

Two provinces, Quebec and Manitoba, provide an escape from the restrictions imposed upon municipal borrowing powers. The agencies by which borrowing in excess of the statutory limitations may be authorized are, respectively, the Quebec Municipal Commission and the Manitoba Municipal and Public Utility Board. In any province, of course, with the concurrence of the legislature, private legislation may provide for exceptions.

Special legislation provides restrictions applying to individual cities. The accompanying chart gives examples of such restrictions. In these

City	*Debt limitation*
London	14% of the assessment
Regina	20% of the net taxable assessment
Toronto	12% of the first $200,000,000 of assessment and 8% of any additional assessment
Vancouver	20% of average aggregate of assessed value of real property of preceding two years*

*Excluding sums required to acquire assets of any utility company, and local improvement debentures.

cases the statutes provide that borrowings for certain purposes are not to be included in determining if the borrowing limits have been attained; it has also been quite a common practice that when the legislature authorizes specific borrowings it at the same time specifies that they shall be excluded when calculating if the debt limit has been reached.

Requirements for provincial approval of debenture issues. Most provinces now require their municipalities to obtain provincial approval before any long-term debt is incurred. In Prince Edward Island towns no provincial approval is required for debenture issues. For New Brunswick cities and counties authorization must be obtained from the provincial legislature. In Nova Scotia the approval of the Minister of Municipal Affairs is necessary and ministerial approval is also required for the issue of debentures by New Brunswick villages. In Quebec, approval must be obtained from the Quebec Municipal Commission and the Lieutenant-Governor in Council. In the provinces west of Quebec such approval is by provincial administrative agents, viz, in Ontario, the Ontario Municipal Board; in Manitoba, the Municipal and Public Utility Board; in Saskatchewan, the Local Government Board; in Alberta, the Board of Public Utility Commissioners; and in British Columbia, the Inspector of Municipalities, from whose decision there is an appeal to the Lieutenant-Governor in Council.

The first prerequisite for the issue and sale of debentures by a municipal corporation is that there be statutory authority for borrowing for the specific purpose contemplated and the proceeds of the sale of the

TABLE 25

STATUTORY MUNICIPAL DEBT LIMITS

Province	Type of municipality	Debt limits
Prince Edward Island	Towns	Five times the total of all taxes of the year last passed actually collected up to the date of the debenture issue (exclusive of issues exempted from the general borrowing power)
New Brunswick	Villages	10% of assessable real property
Quebec	Cities and towns[a]	20% of taxable immovable property
	Villages[a]	15% do
	Rural local municipalities	10% do
	Counties	5% do
Ontario	All municipalities	No more borrowing permitted without approval of Ontario Municipal Board when tax levy (exclusive of levy for schools, local improvements, and certain hospital grants) exceeds 2½¢[b]
Manitoba	All except rural municipalities	$300 per capita, if population 10,000 or over
		$150 per capita, if population 2,000 to 10,000
		$100 per capita, if population under 2,000
	Rural municipalities	Amount provided in its letters patent or fixed by Municipal and Public Utility Board
Saskatchewan[c]	Cities	20% of assessment of land, building and franchises
	Towns	15% do
	Villages	10% do
	Rural municipalities	13¢ an acre
Alberta	Cities	20% of assessment of rateable property[d]
	Towns and villages	20% of assessment of rateable property
	Municipal districts	5% of assessment of rateable property

[a]These limits do not apply to individual borrowings if they are voted on by two-fifths of the proprietors who are electors residing in the municipality and approved by two-thirds in number and real value of all proprietors, whether resident or not, who have voted, and is also approved by the Lieutenant-Governor in Council.

[b]This provision is not of much significance as all debenture issues are now required to be approved by the Ontario Municipal Board.

[c]Certain classes of debentures are excluded when determining if the limit has been reached, e.g. those issued under the Secondary Education Act, for local improvements, and for construction or maintenance of certain public utilities, etc.

[d]Exclusive of school district debt, property owners' share of local improvements, and utility debt.

TABLE 25—*Continued*

STATUTORY MUNICIPAL DEBT LIMITS

Province	Type of municipality	Debt limits
British Columbia	All municipalities	20% of (*a*) average assessed value of taxable land and improvements for previous three years, and (*b*) value of water, irrigation, electrical, telephone, transportation and gas systems constructed or purchased at expense of the municipality as a whole—at cost less depreciation but excluding value of any utility the rates of which have been pledged as security for any borrowings—limit does not apply to borrowings for local improvements and school purposes

debentures may only be used for the purposes for which they were issued.[4] Municipal long-term borrowing is not permitted merely for the purpose of obtaining a general supply of working capital.

Even though there be legal authority to incur a debt the corporation in doing so must comply with the conditions and requirements imposed by statute. Most provinces require that before debentures can be issued the ratepayers must be consulted, in which case a money by-law is submitted to a vote of that portion of the electorate entitled to vote on such by-laws, usually the property owners, unless some other method of consultation with the electors is provided for. Municipalities may be allowed to borrow for certain specified purposes without a vote of the ratepayers.[5] It should be noted that in some provinces, e.g. Quebec and Ontario, approval by the electors is to be obtained before application is made for provincial approval, while in others, e.g. Manitoba, Saskatchewan, and Alberta, provincial approval must be obtained before the electors may be consulted. As provincial administrative boards are given increased jurisdiction, approval of borrowings by the electorate is becoming less important.

[4]British Columbia provides that with the assent of the electors a council may expend for any lawful purpose money borrowed for some other specific purpose.

[5]Such purposes in Ontario, for example, are, in part, grants toward the construction of public hospitals or sanatoria, war memorials, establishment of municipal pension funds, local improvement works, road making and fire fighting equipment, establishment of a refuse collection and disposal system, erection of court houses and gaols, works ordered by the Board of Transport Commissioners of Canada, monies borrowed under the school Acts, bridge construction in certain cases, certain extensions to municipal utilities, certain work carried out under the Public Health Act, etc.

The by-law authorizing each debenture issue sets forth the purpose for which the debt is being incurred, the amount of the debt, the time or times and place of repayment of the principal sum, the rate of interest and dates and place of interest payments during the lifetime or term[6] of the debenture issue, and the amount to be raised annually by the council during the term of the debentures to provide for interest and principal payments. These latter amounts are known as the debt charges, and the annual debt charges of a municipality are the total of all the individual debt charges of the outstanding debenture issues. The by-law usually also specifies the currency in which the payment of principal and the payments of interest will be made. Prior to the World War I it was not an uncommon practice to make such payments payable either in Canadian or United States funds or in gold, thereby improving their salability in England and the United States. Costly experience in making repayments in the United States at times when the discount on Canadian funds was as high as 20 per cent discouraged this practice.

Provincial legislation requires that councils of succeeding years, throughout the term of a debenture issue, raise annually the amount stated in the authorizing by-law, to provide for the interest falling due in the year and the sum to be provided for principal repayment. This is a feature of municipal financing which is in contrast to public financing at the other two levels of government. It assures that there will be a progressive reduction of the outstanding debt, unless new debts are incurred. As a consequence it is not the practice, under normal conditions, to re-fund municipal debts at maturity in such a manner as to result in a continuous addition to the total debt, although some provinces permit a reissue at maturity as in Prince Edward Island towns.

Several inducements are provided to encourage councils to raise these required sums and not to divert them to some other purpose. Ontario and Saskatchewan provide that if a council fail to levy for the money required to be raised for a sinking fund, the members shall be disqualified from office for two years except for those who can show they made reasonable efforts to procure the levying. In these two provinces and in British Columbia, if such money once raised is applied to another purpose, any member who voted to do so is personally liable for the amount so misapplied which may be recovered in any court of competent jurisdiction. In addition, in British Columbia such

[6]The lifetime or term of a debenture issue is the period of years between the date of issue and the date of repayment of the principal sum.

a member is disqualified from office for five years and in the other two provinces for two years. The Municipal Commissioner of Nova Scotia may sue for the amount which a council fails to raise to meet debt charges, and in Quebec and Alberta, if the sinking funds are deposited with the provincial treasurer, a designated provincial officer may sue for any payments missed. The Lieutenant-Governor in Council of New Brunswick may order an assessment if a local council fails to raise the funds required to service its debt.

Sinking Fund Debentures

There are two types of debenture issued by municipalities, the sinking fund type and the instalment or serial type.

The sinking fund debenture derives its name from the method of providing for the repayment of the principal sum borrowed. The authorizing by-law provides that the corporation will repay at a specified date the total amount stated on the face of the debenture and also will pay interest at the stated rate at fixed intervals, usually semi-annually. It further provides that during the term of the debenture the council must raise annually (1) a stated amount, which is the same each year, to meet the interest charges for that year, and (2) an amount which set aside in a sinking fund and invested at an estimated rate, not exceeding a statutory maximum, will at the maturity date equal the principal sum due. Some provinces limit by statute the estimated earning rate of the fund, for if the estimated rate is in excess of the rate actually earned there will be a shortage in the amount available to pay off the debt at maturity. The maximum rate of estimated earning in Manitoba is 5 per cent, in Saskatchewan and Alberta, 4 per cent, and in Quebec, 3½ per cent.

Thus, a by-law to authorize the borrowing of $10,000 at 5 per cent interest, and repayable in thirty years, and with an estimated sinking fund earning rate of 3½ per cent would require the council of each of the thirty years to raise,

For interest	$500.00
For sinking fund	193.71
Annual total	$693.71

If the sinking fund investments fail to earn the estimated rate of interest, the council must make up any deficiency at the maturity date. It sometimes happens on the other hand that where a conservatively estimated earning rate has been used, or where interest rates have risen sharply, as during World War I, large surpluses have accumulated in sinking funds. These surpluses, however, may be deceiving for earnings may drop materially before the final maturity date, as during the forties. The effect of changes in interest rates on the earning power of a municipal sinking fund is illustrated by an examination of the sinking fund of one Ontario city in which, in 1930, 87 per cent of the investments were earning 5 per cent or better, while, in 1939, 83 per cent of the investments were earning less than 5 per cent.

Some municipal sinking funds have earned large surpluses which have on occasion tempted councils beyond resistance. The usual statutory provision is that no money raised for sinking fund purposes may be diverted or expended for current expenditures, but councils, desperate for funds, have sometimes drawn a distinction between the money raised for the sinking fund, and the excess earnings on the investments once they are in the fund. At least two provinces specifically provide for the disposition of surpluses. In Ontario if there is an over-all surplus in the sinking fund (referring to the total of all the individual sinking funds as one fund) such surplus, with the approval of the council and the Ontario Municipal Board, may be applied to the sinking fund of each debt in the proportion which its sinking fund bears to the aggregate of sinking funds, or the amount of the surplus not so applied may with the approval of the Municipal Board be transferred to the general funds of the municipality. Where the amount in a sinking fund is sufficient, with its estimated revenue, to pay the principal of the debt when due, a council, with the approval of the Ontario Municipal Board, may cease to raise any further sum with respect to that particular debt. Saskatchewan provides that if the fund is in excess of requirements, the Local Government Board, on application of a council, may authorize the council to use the excess for such purposes as may be designated by the Board.

Opinions differ as to the proper disposition of such surpluses. It is argued that, since the sinking fund is established primarily to protect the bond holders, neither the money raised for the sinking fund nor its earnings should be diverted to any other purpose; the logical use of any surplus is to redeem outstanding debentures before maturity, thereby reducing the total outstanding liability to the public and indirectly reducing the current tax burden.[7] Those who would have council appropriate the surplus to reduce the current tax levy argue that any surplus results from the efficient handling of the funds and

[7]In the period 1919–46 the city of Toronto redeemed $47,109,058 debentures before maturity, largely by application of earnings of the sinking fund over actuarial requirements.

the bond holders have no claim on it. It is not reasonable, they assert, to hold an accumulating surplus until the expiry of the debentures and to give the taxpayers at that late date the benefit. An argument frequently advanced in the difficult times of the depression was that to build up a surplus or to use it to redeem debentures before maturity at the same time that taxpayers were losing their homes through inability to meet their taxes was like making accelerated payments on a mortgage while the house was burning.

One of the problems associated with the sinking fund type of debenture is that of investing the money in the fund. To prevent losses through poor investments, the provinces have restricted the type of investments for such funds. All provinces except Newfoundland, Prince Edward Island, and British Columbia provide that such funds may be deposited with the province, which will allow interest thereon, or, in Nova Scotia, with a trust company. There are provisions governing investment by the local authorities in most of the provinces, generally with one of two types of restriction: the objects of investment may be restricted either to securities authorized for trustee investment or specifically to stated classes of securities, viz, securities issued or guaranteed by the Dominion or the provinces, or debentures of municipal or school corporations within the province;[8] or provincial approval may be required for action taken with respect to investments. Nova Scotia requires the consent of the Municipal Commissioner for investment of sinking fund money and also approval of the securities by the Lieutenant-Governor in Council. Manitoba, in addition to specifying permissible investments, provides that the fund may be invested as the Municipal and Public Utility Board directs. Saskatchewan requires Local Government Board approval of all investments.

There is a variety of practice in the management of sinking funds. Local management in Nova Scotia rests with the head of the council and the clerk. Some councils designate a committee to work with the treasurer in this matter, or the fund may be under the jurisdiction of the finance committee. In others special bodies called sinking fund trustees are created by statute to manage the funds and their investment. Such a body was the Peterborough City Trust composed of five commissioners, one of whom was appointed annually by the council for

[8]Three special provisions are: in Ontario, the municipality may invest in its own debentures up to the amount of 25 per cent of the sinking fund, with the approval of the Ontario Municipal Board; in British Columbia, the Lieutenant-Governor in Council may authorize the municipality to use its sinking fund to purchase its own securities before maturity; and in Alberta, towns and villages may invest such funds in first mortgages within the municipality for an amount not exceeding one-third of the cash value of the mortgaged property.

a term of five years. Sinking fund trustees are found also in Winnipeg, Regina, and Calgary. Three of the trustees in Winnipeg are appointed by a judge of the Court of Queen's Bench on application by the city and one by council from among the council members. Under general legislation a sinking fund in Saskatchewan cities and towns may be handled either by three sinking fund trustees, two appointed by a judge on application and the third by council; or, alternatively, by a trust company appointed to take charge of such fund. Similar powers are granted to Alberta cities with the additional alternative of appointing a board of permanent officials to exercise the powers of trustees. The major advantage of having these funds in the keeping of an independent body is the protection which it affords against "raiding" of the sinking fund by a council in financial straits.

The sinking fund type of debenture has both advantages and disadvantages. There is a class of investor who wishes to be free from the problem of reinvesting his capital from time to time. The sinking fund type of investment relieves the investor of any problem of reinvestment during the lifetime of the debenture issue. The sinking fund, in its capacity as an investor, also provides a convenient market for odd lots of debentures of the local municipality and in English practice it serves as a temporary loan fund for the municipality.

The problem of safe investment, the danger of mismanagement or even dishonesty in the handling of the funds, the possibility of failure to maintain the fund or its earning power, the task of arranging for investment maturities to coincide with debt maturities, and the cost and bother of sinking fund management have combined to reduce the popularity of this type of issue in favour of the instalment or serial type. In Ontario and British Columbia it is no longer permissible for municipalities to issue debentures on the sinking fund basis although there is a substantial but declining number of sinking fund debentures still outstanding. In practice in Quebec sinking fund bonds are no longer authorized.

Instalment or Serial Debentures

The instalment or serial type of debenture differs from the sinking fund type in that the debentures which are issued do not provide for the repayment of the total principal sum at the end of the term of the debenture issue. Rather, a specified portion of the principal is repaid each year, thus eliminating any necessity for a sinking fund. The authorizing by-law provides that the council shall raise annually sufficient money to pay the interest due each year and also to meet the instalment of principal falling due within the year.

The arrangements with respect to the annual payments of interest and principal may be on several bases. Some debentures provide for repayment of equal amounts of principal each year with a decreasing amount for interest (see Example A below); others provide that the amount of principal to be repaid each year may vary, the amount being increased as the annual interest charges decrease, so that the total annual payment of interest and principal will be approximately equal (see Example B below). There are also various other bases used.[9]

	Example A			*Example B*		
	$50,000—10 years—2%			*$59,000—10 Years—2%*		
Year	Principal	Interest	Total	Principal	Interest	Total
1	$5,000	$1,000	$6,000	$5,500	$1,180	$6,680
2	5,000	900	5,900	5,500	1,070	6,570
3	5,000	800	5,800	5,500	960	6,460
4	5,000	700	5,700	5,500	850	6,350
5	5,000	600	5,600	6,000	740	6,740
6	5,000	500	5,500	6,000	620	6,620
7	5,000	400	5,400	6,000	500	6,500
8	5,000	300	5,300	6,000	380	6,380
9	5,000	200	5,200	6,500	260	6,760
10	5,000	100	5,100	6,500	130	6,630

The instalment or serial type of debenture has the merit of simplicity. There are no worries about investment of sinking funds, no concern about synchronizing maturities of investments with the debentures coming due. They might almost be classed as foolproof. The annual repayment of a portion of the principal provides an automatic reduction of the outstanding debt and creditors are immediately aware of any default, whereas with the sinking fund type a growing deficiency may not come to the debenture holders' attention until the final maturity date when the total principal amount falls due. Not the least of the advantages of the serial debenture is the reduced incentive to consolidate the outstanding debt.

Debt Consolidations

It was a not uncommon practice some years ago that a municipality

[9]Sometimes debentures are issued on the basis that in the early years there is only a token repayment of principal, the amounts being substantially increased in later years. This arrangement imposes a very light burden for a few years while other outstanding debentures are maturing and the total annual burden being reduced.

whose debentures were issued on the sinking fund basis would, from time to time, obtain legislative authority to consolidate or call in all the outstanding debentures and replace them with a new issue, usually on a long-term basis. In such an event the sinking funds, which had been built up to pay off the debentures called in, would be constituted a sinking fund securing the new debenture issues. In this way the annual amounts required for payments into the sinking fund were reduced, since the time for total repayment was projected another twenty or thirty years further into the future. The interest charges over the total period were greatly increased, but there was an immediate relief to the current taxpayer. Repeated consolidations might mean that taxpayers were paying for capital construction years after the actual works constructed had worn out and been replaced.[10] The automatic annual reduction of the principal amount under the instalment plan removes much of the incentive for such a procedure, although issues having a callable feature may be called in and reissued to take advantage of lowering interest rates.

Sale of Debentures

The usual method of selling debentures is to call for public tenders by advertisement or by direct notice to the bond dealers. Calling for tenders is the prescribed method in the province of Quebec, unless some other procedure is authorized by special permission of the Minister of Municipal Affairs. In some cases they are sold by private arrangement between the municipality and a bulk purchaser and under special circumstances they may be sold directly to the citizens through the muncipal treasurer's office, although this last method is not looked on with favour by the bond dealers.

The customary basis of tendering is to offer a price per hundred dollars of the debentures. This may result in the municipality's receiving a premium or obtaining less than the face value of the debentures offered. The practice of offering debentures for sale at par, with the purchasers offering varying interest rates, has not as yet become established in Canada.

The debentures are issued in denominations to suit the convenience of the purchaser. An issue of $500,000 is not ordinarily sold as one instrument with a face value of $500,000 but rather as a number of debentures with face values of $5,000, $1,000, etc., as low as $50 if

[10]One Canadian city consolidated its debt in 1871, 1891 and 1906. The last consolidation provided for the issue of forty-year debentures, so that the taxpayers of 1946 were still paying for capital expenditures made prior to 1870.

desired. Provision also is made for registering the debentures as to principal but the usual practice is to provide for interest payments by attaching interest coupons to the debentures. While the immediate purchasers of most municipal debentures are bond dealers, the ultimate purchasers include private individuals, insurance companies, banks, trustees, municipal sinking funds, and educational and charitable institutions.

Provincial Loans to Municipalities

Several provinces have established loan funds to enable their municipalities to finance certain types of capital expenditures without being obliged to sell their debentures to the public. Except for those with high financial standing this usually results in lower interest costs for the municipalities than would otherwise be obtained. Nova Scotia in 1944 created a School Building Fund in the amount of $200,000 to provide loans to assist school sections in the erection and improvement of school buildings. This fund in 1949 was increased to $1,000,000 and the scope of loans extended to include the equipping of school buildings and the purchase of school buses. In 1948 a Municipal Loan Fund also was provided for to make loans to municipalities for waterworks and sewer construction or for municipal buildings including schools, hospitals, city or town halls, court houses, and jails. The amount of the fund was fixed in 1949 at $4,500,000.

Alberta in 1950 authorized the Provincial Treasurer to make loans to municipalities at 2 per cent per annum to finance the construction of self-liquidating projects. By 1952, $12,000,000 had been set aside for this purpose. The loans are secured by the debentures of the municipality and, if required, a mortgage on the project.[11] In the same year Ontario established The Ontario Municipal Improvement Corporation, composed of three provincial officials, authorized to borrow money by the sale of debentures, treasury bills, or temporary loans. The aggregate amount outstanding at any time may not exceed $50,000,000. The Corporation, with the approval of the Lieutenant-Governor in Council, may purchase the debentures of any Ontario municipality issued to finance waterworks, sewers or sewage works, refuse plants or incinerators, or drainage works, provided the debentures have been authorized and validated by the Ontario Municipal Board.[12]

[11]In October 1951, the Minister of Municipal Affairs reported that 61 loans totalling $9,748,000 had been made and 19 others were pending.

[12]As at March 1952 municipal debentures to the amount of $10,355,141 had been purchased from 35 municipalities.

Municipal Debt

The municipal debt is declining in importance as compared with the debt of the other two levels of government. It gradually declined from a high point of $1,384,000,000 in 1933 to $982,000,000 in 1946, but since that date has been rising.

The prolonged decline in the total municipal debt was due to several factors. The financial difficulties of the depression years limited expenditures on capital construction and were followed by the shortages of manpower and materials during the war years. The repayment provisions of municipal debentures also contributed to the reduction, for as long as municipalities are not incurring new debt their total debt will continuously decrease, because they are required to maintain their annual principal repayments.

The trend toward increased municipal debt is suggested in the figures from a number of the provinces shown in Table 26. Table 27 shows the distribution of the outstanding municipal debt in the years 1944 and 1948 by provinces and by classes of municipalities. It will be seen that municipal debt is largely an urban problem, as 91 per cent of the total debt is urban debt. As might be expected, 71.4 per cent of the municipal debt lies in the two provinces of Quebec and Ontario; this is not far out of line as they contain 61.8 per cent of the population and, as shown in Table 2, are the two most highly urbanized provinces. At the same time, the rural debt, although small in total amount, has almost doubled both in amount and in percentage of the total in the period 1944–8.

Table 28 indicates the major purposes for which the outstanding municipal debt has been incurred.

TABLE 26

MUNICIPAL DEBENTURE DEBT IN CERTAIN PROVINCES, 1945–8
(000,000's omitted)

Year	N.S.[a]	N.B.[a]	Ont.[a]	Sask.[a]	Alta.[b]	B.C.[b]
1945	$15	$13	$195	$17	$32	$104
1946	17	13	182	13	30	109
1947	19	15	193	12	31	116
1948	22	18	225	14	34	129
1949	22	22	260	16	45	142
1950	27	25	331	17	57	152

[a]Net debt.
[b]Gross debt.

TABLE 27

OUTSTANDING MUNICIPAL DEBT (NET) 1944 AND 1948[a]
(000,000's omitted)

Province	Metropolitan municipalities		Other urban		Rural		Total	
	1944	1948	1944	1948	1944	1948	1944	1948
Prince Edward Island	$	$	$ 2	$ 2	$	$	$ 2	$ 2
Nova Scotia			17	23	1	1	19	24
New Brunswick			11	17	3	6	15	24
Quebec	313	245	106	128	10	14	430	387
Ontario	156	145	76	105	14	31	246	283
Manitoba	39	37	1	2	4	4	45	44
Saskatchewan			18	15	4	5	22	20
Alberta			37	41	1	4	39	46
British Columbia	64	73	16	22	2	8	83	105
	572	502	288	359	43	76	904	939
	63%	53%	31%	38%	4%	8%	100%	100%

[a]Based on statistics contained in *Bank of Canada Statistical Summary, 1946 Supplement*, and *1950 Supplement*.

TABLE 28

DISTRIBUTION OF MUNICIPAL BONDED DEBT, 1944 AND 1948[a]
(in millions)

	Metropolitan municipalities		Other urban		Rural		Total	
	1944	1948	1944	1948	1944	1948	1944	1948
Schools (gross)	$106	$ 42	$ 69	$ 81	$ 9	$ 30	$185	$154
Highways (gross)	93	79	77	82	6	6	177	168
Others (gross) excl. utilities	284	267	120	148	16	20	422	436
	483	389	267	312	32	56	784	759
Less sinking funds	61	42	65	59	3	3	130	105
	421	347	201	253	29	53	653	653
Utilities (net)	97	90	75	76	6	8	179	175
Total (net)	520	437	277	329	35	61	833	828
Guaranteed debt (net)	44	47	2	2			46	49
Bank loans	7	17	8	28	7	15	23	60
Total	572	502	287	359	43	76	903	939

[a]Based on *Bank of Canada Statistical Summary, 1950 Supplement.*

Subsidies, Grants, and Shared Taxes

Most grants and subsidies received by municipalities come from the respective provincial authorities, although there have been a few cases of Dominion grants for specific purposes. Provincial grants may be made to the municipal corporation or may be paid directly to special purpose bodies in the municipal organization. The extent to which such grants are made, the purposes for which they are made, and the basis upon which they are paid vary widely from province to province and even within a province.

Provincial grants have been developed for three main purposes: (1) to assist municipalities to carry the general cost of municipal government, or of certain aspects of it, and thereby to relieve the burden of taxation on real property, (2) to induce the municipal council or the special purpose body concerned to undertake certain services, to improve its services, or to maintain a stated standard of service, and (3) to equalize the burden of maintaining certain services at adequate standards as between different municipalities, consideration being given to their relative capacities to carry the cost of these services.

To attain these varied ends, the grants which have been made have had to be determined on different bases, some of which are indicated below. It sometimes happens that the purposes aimed at by different grants may be in conflict. Thus, a grant designed to increase the expenditures in a particular field tends to defeat the aim of a grant intended to reduce the burden upon the ratepayers.

General Subsidy or Unconditional Grants

A general subsidy is a grant or subsidy made by a province for the purpose of assisting the municipality with its financing and is not conditional on the maintenance of specific services or any particular standard of service, nor is it earmarked for any special purpose. Its purpose is to relieve the burden upon the local taxpayer. Such a subsidy may or may not be uniform for all municipalities and may or may not have an equalizing factor in it.

There are different bases for determining the amount of subsidy for individual municipalities. The province of Ontario in the years 1937 to 1948 inclusive paid a general subsidy to all the municipalities.[13] Each municipality received an amount equivalent to the product of a one mill[14] levy on its taxable assessment. The subsidy was "to be

[13]The subsidy was instituted to compensate the municipalities for the loss of the municipal personal income tax which the province took over in 1936.

[14]In the year 1939 the basis was the equivalent of a levy of one and one-half mills, and in 1944 two mills.

applied by the council thereof solely for the purpose of reduction of the general municipal tax rate . . . so that the benefits of such grant or subsidy [would] . . . accrue, directly, to the benefit of the ratepayers of the municipality, and the same [should] . . . not be applied or used by the council for any other purpose." Thus, the amount received by the respective municipalities varied directly according to the total local assessment with the result that the more prosperous the community, as reflected in its assessed values, the larger was the grant.

Allocation on such basis fails to recognize relative capacities to provide services nor does it allow for the variations in the extent and quality of the services which different types of municipalities must provide. One difficulty with a subsidy on this basis is that as assessment is a matter of local determination, based in great part on the judgment of the local assessor, there is no satisfactory common or objective standard against which to measure the respective assessments. There is a constant temptation to adjust assessments upwards as a means of increasing the subsidy, although this tendency is to a degree offset by other pressures to lower assessments for the purposes of reducing the local share of joint municipal costs and by the desire to benefit by other grants which vary inversely as to the assessment.

Another basis was adopted in New Brunswick in 1947 when a system of provincial grants to municipalities was introduced in part to compensate them for their exclusion from the income tax field under a Dominion-provincial agreement. The grants were based upon the population of the municipality and the per capita grant varied according to the type of municipality, a recognition of the difference in burden of cost of local services resulting from difference of function. The annual grants presently are as follows: to cities $12.38 per capita, to towns $6.92 per capita, to villages $4.00 per capita, and to counties $1.56 per capita. One advantage of the per capita basis of distribution is that it provides a unit of measurement that can be applied with much greater objectivity as between municipalities than is possible where an assessment basis is used. It is argued by some that, to the extent that municipal costs are increasingly for social services, the need for assistance is more closely related to population than to any other factor.

Similarly, Ontario, in 1953, introduced a system of unconditional per capita grants to all municipalities other than counties. These grants, effective 1954, consist of a basic unconditional grant of $1.50 per capita "to assist in the provision of welfare services, social services, the administration of justice and other services for its inhabitants." In addition, "in recognition of the larger per capita expenditures that municipalities with large populations are required to make" for such purposes, a further per capita grant is made varying in proportion to population. This additional grant rises from 10c in towns and villages with a population from 2,000 to 5,000 to $1.00 in cities of 75,000 and over and as high as $2.50 in metropolitan municipalities and cities of over 750,000 population. At the same session of the legislature provision for certain conditional grants, previously in effect, was repealed.

The general grants of Newfoundland differ in purpose from those found elsewhere. They are designed primarily to encourage the formation of municipalities and to assist them in the difficult early years. In the first year of operation a town council gets a free grant of $10,000 to enable it to set up office and to begin a public works programme. The province also pays to the towns a revenue grant based on the taxes collected, on the basis shown in the accompanying chart. In addition to the grants noted the province pays one-half the interest charges and principal repayment on town debentures.

For each $1 of taxes collected	*Provincial grant during first 4 years*	*Annually after 4th year*
up to $3,000	$1.50	$1.00
from $ 3,000 to $ 10,000	.75	.50
from $10,000 to $100,000	.30	.20

Conditional Grants

Percentage grants. Percentage grants are variously designed to encourage expenditures on a particular activity which the province desires to promote, to assist the municipality to meet the cost of some service which the province has required the municipality to undertake, to induce the council or other body to maintain a minimum standard of performance in some service, to assist in carrying the cost of some service which may be optional with the local authorities, or to equalize the burden of maintaining certain services as between municipalities of varying financial capacities.

These grants may be (*a*) a flat percentage of the expenditure, (*b*) a percentage which increases as the expenditure increases (*c*) a percentage which decreases as the expenditure increases, (*d*) a percentage which increases as the population decreases, (*e*) a percentage which increases as taxable resources decrease, or (*f*) a percentage which increases as the burden of taxation increases. Those grants which vary as noted in (*d*), (*e*), and (*f*) are frequently referred to as equalization grants designed to give proportionately greater assistance to those municipalities which are less able to bear the costs of the services being subsidized. In some cases the grants toward one function or service combine a number of the above features. Examples of these various types of grants will be found in the Appendix to this chapter.

Flat rate grants. A flat rate grant may either be conditional on the establishment of a stated service or be a grant per unit with the result that the more units provided, the greater will be the total amount of the grant received. In some cases the unit grant may vary according to a number of factors. An example of the first type would be a grant of $500 annually toward a township school-area providing specified instruction in home economics. An example of the second type would be the grant, which in Ontario is made to public libraries, of $600 for each librarian holding a Class A. Certificate of Librarianship or the grant toward indigent inmates of charitable institutions in Ontario which is at the rate of 10c per person per day. An example of a variable flat rate or unit grant is the per pupil grant to Ontario high schools which varies inversely according to taxable resources and to population as shown in the accompanying chart.

Assessment per capita	*In municipalities having a population of* not fewer than 20,000	not fewer than 10,000 but under 20,000 —urban	under 10,000—urban
at least $1,150	$ 40	$ 50	$ 60
at least $1,100 but under $1,150	44	54	64
at least $1,050 but under $1,100	48	58	68
. . . .	...	...	...
at least $250 but under $300	112	122	132
at least $200 but under $250	116	126	136
under $200	120	130	140

Shared taxes. One method of providing provincial assistance is to assign to the municipalities a share of some provincial tax. This practice is not as widely used in Canada as in the United States, but does occur in some instances.

The municipal sales tax in effect in some areas of the province of Quebec as previously noted would appear to be in the nature of a shared tax, though not so designated. Ontario municipalities receive from the province 20 per cent of the licence fees paid to the province by persons licensed to sell alcoholic beverages in the municipality. The twenty-nine cities received as their share in 1947 the sum of $777,857.

An amount equal to one-third of the net proceeds of British Columbia's 3 per cent retail sales tax is distributed among the municipalities as determined by the Minister but substantially in the proportion that the sum of its school population and estimated municipal population, in the case of a city and a district municipality, and in the proportion that its estimated municipal population only, in the case of a village municipality, bears to the aggregate of such populations. The municipalities also receive an amount equal to one-third of the annual provincial licence fees for motor vehicles, less the expenses of administration. The apportionment of this appropriation among the municipalities is also made by the Minister but is substantially in proportion to population. The money so apportioned based on motor licence revenues may be expended only on the construction and maintenance of public roads.

Under the Municipal Assistance Act of 1951, Alberta sets aside 4¢ of the tax collected on each gallon of gasoline to provide a fund to be distributed among the municipalities. Out of the fund the province pays a "tax reduction subsidy" in the form of a grant matching the amount by which the municipality reduces its mill rate below the highest rate levied in any year after 1949. The maximum provincial subsidy will not exceed the equivalent of a rate of three mills on the municipal assessment. After these conditional grants have been met the balance in the fund is divided among all the municipalities in proportion to their respective assessments. This payment is designated "an unconditional municipal revenue grant."[15]

There is wide variation in the percentage of the revenue of different municipalities represented by these grants and subsidies. It is impossible to get an accurate picture from the municipalities' financial reports, for they fail in some cases to record grants made to special purpose bodies. Table 29, however, presents an over-all view of this rapidly developing source of revenue. The purposes toward which provincial grants are more commonly made to municipalities are education, highways, health, and welfare or social services. There is, however, a wide range of special grants for special purposes too extensive to outline here.

The task of working out a satisfactory system of provincial assistance to municipalities is a difficult one. One problem is to find a basis of distribution which will be equitable as between the various municipalities, will adequately protect the provincial taxpayer, will be reasonably simple from an administrative point of view, and will obtain the desired end. It is doubtful if any one single basis can accomplish the varied purposes desired. To do so it would have to be designed to

[15]As at October, 1951, of $4,665,000 in grants under this Act, $1,592,000 had been paid out as "tax reduction subsidy" and $3,072,000 as "unconditional municipal revenue grants."

TABLE 29

IMPORTANCE OF PROVINCIAL SUBSIDIES AND GRANTS[a] IN CANADIAN MUNICIPAL REVENUES

(a) Subsidies and grants to municipalities (000,000's omitted)	1930	1933	1937	1939	1941	1944	1945	1946	1948
Subsidies	$1.2	$ .5	$3.1	$4.6	$3.1	$7.3	$7.7	$7.5	$8.5
Grants for:									
Education	17.3	11.9	15.6	18.2	19.9	40.9	44.6	56.7	83.5
Relief	5.1	36.8	56.5	35.5	5.8	1.3	3.1	3.5	6.0
Transportation		3.2	3.6	7.0	5.1	6.5	7.2	10.0	21.3
Other	.3	.2					3.1	2.9	
Total	23.9	52.6	78.8	65.3	33.9	56.0	65.7	80.6	119.3
(b) Subsidies and grants as a percentage of:									
Municipal current expenditures[b]	8.3	18.2	27.6	22.5	11.8	18.4	20.7	23.1	27.7
Amount collected from the public	7.8	18.0	26.0	20.6	10.2	15.8	18.5	21.3	25.8

[a]Based on *Bank of Canada Statistical Summary, 1950*, p. 36 *et seq.*
[b]Excl. debt repayment.

encourage expenditures on activities which the province wishes the municipalities to promote, to equalize the burden of maintaining mimimum standards of certain services in different municipalities, and at the same time grant some relief from the tax burden on the owners of real property.

Assuming that a system of grants and subsidies could be devised which accomplished these varied and sometimes contradictory purposes there are still further problems to be considered. If the municipalities are to be satisfied that they are being fairly dealt with as compared with one another, the system of grants should be sufficiently simply that it can be readily understood both as it applies to the several municipalities and as it applies to the municipality immediately involved. The more complex the system of grants the more difficult it is for the citizen or councillor to get the whole pattern of grants clearly in mind and to satisfy himself that his town is obtaining its fair share in comparison with others. The problem of determining just how a grant applies to a particular municipality is illustrated by the Saskatchewan equalization road grants formula and "scoring" procedure, as follows:

The total score is 100 points. An almost perfect municipality might score the full 100 points and would therefore get no equalization grant but would receive the minimum of $500. Each municipality is scored according to this formula and in each case the score is subtracted from the total 100 points to get the "working index." The working index is then multiplied by the "log figure" to get the grant. The log figure is the same for all municipalities and is a figure selected so that the total grants to all municipalities come to the approximate total of $450,000.

Example

Mill rate 1947—13 mills	scores	4 points	out of 14
Provincial roads—2.4 mills per twp.	scores	12 points	out of 20
Farm units—31 per twp.	scores	10 points	out of 10
Soil index—poor soil	scores	5 points	out of 24
Topography—rough	scores	1 point	out of 14
Stoniness—quite stony	scores	1 point	out of 6
Bush cover—prairie	scores	12 points	out of 12
Score for this R.M.		45	100

Total score 100 points, minus 45 points, produces a working index of 55. The log figure is 33.5. Multiply 55 by 33.5 and we get the grant for a nine township municipality which is $1,843. But this municipality is only 7½ townships, therefore the grant is 7½ ninths of $1,842 which equals $1,536. This is then taken to the nearest even ten dollars, which is $1,540.

The municipality must in all cases agree to expend $500 of municipal funds with the grant on the location or locations approved by the Department of Highways.[16]

Such a basis of determining grants is far too complex and contains too many variables dependent upon subjective judgments to make it either understandable or satisfactory to the beneficiaries of the grants.

From the municipal viewpoint it is most desirable that the basis of determining grants should be readily understandable, that the revenue to be derived should be predictable with reasonable accuracy, and that the amount of the grants should not vary greatly from year to year. Any conditions attached should not be so onerous as to result in an increase in expenditure which offsets, or more than offsets, the amount of the grant, and the volume of reports, returns, and records required by the granting authority should not be excessive nor too irksome.

Intergovernmental grants give rise to political problems. It is a generally accepted principle that it is not desirable for one level of government to expend funds raised by some other level of government. The responsibility for expenditure should rest with the revenue raising body. Yet, to such an extent have intergovernmental finances become intermingled that we find provinces expending money raised by the Dominion, the municipalities expending money raised by the provinces, and provinces expending money raised by the municipalities. Inevitably, as provincial grants to municipalities increase, the provinces,

[16] *Western Municipal News*, vol. 43, no. 5, 1948, p. 135.

in the interests of their own taxpayers, must assure themselves that these monies are being expended with reasonable efficiency and for the purposes for which they were granted. This leads in turn to increasing provincial interference and supervision of municipal policies and administration.

As the significance of the provincial grants in the local revenues increases, the local authority's power of resistance to provincial direction and interference is proportionately weakened. The amount at stake eventually becomes too great for a municipality to afford the risk of its being cut off because the local authorities are too obdurate. The one who pays the piper will, not unnaturally, expect to call the tune.

A further complication that results is the possibility of the municipality's becoming embroiled in differences which may arise between the Dominion and the provinces. When these differences occur it may be that a province which cannot arrive at a satisfactory financial settlement with the Dominion will make the municipalities actually bear a portion of the cost of such failure. The municipalities may thus become pawns in the Dominion-provincial game. The uncertainty of the future basis of grants may also, under some circumstances, create an acute problem in municipal finance. Such was the case in the thirties, when the annual decisions of the two senior governments as to the basis on which they would contribute toward relief costs were seldom decided prior to the date by which the municipalities had to decide upon their budgets for the year.

While grants may be made by the provinces for the purpose of lightening the burden of real property taxation, the resulting reduction is usually less than the amount of the grant. Municipalities always have more objects upon which to expend their money than they have money to spend. Greater grants, therefore, enable the local authority to incur additional expenditures without requiring higher taxes from the taxpayers. The relief to the taxpayer thus is not reflected in a lowered tax burden for any prolonged period of time but rather in services which, but for the grant, either would not have been undertaken or would have meant an increase in the tax burden. It does not necessarily follow, however, that the additional expenditure would have been incurred if no grants had been available.

Enterprise Earnings

Under the provisions of provincial statutes of general application, and, in some cases, under legislation applying only to an individual municipality, a wide range of activities is carried on which are classed as enterprises. Probably the earliest of such enterprises to be undertaken was the operation of municipal markets but the list has extended over the years to include waterworks, electrical works, gas works, transportation systems (including street and other railways, bus systems, and harbour ferries), amusement centres and dance halls, hospitals, cemeteries, fuel yards, heating systems, abbatoirs, telephone systems, airports, housing, etc.

These enterprises have been undertaken for a variety of reasons. Some, such as waterworks, have been acquired or developed as municipal enterprises to assure satisfactory operation of a function too vital to community life to be left under private control, others, such as the generation and distribution of electricity, to protect consumers against unduly high charges; in yet other instances a municipality has assumed responsibility for activities previously carried on by private undertakers with unsatisfactory results or to meet a need which private enterprise has failed to meet.

The importance of enterprise earnings in the municipal revenues depends on several factors. The revenues shown in individual municipal reports depend in part on the accounting practices of the municipality, for some show the gross revenues of an enterprise as a municipal revenue, while others take into consideration only the net results. Moreover, not all municipal enterprises operate at a net profit, so although a municipality may carry on a number of such activities it may receive little or no net revenue. Even where an enterprise is able to operate at a profit the extent of that profit is to a degree determined by the policy of the authority under which it operates.

Some authorities follow a policy of so operating some of their enterprises that they will show a profit which can be used to reduce the burden of taxation on the taxpayers. Such a policy is based on the argument that the risks of the enterprise are taken by the taxpayers who supply the initial capital funds, or at least the credit upon which such funds are borrowed, that if there are losses it is the taxpayer who must make good the losses, and alternatively that if there are profits he is entitled to the benefit. It is based too, on the belief that there is nothing wrong in principle in operating public enterprises at a profit provided the operating authority does not take advantage of what is usually a monopoly position to charge exorbitant rates. Some justify the operation of municipal utilities at a profit as a means of taxing tenants and thereby relieving the burden on real property owners.

A widely held view, however, is that such public enterprises should sell their service or product to the consumer at cost or as nearly at cost as is feasible. The proponents of this view hold that when the consumers, through their rates, have repaid the capital which the ratepayers may have supplied or guaranteed they owe nothing more to the ratepayers, and that the ratepayers have no justifiable claim to any profit. The supporters of "service at cost" are more likely to be adamant in the case of a profit-making enterprise than in the case of an enterprise which operates at a loss. Thus, while it is popularly argued that municipal taxpayers have no right to any profit on the sale of electrical power to the consumers in the municipality, it is also argued that if the fares on a transportation system will not enable it to meet its costs of operation the taxpayers should subsidize the system rather than raise the fares. The basis of either view is often one of expediency, and the taxpayer in most cases ends up in his customary position.

Even where the prevailing policy is one of service at cost, surpluses may develop, for it is not always feasible to adjust rates constantly as business fluctuates. Thus, some municipalities which under prevailing rates were normally just able to meet the costs of operation of their waterworks, or even showed a loss in the depression years, received large net profits from their operations during the war years in spite of rate reductions and, in some cases, the remission or cancellation of bills for stated periods.

The net surpluses from some enterprises are not available to the municipality for general purposes but under statutory provisions must be held for the extension and improvement of the enterprise, as is the case of electrical authorities forming part of the hydro electric power system in Ontario.

More of such enterprises are carried on by the larger urban municipalities than by the rural and smaller urban centres. A survey of the reports of forty larger Canadian urban centres shows the following number in which the enterprises indicated are operated, either by the municipal corporation or by some special purpose municipal body: waterworks, 39; cemeteries, 17; transportation systems, 13; gas works, 7; exhibitions or fairs, 6; airports, 4; ferry service, 4; telephone systems, 2; and the following occur once: abbatoir, harbour, arena, stadium, stockyard, and steam heat production and distribution. There are other activities such as golf courses and housing which might also be considered as enterprise operations. The cases shown in Table 30 are only a portion of the total municipal enterprises throughout Canada but they give some indication of the extent of such operations, the existing policies with respect to the earning of surpluses, and some measure of the success of municipal operation of various types of enterprises.

A factor to be kept in mind in judging the results of the operation

TABLE 30

SOME MUNICIPAL ENTERPRISE OPERATIONS[a]
(000's omitted)

Enterprises	No.	Total expenditure	Surplus or deficit	No. with deficit	Surplus or deficit as % of expenditure
Waterworks					
Nova Scotia	32	$ 1,106	S $ 5	14	S .45
Quebec	105	9,815	S 4,071	38	S 41.40
Ontario	263	17,617	S 3,138	74	S 17.80
Alberta	50	3,675	S 22	25	S .59
British Columbia	33	5,837	S 990	10	S 16.96
Electricity					
Nova Scotia	17	1,335	S 121	1	S 9.06
Quebec	26	2,073	S 620	2	S 29.90
Alberta	14	6,914	S 901	0	S 13.03
British Columbia	14	1,733	S 944	0	S 54.47
Gas					
Alberta	1	246	S 139	0	S 56.50
British Columbia	1	47	D 12	1	D 25.50
Transportation					
Alberta	3	4,881	D 42	2	D .86
British Columbia	1	306	D 12	1	D 4.14
Telephone					
Alberta	1	1,236	S 174	0	S 14.07
British Columbia	1	112	S 10	0	S 9.14
Cemeteries					
Alberta	4	33	D 13	2	D 39.39
Ferries					
British Columbia	1	211	D 33	1	D 15.78
Irrigation					
British Columbia	2	110	D 32	2	D 29.09
	569[b]	57,287	S 11,135 D 112	173	S 19.20

[a]Figures for all provinces except Quebec are for 1950; Quebec figures are for 1943.

[b]This total only includes municipal enterprises for which information is available from provincial reports and is far from complete, e.g. while the above only accounts for 464 municipally operated water systems there are 629 in municipalities of 1,000 population and over.

of most municipal enterprises is that, except in the case of utilities in Ontario, Alberta, and some Nova Scotia municipalities, they are free from municipal taxation and also from corporation taxes imposed by the senior levels of government. As yet no thorough study of the operation of municipal enterprises by Canadian municipalities has been made.

The significance of the revenue from enterprise earnings in the total municipal revenues requires analysis to determine whether or not the revenues shown in municipal reports are net revenues available to reduce the tax burden, or are payments which are largely absorbed in payment of debt charges attributable to the respective enterprises. It is probable that they will be of increasing importance, for the trend would appear to be in the direction of expanding such municipal activities[17] and it may be that increasing pressure on municipal finances will result in a modification of the policy of service at cost, in favour of a planned use of enterprise rates and charges as a means of shifting the burden from the real property owner, as such, to the utility consumer.[18]

Miscellaneous Revenues

Miscellaneous revenues are those which do not fall under the headings of taxes, subsidies or grants, or enterprise earnings. They are of greater importance in the larger urban municipalities, but are not of great significance in the total financial picture in any municipality. Table 31 sets out the more important sources of revenue under this heading in a number of cities and shows the percentage of the total revenue which they represent. Under this heading also are to be found a wide variety of items such as earnings on investments, sinking fund surpluses transferred to current account, profits on the sales of tax title properties, and many others peculiar to individual municipalities.

Licences, Permits, and Privileges

Licensing has been defined as the "administrative lifting of a legislative prohibition, in which the basic idea is not to prohibit but to regulate." The power to require the taking of a municipal licence as a condition of carrying on any particular type of business is granted to the municipalities by provincial legislation and the range of activities which may be licensed is greater in the larger municipalities. The person obtaining a licence must pay an amount fixed by the council, although in some cases this amount may be subject to the approval of a provincial administrative agency or the maximum amount chargeable may be fixed by statute. Most licences are issued on a yearly basis

[17]Saskatchewan in 1947 authorized cities and towns to provide for the distribution and delivery of dairy and baking products, to acquire and operate dairies and bakeries, to acquire and operate gas and oil service stations, and to acquire and operate exhibitions, theatres, and places of amusement.

[18]In Saskatchewan utility profits as a percentage of municipal revenues in all urban municipalities increased from 5 per cent in 1922 to 30 per cent in 1947 and was as high as 41 per cent in the cities in the latter year. In British Columbia cities, exclusive of Vancouver, utility surpluses increased from 6.1 per cent of the gross receipts in 1936 to 13.8 per cent in 1945.

TABLE 31

COMMONLY RECURRING "MISCELLANEOUS" REVENUES IN 10 CANADIAN CITIES, 1946
(000's omitted)

	Licenses and permits		Fines		Rents	
Municipality	Amount	% of total revenue[a]	Amount	% of total revenue	Amount	% of total revenue
Saint John	$ 15	.4	$ 45	1.4	$ 19	.6
Moncton	16	1.3	19	1.6	3	.3
Montreal	1,492	2.4	410	.5	296	.4
Ottawa	76	1.0	50	.6	19	.2
London	52	1.1	43	.9	12	.2
Winnipeg	291	2.3	113	.8	16	.1
Saskatoon	180	11.8	15	.9	17	1.1
Calgary	152	5.2	24	.8	75	2.5
Victoria	202	8.6	39	1.6	33	1.4
Vancouver	1,492	8.4			112	.6

[a]The revenue used here is the total revenue of the year less any surplus brought forward from a previous year.

and the licensee must pay for each annual renewal. In practice, the charge may be nominal if the purpose of licensing is primarily for the purpose of control, or it may be larger where it is designed to discourage applicants or to raise a revenue. As noted in Table 31 the percentage of the total revenue received for licences and permits in some of the western cities is many times that of the cities in the easterly provinces. This is owing to the fact that certain business licences in cities where there is no business assessment are designed to be revenue producers and are really a form of business tax.

The charges for the issue of permits are commonly referred to as fees, which are defined as "payments exacted for specific acts of some governmental agency, usually of a clerical nature, such as the recording of a deed, which is required in the public interest, and which confers some actual or constructive benefit on the payer."

There is a wide range of activities in many municipalities for which either a licence or a permit is required. The extent to which the purpose is that of revenue, rather than mainly of control, is indicated by the amount of the charge. Thus, in Montreal the charges range from $1.00 for an ice merchant with a hand cart, to $1,000 for certain types of money lenders, and in Toronto, from $1.00 for each driver of a cab, to $500 per day for a circus travelling with over twenty-five cars. Most licences are primarily for the purpose of control. Permits are in most cases issued to cover a particular operation and the charge may either be a flat fee or one which varies according to the service involved. So the fee for a tax search is the same regardless of the value of the property, while the fee for a building permit may vary according to the value of the building to be constructed, for it is reasonable to expect that the larger building will require more inspection service and the fee is designed to cover, or partially cover, the cost of the service rendered.

Fines and Penalties

The revenues from fines represents the share of the fines in the magistrate's court which is received by the municipality, but the basis upon which the municipality shares varies greatly. In Quebec cities and towns in which the Recorder is paid by the municipality, any fines under the Cities and Towns Act, the municipal charter, or any by-law of the council belong to the municipality. In other cases before the district magistrate such fines are shared equally by the municipality and the prosecutor. Ontario cities in which the magistrate is paid by the city rather than by the province, receives the fines and fees, but where the magistrate is paid by the province, 40 per cent goes to the province and 60 per cent to the municipality. Saskatchewan cities and towns receive the penalties imposed under the provisions of their by-laws. In British Columbia, if the magistrate is paid by the municipality, it receives the fees as well as fines under municipal by-laws and provincial statutes unless otherwise provided, but if the magistrate is not paid by the municipality, only penalties under municipal by-laws are paid to the municipality. In addition to these general provisions there are individual arrangements for cities with special charters, as in Winnipeg where all fines and penalties under the charter or city by-laws accrue to the city.

Rents

Rental revenues are derived from two main sources. The first of these is the rental of real property owned by the corporation. Such real property may be acquired in a number of ways. Much real property in times of depression comes into the possession of the municipalities through tax sale if no other person buys such properties; in some cases lands or buildings once used for municipal purposes may have ceased to be used, or the municipality may have acquired lands for future use, holding the property for rent in the interim; some municipalities acquire properties from elderly persons who transfer them to the corporation in return for an undertaking on the part of the municipality to maintain them in their declining years. A major source of rental income in some municipalities is the rent paid by tenants of dwellings provided by the corporation under a housing plan. Such revenues are obtained only in a limited number of municipalities for Canadian cities have not entered the housing field to any great extent.

There is another source of such revenues which may be differently classified in various municipalities. It includes a variety of charges for the use of, or encroachments on, the highways within the municipality for such things are areaways and coal chutes in the sidewalks, canopies, signs, and private bridges over highways, and tunnels, conduits, heating mains, etc. under the highways. The rate charged may be a flat rate or one which varies according to the area or extent of the encroachment on the highway. The annual rates charged in London, for example, are as set out in the accompanying chart. A rapidly developing additional source of revenue of this type is that from parking meters which have been installed in many urban municipalities in the last ten years. This revenue in some cities runs as high as 70¢ to 80¢ per capita.

London Street Encroachment Charges

Areas[a] in central portion of city	10¢ a sq. ft.
in other portions of city	7¢ a sq. ft.
Coal chutes in the street	$1.00
Tunnels under the street (maximum charge $25)	5¢ a sq. ft.
Signs, overhanging (minimum $1, maximum $10)	25¢ a sq. ft.

[a]An area or areaway is an opening in the street usually used for basement lighting or for delivery of goods.

Poll Tax

A poll tax is levied in most of the provinces, although the basis of the tax varies and the tax is not always designated as a poll tax. The terms under which the tax may be levied and the persons liable are fixed by statute but it may be optional with the local council whether or not such a tax will be imposed.[19] In Nova Scotia municipalities and towns, New Brunswick municipalities of all types, Saskatchewan cities and towns, and Alberta municipal districts the imposition of the tax is mandatory. Councils in many cases are free to vary the amount of the tax within fixed limits. The tax usually ranges from $1.00 to $5.00, but in some cases is higher, as in Saint John, N.B. where the rate is $12.00.[20]

[19]In 1947 only thirteen of twenty-eight cities in Ontario levied a poll tax.

[20]The Fredericton poll tax is $15 for males over 21 years who are not assessed for an occupancy tax and $10 for all other inhabitants over 21 years, with the exception of non-employed married women whose husbands pay poll tax, and recipients of old age or blind pensions, mothers' allowance, or war veterans allowances.

In Manitoba and the provinces to the east only males are liable to the tax under the general statutory provision. In Fredericton, Saint John, and a number of other New Brunswick municipalities, however, under special legislation, all inhabitants of twenty-one years or over, both male and female, are liable except paupers, housewives, and domestics. The Newfoundland municipal service fee, the Alberta minimum tax, and the Saskatchewan poll tax apply to both sexes but in British Columbia the council may define who, among the persons over twenty-one years of age, shall be liable.

These taxes are usually imposed only on those between twenty-one and sixty years of age but in Quebec, Saskatchewan, and Alberta no maximum age limit is fixed. In Nova Scotia, although the age limits extend from eighteen to sixty years, the council may reduce the amount or grant exemption for those between eighteen and twenty-one. Various classes of persons are granted exemption from the poll tax in the different provinces, such as persons who have paid a poll tax in another municipality, members of the armed forces, volunteer firemen, paupers, etc. Saskatchewan cities may exempt a married person whose income is less than $900 a year and an unmarried person whose income is less than $480 a year, or such lesser amount as the council may determine.

The amount of the poll tax, which is levied annually, is usually a small fixed uniform amount and the revenue produced is small. A variation from the usual practice occurs in New Brunswick where a council may, if it chooses,[21] levy upon all persons liable to pay poll tax, by an equal rate per capita, for a sufficient amount to raise one-sixth of the total amount required to be raised by taxation in the year.

Newfoundland does not provide for a poll tax by that name but permits councils to levy a municipal service fee not less than $5.00 nor more than $10.00. The fee is levied upon all males of twenty-one years or over residing or employed in the municipality for a period of three months or more, and on all non-residents, personal or corporate, who own real property within the municipality to the value of $100. It applies also to all females, twenty-one years of age or over, who reside or are employed in the municipality and whose income is $600 or more. A person who has paid a real property tax in the same financial year, however, is not liable to the municipal service fee.

The Charlottetown poll tax, which is a mandatory tax of $3.00 which the council may increase to $5.00, is levied on all males between

[21]This is compulsory in towns except those which by special legislation may levy a fixed poll tax.

twenty-one and sixty years who are resident in the city, do business therein, or are employed or live in the city for a period of two months. In Prince Edward Island towns every male who is resident or engaged in business or employed in the town for two months within the assessment year is liable to a poll tax or taxes not exceeding in the aggregate $10.00 annually. There may be a general poll tax and also additional poll taxes for special purposes. These additional poll taxes may be applicable to any class of taxpayer and may be levied on female property owners. A council may exempt from the payment of poll taxes all persons over a stated age, not less than sixty years.

Alberta does not provide for a poll tax but has a minimum tax which is optional with cities, towns, and villages but is mandatory to a degree for municipal districts. The urban councils, with the approval of the Minister in the case of towns and villages, may impose a minimum tax on all residents who are gainfully employed but are not otherwise assessed and may also impose a minimum tax on any resident who is otherwise assessed but whose taxes are less in amount than the minimum tax. There may be a minimum tax for municipal purposes, one for school purposes, and one for hospital purposes. In the municipal districts a minimum tax of $4.00 is mandatory for all persons gainfully employed and who are not assessed and for assessed persons whose taxes are less than $4.00. Further minimum taxes of $4.00 for schools and also for hospital purposes are optional but if provided for must be approved by the Minister. The British Columbia tax, which is referred to as a road tax, is optional with the council.

The poll tax is difficult to administer and is often not very productive although its productivity depends considerably on the local efforts to make it produce.[22] In several provinces, Nova Scotia, Manitoba, Saskatchewan, and Alberta, employers may be required to furnish a list of their employees to assist the taxing authority in obtaining a record of persons who might be liable to poll tax. In Nova Scotia municipalities, in Ontario, and in Saskatchewan, the employer also may be required to withhold from any money owing to any employee sufficient to pay his poll tax if the employee has not paid. The Manitoba poll tax constitutes a lien on the personal property of the individual liable and is recoverable by distress and sale, and the municipality also can take proceedings to attach money owing to a poll tax payer who is in default.

[22]In Ontario cities in 1949 the per capita yield from the poll tax, where it was used, varied from 4.4¢ to 42.5¢. In New Brunswick on the other hand poll taxes provide about 15 per cent of all locally raised funds.

Dog Tax

A minor source of revenue but one which occurs in many municipalities is what is commonly referred to as a dog tax. Practice varies as to whether it is handled as a tax or as licence fee and even within one province it may be differently classified in different types of municipalities, as in New Brunswick where counties and villages are authorized to impose a tax on the owners of dogs while in towns the municipality may require dogs to be licensed. The power to tax or license is optional in New Brunswick, Quebec, Manitoba, and British Columbia but is mandatory in Ontario. The amount of the tax or licence fee rests with the local councils, although frequently within limits fixed by statute. Ontario requires that an annual tax be levied on the following basis: one male dog, $2.00, each additional male $4.00, one female $4.00, each additional female $6.00; but an Ontario council may increase the rate or, as an alternative to the tax, may require the licensing of dogs in which case the licence fee for females may be larger than for males and the rate may be increased where more than one is kept.

Other Miscellaneous Revenues

There is a wide variety of other miscellaneous revenues which vary greatly from one municipality to another, but in most cases the total amount of such revenue is not great. It is not possible here to deal with these items in detail.

APPENDIX

Examples of Percentage and Unit or Flat Rate Provincial Grants toward Municipal Costs

(in effect in Ontario in 1952 except as noted)

I. Grants which are a flat percentage of the expenditure:
  A. A uniform flat percentage grant:
    Under the Children's Protection Act the province pays to a municipality an amount equal to 25 per cent of the amount of the net expenditures of the municipality for the maintenance of a child made a ward of a Children's Aid Society.
  B. A uniform flat percentage which varies according to the type of municipality:
    Under the Highway Improvement Act the Minister may direct payment to a municipality of an amount equal to the following portion of its approved expenditures on highways:
      1. in the case of a city or separated town, 33⅓ per cent; and
      2. in all other cases, 50 per cent.

II. Percentage grants under which the percentage increases as the expenditure increases:

One provincial grant toward public libraries in cities of 10,000 to 14,999 population varies according to the expenditure per capita as follows:

expenditure per capita	50¢–60¢	61¢–70¢	71¢–80¢	over 80¢
grant	10%	12%	25%	30%

III. Percentage grants under which the percentage increases as the population decreases:

Grants toward the cost of police and fire department are paid on the following basis:

Population	*Grant*
70,000 or over	10%
25,000–70,000	15%
10,000–25,000	20%
under 10,000	25%

IV. Percentage grants under which the percentage increases as the taxable resources decrease:

One of the grants towards approved costs of public and separate schools in rural areas and certain other cases varies from 40 per cent to 92 per cent according to the assessment in the area per class room unit, as follows:

Assessment per class room unit	*Grant*
at least $125,000	40%
at least $120,000 but less than $125,000	42%
at least $115,000 but less than $120,000	44%
. . . .	. .
at least $30,000 but less than $35,000	84%
at least $25,000 but less than $30,000	89%
less than $25,000	92%

V. Percentage grants under which the percentage increases as the tax rate increases:

This basis which was in effect in Ontario a few years ago is not being used at the present time. Certain grants were made to secondary schools on the following basis:

School mill rate	*Grant as a percentage of approved cost*
under 4 mills	15
at least 4 but under 5 mills	20
. . . .	. .
at least 13 but under 14 mills	65
at least 14	70

VI. Percentage grants under which the percentage varies according to more than one factor:

The grant towards public libraries noted in II above is part of a percentage grant in which the percentages vary directly according to the expenditures and inversely according to population, as follows:

Population of municipality	*Grants as a percentage of expenditure where the public library municipal rate per capita is—*			
	50¢–60¢	61¢–70¢	71¢–80¢	over 80¢
less than 1,000	25	30	50	70
1,000–1,999	20	30	50	65
2,000–4,999	15	20	40	60
. . . .	. .	. .	. .	. .
25,000–49,999	10	12	15	20
50,000 and over	7	10	12	12

CHAPTER XIII

ASSESSMENT

Purpose and Importance of Assessment

The process of assessing serves two major purposes: it determines what objects or properties in the municipality are liable to taxation, and thereby the total tax base upon which the tax rate is to be levied to raise the taxes required for the year, and at the same time it determines the share of the total tax burden which each taxpayer will be required to bear.

In practice, the term "assessment" has several connotations. In one sense an assessment is the equivalent of a tax or a levy. From the individual's point of view, municipally, it means the valuation for taxaation purposes placed upon the taxable object, while from the viewpoint of a council, it means the total of the values for taxation purposes of all the taxable units in the municipality.

To the citizen, the important factor of the assessment is its equity. It matters little ultimately to the individual whether his property is assessed at too high or too low a figure, as related to actual value, provided his assessment is equitable as related to the assessments of all the other properties, for, from his point of view, the assessment merely determines his share of the total tax burden. If all are assessed at 50 per cent of value, his share is no different than if all are assessed at 100 per cent.

While councils are interested in an equitable distribution of the tax burden, they are also concerned with the tax rate. Advertising, propaganda, and election appeals have led the voters to concentrate their attention on the rate, rather than the tax burden, as the measure of municipal extravagance or efficiency. Yet it is the tax burden which should be of real concern to the taxpayer. The tax burden is a product of two factors, the taxable assessment and the tax rate. Accordingly, for any given amount of tax burden, if the assessment is low, the tax rate must be high or, if the assessment is high, the tax rate will be low. Because taxpayers have been educated to concentrate their attention on the rate is is of political interest to councillors that the assessments should be higher rather than lower and the rate correspondingly lower provided the particular council do not have to bear the blame for an increase in assessment. There are other factors which enter into the problem, as a matter of expediency, which will be discussed later.

Assessment of real property for municipal purposes in most Canadian provinces is on a capital value basis. In St. John's, Newfoundland, the rental value is the basis[1] but other local councils in that province may determine whether the basis to be used shall be capital or rental value. Assessors in Quebec cities and towns are required to assess both on a capital value and on a rental value basis, the latter being subsequently used only for the purpose of the tenants' tax. Rental value assessment is also required as the basis for business assessment purposes in some provinces.

The capital value basis prevails also in the United States. It is in contrast to the rental or annual value basis which is used in England and the varied bases found in Australia or in New Zealand where a municipality may use either the capital value basis or the annual value basis or the unimproved land value basis and where in some instances two different bases are used within the one municipality for taxing for different purposes.

The proponents of both the annual and the capital value systems of assessing advance arguments in support of the basis to which they have become accustomed. Inasmuch as the annual or rental value assessment is not based on the actual rental paid but rather on a rental which, governed by precedents and judicial decisions, is in the opinion of the assessor a proper rental, and the capital value assessment is not based on the sale or market value but rather on a capital value which, governed by precedents and judicial decisions, is in the opinion of the assessor the proper capital value, the results in both cases come finally to depend on the judgment of the assessor, guided, to the extent that he is acquainted with or recognizes them, by the precedents and judicial decisions which exist.

Regardless of the basis used in determining the assessment of individual taxable units, the essential steps in the process of assessing are similar under all systems. They are (1) to discover the assessable property, (2) to record the assessable property, and (3) to value the assessable property. While the first two of these duties are important it is the third which is the most difficult.

[1]Rental value for St. John's is defined as "the annual rent at which the property might reasonably be expected to let from year to year, notwithstanding the existence of any lease or agreement to let the same for a greater or lesser sum, without any deduction from such rent being made or allowed in estimating such rental values other than the expenses of any services supplied to the tenant of such property."

Assessors

The assessing function is a municipal one in all the provinces except Manitoba. That province is divided into municipal assessment districts and the assessment in the various municipalities is made by or under the direction of the Provincial Municipal Assessor rather than by municipal assessors. These districts, however, do not include the cities or such urban municipalities and such towns as the Municipal Commissioner decides should be excluded.[2] One-half of the cost of making the assessment is apportioned among the municipalities and local government areas assessed, on the basis of the equalized assessment, and forms part of the Municipal Commissioner's levy.

In the other provinces each municipality is an assessing authority except the county municipalities in Quebec and Ontario. Ontario has county assessors in twenty of the counties[3] but their appointment is optional with the county and they have no original assessing power. Their duties are primarily to supervise and advise the assessors of the local municipalities and they have certain rights of appeal against assessments.

The task of discovering, recording, and valuing the units which will comprise the tax base is done by assessors.[4] They are appointed by the municipal council and are officers which a council must appoint. Usually a council is free to appoint whom it will, but in some cases restrictions may be imposed by statute. In Charlottetown, an assessor must have qualifications similar to those of a councillor; in New Brunswick towns an assessor must be a resident and qualified voter, and parish assessors must be British subjects and ratepayers in the parish; in Alberta municipalities, other than cities, the appointment is subject to the approval of the provincial Minister, unless the secretary-treasurer is the appointee. While several provinces require that a council appoint an assessor annually it is a general practice to reappoint assessors from year to year, and in most larger municipalities the appointments are at pleasure without any definite date of termination.

In some provinces the number of assessors to be appointed by a municipality is specified, in others the council has some discretion as to the number. Usually, however, the council may appoint one or more

[2]It is contemplated by the Department of Municipal Commissioner that eventually all the municipalities will be assessed by the Provincial Municipal Assessor except Winnipeg and possibly St. Boniface.

[3]The appointment of county assessors by county councils was authorized in 1940. The first appointment was made in 1943 and by 1951 twenty of the thirty-eight counties had made such appointments.

[4]Known as appraisers in Newfoundland.

assessors according to the need as determined by it. Where more than one is appointed, the council may assign each to a designated portion of the municipality with each assessor responsible for the assessing which he does, or the assessors may work as a group under the direction of a chief assessor or assessment commissioner.

The responsibility for assessing is a joint one in New Brunswick counties and in Quebec municipalities. New Brunswick county councils may appoint either (*a*) a chairman of assessors and two additional assessors for the county, or (*b*) a chairman and vice-chairman for the county and one assessor for each parish, or (*c*) a chairman of assessors for the county and two assessors for each parish, or (*d*) a chairman and two assessors for each parish.[5] In any case the assessment is a joint responsibility. Similarly, Quebec councils are required to appoint three assessors annually in cities and towns, and every second year in the municipalities under the Municipal Code, and the valuation roll must be signed by two of the three appointees in all cases.

Assessors' duties are set out in detail in provincial statutes which substantially restrict their discretion as to the manner in which they assess, assessment procedures, and the basis of valuation to be used in assessing. In practice, however, the vital task of valuation remains largely a matter of subjective judgment. Assessors are statutory officers and their first duty is to comply with the directions contained in the statute which, as suggested above, may give rise to difficulties in the relationships between councils and assessors. Municipal councils retain jurisdiction in the matter of dismissal and the rate of remuneration of assessors although, at least in the larger municipalities, there is no evidence to indicate that assessors have any less degree of security of tenure than other municipal officers. Because of the probable public reaction to any attempt to penalize an assessor for faithfully carrying out his statutory duties, a council would have to be amply justified before taking drastic action. It may be that in the very delicacy of his position lies the assessor's greatest security.

The Assessing Process

The assessor's function is to prepare an assessment or valuation roll, which involves two tasks. The first, as previously stated, is to discover, record, and value for taxation purposes the assessable property, usually both taxable and exempt, in the municipality. The second is to gather additional information such as the names of the owners or

[5]Of these alternatives (*a*) is not used, (*b*) is used in one county, (*c*) is used in twelve counties, and (*d*) is used in St. John and Kings counties.

occupiers of properties, their occupations, ages, citizenship, status in life, eligibility to vote, religious persuasion, in some cases the classification of schools which they support, etc. This latter task might for brevity be referred to as their census-taking function. Provincial statutes or regulations set out in detail, in most cases, the type of information required in the assessment roll[6] which is obtained for purposes other than taxation, such as the preparation of voters' lists, the selection of jurors, or the allocation of school taxes.

All the provinces except Newfoundland require the annual preparation of an assessment roll but the majority of the provinces do not require an annual revaluation of real property for assessment purposes. In Charlottetown, in the province of Nova Scotia, in Quebec municipalities under the Municipal Code, and in Saskatchewan, the making of an annual assessment is compulsory. The other provinces permit a certain discretion on the part of the municipal council as to whether or not the annual preparation of a roll involves an annual valuation. In Newfoundland, the appraisers must make a return not less frequently than once in every three years; Quebec city and town councils may provide that the valuation roll be prepared not more often than every three years; in Ontario valuation may be on a rotary basis, the valuation of one-half or one-third of the properties being ascertained each year and the balance of the properties being assessed at the last valuations ascertained[7]; Manitoba councils which retain an assessing function, in any year, with the approval of the Provincial Municipal Assessor, may adopt the assessment of the previous year, but not for more than six years following an actual valuation; in Alberta, similarly, a council may adopt the assessment of the previous year but such action may not be taken for more than four consecutive years; British Columbia councils also may adopt the assessment of the previous year, apparently without limitation. Where councils are permitted to adopt the assessment of the previous year, provision is made for annual adjustments to deal with properties which have been added or removed since the last assessment was made.

In practice, however, it is impossible for the assessors to actually revalue each year all the properties to be assessed in the municipality.

[6]In Ontario the Assessment Act provides for twenty-eight items of information to be contained in the assessment roll. In other provinces, such as Manitoba and Saskatchewan, the detail is determined by regulations of a provincial administrative agency.

[7]Where a municipality first adopts the rotary system the valuation thus made is not to be used as the basis of taxation until the entire municipality has been revalued. This provision has not been widely used and in practice there is usually a nominal annual valuation.

The result is that to a great extent, so far as real property is concerned, the various parcels are recorded in the roll in each assessment period at the values of the previous year, with adjustments for any additions or improvements or for any structures which have been removed. An actual valuation is made of new structures which have been erected. If, after the assessment for the year has been completed, there is time available the assessor may revalue properties which he considers require revaluation and will use such revaluation in the assessment of the following year. At irregular intervals there may be a general revaluation of all the lands and buildings in the municipality but this involves such a vast amount of work in proportion to the number on the assessment staff of any municipality, and is so frequently accompanied by violent political repercussions, that there is normally great reluctance to attempt the task.[8]

The usual practice is that the roll is prepared by the assessors and is then "returned" to the municipal clerk.[9] Saskatchewan assessors, however, turn over their rolls to an Assessment Board. This board is a body of three to five persons appointed by the council on which the assessor may sit as a member as may also one or two members of the council. The Assessment Board reviews and corrects the roll.

Notice of Assessment

The assessor must notify the persons assessed, specifying the amount of their assessment and other information and also advising of the date by which any appeal against the assessment must be made. This matter of giving such notice as is required by statute is of prime importance, for, unless the person assessed is notified, he has no knowledge of the amount or equity of his assessment nor has he an opportunity to appeal against any error or inequity. In any subsequent action to enforce the collection of a tax based upon the assessment, the courts will ordinarily hold that a condition precedent to enforcing the tax is that the person liable to taxation must have been notified of the facts with respect to his assessment.

The method of serving assessment notices, the officer who gives the notice, and the persons to be notified, vary from province to province. Newfoundland municipal councils are required to give public notice

[8]"Although the law required that assessment be based on "actual value," it has been admitted to the Commission by a number of municipalities that they have not reassessed real estate for periods of more than ten, twenty, or even thirty years!" H. Carl Goldenberg, *Provincial-Municipal Relations in British Columbia* (Victoria 1947), p. X62.

[9]In Newfoundland the roll is returned by the appraisers to the chairman of the council.

of the filing of the roll but need give individual notices only to persons whose appraisement has been increased, indicating the amount of the increase, and to persons newly appraised, indicating the amount of the appraisement. In Quebec there is a general public notice or advertisement that the roll has been prepared and is open for public inspection. In Nova Scotia "municipalities" and in New Brunswick notice is given by the posting up of a copy of the roll. The other provinces, except in Prince Edward Island towns,[10] provide for individual notification to all persons named in the assessment roll, and, in most cases, a general public notice. Saskatchewan and Alberta, however, provide that in those years in which a council uses the assessment of a previous year, only those individuals need be notified with respect to whose properties there are any changes in assessment or where new properties have been assessed.

The individual notices are sent out by the assessor, except in a few instances such as Charlottetown, Nova Scotia towns, and Alberta municipalities where this is one of the clerk's duties. In Saskatchewan such notices are not sent out until after the roll has been reviewed by the Assessment Board.

Special mention should be made of the New Brunswick procedure where the assessors, on receipt of a warrant for assessment[11] from the council, require by public notice that all persons liable to be rated file with them statements of their assessable property within thirty days.[12] Although the assessor is not bound by these statements, any person who fails to give all necessary information is not entitled to appeal with respect to overvaluation.

The assessors then make a list of the persons assessed and the valuations of their properties, both real and personal, and post copies of the lists for public inspection. Within twenty days appeals may be filed with the assessor by any person on the grounds of overvaluation of his

[10]In Prince Edward Island towns the clerk sends to each taxpayer one notice indicating the amount of his taxes and the assessment upon which he has been taxed. Either the assessment or the taxes may be appealed against within twenty days.

[11]The word assessment as used here is equivalent to the word levy, the warrant stating the amount of money required to be raised.

[12]The Royal Commission on the Rates and Taxes Act reporting in 1951 suggested the difficulty of generalizing respecting New Brunswick procedures as follows: "Although the Act is designed to extend and apply to all parishes, cities and towns in the province and to form the basis for local taxation of all incorporated areas, so many modifications and changes are embodied in other acts and so many of the cities and towns have special legislation governing their taxation authority that the Act now applies to rural municipalities and a few of the towns whose acts of incorporation and other special legislation are not inconsistent with it."

own property, or against undervaluation in the case of another person's property, in which latter case he must state the amount at which he thinks such property should be valued. If the person whose assessment is objected to admits the undervaluation, the assessor adjusts the valuation accordingly and if he does not so admit, the assessors hear the complaint and fix the valuation as to them seems just.

There is an appeal from the decision of the assessors to the county valuators, except that in the case of an appellant whose original return to the assessor was not voluntarily given under oath no appeal is sustained unless the assessor's valuation is more than 15 per cent in excess of the correct amount. A further appeal is provided from the decision of the valuators to the county court judge. Only after such appeals against the valuation lists have been dealt with do the assessors prepare an assessment roll. Any further appeal resulting from individual notification in New Brunswick must be taken on notification of the rates levied.

The New Brunswick procedure has been outlined in some detail here because it differs from the more generally prevailing procedure under which an assessment roll is prepared first and the amount of taxes to be raised is determined later. When the amount to be raised has been fixed by council, it is then levied upon the assessments recorded in the roll which has already been prepared.

Appeals against Assessment

The notice of assessment advises the person assessed of the date before which he must enter an appeal if he is not satisfied with the amount or other detail of his assessment. The matters which are usually the subject of appeal are (1) that a person's name or a property has wrongfully been inserted in or omitted from the roll, (2) that a property is assessed at too high or too low an amount, or (3) in the case of business assessments, that the business has been classified incorrectly. In Quebec cities and towns, where the complaint is that the valuation is too high, the complainant in his notice of complaint must state what he considers to be a just valuation.

Appeals in most cases may be made by any person with respect to either his own assessment or that of any other person, although in Nova Scotia the right of appeal is limited to ratepayers, and in Alberta, to persons whose names appear on the assessment roll. In addition, a specific right of appeal is given to an assessor in Manitoba, a county assessor in Ontario, and a municipal council in Newfoundland and British Columbia. An Ontario county assessor may enter an appeal against an assessment in any municipality forming part of the county and may appeal either against an individual assessment, or in general with respect to all assessments, or to all assessments in certain areas of the municipality, and in either case with respect to land only or improvements or business assessment only.

Appeals must be filed with a designated official, usually the clerk, within a stated period after publication of notice that the assessment has been completed, or after individual notice to the persons assessed. The period varies from fourteen days in Ontario to thirty days in Quebec and in Saskatchewan urban municipalities. The assessment rolls in the interim are open for public inspection. Some provinces provide for a fixed date before which appeals must be filed, as in Nova Scotia "municipalities," eight days before the fourth Tuesday of January, or as in Manitoba and British Columbia, at least ten days before the first meeting of the court. It is the usual practice that all persons entering appeals or whose assessment is the subject of an appeal are notified by the clerk of the date at which the appeal will be dealt with by the court.

Court of revision. The court of first appeal in the matter of assessments is usually designated as a court of revision. The constitution of these courts is as set out in Appendix A to this chapter.

There are some significant differences that should be noted. In most cases the municipal clerk is the clerk of the court, but in Saskatchewan cities and towns the assessor acts in that capacity, and in British Columbia the court selects its own clerk. It is a widespread practice to have the whole or a portion of the council, which might well be considered as an interested party, act as the court. In Charlottetown and Prince Edward Island towns, in Nova Scotia "municipalities," and in Ontario cities and counties members of council are specifically barred from appointment to the court. In a few cases qualifications are established for appointees; thus in Charlottetown they must be residents, in Nova Scotia "municipalities" they must be ratepayers, and in Charlottetown and in Ontario municipalities, other than cities, they must be persons eligible to be elected a member of council.

The extent of the powers of these courts varies. In Ontario and Manitoba the court may not make alterations in the roll except on a complaint formally made, and in several of the other provinces, while there is no such stated limitation, no provision is made for action except on complaint. A Nova Scotia court has power on its own motion to add to the amount of any assessment, from which action there is an appeal to the county court or, in the case of towns, an alternative appeal to the town council, which after a hearing may, if good cause is shown, reverse or modify the decision of the court. In Quebec, however, the court (council) is required to "revise and homologate" the roll whether it be complained of or not, and in British Columbia, in addition to dealing with complaints, the court is required to investigate the roll and assessments, whether complained of or not, "and so adjudicate upon the same that the same shall be fair and equitable and fairly represent the actual value."

In three cases notable limitations are placed upon the courts' powers to deal with complaints. Manitoba provides that the assessment of property complained about is not to be varied by the court if the assessed value bears a fair and just relationship to the value at which other property in the municipality is assessed; but where the assessment was made by a municipal assessor, rather than the Provincial Municipal Assessor, the court, without determining the complaint, may order a new assessment of the whole municipality or of any ward, block, or portion thereof which includes the property complained against. A similar provision is in effect in Alberta. British Columbia does not allow a complaint on the grounds that any lands or improvements are assessed at too high an amount if, in the case of land, the assessment complained of is at least 10 per cent less than its assessment in the previous year and in the case of improvements, if they are assessed at least 5 per cent less than in the previous year.

The court of revision is sometimes described as a poor man's court because, except where large amounts are involved, most parties present their own case rather than incur the expense of being represented by solicitors, there are usually no costs, and the business of the court is conducted in an informal manner to give the complainant every opportunity to present his claims and arguments. While the complainants have the right to be heard, the court also has the right to deal with complaints in the absence of the complainant, provided he has been properly notified that his appeal or complaint is to be dealt with. The assessor in most cases is in attendance at the court to present the evidence or arguments to support the valuation as assessed.

Further appeals. Most provinces provide for an appeal from the decisions of this original court of revision by any person assessed or any other party interested and in Ontario both the assessor and the municipal corporation are given a specific right of appeal. The grounds of appeal may be either the decision of the court or the refusal or neglect of the court to hear the original appeal. Provision is made that the costs of the appeal are to be in the discretion of the judge or other body before whom the appeal is heard, but they are usually limited to the costs for witnesses. There is a provision in Nova Scotia, however, that if the assessment is lowered on appeal the costs shall be paid by the municipality. Both Nova Scotia[13] and Manitoba[14] require a deposit with the appeal, as security for the costs. Persons who wish to appeal from the decision of the court of revision must do so within a fixed time after the date of the decision of the court, varying from a week in British Columbia to thirty days in Quebec.

There is considerable variation in the number of appeals which may be taken on any particular case before the final court of appeal is reached. Except, as indicated in Appendix B to this chapter, where an appeal is limited to a matter of law, the general procedure is that at each stage of appeal the authority hearing the appeal may reopen the whole matter under appeal and deal with the matter *de novo*, and is not limited to the issues raised at the previous level of appeal. The taxpayer is thus given ample opportunity to obtain a hearing in any case where he feels that his assessment is inequitable. The bulk of the appeals or complaints are disposed of at the original court of revision. The number of appeals tends to be higher when economic conditions are poor as it becomes worth the citizen's time and effort to obtain minor adjustments in assessment. There also is a larger number of appeals immediately following any general revaluation of properties with the consequent upward adjustments in assessment. When all the appeals have been disposed of the assessment roll is said to be "finally revised."

Regular Review of Assessments

Some provinces, in addition to providing for appeals by individuals, provide for a review of the assessments even though there has been no appeal. Quebec city and town councils are required to "revise and homologate" the roll whether complained of or not and in Quebec municipalities under the Code the council is more specifically authorized to fix "at such sum as it thinks reasonable any valuation of taxable property which it believes to have been made under or above its true, real or annual value."

Saskatchewan city councils appoint an assessment board, composed of three to five members, one of whom is the assessor and one or two of whom may be members of council. This board, before any assessment notices are sent out, makes corrections and amendments which

[13]$100.
[14]$5.00 for the first appeal and $2.00 for each additional appeal.

it deems necessary to maintain equity between assessments. Similar boards occur in other Saskatchewan municipalities but in these latter cases they have no authority to alter the amounts of assessments.

While Alberta does not provide for such a review as a normal procedure, the Alberta Assessment Commission on the hearing of an appeal, if in its opinion the assessment is so inequitable that substantial justice cannot be done by adjusting the assessment in the cases then on appeal, may order that the whole assessment be quashed and a new assessment made. Courts of revision in British Columbia also may investigate the various assessments made in the roll, whether or not they have been appealed against, and may alter the assessments so that they shall be fair and equitable and fairly represent the actual value.

Special Review of Assessments

In a few cases provision is made for a special general review of assessments in addition to the regular type of review mentioned above. Charlottetown legislation permits the council at intervals of not less than five years to appoint for a single year a General Assessment Board of not less than three members, to be appointed by council and approved by the Lieutenant-Governor in Council. This board assumes all the duties of the assessor who, during such year, has no official authority or responsibility for the assessment but is retained in office to give assistance and information to the board and resumes his active duties and responsibilities after the board had completed its general valuation. It is the board's duty to examine and review all valuations and assessments to effect reasonably equitable valuation generally throughout the city and to make the regular annual assessment for the ensuing year as the city assessor would otherwise do.

The Board of Revision in Nova Scotia "municipalities," in the course of personally valuing properties for equalization purposes (see below), may reduce or increase individual assessments which they are satisfied are disproportionate or unjust.

Saskatchewan and Alberta provide for provincial review of assessments. In the former province a general revaluation of all rural municipalities was started in 1939. In 1948 this work was transferred to the Department of Municipal Affairs and extended to all municipalities except cities over 15,000.[15] The revaluation of the rural municipalities had been completed by 1948 and the urban municipalities by 1950. The cost of such revaluation is repaid to the province by the munici-

[15]The Assessment Branch of the Department of Municipal Affairs will undertake the revaluation of cities over 15,000 on request and did so in Moose Jaw in 1951–2.

palities. In Alberta, if the provincial Director of Assessments is of the opinion that it is in the public interest to have a new assessment in any municipality because it is not in substantial conformity with the law or is not fair and equitable, he may so certify to the Minister of Municipal Affairs who may then declare the whole or any part of the assessment to be null and void, and direct a new assessment to be made. If in the Minister's opinion, after inquiry, the assessor of the municipality is incompetent or unsuitable, he may order the council to replace the assessor with an appointee approved by the Minister, and if the council fail to do so within thirty days, the Minister may dismiss the assessor, appoint another in his place, and fix his remuneration.

Equalization of Assessments

Although provincial legislation provides in a general way for the basis on which values for assessment purposes are to be determined, there are wide variations in the results in different municipalities. Because the element of human judgment is so important in this work, comparable properties in adjacent municipalities operating under the same provincial laws may be assessed at vastly different amounts. This would be of little significance were it not that there are many instances where the taxpayers of a number of municipalities, in addition to paying taxes to maintain the local municipal services, are taxed also for their share of expenses which are borne jointly with the taxpayers of other municipalities, as is the case in the local municipalities comprising a county.

To obtain a greater degree of equity in sharing these joint expenditures it is necessary to bring the assessments of the various municipalities to a comparable basis by the process usually referred to as equalization. Such equalization, however, is necessary not only as a basis for sharing of joint municipal expenditures but for several other purposes. It is needed to establish a fair basis for the distribution of charges which some provinces make against their municipalities, such as judicial district expenses in Manitoba, which are allocated to the municipalities comprising the district according to their equalized assessments. It is also required to provide a fairer basis for provincial real property taxation where such taxes are collected by the municipalities on behalf of the province, as in the Saskatchewan public revenue tax. It is desirable also where provincial grants to municipalities are related to the assessment.

All the provinces except Newfoundland, Prince Edward Island, and British Columbia provide for a system of equalization, but the machinery varies. In Nova Scotia assessments are equalized by the board of revision, the body which hears original assessment appeals; in New Brunswick, by special valuators appointed by each county; in Quebec and Ontario, by the county councils; in Manitoba, by the Municipal Assessment Equalization and Appeal Board; in Saskatchewan, by the Minister of Municipal Affairs; and in Alberta, by the Alberta Assessment Commission. The equalization is of less significance in Manitoba and Saskatchewan than in the other provinces to the extent that the original assessments are made by provincial assessors.

A Nova Scotia board of revision is required to equalize the assessments of the various districts in the "municipality" (county) annually, although the council may suspend the work of revision for any year. The members of the board are required to examine the various assessment rolls, to visit the various districts, and personally to value as many properties as are necessary to verify the valuations of the assessors. The board may increase or decrease the aggregate valuation of real and personal property in any district sufficiently to produce a just relation between the various districts, but may not reduce the aggregate valuation for the whole "municipality" as made by the assessors. The board has the power, however, to reduce or increase individual assessments that are disproportionate or unjust, subject to a right of appeal to the County Court. In addition to the problem of equalizing the assessments within the "municipality" there is in Nova Scotia the problem of sharing joint costs between the "municipality" and any cities or towns. To deal with this problem the council of each "municipality," city, and town annually appoints an arbitration committee of not more than five of its own members. This committee has power to adjust the objects of joint municipal expenditure and the proportion of such expenditure which, having regard to a uniform standard of assessment, should be borne by each. If an arbitration committee fail to agree, the matter is finally settled by an arbitration board composed of one arbitrator appointed by each party, and a third member being selected by the two appointees.

In New Brunswick three county valuators[16] are appointed by each county council for a term of three years. A valuation is supposed to be made at intervals of not less than five years or more than ten, but at the request of the council the Lieutenant-Governor in Council may extend the time for a further period up to two years. The assessors are required to supply the board of valuators with schedules setting out the

[16]Nine for the County and City of Saint John—five from the City of Saint John, and one from each of four parishes.

taxable property and other information required and the valuators in revising the schedules must value personally as many properties as are necessary to secure a uniform standard of valuation. The valuators then make a list for each parish, city, or town which is to be used as the basis for apportionment of county rates until the next valuation. There is an appeal to a provincial board of revision, composed of three members, if it is made to appear to the Lieutenant-Governor in Council that the county valuators have not observed a common standard of valuation, or have not applied the principles of the governing legislation, to the substantial prejudice of any municipality. The decision of the provincial board is final and any expense of the provincial board is payable by the county.

Quebec county councils annually examine the valuation rolls of the local municipalities and increase or decrease the valuation roll in any case by any percentage the council consider necessary to establish a just proportion between all the rolls but it may not reduce the total amount of all the valuation rolls. The valuation rolls as thus amended serve only for county purposes.

The plan of having special county valuators equalize assessments at intervals was abolished in Ontario in 1944. Counties now may appoint a county assessor whose function is to supervise and advise the local assessors for the purpose of making more uniform the methods of preparing assessment rolls in the different municipalities and to find out whether the valuations of real property in the municipalities bear a just relation to one another. Where a county assessor has been appointed he reports to the county council annually and his report forms the basis for equalization. The county council annually examines the rolls of the various local municipalities for the previous year, adding or deducting such percentage as is necessary to produce a just relationship, but without reducing the aggregate valuation. Any municipality may appeal against the equalization. The appeal may be to the county judge or, if either party objects to having the matter dealt with by the county judge, the Lieutenant-Governor in Council appoints a special court of three persons to make the final equalization. There is also an appeal from either the county judge or the special court to the Court of Appeal on a question of law or the construction of a statute.

In the western provinces the task of equalization is approached with a much wider view for, while in the more easterly provinces equalization is limited to the county area, the Prairie Provinces attempt to attain province-wide equalization. The Municipal Assessment Equalization and Appeal Board of Manitoba is required to equalize biennially the assessment of all property liable to assessment in all the municipalities, including cities, and local government districts. The basis of equalization is the full value of all real property and two-thirds the value of all buildings. This equalization is the basis of apportionment of the Municipal Commissioner's annual levies.

Prior to 1948, in Saskatchewan, equalization was the function of the Saskatchewan Assessment Commission but in that year was placed under the Minister of Municipal Affairs. A municipality, however, may appeal to the Commission from the equalized assessment as determined by the Minister and it may alter the assessment accordingly.

Alberta has a provincial Director of Assessments assisted by inspectors. His duty is to establish equalized assessments for all municipalities and the director or an inspector may cancel the assessment of any parcel of property and make a new assessment of it. The secretary-treasurer of each municipality makes an annual return of the detail and the aggregate of the local assessment which the director compares with all such returns so that the assessments of ratable land in all municipalities shall be on a common basis of valuation and shall be fair and equitable as between one another. He confirms the assessment or varies it by making such decrease or increase as he thinks necessary and then confirms the assessment so varied. This confirmed assessment becomes the equalized assessment. Where in a municipal district the equalized assessment differs from the total as fixed by the local assessor, the difference is divided by the secretary-treasurer among all the parcels of land separately assessed in the district, in proportion to their assessment. The assessed value so determined is the value to be used for taxation of land, exclusive of improvements, by the municipal district or by collecting school districts. In the case of urban municipalities the director, in determining the equalized assessment, is required to consider the area, population, land values, the business transacted within the limits of the municipality, the equalized assessments of contiguous municipal districts, and such factors as in his opinion should be considered in order to equalize the bearing of taxes upon the different classes of municipalities. An appeal from any order of the director, with respect to equalization, may be made by any municipality to the provincial Assessment Commission.

APPENDIX A

Constitution of Municipal Assessment Appeal Courts or Courts of Revision

(under general legislation)

Newfoundland	
All municipalities[a]	The stipendiary magistrate or other person appointed by the Lieutenant-Governor in Council
Prince Edward Island	
Charlottetown	3 members—one appointed by the Lieutenant-Governor in Council and two residents appointed by council
Towns	The magistrate and two persons appointed by council
Nova Scotia	
Municipalities	3 members—ratepayers appointed by council[b]
Towns	4 members—three councillors and the town solicitor
New Brunswick	
All municipalities[c]	The assessors; for non-residents, the county valuators
Quebec	
All municipalities	Whole council
Ontario	
Cities over 200,000	One member—a barrister appointed by council[d]
Other cities	3 members—one appointed by council, one by the mayor, one ex-officio, or in some cases appointed by council[e]
Other local municipalities	5 members—appointed by council, may be councillors or others
Counties	Where there is a county assessor the county council may appoint five non-councillors in which case the local courts are not appointed
Manitoba	
All municipalities	Whole council
Saskatchewan	
Cities	3 to 5 members of council, or council may appoint the city commissioners to be the court
Other municipalities	Whole council
Alberta	
Cities	Council may appoint a court of three non-council members or 3 to 5 members of council
Other municipalities	Whole council
British Columbia	
All municipalities	Whole council, or council may appoint five of its members

[a]The St. John's court of revision consists of two or more persons appointed by the Lieutenant-Governor in Council.

[b]No two of the members may be residents of the same district.

[c]The Fredericton court consists of three members appointed by council who are neither members of council nor its employees. They deal with appeals from the decision of the assessor on appeal.

[d]Alternatively council may provide for one or more three-man courts.

[e]The third member is the official arbitrator, but if there is no such officer or if he is the county judge, the sheriff is the third member, except that where the city is not the county town the council appoints the third member.

APPENDIX B

Appeal Procedure on Assessments beyond the Original Court of Revision

	First appeal to	Second appeal to	Third appeal to
Newfoundland	Supreme Court		
Prince Edward Island[a]	Supreme Court		
Nova Scotia	County Court		
New Brunswick	County valuators (in counties)	County judge	
Quebec	Circuit Court of county or district	Court of Queen's Bench[b]	
Ontario	County judge[c]	Ontario Municipal Board[c]	Court of Appeal[d]
Manitoba	Municipal Assessment Equalization and Appeal Board	Court of Queen's Bench[e]	
Saskatchewan	Saskatchewan Assessment Commission	Court of Appeal[f]	
Alberta	Alberta Municipal Assessment Commission		
British Columbia	Judge of County or Supreme Court	Court of Appeal[g]	

[a]This refers to Charlottetown: in the towns the decision of the court of revision is final.

[b]Limited to cases where the real estate tax based on the contested valuation amounts to $500.

[c]There is also a right to appeal directly to the Ontario Municipal Board from the court of revision without first appealing to the county judge. A recent decision of the Court of Appeal determined that the Board has no jurisdiction to decide whether a person is liable to assessment or exempt therefrom (*Quance* vs. *Thomas A. Ivey & Sons, Limited*)

[d]Appeal is limited to questions of law or the construction of a statute, by-law, written agreement to which the municipality is a party, or an order of the Ontario Municipal Board. There is also an appeal direct from a judge on similar grounds by way of a stated case, at the request of a party on the hearing of the appeal.

[e]The Municipal Assessment Equalization and Appeal Board may submit a stated case on a question of a law to the Court of Queen's Bench and any person affected by the Commission's decision, including the municipality, may within seven days of decision require the submission of a stated case on a question of law only, not involving a question of valuation.

[f]A provision similar to that in Manitoba is made with respect to a stated case on a question of law except that the appellent "may request" submission of a stated case within 30 days. There is a right of appeal to the Court of Appeal on the matter of public or separate school assessment.

[g]Limited to points of law raised on the hearing before the judge.

CHAPTER XIV

REAL PROPERTY ASSESSMENT

THE THREE TYPES or classes of assessments which are of major importance as indicated in Table 19 are the real property assessment, personal property assessment, and business assessment.

Two main points of interest with respect to real property assessment are what constitutes real property for assessment purposes, and the basis upon which it is to be valued. The statutory definitions of land[1] for assessment purposes vary somewhat from province to province in detail. The Ontario definition, for example, provides that the term includes "(i) Land covered with water; (ii) all trees and underwood growing upon land; (iii) all mines, minerals, gas, oil, salt quarries and fossils in and under land; (iv) all buildings, or any part of any building, and all structures, machinery and fixtures erected or placed upon, in, over, under, or affixed to land; (v) all structures and fixtures erected or placed upon, in, over, under, or affixed to any highway, land, or other public communication or water; but not the rolling stock of any transportation system." While this definition is more extensive and detailed than some, the essential content of the term as used in the various provinces does not differ greatly. Thus, land or real property includes both the ground and the improvements or buildings attached to the ground.

Somewhat more variation appears when the provinces attempt to determine the basis of valuation for land. The basis for valuation of buildings sometimes differs from that provided for land in its restricted sense. Each province has attempted to put into words in the statute the conception of the basis to be used in valuing land. In no case are the terms used of much real guidance to an assessing officer. The terms used are as follows: value (Manitoba), fair value (Saskatchewan), actual value (Ontario and British Columbia), real value (Quebec), fair actual value (Alberta), actual cash value (Prince Edward Island and Nova Scotia) and full cash value (New Brunswick).[2]

Some provinces have attempted to amplify or define these general terms. Nova Scotia provides that the term "actual cash value" is the

[1]The terms "land," "real estate," and "real property" are used interchangeably in most cases.

[2]In Charlottetown the basis is "full, true and real value."

amount which in the opinion of the assessor it would realize in cash, if offered at auction after reasonable notice, but in forming such opinion the assessor is to have regard to the assessment of other property of the like class in the municipality. New Brunswick interprets "full cash value" assessment to be the same as if the property were "to be appraised as belonging to the estate of a deceased person." Saskatchewan's statutory comment on "fair value" is that the "dominant and controlling factor shall be equity."

Several of the other provinces, instead of defining the terms used, have set out the factors to be considered by the assessor in arriving at a value. Thus, in Ontario consideration is to be given to the present use, location, revenue, normal sale value, and any other circumstances affecting the value. A Manitoba or Alberta assessor is to consider, among other things, the advantages and disadvantages of the location, the quality of the soil, the annual rental value the lands are reasonably worth for the purpose for which they may be used, the value of the standing timber, and such other considerations as the Assessment Commission directs. British Columbia provides that an assessor may give consideration to present use, location, original cost, cost of replacement, revenue or rental value, the price which the land and improvements might be reasonably expected to bring if offered for sale in the open market by a solvent owner, and any other circumstance affecting the value. Prince Edward Island and Quebec, perhaps wisely, do not attempt to interpret the meaning of their own words.

In practice, value for assessment purposes ultimately is determined by the judgment of the assessor involved, subject to any decision of a higher authority on appeal. Numerous systems of arriving at valuations for both land and buildings have been worked out but even these when applied do not completely solve the problem, for the weight to be given to each of a wide variety of factors influencing value still remains a matter for the assessors' judgment.

The basis of valuation for assessment of buildings and improvements is different from that for land in the five westerly provinces and is as shown in Tables 32 and 33.

Just what is the actual basis of valuation, as distinct from the legal basis, is difficult to determine because of the difficulty of precisely defining a basis of valuation and because of varying local practices and changing conditions.[8] Even per capita assessments, while useful in roughly comparing the taxable capacities of municipalities, give no

[8]Records kept by the city of London show that for 1,033 properties sold in 1936 the assessment was 99.1 per cent of the selling price while for 3,226 properties sold in 1949 the percentage was 46.1.

measurable indication of assessing standards because numerous other factors enter into such per capita figures.[4] There are, however, several generalizations that are agreed upon by those who have studied assessments. One is that there is a general tendency to under-assess and that this tendency is probably more marked in rural and smaller urban municipalities. Another is that there is a tendency toward greater under-assessment of more valuable properties than in the case of less valuable properties.

Two major factors to be considered in determining the value of land, as distinct from buildings or improvements, are fertility and location. In rural areas the factor of fertility is of greater importance while in urban areas the location or site value is the more important. In either case there are numerous qualifying factors to be considered. While fertility is the dominant factor in arriving at a valuation of rural land, that value is influenced by accessibility to markets and highways, water supply, schools, etc. On the other hand in assessing urban land such factors as proximity to schools, parks, paved streets, and transportation and the type of neighbourhood may affect the value of land used for residential purposes, and for land for commercial or industrial use numerous other factors have an influence on value. One difficulty in the valuation of land as compared to buildings is that "no two pieces of land are identical; since one of the principal characteristics of land is location, and this is not subject to duplication." Even the other factors which influence land value, such as fertility, accessibility, etc., are seldom found in the same combination in any two parcels.

TABLE 32

BASIS OF VALUATION OF BUILDINGS AND IMPROVEMENTS FOR ASSESSMENT IN PROVINCES WHERE BASIS DIFFERS FROM THAT FOR LAND

Province	Basis of valuation of buildings and improvements
Ontario	The amount by which the value of the land is thereby increased
Manitoba	Two-thirds of the value (buildings on land used for grain growing, stock raising, and market gardening where income from such is chief source of livelihood of owner or tenant not be be assessed)
Saskatchewan	Not more than 60 per cent of fair value (buildings used for agricultural operations of land not to be assessed)
Alberta	In cities at 60 per cent of fair actual value, in other municipalities at 100 per cent (farm buildings and improvements not to be assessed)

[4]E.g., per capita figures will show wide variations as between a heavily industrialized municipality and one that is largely residential.

TABLE 33

LEGAL BASIS OF ASSESSMENT OF REAL PROPERTY FOR TAXATION AS RELATED TO VALUE

Province	Land	Buildings and improvements
Prince Edward Island	100%	100%
Nova Scotia	100	100
New Brunswick	100	100
Quebec	100	100
Ontario	100	100
Manitoba	100	66⅔
Saskatchewan	100	Cities and towns 60% maximum[a] Villages and rural municipalities 60%
Alberta	100	In cities 60% of fair actual value to be entered on the assessment roll Town and villages 100% Municipal districts 100%
British Columbia	100	75% maximum[b]

[a]Council may fix a lower percentage, e.g. Regina assessment is on a 30% basis.
[b]Council may fix a lower percentage, e.g. Vancouver, 1895–1905, 50%; 1906–9, 25%; 1910–1917, nil; 1918, 25%; 1919 to date, 50%.

The determination of values for buildings for assessment purposes is, in theory, a more simple task for "the maximum value of reproducible property may be said to equal the cost of reproducing it" and the "lower end of the range is the salvage value the improvement may have in the form of materials, less the cost of removing it."

There are many practical problems involved, however, in the valuation of a particular building or improvement within the range indicated. Without going into the details of the various systems used in determining values of buildings and improvements for assessment purposes it is generally accepted, though not always applied, that a sound basis is reproduction cost less due allowance for depreciation and obsolescence. Depreciation here referred to is physical depreciation and there are several methods of determining the depreciation factors which are used. Obsolescence, for assessing purposes, is defined "as a loss in value resulting from shifting demands which are not offset by similar changes in supply."

Carefully prepared and intricate methods of arriving at proper assessable values and elaborate tables of allowances for depreciation and obsolescence have been worked out and are applied in some of the larger municipalities. The difficulty with which most of the smaller municipalities are met is the cost of providing sufficient staff competent to make what is sometimes referred to as a scientific assessment. It is doubtful if there are sufficient men so qualified to meet the needs of the municipalities if they could afford the cost.

An attempt is being made in some of the provinces, both by the provincial authorities and by professional associations of assessors, to raise the standards of assessment and the qualifications of those engaged in this work. Examples of what is being done are the schools for assessors encouraged by the New Brunswick Department of Municipal Affairs and the *Manual* issued by the Ontario Department to assist local assessors. Increasing pressure of municipal taxation, together with the problem of the distribution of certain provincial costs, grants, and joint municipal expenditures, have combined to compel a general trend toward improvement in a field which in the past has been somewhat less than satisfactory, and with it has come a greater appreciation of the importance of assessment in municipal finance.

UNDER-ASSESSMENT

The tendency for assessors to under-assess properties is based on several factors. An assessor must always be prepared when there is an appeal to the court of revision to justify the valuation which he places upon any property and it is only to be expected that, with every desire to carry out the full intent of the Act under which he operates, he yet will err on the safe side so that if possible his valuations will not be upset on appeal; nor are the property owners as likely to appeal if their assessment is lower than the value which they themselves place on their property. Not infrequently assessors, who are under constant pressure, uttered or unexpressed, both from their councils and the taxpayers, may justify a policy of under-assessment by the fact that equity in assessment is the primary aim and that if all are equally under-assessed there is no inequity.

The difficulty is that, once there is a departure from the standard of valuation established by statute, it is impossible for the citizen to have any assurance that other taxpayers may not be under-assessed to an even greater extent than he is. Even though he may know that his assessment is relatively high he is hesitant to appeal his assessment for he knows that according to the statutory basis of valuation his appeal is not on sound grounds to start with.[5]

Even though the assessor who follows a policy of under-assessment

[5]This would not apply in Saskatchewan municipalities where the statutory provisions are that "the dominant and controlling factor in assessment of lands and buildings shall be equity" and that where the value in specific cases appears to be more or less than the fair value the assessment is not to be varied on appeal if the assessed value bears a fair and just proportion to the value at which other lands or buildings in the municipality are assessed. It is of interest to note that the Tax Commission in 1936 found that these provisions in large part had been responsible for maintaining assessed values above actual values.

may be scrupulously fair in his application of the policy, he sacrifices one of the essentials of satisfactory assessing. The citizen who realizes that he is under-assessed may feel that such a situation enables him to shift some of his share of the burden of taxation but at the same time it leaves in his mind the thought that others are obtaining even greater benefits. This in turn breeds distrust of the whole job of assessing and nothing is more damaging to public confidence in the assessor than the suspicion that there is not uniformity of treatment for all.

In addition to the desire of the individual to have his property under-assessed in the hope of getting a relative advantage over his fellow taxpayers there is a further incentive to collective under-assessment. This occurs when municipalities share with other municipalities in the cost of joint expenditures, as in a county. Despite the existence of systems of equalization designed to bring assessments in municipalities which share in joint expenditures to an approximately common standard, there is still the underlying hope that by holding down the total assessment of the municipality there may be some advantage gained, as compared with others, in bearing these joint costs. This tendency is somewhat offset where provincial grants are directly proportionate to assessment, for in such cases the municipality which is under-assessed loses a portion of the grant which it might otherwise receive. On the other hand, however, the tendency is accentuated where grants vary inversely as to the assessment.

It is generally agreed by those who have studied assessment problems that the only satisfactory basis of assessing, if equity is to be attained and public confidence inspired, is full value as specified by law. There are many points at which the assessor is expected to use his judgment, but the application of the standard established by statute is not one in which he is justified in exercising his discretion.

Assessment Lag

Assessment values tend to lag behind general upward and downward trends in market values with the result that in periods of economic depression assessments will be relatively high compared to current sale prices and in periods of high sale prices the assessment values will be relatively low. Assessors argue that sales are not a true indication of value, and that sale price is only one of the factors to be considered in determining value. They aim to maintain an even level of assessment free from the violent fluctuations which occur in the real property market, in part with a view to greater stability in municipal finance and in part to give the assessor an opportunity to determine if the peak or low sale prices are the result of short-run movements or if the changed levels, either upward or downward, represent a relatively permanent adjustment of values.

Councils, and those who are responsible for the spending policies of the municipality, when faced with soaring costs in a period of rising prices, argue that as a means of keeping the tax rate relatively stable assessments should be adjusted upward in recognition of the rising values of real property.[6] When the real property market is depressed, however, there is not the same enthusiasm for following the trend the other way, for there is more public appeal in a reduction of a tax rate than in accomplishing the same end by a reduction in assessment. The possibility of adjustment downward is complicated by the fact that it would normally come at a time when councils are desperate for revenues and when it would not be feasible to reduce the tax base.

The official attitude of assessors appears to be that while they are not prepared to follow the upward and downward swings of sale values they must recognize what appear to be established changes in the levels of values. Their position in relation to the rapidly rising value in the 1940's has been described as "mid-way between an ostrich-like attitude of refusing to believe that real estate values have increased at all and the other extreme that even the wildest prices are a fair reflection and determinant of value for tax purposes."[7]

Comparative Taxable Real Property Assessments

There is wide variation in the per capita assessments between different classes of municipalities and also between different municipalities within any one classification as indicated in Tables 34 and 35. The average per capita assessment is greater in larger municipalities than in smaller ones in the eastern provinces, owing in part to the concentration of industrial and commercial properties in the larger places and in part to the fact that the necessity of raising proportionately larger revenues has resulted in the standard of valuation in the larger places being brought somewhat closer to full-value assessment. Similar influences result in marked variations between municipalities within the same population class. Such difference may be accounted for also by other factors such as the extent of exempt properties, the number of fixed assessments, the nature and extent of the industrial or com-

[6]"Until a practical attitude is adopted toward establishing a realistic relationship between actual and assessed values . . . the municipalities are leaving untapped a legitimate source of revenue." The Municipal and Public Utility Board, Manitoba, *Twenty-third Annual Report* (1950), p. 2.

[7]*Assessment Administration* (National Association of Assessing Officers, 1946), p. 11.

TABLE 34

PER CAPITA TAXABLE ASSESSMENTS OF REAL PROPERTY IN VARIOUS CLASSES OF MUNICIPALITIES IN CERTAIN CANADIAN PROVINCES[a]

Province	Cities	Towns and/or villages	Basic rural unit
Nova Scotia	$ 774	$ 367	$ 133 (municipalities)
New Brunswick	792	699	411 (counties)
Quebec	904	681	398 (townships, etc.)
Ontario	1,123	514	686 (townships)
Manitoba	1,004	503[b]	
Saskatchewan	638	512	1,348 (rural municipalities)
Alberta	638	617	1,049 (municipal districts)
British Columbia[c]	632	400	559 (district municipalities)

[a]All figures are for the year 1949 except those for Quebec which are for 1946.
[b]Based on sixteen towns.
[c]Assessments used are those actually taxed.

TABLE 35

PER CAPITA TAXABLE ASSESSMENTS OF REAL PROPERTY IN CITIES OF 10,000 OR OVER (1950)

Province	No.	High	Low	Average
Nova Scotia	2	$ 906	$564	$735
New Brunswick	3	1,059	672	920
Quebec[a]	22	2,539	399	856
Ontario	29	1,635	504	856
Manitoba	3	1,118	560	791
Saskatchewan	4	766	575	646
Alberta	4	808	600	727
British Columbia[b]	9	759	370	576

[a]Figures are for the year 1944.
[b]Assessments actually taxed.

mercial development, etc. In comparisons between provinces the extensive exemption of improvements in the western provinces must be kept in mind.

EXEMPTIONS

Each province provides that properties owned by certain classes of owners or devoted to certain uses shall be wholly or in part exempt from municipal taxation. The municipalities consider that these exemptions constitute one of their major financial problems, for although the exempt properties receive the benefit of the municipal services they make no contribution toward the cost. The owners of properties liable to taxation are thus required to subsidize the owners of exempt property to the extent of what would otherwise be their share of the municipal taxes.

The proportion of such exempt property is usually greater in the larger urban municipalities than in the smaller and rural communities although there are exceptions to this generalization. There is also considerable variation in the proportion of exempt property between municipalities of comparable size even within one province.

The exemptions can be divided into two classes, those that are compulsory under general legislation of the province or under some special or private Act and those which are optional with the local council. This latter group would include what are known as fixed assessments.

Compulsory Exemptions

Somewhat in excess of fifty different types of otherwise assessable and taxable properties are declared by law to be exempt from municipal taxation in the various provinces. The more frequently recurring types or classes of property specifically exempted by general legislation are shown in the accompanying chart.

	Types or classes of land exempt from municipal taxation	*Provinces in which such exemptions occur*
1.	Property of the Crown	10
2.	Churches and places of worship	10
3.	Municipal property	9
4.	Cemeteries	8
5.	Common schools	8
6.	Colleges and institutions of learning	8
7.	Property of agricultural societies	7
8.	Charitable institutions	6
9.	Public libraries	5
10.	Registry offices	5
11.	Property of the Canadian Legion	4
12.	Buildings used in agricultural operations	3
13.	Property of agricultural exhibitions	2
14.	Property of literary societies and institutions	2
15.	Property of children's aid societies	2
16.	Community halls	2
17.	Sites of historic buildings	2

There are a few cases of compassionate exemptions, as in Nova Scotia where widows have a statutory exemption up to $400 which a local council may increase to $1,000. Similarly in New Brunswick a female who is not supported by her husband is entitled to an exemption of her interest in real property up to $500 provided her total interest therein does not exceed $5,000. This has resulted in numerous attempts at tax evasion by the deeding of property to females.

The classes of exempt property which are of major importance in amount are properties owned by the municipality, the Dominion and provincial governments, school authorities, churches, and in western provinces the improvements, in both rural and urban municipalities. The relative importance of these different classes varies according to local conditions. The total extent of the exemptions in effect is indicated on Table 36. In interpreting the table it must be kept in mind that optional exemptions are extensive in the western provinces.

While the percentages of exemptions as between provinces differ greatly, there is also a wide variation between comparable municipalities within a province and also between different classes of municipalities. In seven Quebec cities studied the percentage of exempt property varied from 17.4 to 37.7, and in twenty-eight Ontario cities, from 10 to 42. Again, comparisons within the western provinces are complicated by optional exemptions, which will be discussed below, in addition to statutory exemptions.

Table 37 indicates the distribution of real property exemption in a number of Canadian cities. Within the city group where the proportion of the total assessment which is exempt is excessively high, it is usually due to the extent of Crown property, as in Halifax and Saint John where the exempt properties constitute 51.2 and 55.6 per cent respectively of the total assessment and in which cases the exemptions of Dominion property constitute 61.2 and 74.5 per cent of the total exemptions. Similarly in Ontario, where the average percentage of exempt property in twenty-eight cities is 19.7, the percentages in the cities of Ottawa, Kingston, and Niagara Falls, where there are ex-

TABLE 36

REAL PROPERTY EXEMPTIONS FOR TAXATION PURPOSES—1946[a]
(000's omitted)

Province	Taxable assessment	Exemptions[b]	Total assessment	Percentage exempt
Prince Edward Island	$ 10,984	$ 6,101	$ 17,085	$35.6
Nova Scotia	157,154	93,799	250,953	37.3
New Brunswick	172,431	see below[c]	172,431	
Quebec	2,436,210[d]	834,183	3,270,393	25.5
Ontario	2,890,673	440,985	3,331,658	13.5
Manitoba	445,388	159,400	604,788	26.3
Saskatchewan	782,937	98,992	881,929	11.2
Alberta	516,607	65,334	581,941	11.2
British Columbia	448,357	433,520[e]	881,877	49.1
Total	$7,860,741	$2,132,314	$9,993,055	21.3[f]

[a]Based on the *Canada Year Book, 1948–49*, p. 1000.
[b]The figures for Manitoba, Saskatchewan, and Alberta do not include the values of non-assessable improvements used for agricultural purposes.
[c]Information not available.
[d]This figure is for 1945 and includes all types of assessment.
[e]Consists of $188,328,203 valuation of exempt properties and $245,192,116 exemption of taxable improvements.
[f]This percentage is less than it would be were the information respecting New Brunswick available.

TABLE 37

REAL PROPERTY EXEMPTIONS IN CERTAIN CANADIAN CITIES
(in millions of dollars)

City	*City owned*	*School*	*Dominion*	*Provincial*	*Churches*	*Other*	*Total*
Halifax	$ 5.6	$ 8.3[a]	$35.4	$ 3.4	$	$ 4.9	$ 57.8
Saint John	2.7	2.3	27.4	.4	2.7	1.0	36.8
Moncton	1.5	1.9	14.3		1.5	.1	19.4
Montreal	113.1	64.6	71.1	15.0	35.0	49.8	349.7
Westmount	5.6	1.8	.9	.5	4.2	1.4	14.7
London	4.0	3.1	2.0	1.9	1.7	1.5	14.4
Winnipeg	16.0	5.4	3.9	6.8	2.9	18.5[b]	53.8

[a]Includes education, religious, and charitable exemptions.
[b]$15,120,000 of this amount is made up of railway property exemptions.

tensive Crown properties, are 42, 32.9, and 38 respectively. That this is not exclusively an urban problem is evidenced by Sidney Township in Ontario in which 65 per cent of the assessment is exempt and 95 per cent of the exempt property is Crown property.

Optional Exemptions

In Saskatchewan and British Columbia, provincial statutes establish the maximum percentage of the value of improvements at which they may be assessed. But the local councils in Saskatchewan cities and town and in all British Columbia municipalities may provide for the assessment of improvements at a lower percentage than the statutory maximum or even for complete exemption. The extent to which local councils have used this privilege in two of the provinces is shown in Table 38. It suggests the difficulty of comparisons between municipalities in different provinces.

The practice of permitting extensive exemptions of improvements in the western provinces developed in the early years of rapid expansion as a result of the popularity of the single tax idea, but has been severely criticized. The Commission of Inquiry into Provincial and Municipal Taxation reported in 1936:[8]

> The Commission believes that buildings and improvements should be assessed at 100 per cent of value. . . .
>
> To encourage the improvement of land it has long been the policy in Saskatchewan to either exempt other forms of property value than land from taxation, or to treat other forms of property more favourably than land. During the first two decades of the present century buildings and improvements were assessed at an even lower percentage of full value

[8]*Report of the Commission of Inquiry into Provincial and Municipal Taxation to the Government of the Province of Saskatchewan* (1936), p. 178.

TABLE 38

TAXED ASSESSMENT OF BUILDINGS AND IMPROVEMENTS AS A PERCENTAGE OF ASSESSED VALUES IN ALBERTA AND BRITISH COLUMBIA MUNICIPALITIES, 1946

Municipalities	Percentages																					
	0	10	15	20	25	30	33⅓	35	40	45	50	55	58⅓	60	65	66⅔	70	75	80	85	90	100
Alberta:																						
Cities											3		1			2						
Towns														3		26	1	3	4	1	1	14
Villages											1					45		2			1	80
Districts																all						
British Columbia:																						
Cities	2	1	1	1	1	2	2	2	2	1	16	1			1							
Villages											all											
Districts				1	1	1	1		2	1	14	1		2			1	2				

than they are at present. More recently the trend has been to assess a larger fraction of these values, as it has been apparent that land owners as a class and building owners as a class are not necessarily identical.

Exclusion of the value of buildings or improvements from assessment represents a departure from the theory underlying the *ad valorem* taxation of property. By excluding almost entirely the value of buildings and improvements from the assessment base in rural municipalities and by making a partial exclusion of these values in urban municipalities, the burden of taxation has been thrust inordinately upon land owners. This has reduced the desirability of investment in land, and the security of tenure of land holders. Assessment of buildings and improvements at 100 per cent of fair, actual value would remove the present tax discrimination against the land owner, a factor that has driven thousands of parcels of land—particularly unimproved lots in urban municipalities—into tax sale and the hands of the municipalities and further narrowed the tax base. One hundred per cent assessment of buildings and improvements will *not* by itself increase the aggregate tax levy. It will merely apportion it differently than at present.

Similarly Goldenberg in his report on British Columbia[9] pointed out that land had proved to be an unstable basis for taxation since it is subject to a high degree of inflation and deflation and that, while the argument that the exemption of improvements stimulates building and penalizes the land speculator may have merit in the period of early development of a community, it is not as applicable to the later period when the community has been developed. The results, he advised, were to restrict taxation to a narrow and unstable base which could not satisfy the requirements in the developed stage of community growth, and to subsidize the holders of large improved properties

[9]*Provincial-Municipal Relations in British Columbia*, p. X68.

whose properties require extensive municipal services and who in most instance have greater tax paying capacity than the owners of smaller properties and vacant land. He also pointed out that the variation in the percentages of taxes on improvements in the different municipalities resulted in an uneven distribution of the tax burden as between municipalities and created serious problems in the allocation of provincial grants where such are related to the tax yield on the local valuation. His report recommended a mandatory uniform policy providing that municipal taxes should be levied on 75 per cent of the assessed value of improvements.

The Appendix to this chapter indicates the distribution of real property assessment between land and improvements in several provinces. The results of the different assessment policies are most apparent in comparing the proportion of the total assessment represented by improvements in Ontario rural municipalities with that in rural municipalities in Saskatchewan and Alberta, and also in comparing the distribution in Ontario cities with that in British Columbia cities.

There are several other classes of optional exemptions authorized by statute which should be noted, although the total of these exemptions is not great. In some of the cases the exemption is stated to be an exemption from taxation but they are discussed here as the end result for the municipal corporation is the same as if the exemption were from assessment.

One class comprises exemptions based on charitable or patriotic grounds. Thus, in Quebec a council may exempt the poor from payment of taxes; in Ontario, with the approval of the Department of Municipal Affairs, a council may exempt from taxation, except for local improvement and school taxes, for a period of ten years, premises used by veterans as a memorial home, club house, or athletic grounds. Manitoba municipal corporations, with a vote of the ratepayers, may exempt buildings and a limited amount of land used exclusively as a charitable institution and also a Y.M.C.A. or a Y.W.C.A., and Saskatchewan cities and towns may grant exemption from taxation for a period up to ten years to educational and charitable institutions, subject to a majority vote of the burgesses. Such exemptions for education and charitable institutions in the eastern provinces are obligatory and not optional with the municipalities.

Another class of exemptions is designed to encourage improved or low cost housing, as in Quebec cities and towns where councils may provide that if a proprietor repairs, improves, or rebuilds his house the valuation for taxation purposes will remain for five years at the value established before such work was started.[10] The provision, however does not apply to work designed to increase the number of lodgings in the building. Since the war of 1914–18, Ontario has permitted urban councils, with the assent of the electors entitled to vote on money by-laws, to provide that taxes, other than school taxes, to be levied on low cost dwellings should be levied only on a percentage of the assessed value, but on not less than a minimum percentage fixed by statute.[11] Only two municipalities have taken advantage of this legislation, although it was put into effect in the largest municipality, Toronto. In St. John's, Newfoundland, if the assessor determines that the annual rental value of a dwelling is less than $250, he must deduct 20 per cent from the estimated rental for taxation purposes. Saskatchewan cities and towns have a general power to grant exemptions from taxation for the year current at the time the power is exercised.

Fixed Assessments or Industrial and Commercial Exemptions

Another class of exemptions are those which a municipality, under statutory authority, may grant to encourage an industry or business to locate in the municipality or to assist a business newly established. The authority may be either by general legislation applicable to all municipalities in a province or by special legislation applying only to one municipality and sometimes applying to a named industry or business.

Provision may be for complete or partial exemption from taxation or may take the form of fixing the assessment at an agreed figure for a stated period of years. As a result of the difficulties arising from the exploitation of municipalities in the matter of fixed assessments and from inter-municipal competition for industries and because such exemptions or fixed assessments really are a compulsory subsidizing of the business by all the other taxpayers, the exercise of council discretion in this matter is usually subject to statutory regulations.

The benefit granted in Charlottetown and in Prince Edward Island towns, in Quebec urban municipalities, and in Manitoba takes the form of partial or complete exemption from taxation and in Nova Scotia, Ontario, and Alberta urban municipalities the provision is for a fixed assessment. The Charlottetown Charter limits such exemptions to a new hotel or any new industry coming into the city and not in

[10]Saint John, N.B., exempts dwelling houses during the period of construction and for two calendar years after any part is habitable. This exemption is statutory and not optional.

[11]Where the assessment is not more than $2,000, a minimum of 50 per cent. The minimum percentage increases by 10 for each increase of $500 in the assessed value.

existence at the time of application for exemption; in Nova Scotia the fixed assessment may apply to any person carrying on or proposing to carry on an industry or business; in Quebec the exemption applies to any railway company having a station in the municipality; in Ontario the statute sets out the types of industry to which a fixed assessment may apply, e.g. iron works, rolling mills, grain elevators, sugar factories, tobacco driers, etc.; and in Manitoba and Alberta the exemption may apply to any industry.[12] Quebec and British Columbia prohibit the granting of exemptions from taxation to any industrial or commercial establishment.

In Nova Scotia, Ontario, and Manitoba the benefits granted may not be for a greater period than ten years, and in the first two provinces are not renewable. The exemptions in Charlottetown may be for five years for an industry and fifteen for an hotel, for railways in Quebec may be for twenty-five years, and the maximum period for a fixed assessment in Alberta is twenty years and it is not renewable.

The granting of a fixed assessment in Nova Scotia must be approved by a three-quarters' vote of all the members of the council and in cities and towns must receive the assent of three-quarters of the ratepayers entitled to vote in the matter. Quebec merely requires that the action of council be approved by a vote of the property owners. Ontario and Alberta require a three-quarters' vote of all the members of the council and a two-thirds' vote of the qualified electors voting on the matter, while Manitoba requires the assent of three-fifths of the ratepayers voting on the question. No by-law dealing with a proposed fixed assessment in Alberta may be submitted to the electors unless it has first been approved of by the Minister of Municipal Affairs.

No fixed assessment may be granted in Nova Scotia, Ontario, or Alberta in respect of any industry or business established elsewhere in the province or which has removed to the municipality from another municipality in the province, and Ontario further prohibits a fixed assessment in respect of a branch of an industry of a nature similar to one already established in the municipality except with the written consent of the locally established industry.

The Ontario and Manitoba exemptions do not apply to school or local improvement taxes, nor in Ontario to taxes for unemployment relief. In Nova Scotia and Alberta the fixed assessment applies only to the improvements and not to the land and in the latter province does not apply to special taxes or business taxes.

[12]Instances will be found of fixed assessments applying to enterprises other than those noted. Such cases usually will have been authorized by special legislation.

The Nova Scotia and Alberta legislation provides that the fixed assessment must not be less than 25 per cent of the actual value of the improvements or of the approximate cost of the proposed improvements. This amount is determined by the Board of Commissioners of Public Utilities in Nova Scotia and in that province the fixed assessment is to be increased annually by such amount as the council determines, but in any case by not less than 10 per cent, so that at the end of the period of fixed assessment the property will be assessed in accordance with the Assessment Act.

In addition to these official and legitimate exemptions and fixed assessments there are unofficial and extra-legal arrangements in many municipalities whereby industrial and business properties are assessed at less than full value. Such arrangements, to which the council is an off-the-record party, are not difficult to maintain, particularly where the court of revision is composed of council members.[13] It is obviously impossible to arrive at any figure which would indicate the number or the extent of these unofficial exemptions.

Crown Property Exemptions

The municipalities have been persistent in their requests that Crown property, whether in the right of the Dominion or of the provinces, should be subject to municipal taxation or that grants should be made in lieu of such taxation. Their claims have been endorsed in recent years by a number of Royal Commissions. The Dominion Rowell-Sirois Commission recommended:

that the senior governments should make payments *ex gratia* in place of taxation in respect of all property (other than commercial enterprises which should be assessed and taxed on the same basis as private property) held by them in municipalities, but that the amount of these payments should depend on the nature of the property and the extent to which it benefits from municipal services. It may be expedient for both senior governments to lay down some general principles to govern these payments and to employ arbitrators to apply them to individual properties in the event of being unable to reach an agreement with the municipality. The principle is clear that the burden of providing services for government properties should be spread widely by federal or provincial taxation, as the case may be, and not charged against neighbouring properties. But the amount of the payment appropriate in each case will depend on a number of circumstances of which the assessable value of the property may not be one.[14]

[13]In practice such unofficial undertakings given by a council as an inducement to secure an industry are carried out by succeeding councils even though the undertaking is not legally binding.

[14]*Report of the Royal Commission on Dominion Provincial Relations*, book II, *Recommendations* (Ottawa, 1940), p. 146.

The Saskatchewan Commission on Taxation in 1936 recommended that provincial or municipal property used for proprietary activities should be assessed and taxed to the same extent as other property.[15] Goldenberg also distinguishes between Crown property used for ordinary governmental purposes, such as legislative buildings, post offices, court houses, etc., and Crown property used for commercial or profit making purposes, such as electric power distribution or government liquor stores. With respect to government commercial enterprises he recommended that the Crown should make payments in lieu of municipal taxes equivalent to the taxes payable if the enterprise were privately owned. With respect to Crown property used for ordinary governmental purposes he pointed out that, while the property benefits from municipal services, the municipalities also benefit from the location of certain government properties within their boundaries and that it is not unreasonable to expect the local taxpayers to provide some services for such properties. He conceded, however, that where there is an undue concentration of Crown property making wide use of municipal services in a municipality it places an unfair burden on the local taxpayers and also that where the Crown acquires large properties which had been producing municipal tax revenues the municipality may be adversely affected. In such cases, or where a municipality can establish other reasons which warrant special consideration, he recommended that the government, whether provincial or Dominion, should make a grant in aid of local taxes.[16]

The Judge *Report* similarly classifies Crown properties according to their use, recommending that government commercial enterprises should be assessed or taxed as other properties or, alternatively, that an amount equivalent to the taxes be granted to the municipality, but the Commission was of the opinion that all administrative offices necessary to the functions of government should continue to be exempt.[17] The Britnell *Report*, 1950, went a step further, for it recommends not only that Crown property of a commercial nature, both provincial and Dominion, should be liable to municipal taxation but that the province should enact legislation under which Saskatchewan Crown companies or commercial agencies shall pay municipal taxes and levies to the same extent as private owners. The *Report* also suggested that attention should be given to the making of a contribution

[15] *Report of the Commission of Inquiry into Provincial and Municipal Taxation to the Government of the Province of Saskatchewan* (1936), p. 183.

[16] *Provincial-Municipal Relations in British Columbia*, p. X79.

[17] *Report of the Royal Commission on Taxation*, J. W. Judge, Commissioner, Alberta Sessional Paper no. 71 (Edmonton, 1948).

to municipal revenues in the case of non-commercial buildings on the basis of payment for services rendered.[18]

Perhaps the greatest progress in this matter at the provincial level has been made with provincially owned electrical enterprises. As early as 1917 lands owned by the Hydro Electric Power Commission of Ontario were made taxable for municipal and school purposes at their actual value, but buildings and improvements continued to be exempt except that after 1925 both lands and buildings used for retail selling of electrical supplies were assessable to the same extent as a retail merchant carrying on the same business. Under the Quebec Hydro Electric Commission legislation of 1944, properties owned or occupied by the Commission for the generation, transmission, and distribution of power were made subject to municipal and school taxes and properties used as retail stores and office buildings or for manufacturing apparatus were taxable as if held by an ordinary ratepayer, including business and tenant's tax. It also provided that where an undertaking for the generation or distribution of power had been paying a greater amount of taxes prior to its acquisition by the Commission than it would yield as Commission property, the Commission was required to pay municipal and school taxes for a period of twenty years at least equal to the taxes payable during the year preceding its acquisition. The British Columbia Power Commission in 1945 was also made subject to municipal and school taxes on land, though not on buildings and improvements. Where, however, it distributes or sells power within a municipality it must pay to the municipality an amount equal to 3 per cent of the gross cash revenues from the sale of power, other than power for resale, in lieu of taxes on improvements. A provision similar to that of Quebec requires the Commission, after acquiring an undertaking, to continue to pay to any municipal authority an amount in taxes at least equal to that payable on the undertaking in 1944.

In some provinces provincial enterprises do pay municipal taxes, by consent, on the same basis as private businesses, as do the retail outlets of the Liquor Control Board of Ontario, or make grants in lieu of taxes, as does the Manitoba Telephone System which since 1947 has made grants to municipalities equivalent to the realty taxes, although it does not pay business tax. Saskatchewan in 1945 authorized towns and cities, subject to the approval of the Local Government Board, to levy a charge against owners of exempt property in lieu of taxes which otherwise would have been levied for police and fire pro-

[18] *Report of the Committee on Provincial-Municipal Relations* (Regina, 1950), p. 100.

tection, street lighting, and the maintenance of streets and sidewalks. By-laws of four cities and three towns enacted under this legislation were approved by the Board with rates varying from four to thirteen and one-half mills. Although the province signified its intention to pay the charges on certain government properties the legislation was repealed in 1946.

Ontario in 1952 enacted legislation to provide for payments to the municipalities in lieu of taxes. The legislation did not confer any right to a payment nor did it authorize a municipality to levy taxes on provincial property. To arrive at the basis of such payments the provincial property is valued each year by the Department of Municipal Affairs on the same basis as real property which is liable for municipal taxation in the municipality. There is provision for an appeal from this valuation to the Ontario Municipal Board either by the municipality, the Department of Municipal Affairs, or any Crown agency involved.

Under this legislation the Department of Municipal Affairs is authorized to pay annually to each municipality the amount which the general municipal rate (exclusive of educational and business tax levies) would produce if levied on real property owned by the province other than property occupied by a Crown agency. Certain classes of provincial property are excluded from consideration, such as unpatented lands, highways, parks, hospitals, penal and educational institutions, experimental and demonstration farms, etc. Every provincial Crown agency may make similar payments with respect to provincial property owned or occupied by it. Where the province or its agencies occupy or use land for business purposes an additional amount equivalent to the current rate for general municipal purposes on business assessment may be paid but the legislative, executive, and administrative activities of the government are not considered to be in the nature of carrying on a business. Both the Department and the Crown agencies may also pay local improvement assessments.

Prior to 1950 certain Dominion Crown corporations, usually those operating war industries and housing projects, had made payments to municipalities in lieu of municipal taxes, and government departments in a few special cases such as Ottawa and municipalities which were sites of penitentiaries had also made such payments. In 1950, however, the Dominion put into effect a general policy on the matter of contributions by the government to municipalities. The policy is based on three general principles, (1) that the constitutional exemption of federal property from municipal taxation must be maintained, so that any grants in lieu of taxes are to be made solely as a matter of grace and are subject to discretionary determination by an agency of the federal government, (2) that to be fair to all municipalities it should be recognized that the presence of federal property normally brings certain benefits to a municipality, and (3) where there is an abnormally large concentration of federal property the benefits to the municipality may not be sufficient to compensate for the resulting added costs.

The formula on which the grants are calculated is based on the assumption that the total assessment of federal property in all Canadian municipalities is approximately 4 per cent of the taxable assessment. The annual grants to individual municipalities are arrived at on the following basis: the percentage which the total assessment of federal property in the municipality bears to the total assessment of the municipality is determined and is reduced by four. A sum is then determined by applying that percentage to the general tax levy for municipal and school purposes, but excluding business taxes. The grant is equal to 75 per cent of this latter amount. In announcing the policy the Minister of Finance explained that payment was limited to 75 per cent in consideration of the benefits accruing to the municipality from the location of federal property within its limits and because there is a proportion of other exempt property in any municipality. Certain types of federal property such as parks, harbours, and self-contained defence establishments are excluded in determining the value of Crown property and the properties of Crown corporations are also excluded as the policy is that such corporations will work out their own arrangements with the municipalities.

At the same time provision was made for temporary adjustment grants to be payable when the Dominion acquires new property. Where such property is acquired in a municipality which receives payments in lieu of taxes, a grant is made to ensure that the municipality receives full taxes for the year in which the property is acquired, and in the succeeding year and one-half the amount of the taxes for the next following year, after which the assessment of the property is to be included in the total assessment of federal property and the payment in lieu of taxes is adjusted accordingly. In municipalities which, owing to the small amount of federal property, are not receiving payments in lieu of taxes, the Dominion pays full taxes on newly acquired property in the year it is acquired and in the succeeding year, and in each of the three succeeding years grants equal to 75, 50, and 25 per cent of the taxes respectively. These temporary grants are intended to permit the municipality to adjust itself to the loss of tax revenue resulting from property's being acquired by the Crown.

When these policies were announced it was estimated that about 100 municipalities would benefit. During the first year of operation, 1950-1, however, payments in lieu of taxes, other than on newly acquired properties, amounted to $1,059,279, but only nine municipalities benefited, with 90 per cent of the total being paid to Ottawa and Halifax.[19] The significance of the Dominion policy, however, from the viewpoint of the municipalities lies in the recognition of the problem and the acceptance of the principle, even to a limited degree, that municipalities should not be expected to carry the whole cost of servicing federal properties within their limits. It is not unreasonable to expect that the action of the Dominion will have an influence on the attitude of the provinces respecting their responsibility for payments in lieu of taxes on provincially owned properties within municipalities.

The exemption of Crown property is of major importance because of the extension of the commercial and trading activities of all levels of government and the hardship which it causes in some municipalities where Crown holdings are a considerable proportion of the total real estate in the municipality. The municipalities claim that exemptions as a whole are increasing at a faster rate than the total of the taxable portion of the real property assessment, although the available statistics might be misleading as heretofore there has been little incentive to bring assessed values of exempt properties up to current levels.

Statutory Assessments

The assessment or valuation of utilities is sometimes fixed by statute rather than by the local assessor. Few municipal assessors are sufficiently experienced to determine values of such properties and in many cases the property of a utility located in any one municipality may only be a portion of the whole real property essential to the entire operation. In the interests of simplicity and uniformity an arbitrary figure is fixed by law.

Thus, in Ontario the statutes determine the amount per mile at which telephone and telegraph lines are to be assessed[20] and in Quebec municipalities under the Municipal Code the values of towers and

[19]The payments were as follows, Amherst $6,646, Halifax $197,394, Pictou $2,690, Moncton $23,161, Saint John $42,210, Lauzon $2,324, Little Current $2,195, Ottawa $762,392, Esquimalt $19,175. *House of Commons Debates,* February 26, 1951, p. 664.

[20]$135 per mile for first telephone circuit on any pole line and $7.50 per mile for each additional circuit; telegraph lines at $40 per mile for the first wire and $5 per mile for each additional wire.

poles of electrical transmission lines are similarly fixed.[21] Manitoba and Saskatchewan place a statutory valuation on railways which varies according to the type of municipality.[22] In Ontario urban municipalities the problem of assessing telephone and telegraph companies is simplified by substituting for the valuation of their poles and line, their gross receipts in each municipality. These gross receipts are declared to be real property and telephone companies are assessed for 75 per cent of gross receipts in cities over 100,000 population, and 60 per cent in other urban municipalities. The assessment of telegraph companies is 50 per cent of the gross receipts. The same tax rates are levied on these assessments as are levied on other forms of real estate. These companies, however, remain subject also to taxation on their lands and buildings.

British Columbia also uses the statutory assessment method for poles and wires of telegraph companies[23] and for railways[24] but has substituted a 2 per cent tax on the rentals, revenues, and fares of telephone, light, power, gas, and street railway companies, in place of the previous statutory assessments of their poles, lines, mains, and trackage.

A unique provision of the Winnipeg Charter fixes the assessment of poles, wires, and other property of electric light, gas, telegraph, telephone, and electric railway companies at total amounts.[25] These valuations vary according to population, being increased by one-ninth for every increase of 20,000 in population over a base population of 180,000.

[21]For each tower $500, for each wooden pole $20, and for other than wooden poles $50.

[22]In cities $6,000 a mile, in towns $5,000, in villages $3,000, and in rural municipalities in Manitoba $2,000, and in Saskatchewan $800.

[23]$800 per mile in municipalities of 10,000 or over, $500 per mile in other municipalities.

[24]$5,280 per mile for main or branch line track and $3,250 a mile for all other track.

[25]Company supplying gas at $540,000, electric light at $900,000, telephone company at $900,000, street railway at $1,300,000, and telegraph at $72,000.

APPENDIX

Real Property Assessments on Which Taxes are Levied in Certain Canadian Provinces (1950)[a]
(000's omitted)

Province	Municipalities	Land		Improvements		Total real property assessment
		Assessment	Percentage of total real property assessment	Assessment	Percentage of total real property assessment	
Ontario	Cities	$ 673,276	30.7	$1,514,389	69.2	$2,187,665
	Towns	94,024	24.8	284,101	75.1	378,125
	Villages	26,019	22.8	87,793	77.1	113,812
	Townships	559,082	54.4	468,403	45.5	1,027,485
		1,352,401	36.4	2,354,686	63.4	3,707,087
Saskatchewan	Cities	56,014	45.6	66,769	54.6	122,873
	Towns	13,353	29.2	32,362	70.7	45,715
	Villages	9,637	19.7	39,021	80.1	48,658
	Rural municipalities	604,516	96.9	19,129	3.0	623,645
		683,610	81.2	157,281	18.7	840,891
Alberta	Cities	78,202	33.1	157,836	66.8	236,038
	Towns	13,435	19.9	53,819	80.0	67,254
	Villages	4,529	14.2	27,276	85.7	31,805
	Municipal districts	319,877	92.9	24,245	7.0	344,122
		416,043	61.2	263,176	38.7	679,219
British Columbia	Cities	199,768	46.3	231,454	53.6	431,222
	Villages	7,111	33.4	14,177	66.5	21,289
	District municipalities	67,689	39.8	102,239	60.1	169,929
		274,568	44.1	347,870	55.8	622,440
Total of 4 provinces		2,726,622	46.6	3,123,013	53.3	5,849,637

[a]The provinces included in the table are those for which statistics are available indicating the land and improvement portions of real property assessment.

CHAPTER XV

PERSONAL PROPERTY AND BUSINESS ASSESSMENT

PERSONAL PROPERTY ASSESSMENT

THE ASSESSMENT of personal property as a basis for municipal taxation occurs in Newfoundland, Prince Edward Island, Nova Scotia, New Brunswick, Manitoba, and Alberta and to a limited extent, in the form of a stock-in-trade tax, in Quebec. It was at one time in effect elsewhere but was abandoned in favour of a business tax as in Winnipeg in 1893 and in Ontario in 1904. While Saskatchewan does not assess or tax personal property, the Saskatchewan Tax Commission in 1936 recommended "that tangible personal property be assessed for taxation at full, fair, actual value." Despite representations made to the Commission by municipal officials with respect to the accompanying serious administrative difficulties the Commission considered that the administrative problems incidental to assessment and collection of personal property taxes were not insuperable.

The MacLennan Commission in Ontario in 1902[1] reported:

> The conclusion would seem to be that in Ontario, as everywhere else, the direct taxation of personal property generally fails to reach the new kinds of property or wealth which modern civilization has produced. The more comprehensive general property tax which prevails in most of the States of the American Union fails in spite of the most stringent provisions for the discovery of personal property. The various attempts to compel its enforcement by stricter inquiries and greater penalties have only brought a train of moral evils upon the community, without reaching the property intended to be taxed. As Professor Ely has said of it: "The more you perfect it the worse you make it." . . . One conclusion which can unhesitatingly be drawn is that the tax on personal property is a failure, and that it is a hopeless task to perfect it by further legislation. It should therefore be abolished; and if taxation is not to be borne by land alone some substitute for it must be devised.

Almost fifty years later, in 1947, the Commission investigating taxation in the City of Fredericton[2] reported that "intangible property cannot be reached despite the most conscientious efforts of the assessor. Personal property never bears its fair proportion of the tax burden, and when it is remembered that the aggregate value of personal property

[1]Sessional Papers, vol. XXXIV, part IX, 1902, no. 48, p. 15.

[2]*Report of the Commission to Investigate Taxation in the City of Fredericton* (1947), p. 7.

in an industrial society exceeds by far the value of reality, assessment ratios become ridiculous. In none of the three Maritime Provinces, where the general property tax is still in use, is the ratio of the assessed value of personal property to real estate as high as 20 per cent, and during the twenty years before the outbreak of the war personal property valuations declined relatively as well as in absolute amount." The Commission recommended that all personal property be exempt from taxation.

The relative importance of the personal property assessment is indicated in Table 19. While it represents as much as 28.6 per cent of the total assessment in the province of Prince Edward Island and 41 per cent in one Nova Scotia town, it is only one per cent of the total municipal taxable assessment in the Dominion as a whole.

The task of the assessor with respect to personal property is the same as that in dealing with real property, viz, to locate, to value, and to record the assessable property. But the task in this case is a more difficult one. Land and buildings are readily located and cannot be hidden, but it is quite a different matter to locate personal property both tangible and intangible. Even such as is located presents difficulty in valuation. Except for the more obvious types of personal property, the assessor is forced to rely on the honesty of the citizen, a somewhat elastic quality in the individual when acting in his capacity as a prospective taxpayer. "The discovery of personal property is at once one of the most difficult and one of the least satisfactorily performed duties of an assessor. This is a task which calls for ingenuity, resourcefulness, energy and courage."[8]

The tax rate levied on the personal property assessment is usually the same as that levied on the real property assessment although there are exceptions, as in Prince Edward Island towns where the council may fix different rates for real property and personal property taxation or as in the Quebec stock-in-trade tax noted below, in which case the tax is limited by statute to a maximum of one per cent of the estimated average value of the stock-in-trade.

Personal property assessment is mandatory in Prince Edward Island, Nova Scotia, and New Brunswick; the stock-in-trade assessment in Quebec is optional with the local council; in Manitoba the municipal councils may elect either to assess personal property or to use a business assessment; and Alberta municipalities may, with respect to persons in business, provide for a business assessment in lieu

[8]*Assessment Principles*, National Association of Assessing Officers (Chicago, 1938), p. 70.

of the assessment of any stock-in-trade or other personal property. It is not the practice in any case to use both a personal property assessment and a general business assessment.

Definition

There is considerable variation as to the property included in the term "personal property" in the six provinces. In general it includes all goods and chattels and property not included in the term real estate, including the average stock-in-trade of merchants, manufacturers, etc. subject to the exemptions mentioned below. In Quebec it is limited to articles of commerce kept by merchants and dealers.

Valuation

The basis of valuation of personal property for assessment is variously established as "the full, true and real value" (Prince Edward Island), "actual cash value" (Nova Scotia), "real and true value" (New Brunswick), "actual cash value as it would be appraised in payment of a just debt" (Manitoba and Alberta). In Nova Scotia, stock-in-trade valuation is to be "estimated at cost" and in Quebec at the "estimated average value."

Exemptions

The major exemptions applicable in the various provinces might be classified as follows:

Compassionate exemptions. In Charlottetown personal property is exempt if the aggregate assessment is under $200, and in Alberta, if not in excess of $300; in Nova Scotia the property, both real and personal, of widows, unmarried women, and wives deserted by their husbands is exempt to the value of $400.

Household effects exemptions. New Brunswick, Manitoba, and Alberta exempt household effects and furniture, books, and wearing apparel used by a person or his family.

Occupational exemptions. These exemptions vary from province to province reflecting in some cases the more important local types of industry. In many cases the exemption is not total but applies only up to a stated amount or value of the chattels required for the particular operation, thus:

Farmers: farm implements and machinery used for farming; in Manitoba and Alberta, to the full amount; in New Brunswick, to the value of $1,500 (not including tractors); in Nova Scotia to the value of $200.

Mechanics: tools owned by a mechanic, necessary for his business; in both Nova Scotia and New Brunswick to the value of $200.
Fishermen: boats, nets, etc.; in New Brunswick to the value of $500; in Nova Scotia to the value of $200.

Natural products exemptions. In Nova Scotia the produce of the farm or sea is exempt if the property of the producer or person catching the same; in Manitoba and Alberta the produce of land occupied as a farm or garden and all farm livestock.

Money, securities, etc. exemptions. In Nova Scotia, funds invested in provincial debentures are exempt; in New Brunswick, money on hand or on deposit, debts and loans, commercial or negotiable paper, bonds and debentures, mortgages or securities for money, stocks and shares; in Alberta, money, bank notes, cheques, bills of exchange, promissory notes and choses in action.

Miscellaneous exemptions. Railway plant and rolling stock and one-half the value of ships and shares in ships in Nova Scotia; motor vehicles in Alberta.

Alternative Assessments

As noted above, Manitoba and Alberta provide for business assessments as an alternative to personal property assessment at the option of the local council. Table 39 indicates the extent to which this optional basis has been used in these provinces.

TABLE 39

PERSONAL PROPERTY ASSESSMENT

Province	Cities		Towns		Villages		Others—rural	
	Total no.	Number assessing personal property	Total no.	Number assessing personal property	Total no.	Number assessing personal property	Total no.	Number assessing personal property
Nova Scotia	2	1	42	42			24	24
New Brunswick	3	3	19	19	2	2	15	15
Manitoba	4	2	31	5	23	15	116	101
Alberta	7	1[a]	53	4[b]	134	67[c]	60	17[d]
Total	16	7	145	70	159	84	215	157

[a]One additional city assesses personal property of city owned utilities only.
[b]In two of these cases the personal property assessment is for school purposes only.
[c]Twenty-eight of these have personal property assessment for school purposes only.
[d]One of these uses personal property assessment for school purposes only.

Business Assessment[4]

A municipal business assessment or business tax occurs in every province. It is of general application in Ontario and Saskatchewan where municipalities are required to levy a business tax, as is also the case in Prince Edward Island towns. The use of such a tax is optional in Quebec, Manitoba, Alberta, and British Columbia, but in Quebec is applicable only in cities and towns. In Prince Edward Island, Nova Scotia, and New Brunswick a business tax is levied in certain cities, and in the larger cities of Quebec, Manitoba, and Saskatchewan there are special provisions applicable to the individual cities.

While the terms "business assessment" or "business tax" are used as general terms they mean materially different things in the different provinces and there is little in common in the various types of taxes so described. In general the various business taxes in effect may be classified as follows:

Specific Taxes

These taxes are found in Newfoundland, Charlottetown, Prince Edward Island towns, Halifax, and in Quebec cities and towns. Specific taxes take the form of a fixed amount to be paid annually. In Charlottetown and Prince Edward Island towns and Halifax the types of business liable to such charges and the amounts are determined by statute. In the Island municipalities, these businesses include financial and insurance institutions, utilities, express companies, and dealers in gasoline and oils, and the tax varies from $1 to $115. In Halifax specific taxes apply to telegraph and cable companies, insurance and financial businesses, real estate agents, steamship companies, etc., with taxes varying from $50 to $250 per annum. Newfoundland municipalities may levy an annual tax not exceeding $10 on non-resident commercial agents or commercial agents of non-resident firms.

Quebec city and town councils may levy specific annual dues or taxes, which may take the form of a licence fee, on trades, manufactures, financial and commercial establishments, occupations, arts, professions, callings, or means of earning a profit or a livelihood. The amount is fixed by council subject to the statutory maximum of $200 which may be increased by not more than 50 per cent in the case of non-residents or those with less than twelve months' residence. Individual cities have special legislation providing for special specific taxes; e.g., in Montreal there is a municipal tax on chain grocers of $100 for

[4]For an extensive discussion of the business tax in Canadian municipalities see Robert M. Clark, *The Municipal Business Tax in Canada* (Toronto, 1952).

each store in excess of one and up to five inclusive, $200 for each over five and up to ten inclusive, $300 for each over ten.

Special Franchise Taxes

These occur in Saskatchewan, in Calgary, Alberta, and in British Columbia. They differ from the franchise taxes referred to in chapter XI in that they do not arise out of individual franchise agreements but by authority of general statute. That they are considered as a type of tax is evidenced by the provision that where a special franchise assessment is made the person liable shall not be liable for the normal business assessment.

In Saskatchewan municipalities, in addition to the assessment for land, the holder of a special franchise is to be assessed for buildings and improvements at a fair value (as compared with the regular basis of 60 per cent of value for assessment of improvements) and is also assessed on the basis of 10 per cent of the value of the franchise. The legislation with respect to special franchise assessment in Calgary similarly provides for assessment at full value (rather than 50 per cent) on all buildings, improvements, plant machinery, equipment, and apparatus used. It is arrived at by estimating the actual cost and deducting a reasonable amount for depreciation. The general levy mill rate is levied on such assessment in both cases.

British Columbia in 1947 provided for a special basis for municipal taxation of utilities in lieu of both business taxes and real property taxes on plant and equipment, other than local improvement rates and other special rates. This tax is a 2 per cent levy on revenues as noted above.

Ad Valorem Taxes

These may be classified according to the basis upon which the assessment of the business premises for business tax purposes is determined.

Capital value basis. In Halifax 50 per cent of the assessed value of the premises occupied is taken as the business assessment, except that for premises valued under $2,000 or where the business is that of selling merchandise at retail, or is a rooming or boarding house, the business assessment is 25 per cent of the assessed value.

In Saint John, except for merchants subject to the turn-over tax, and in Fredericton and in all Ontario municipalities the various types of business are classified by statute and the business assessment is fixed for each class at a percentage of the real property assessment of the premises occupied. The percentages for the various classes are as follows: Saint John 60, 100, 112, 150; Fredericton 20, 25, 35, 40, 50; Ontario municipalities 10, 25, 30, 35, 50, 60, 75, 150.

The tax rate levied upon these assessments, except in Halifax, is the same as the real property tax rate. The business tax rate in Halifax, however, is arrived at by a somewhat more complicated process. The total sum required to be raised by the council having been determined, there is deducted the total of the following three items: (1) the revenues from licences, company taxes, and special and specific taxes, (2) the revenues from the real property tax (fixed by statute at 3½ per cent on residential property) and the household tax, and (3) the revenue from the poll tax and non-resident's tax. The balance remaining is raised by the rate which is required when levied on the total of (*a*) the assessed valuations for real property other than that of a residential nature, and (*b*) assessed valuations for business taxes and other occupation taxes, other than the household tax, at the percentages specified.

Rental value basis. The St. John's, Newfoundland, business assessment is 50, 100, 150, or 200 per cent of the appraised rental value of the premises occupied according to the statutory classification of businesses. On this assessment the council levies an annual business tax the rate of which need not be the same as the real property tax.

Montreal business assessment is the assessed rental value upon which is levied a business tax of 10 per cent with a surtax of 8 per cent; there are special rates for hotels, restaurants, distillers, breweries, banks, and bank branches. In Lachine the rate is 8½ per cent on the annual rental value with a maximum in the case of manufacturers of $600.

The general optional provisions which apply in Manitoba fix the business assessment at the rental value of the premises occupied. The tax rate to be levied on this assessment is fixed by council, but may not exceed 15 per cent.

The Winnipeg business assessment is the rental value of the premises occupied but the tax rates which are fixed by statute vary according to the classification of the business. The 352 types of trades, businesses, or occupations dealt with are classified into fifteen classes and the business tax rate applying to any particular business is a percentage which varies according to the class into which it falls, but within the class there may be either a uniform percentage (Class K), a percentage which varies progressively according to the assessment (Class A and B), or a percentage which varies according to the type of business (Class

M). Examples of these rate variations are as set out in the accompanying chart.

Class A

Assessment	Rate
up to $500	6%
$501 to $1,000	7
$1,001 to $2,000	8
$2,001 to $20,000	10
$20,001 to $100,000	12½
$100,001 and over	14½

Class B

Assessment	Rate
up to $500	6%
$501 to $1,000	7½
$1,001 to $2,000	9
$2,001 and over	10

Class K

Flat rate of 12½%

Class M

Grain merchants or brokers, finance, loan mortgage or investment or land companies assessed up to $5,000	12½%
Assessed up to $5,001 and over	17
Investment bankers	17
Insurance companies	18½
Stock brokers	12½
Banks	20
Mail order business	10

The Alberta general legislation also provides for business assessment on a rental value basis in certain cases as noted below. In Edmonton, however, the business assessment is the full annual rental value of the premises occupied and the tax is a percentage which varies according to the classification of the business as classified by the council. The maximum rate is fixed by statute at 25 per cent. At present the council has provided for five classes with rates at 6, 10, 12, 15, and 20 per cent; e.g., in the class liable to a 6 per cent tax are manufacturers, repair shops, greenhouses, hotels, dairies, dressmakers, barbers, coal mines, and brick yards, while in the 20 per cent class are banks, cabarets, express companies, and telephone and telegraph companies. The basis of the Calgary business assessment and tax is similar except that the statutory limitations are that the percentage rates shall not be less than 6 per cent nor more than 15 per cent, the current rate being 8 per cent.[5]

British Columbia in 1947 provided for a business assessment and a business tax, the use of which is optional with the municipalities. It permits an annual tax on persons using real property or any building or structure for carrying on within the municipality any business, trade, profession, or other occupation. The tax is levied on the annual

[5]In 1916 and 1917 the rate was 6 per cent; in 1918–20 graduated rates of 6, 8, and 10 per cent applied; 1921–27 a uniform rate of 10 per cent, reduced in the year 1928 to 9 per cent and for the ears 1929–51 to 8 per cent.

"rental value" of the property occupied. The local councils have authority to classify the various occupations and businesses and to fix the rates applicable to each class. Only New Westminster has used this legislation, under which it levies a uniform 9 per cent tax. Vancouver, operating under similar private legislation, uses the annual rental value of the premises occupied as the business assessment with a uniform business tax of 6 per cent.[6] Under the Vancouver by-law some twenty-four types of business are specifically exempted from the business tax. Among others, these exempted businesses include parks, auto camps, dressmakers, private schools, private hospitals, and lodging houses, including hotels.

Area occupied basis. In Saskatchewan and Alberta there is yet another method of determining the assessment on which the business tax is to be levied. Under this plan the various trades, occupations, and businesses are classified and a rate of assessment per square foot of the premises occupied for various types of business is determined by the assessor or the council. This rate, multiplied by the number of square feet of space so used, determines the assessment for the respective businesses. The rates used may be varied for different classes of business. In Saskatchewan, however, there is a statutory maximum of $8 a square foot, except in the case of banks and other financial institutions, the maximum for which is $15 a square foot, and in the case of yard space, the maximum for which is set at $4 per square foot. The business tax rate which is levied upon these assessments is the general levy mill rate.

Regina classifies 284 types of businesses to provide for the application of fifteen different assessment rates. The assessment rates per square foot provided for are 1¢, 15¢, 20¢, 50¢, $1.00, $1.50, $2.00, $2.25, $3.00, $4.00, $4.50, $5.00, $8.00. The lowest rate of 1¢ applies to fuel dealers' trackage and driveways, while the $8.00 rate applies to banks, financial institutions, and stock or grain brokers. Moose Jaw classifies 184 types of businesses to provide for forty different assessment rates, viz: 20¢, 25¢, 30¢, 35¢, 40¢, 50¢, 55¢, 60¢, 65¢, 70¢, 75¢, 80¢, 85¢, 90¢, 95¢, $1.00, $1.10, $1.25, $1.40, $1.50, $1.70, $1.75, $2.00, $2.20, $2.25, $2.40, $2.50, $2.60, $2.90, $3.00, $3.25, $3.40, $3.50, $3.90, $4.00, $4.50, $5.00, $6.00, $8.75.

The Saskatoon by-law dealing with business taxes provides that they are to be considered as licence fees charged according to the rates fixed by the by-law applied to the number of square feet of the premises occupied for the particular business. Under this plan the tax or fee is

[6]For the year 1951.

determined directly by the product of the rate and the area in square feet, in contrast to Regina and Moose Jaw where an assessment is first determined by a factor applied to the area involved and the general mill rate applied to that assessment. Saskatoon has classified 138 types of business to provide for twenty-four rates as follows: .38¢, .475¢, .665¢, .95¢, 1.045¢, 1.14¢, 1.52¢, 1.9¢, 1.99¢, 2.09¢, 2.375¢, 2.85¢, 4.275¢, 5.7¢, 8.55¢, 10.45¢, 11.4¢, 12.35¢, 13.3¢, 15.2¢, 21.85¢. Provision is also made for a minimum charge of $10.00 in all cases and in special cases a higher minimum charge, e.g., wholesale fruit and vegetable dealers, $100; wholesale auto supplies, $50; auto filling stations and restaurants, $25.

The problem of classifying various types of businesses and fixing different rates for the different classes to obtain a degree of equity in the incidence of the business tax would appear to be a particularly difficult one. Certain refinements which have been introduced might be noted. In Regina, not only are there fifteen different rates but in many cases the various activities carried on within one business are assessed at different rates, as shown in the chart.

Cement block and pipe works	*Assessment per sq. ft.*	*Sales garage*	*Assessment per sq. ft.*
Office	$3.00	Office	$5.00
Works	1.00	Show room	2.25
Sheds	.50	Stock room	2.00
Yards	.15	Work shop	1.00
		Live car storage	1.00
		Dead car storage	.50

Saskatoon follows this practice to a lesser degree but is unique in its provision for a minimum charge in certain cases as noted above. Moose Jaw, which also in a few cases provides for different rates for different activities within the same business, in addition provides in some cases for a variation of rates according to the location, e.g., general store, first floor, $3.00, other than first floor $1.75; music stores, first floor $2.00, other than first floor $1.25.

Multiple basis. Alberta provides by general legislation for the optional use of a business assessment and business tax for either municipal or school purposes or both in urban municipalities. The local council may classify the various businesses, trades, and professions and may provide that the business assessment for any class shall be the full annual rental value of the premises occupied. Introducing a new basis, the council may also provide that grain dealers, elevator operators, coal dealers, gasoline and oil distributors, and storage businesses shall be assessed on the basis of the available storage capacity of the premises at a fixed unit rate per cubic foot, cubic yard, bushel, gallon, or other appropriate unit of weight or measure. It may further provide that businesses not assessed on either of the above bases may be assessed on the basis of the floor space occupied at a rate per square foot. The rates of assessment may vary according to the type of business, to the purposes for which the floor space is used, to the situation of the business in relation to that of other places of business, and to the extent to which the floor space or storage capacity is profitably used.

Where the business assessment is on the rental value basis, the council fixes the tax rate which, however, may not exceed 15 per cent. If the business assessment is other than on a rental value basis the business tax is a uniform rate fixed by council, but may not exceed the rate levied on land. In any case a by-law imposing a business tax must be approved by the Minister.

A tabulation of the business taxes in effect in the various provinces is set out in the Appendix to this chapter. The varying importance of the business tax in different classes of municipalities in several provinces is indicated in Table 40. Within the city group there is also great variation in the relative importance of the business tax as a part of the total tax revenue. The range in the four provinces referred to in Table 41 is shown in Table 42.

TABLE 40

BUSINESS ASSESSMENT AND TAXATION IN CANADIAN MUNICIPALITIES

Province	Cities		Towns and villages		Rural municipalities		
	No.	No. using business assessment	No.	No. using business assessment	No.	No. using business assessment	
Prince Edward Island	1	1	7	7			
Nova Scotia	2	1	42	0	24	0	
New Brunswick	3	1	19	0	15	0	
Quebec	26	17	426	26	1,061	0	
Ontario	28	28	303	294	569	528	
Manitoba	4	2	54	36	116	16	
Saskatchewan	8	7	478	473	303	282	
Alberta	7	7	197	72	60	12	
British Columbia	34	2	23	0	28	0	
Total municipalities	113		1,549		2,176		3,838
Total using business assessment		66		908		838	1,812
Percentage using business assessment		58		59		38	47

TABLE 41

BUSINESS TAX AS A PERCENTAGE OF TOTAL TAX REVENUE
(EXCLUDING WATER AND LOCAL IMPROVEMENT TAXES)

	Cities	Towns	Villages	Rurals
Quebec[a]	10.5	1.1		
Ontario[b]	12.2	9.9	4.9	1.5
Saskatchewan[b]	8.4	20.9	27.4	1.1
Alberta[b]	4.8	7.1	3.3	.1

[a]Based on business tax revenue compared with total tax revenue.
[b]Based on business assessment compared with total taxable assessment.

TABLE 42

RANGE OF BUSINESS TAX AS A
PERCENTAGE OF TOTAL TAX REVENUE IN CITIES
(EXCLUDING WATER AND LOCAL IMPROVEMENT TAXES)

Province	Low	High
Quebec	.5%	19.2%
Ontario	6.5%	15.2%
Saskatchewan	.9%	18.5%
Alberta	2.5%	5.3%

APPENDIX

BUSINESS TAXES IN CANADIAN MUNICIPALITIES[a]

	Basis of assessment	Basis of taxation
Newfoundland		
Towns		Specific taxes
St. John's	Percentage of rental value as classified, rates 50%, 100%, 150%, 200%	Not necessarily same as general tax rate
Prince Edward Island		
Charlottetown		Specific taxes
Nova Scotia		
General provision	None	None
Halifax	50% of capital value assessment of premises occupied	Variable—see text for explanation
New Brunswick		
Saint John and Fredericton	Percentage of capital value as classified, rates from 10% to 150%	General tax rate
Quebec		
Cities and towns general		Specific taxes
Montreal	Assessed rental value	10% plus 8% surtax; also specific taxes

[a]Reference to exceptions and qualifying provisions have been eliminated from this table for greater simplicity.

APPENDIX—*Continued*

	Basis of assessment	Basis of taxation
Ontario		
General provision	Percentage of capital value assessment varying according to classification, rates 10%, 25%, 30%, 35%, 50%, 60%, 75%, 150%	General tax rate
Manitoba		
General provision	Assessed rental value	Maximum 15%
Winnipeg	Assessed rental value	Percentages vary according to classification. Rates range from 6% to 20%
Saskatchewan		
General provision	Rate per square foot of floor space according to classification. Maximum rate $8.00	General tax rate
Regina	Rate per sq. ft. of floor space according to classification, rates range from 1¢ to $8.00	General tax rate
Saskatoon		Charged as licence fees at rates per sq. ft. according to classification, rates range from .38¢ to 21.85¢
Moose Jaw	Rate per sq. ft. according to classification; rates range from 20¢ to $8.75	General tax rate
Alberta		
General provision	Rental value	Maximum 15%
	or	
	Rate per unit of capacity according to class	Not in excess of rate levied on land
	or	
	Rate per sq. ft. according to classification	Not in excess of rate levied on land
Edmonton	Rental value	Rate may vary according to classification; rates, 6%, 10%, 12%, 15%, 20%
Calgary	Rental value	Rate may vary according to classification; 1948 rate—uniform 8%
British Columbia		
General provision	Rental value	Rate may vary according to classification; in practice is a uniform rate

CHAPTER XVI

TAXATION

GENERAL TAXATION

WHEN THE ASSESSMENT upon which the municipal taxes are to be levied has been determined, the municipal council or other tax levying body fix the rate of taxation. This rate, usually expressed in mills on the dollar of assessment, is the rate which, when levied upon the taxable assessment,[1] will produce the amount it is desired to raise. In most cases the same rate of taxation applies to both of the major classes of assessment which are used in the particular municipality, viz, real property and business or personal property, although as previously noted there are exceptions to this general rule both with respect to the tax levied upon business assessment and as in Halifax, where the rate to be levied on residential real property is fixed by statute as 3½ per cent and the rate to be levied on the balance of the real property assessment and on the business assessment varies according to the revenue required.

The rate of taxation is fixed annually and the authority to levy or impose the tax is contained in a by-law passed by the council or other taxing authority. Such taxing by-laws usually recite the amount of the taxable assessment, the amount of money required to be raised, the tax rate or rates to be imposed, and the terms of payment, such as the date of payment, the provision, if any, for instalment payments, discounts, penalties, etc. It is important that all the procedural details prescribed by statute with respect to the imposition of a tax and the subsequent methods of collection be followed carefully for there is always the possibility that the action of the taxing authority may be called in question before the courts. This is more likely to be the case with respect to the levying of taxes than in other actions taken by a council because the action impinges so painfully upon the individual taxpayer.

While it has been said that there are no special rules for construing taxing Acts, as distinct from other statutes,

[1]The taxable assessment is the total assessment less the assessment of exempt properties. The actual rate of taxation, whether it be the general tax or any other tax to be levied on the assessment, is obtained by the application of a very simple formula, viz:

$$\frac{\text{Amount to be raised}}{\text{Taxable assessment}} \times 1{,}000 = \text{tax rate in mills.}$$

. . . there do seem to be certain special principles applicable especially to the construction of taxing Acts. The fundamental rule is the rule of strict construction in favour of the subject. The presumption is against and not in favour of the validity of the charge. The municipality must have a clear right to impose the burden and must have duly exercised the power. It is the creature of the statute and has only such powers as are conferred upon it. Such powers can be exercised only in the way or ways indicated in the statute. There is no such thing as an equitable construction of a taxing Act. The tax, it is sometimes said, must be expressly imposed and the words imposing the tax must be clear. Speculation as to intention is not permissible, and the burden is on those who seek to enforce the tax.[2]

Although in general the tax levy or rate is a matter within the jurisdiction of the municipal council some provinces have imposed maximum limitations, with provisions in certain cases for exceeding the prescribed limits as shown in Table 43.

Tax or Collector's Roll

Once the tax rate has been determined, it is necessary to calculate the amount of the tax levy for each individual taxpayer or property. In most provinces this is done by the clerk or secretary-treasurer. In Quebec cities and towns, however, it is the responsibility of the treasurer, and in Saskatchewan cities and towns and in New Brunswick municipalities the assessor, although as will be noted the New Brunswick procedure differs materially from that of the other provinces.

The usual procedure is that the designated officer prepares a tax roll, rate book, or collector's roll in which are listed the assessments as recorded in the assessment roll and he enters in the proper columns the various taxes levied against the assessments. This roll becomes the authority under which the proper officer proceeds to collect the taxes shown to be owing. In Saskatchewan villages and rural municipalities and in Alberta municipal districts a separate tax roll is not prepared but the taxes levied against the various assessments are entered on the assessment roll.

When the tax roll has been completed it is turned over to the officer whose duty it is to collect the taxes—in Charlottetown, Nova Scotia municipalities, Ontario, and British Columbia, to the collector, and in Quebec, Manitoba, Saskatchewan, and Alberta to the treasurer or secretary-treasurer. In the case of Quebec municipalities, Saskatchewan villages and rural municipalities, and Alberta municipalities both the work of preparing the roll and collecting the taxes is performed by the same official.

[2]H. E. Manning, *Assessment and Rating* (3rd ed., Toronto, 1951), pp. 21–2.

The officer whose duty it is to collect the taxes is required to serve a notice, in most cases by mail, upon each person taxed, indicating the amount of the tax and the date when it must be paid. In Quebec municipalities the treasurer publishes a notice of the completion of the roll, requiring all persons to pay the sum owing by them within twenty days. He sends individual notices only to those who have failed to pay

TABLE 43

STATUTORY MUNICIPAL TAX LIMITS

Province	Limit	Authority which may authorize exceeding limit
Newfoundland	Rate is subject to approval of the Lieutenant-Governor in Council	
Quebec		
Cities and towns	2% on lands and buildings	Lieutenant-Governor in Council
Ontario		
All[a]	2½% excluding school, local improvement and hospital taxes	
Manitoba		
Rural	3% excluding schools, Municipal Commissioner's levy, local improvement and debt charge taxes	Municipal and Public Utility Board[b]
Others[c]	2% excluding schools, Municipal Commissioner's levy, local improvement and debt charge taxes	
British Columbia		
All[d]	2% excluding school and debt charge taxes	

[a]The statute provides that when the 2½ per cent limit is exceeded the municipality may not incur further borrowing without approval of the Ontario Municipal Board, but as such approval is mandatory for all borrowing the limitation is not significant, as evidenced by tax rates as high as 39 mills exclusive of schools, local improvement, and hospital taxes.

[b]With approval of the Municipal and Public Utility Board a council may raise money for permanent improvements, increasing the indebtedness, but so that the total to be raised including principal and interest for all municipal purposes, exclusive of schools and the Municipal Commissioner's levy and local improvements, shall not exceed 4 per cent in rural municipalities and 3 per cent in other municipalities.

[c]Winnipeg rate may not exceed 12 mills excluding amounts required by or for interest on outstanding debentures, sinking fund, schools, police, Public Parks Board, Greater Winnipeg Water District, Greater Winnipeg Sanitary District, and any general statute of the province levying any additional rate provided that if the assessed value of real property in any year is less than $200,000,000 the rate may be increased for that year, but so that no more than $1,600,000 is levied on real property for the purposes in respect of which the 12 mill limit is imposed.

[d]Vancouver limit is 1⅜ per cent exclusive of amount required for payment of interest on debentures and the amount required for sinking fund and school purposes if any. It may be increased to 1½ per cent if improvements, machinery, and plant, being fixtures on any land, are not to be taxed in any year on more than 50 per cent of assessed value.

within the twenty days. These notices are sent by registered mail and there is an added charge of twenty-five cents in cities and towns and thirty-five cents in other municipalities.

As previously noted, New Brunswick combines in one series of operations both the assessing and taxing procedure. When a council decides to levy a rate it directs the assessors by warrant to assess and levy the rate; the warrant sets out the total of the sum of money to be raised rather than a tax rate. The assessors, after receiving the warrant, prepare an assessment roll, listing the persons and properties assessable, the valuations, and the amount of the tax to be paid on such valuations or other assessments. In counties their lists are then delivered to the collectors, and in towns and villages, to the treasurer, whose duty it is to collect the taxes shown on the list. The county collectors are required to notify each ratepayer by personal demand or by mailed notice showing the taxes owing and in towns and villages the treasurer must give public notice of the completion of the list and also give each ratepayer notice of the taxes owing by him.

Tax Collection

Most people look upon the payment of taxes as a necessary evil to be deferred as long as possible so various inducements and devices are used to encourage taxpayers to pay their taxes. These inducements may be grouped into three classifications: (1) those which are used prior to the date on which the taxes are payable, (2) those which are used if the taxes remain unpaid after the due date, and (3) those which are used as the ultimate or final method of securing the payment of the amount due.

The date on which taxes are to be paid is usually in the discretion of the local council although in some cases the date is fixed by statute.[3] The date, or dates, fixed for the payment of taxes is usually in the first half of the year in urban municipalities, but in rural municipalities, owing to the fact that the cash income on the farm is largely received after the harvest, it is commonly in the latter part of the year.

Three devices are used to encourage the payment of taxes on or before the due date.

Payment by instalment. Many urban municpalities in recent years have provided for the payment of taxes by instalments. They usually provide for two, three, or four instalments although some have as

[3]Newfoundland, April 1 and October 1 unless council otherwise determines; Charlottetown, August 1 or ten days after notice; Halifax, May 1; Manitoba, October 31, unless earlier date fixed by council.

many as ten. Payment by instalments is more useful in urban municipalities where most citizens receive their incomes in equal weekly or monthly payments throughout the year. The instalment plan developed partly in imitation of private business and partly as a result of competition for the taxpayer's dollar by instalment vendors.

Payments in advance of due dates. Some provinces permit their municipalities to accept payment on account of the current year's taxes, even though the taxes have not been levied. Where there are many competing demands upon the taxpayer every dollar collected is one which will not be subject to competition from other sources. Such sums as are paid in advance of the due date also serve to reduce the extent of the loans that the council must incur to finance its operations in the period between the commencement of the fiscal year and the date when taxes are due. Some municipalities have been able to eliminate outside financing by reason of the substantial amounts paid on account of taxes in this manner.

As an inducement to taxpayers to make such payments in advance of the due date, councils, subject to the limitations imposed by provincial statutes, may pay interest on money so paid or may allow a discount on taxes so paid in advance. The most commonly occurring rate is at 6 per cent per annum or one-half of one per cent per month.

Discounts for prompt payment of taxes. As a further inducement to pay taxes promptly, most provinces authorize municipalities to allow a discount off the amount of taxes payable if they are paid on or before the due date. In Nova Scotia the amount of such discount is in the discretion of the council; in other provinces a maximum is usually fixed by statute and local discretion permitted within that maximum. The maxima range from 5 to 10 per cent.

Penalties

If taxes are not paid voluntarily by the due date, an added inducement is provided by the imposition of penalties in the form of percentages added to the amount owing. These percentages become part of the taxes and are collectible in the same manner as taxes. The percentages to be added may be fixed by provincial statute or may be in the discretion of the council within maximum limits fixed by statute. The percentages continue to apply until the taxes are paid. Appendix A to this chapter indicates the penalty provisions in the various provinces.

The imposition of penalties is a source of irritation and complaint on the part of taxpayers, in many cases because the purpose of the penalty is not appreciated. Most delinquent taxpayers regard the penalty as a punishment rather than a means of effecting equitable treatment among all the taxpayers. Municipalities have to borrow money to finance their operations in the interim between the start of the fiscal year and the time when taxes become due, which involves costs for the taxpayers as a whole. When the taxes are paid they are used to pay off the loans previously incurred but to the extent that the taxes of any individual are not paid on the due date that amount is not available to reduce the loans. It is inequitable that those who pay their taxes on the due date should have to pay also for the cost of financing those who do not or who cannot pay on time. The penalties encourage the payment of taxes and they also make the delinquent taxpayer bear the cost of financing the loans required as a result of his delinquency.

Citizens frequently complain of the rigidity of enforcement of penalties but any leeway allowed in the enforcement of penalties in individual cases defeats the aim of equality of treatment, and although the individual benefitted by a special extension of time for payment of his taxes may be satisfied, a question is raised in his mind as to whether or not others may be getting the same or even greater concessions. One important factor in satisfying citizens, particularly in matters of taxation, is to convince them that there is uniform and equitable treatment for all under established rules.

While the provisions for discounts and penalties assist tax collection they should not be allowed to become a substitute for a consistent and active programme of tax collection. The accumulation of unpaid taxes introduces an unsound element into the finances of a municipality, for although such arrears may appear in the books of the municipality as an asset they may prove to be of dubious value, as many municipalities discovered in the depression of the thirties. It is not always a kindness to the taxpayer to be lenient in collection, for the longer he delays payment the less becomes the probability that he will be able to pay the taxes together with the accumulating penalties. If the load he is trying to carry is beyond his financial capacity, it may be better for the taxpayer to find it out sooner rather than later and not continue year after year vainly trying to overtake a steadily increasing burden of interest and penalties. On the other hand, if the reason for non-payment is not financial inability but rather a preference for paying other and more pressing creditors first, a lenient collection policy is unfair to the taxpayers who pay on time.

If a taxpayer fails to pay the taxes imposed, and such penalties as may be added, there are a number of methods of collection provided for in the various provinces as follows:

Collection by distress. Where the municipality collects taxes by the process of levying by distress, the authorized municipal official applies to a magistrate, a justice, or some other designed officer for a warrant of distress[4] which authorizes him to seize the goods and chattels of the delinquent taxpayer and to sell them by public auction. The proceeds of the sale are then applied to payment of the taxes[5] and any surplus, in excess of the amount required to pay the taxes and costs, is paid to the owner of the chattels. Provisions as to what goods and chattels may be seized and what are exempt from seizure vary from province to province. Two special provisions might be noted, however. In Halifax such a levy may be made upon goods and chattels and on coin, debentures, bank notes, bills of exchange, promissory notes, cheques and bonds, etc., and in Manitoba the term goods and chattels is defined to include growing crops on the premises in respect of which the taxes are levied.

This method of collection is provided for in all the provinces with the exception of Newfoundland and British Columbia. Normally such action cannot be taken until a certain period has elapsed after the mailing of the demand for payment, varying from six days in New Brunswick to thirty days in the three Prairie Provinces. Special provision, however, is made for "anticipatory distress" in Manitoba, Saskatchewan, and Alberta. This permits such a levy to be made on the authority of the head of the municipality or a justice if the treasurer believes that the goods and chattels liable to be distrained are about to be moved out of the municipality. Action can be taken at any time after the demand for taxes, even before the due date.

In Nova Scotia and New Brunswick the warrant or execution obtained is one of "distress and committal" with the result that in default of there being goods and chattels to seize, the person named in the warrant may be committed to jail. In New Brunswick, if the goods taken fail to satisfy the claim, the taxpayer may be imprisoned for the balance but a ratepayer so imprisoned may not be detained for more than one day for each dollar levied and expenses, and in no case for more than fifty days.

The use of this method of levying taxes by distress is not uncommon.

Collection by suit. In all the provinces except Newfoundland and Prince Edward Island the municipality may sue the taxpayer for the amount of taxes owing in the same manner as if suing for an ordinary debt. This method of collection is not commonly used.

[4]In some cases the municipal official is not required to obtain a warrant.

[5]In Saskatchewan a city may bid at such sale up to the amount due for taxes and costs.

Collection by collecting rents. New Brunswick, Ontario, Manitoba, Saskatchewan, and Alberta provide that where the property taxed is occupied by a tenant, and the taxes are overdue and unpaid, the tax collector may require the tenant to pay his rent to the municipality to be applied on the taxes. The tenant must comply with the notice but is relieved of any liability to his landlord for rent to the extent that he has paid it to the municipality.[6] Some provinces further provide that where such notice has been given, the collector has the same rights to procedures for the collection of the rents, such as distress, as the landlord would have.

This method of collection has been quite commonly used in urban municipalities in periods of depression.

Collection by claim on insurance. In New Brunswick, Manitoba, Saskatchewan, and Alberta the claim of the municipality for unpaid taxes is made a first charge on any insurance payable on account of the destruction or damage to buildings on the property. An insurer is required, within forty-eight hours, to notify the municipality of claims and the municipality is required to notify the insurer, usually within ten days thereafter, if there are any unpaid taxes, in which case the insurance is payable to the municipality up to the amount due, irrespective of the directions in the insurance policy. In Manitoba the insurance is to be so applied only to the extent that it is not used to rebuild or repair the building, and in Alberta the provision does not apply if the insurance has been effected and maintained by a mortgagee for his protection.

Collection by set-off. The Halifax Charter permits the treasurer to pay to the collector, to be applied on taxes, any money owing by the city to a person whose taxes are overdue and unpaid, including any person whose salary is paid directly or indirectly by the city. Similarly, under the general law of New Brunswick,[7] if a county treasurer has money payable by order of the county council to a person indebted for county or parish rates, he is required to set-off against such money any rates owing.

Collection by publication and execution. In Prince Edward Island towns and in Charlottetown, the clerk or collector is required to publish in a newspaper, once a week for three successive weeks (four weeks in towns), a list of ratepayers who have failed to pay taxes due.

[6]In Saskatchewan cities, where heat and other services are supplied to the tenant by the landlord, the city may supply such services out of the money received from the tenant and, on request of the owner, may pay premiums for insurance on the buildings.

[7]A similar provision occurs in the Fredericton Charter.

Thereafter he applies to a magistrate or judge by general application for a judgment against the listed individuals who have not paid their taxes in the interim. The magistrate or judge may issue an execution directed to the sheriff.

Collection by deductions from pay. If a ratepayer who is a workman in the coal mines in certain parishes in New Brunswick[8] fails to pay his taxes within six days of demand the collector may require his employer to deduct the rates from any pay due the ratepayer. This method of collection is also used in other provinces as a means of collecting poll taxes.

Collection by transfer of lien to new site. Manitoba provides that if a building is moved from one location to another, and the taxes on the building or on the land from which it was moved are unpaid, the taxes may be transferred to the land at the new location, and are collectible as if originally levied on the new location. The person who removes a building without the consent of the municipality is liable to a penalty if the taxes are unpaid. Similarly, in Saskatchewan, where taxes are outstanding, a building may not be demolished or removed without the consent of the municipality, subject to a penalty of $100 and damages not exceeding the amount of the outstanding taxes. If, however, a building is removed, it may be seized at its new location and restored to its previous location, the expense being added to the tax roll or, within three months, the municipality may distrain upon the building or material.

Impounding motor vehicles. Prince Edward Island municipalities may by by-law authorize their officials to impound motor vehicles or their registry number plates if the personal property tax on such vehicles is overdue. The vehicle or plates may be retained until the tax and costs are paid or the vehicle has been taken in execution on application of the municipality.

Working out taxes. The Charlottetown council is authorized to establish an arrangement whereby taxpayers assessed for poll tax shall be entitled to discharge such tax by work on some project of the municipality.

Tax Sales and Tax Liens

In the case of real property taxes there is yet a further or ultimate provision for the collection of taxes. Real property taxes in most provinces constitute a lien upon the real property involved and as stated in the Ontario legislation "shall be a special lien on the land in priority to every claim, privilege, lien or incumbrance of every

[8]Parishes of Northfield and of Canning.

person except the Crown. . . ." If, therefore, the taxes on land have not been collected by any of the means outlined above, there remains the final procedure for collection, commonly referred to as tax sale of the land.

This final method of collecting arrears of taxes consists of the seizure or sale of the lands against which the municipal taxes constitute a lien. Its use is limited to the collection of real property taxes and it is not available for the collection of business taxes or personal property taxes. The use of this method may be mandatory or may be optional with the local council and action to exercise the power to collect by this method may be automatic under statute or may require initiating action by the council or head of the municipality.

The time when the procedure for thus collecting taxes shall start and the procedures to be followed vary from province to province and cannot be detailed here. The various steps to be taken are set forth by statute in each province and must be meticulously observed if the seizure or sale is not to be upset by action in the courts. As a consequence it is a common practice, after the procedures have been carried out and a reasonable time has elapsed to enable persons concerned to take legal action to protect their interests, to have the provincial legislature validate a tax sale, either by general legislation or by a private Act.

Not all municipalities have the power to sell lands for the purpose of collecting arrears of taxes. In Quebec such action is taken by the county on behalf of the local municipalities in the county, other than cities and towns, and in Ontario the power is exercised by counties, cities, and towns, and a few townships specified by statute. However, an Ontario county may place the responsibility on townships and villages, a practice which is gradually being extended.

The methods used to collect arrears of taxes falls into three classes according to the procedures followed, the tax sale procedure, the registration or tax lien procedure, and foreclosure. It is only possible to deal with the more important aspects of these so that reference to many points which are vital in practice are omitted.

There is considerable variation in the time which may elapse after taxes became due before proceedings for collection by sale or registration can start. The period ranges from one to three years.

There may again be great variation in the length of the interval between the time when sale proceedings start and the time when tax sale actually takes place, or when the property comes into the possession of the municipality. This depends in part on how involved the procedures may be. Thus, in Charlottetown the collector after thirty days from the date of publishing the list of unpaid taxes applies to a judge who issues an order to the sheriff to sell the lands involved at public auction. In contrast, the Alberta procedure is as follows: the treasurer each March prepares a list of all properties on which the taxes are in arrears for more than one year, which list he submits to the chief officer of the municipality who signs the list and returns it to the treasurer; before April 1 the treasurer sends a copy to the Land Titles Office, and the Registrar of the Land Titles Office then places a certificate of notification against each parcel on the list; not later than August 1 he notifies the owners and encumbrancers that the certificate or notification has been recorded and advises that unless the arrears are paid by a stated date the parcel may be offered for sale by public auction; the sale, which must be advertised, may not take place until after one year from April 1 in the year in which the notification was registered and the land must be offered for sale within three years of such date.

Most provinces provide that the owners and encumbrancers concerned be notified that their properties are liable to be sold unless the arrears are paid by a stated date and it is usually required also that a sale of land for arrears of taxes be amply advertised.

In most cases the procedure to collect by tax sale or tax lien is automatic in its functioning, in accordance with statutory provisions, but in some provinces may be subject to council discretion on some points. Where, as in the cases of Nova Scotia municipalities (including Halifax), Ontario, Manitoba, Saskatchewan, and Alberta, the procedure is initiated by a warrant signed by the head of the council, his refusal to sign the warrant may arrest proceedings. Quebec city and town councils, after examining the list of arrears submitted to them, may order the clerk to sell such lands at public auction. Ontario councils may direct that no warrant be issued until after a longer period than three years and may direct that only land on which the arrears exceed a certain sum shall be included in the list to be sold, or that only lands belonging to any specified classification or of a named character be included. A rural municipal council in Saskatchewan may instruct the treasurer to file a tax lien only with respect to lands which are subdivided into building lots, or those without buildings, or those not being farmed or used for grazing or haying.

Tax Sale Procedure

Provision for the sale of lands for arrears of taxes occurs in all the provinces except Newfoundland and Saskatchewan. Where tax sale procedure applies, the lands with respect to which taxes have remained unpaid for the required length of time are offered for sale by public auction. In Nova Scotia, Quebec counties, Ontario, Manitoba, and Alberta the treasurer is responsible for conducting the sale; in Halifax, Saint John, and British Columbia, the collector; in Prince Edward Island and usually in New Brunswick, the sheriff; and in Quebec cities and towns, the clerk.

The lands offered for sale are sold to the highest bidder in some cases,[9] and in others they are sold to the highest bidder subject to a reserve bid.[10] Another method occurs in Nova Scotia (including Halifax), and in Quebec municipalities other than cities and towns. Nova Scotia requires that the treasurer sell so much of the land as is sufficient to satisfy the taxes, interest, and expenses, selling "in preference such part of the lot as he considers best for the owner to be sold first." In the Quebec municipalities the land is sold to the person offering to pay the amount owing and to take the least amount of the land. This method of sale has advantages in dealing with farm land for it leaves the original owner with the balance of the land upon which he depends for his living. It has complications, however, when used in selling urban lands where the remnant of a city lot may be of no real value. In Ontario, the treasurer may use either the highest bidder basis or that which awards the land to the person who will take the least amount of the land and pay the taxes owing.

The purchaser at a tax sale either is required to pay the full amount of his bid immediately[11] or in some provinces, if the bid exceeds the amount owing, must at least deposit an amount equal to the taxes owing. In Manitoba a purchaser is only required to pay at the time of the sale the amount standing against the property and the balance need not be paid until after the expiry of the redemption period. Alberta requires payment in cash within thirty days unless the council authorizes payment on the instalment plan or the taking of a mortgage for any balance not paid at the sale, but the appropriate Minister may make an order relating to conditions of sales. Most provinces provide for adjourning a tax sale to a later date or dates in cases where there are no bids or where the bids are less than the amount owing, with provision in some cases that at the adjourned sale the lands shall be sold for whatever is offered and the amount obtained is to be accepted in full payment of the taxes owing.

[9] Prince Edward Island, New Brunswick, Quebec cities and towns, and British Columbia.

[10] In Manitoba the municipality has a prior right to purchase a parcel of land for the amount of the arrears and costs; in Alberta each municipality is required to fix a minimum price for each parcel as a reserve bid, subject to any general order of the Minister governing the matter.

[11] Quebec cities and towns, Ontario municipalities.

The purchaser at a tax sale usually receives a certificate of sale but does not receive a deed to the property until after a period of one year, or longer if the period of redemption exceeds a year. Where the sale is conducted by a sheriff, as in Prince Edward Island and New Brunswick municipalities, the sheriff executes a deed forthwith to the purchaser but the land still remains subject to redemption.

Except in New Brunswick, the only lands to be sold at tax sale are those in respect of which there are taxes outstanding but in that province[12] all the real property owned by the taxpayer is liable to sale and not just that parcel on which there are taxes owing.

Purchaser's rights. The rights which the purchaser at a tax sale enjoys with respect to the land purchased, pending the expiry of the redemption period and the issue of a deed, vary greatly. Usually he has the right to prevent waste but has not the right to injure the property nor to cut timber or remove buildings. In Nova Scotia his rights are stated to be those of a first mortgagee and in Manitoba and British Columbia he has no right to the possession of the property. In Halifax, however, and in New Brunswick, Quebec, and Ontario the purchaser becomes the owner and has the right to possession and the enjoyment of the benefits of the land subject to the general prohibition of injury to and dispoiling of the land and, in all cases, subject to the right of redemption.

Redemption. Within the period fixed by law, the original owner of land sold at a tax sale, or someone on his behalf, or some one who had an interest in the land, may redeem the land by paying to the proper officer the amount for which the land was sold, plus certain percentages; if the land was sold for less than the amount owing, the amount required to redeem the land is the equivalent of the amount owing on it at the time of sale, plus the required percentages. The redemption money and the percentages are payable to the person who purchased at the tax sale and on such payment his rights and interest in the property cease. Appendix B to this chapter sets out the more important conditions for redeeming land sold at a tax sale but omits many of the less important details. The period for redemption varies from one to four years but one year is the usual period. The percentage added to the purchase price ranges from a rate of 6 per cent per annum to a straight 15 per cent.

Where lands sold at tax sale have not been redeemed within the statutory period the purchàser, after complying with any necessary formalities, is entitled to a deed to the property, commonly known as

[12]This does not apply to Saint John and may not in some of the other cities and towns.

a tax deed. In Manitoba, unless the purchaser at a tax sale applies for title within a period of one year from date of sale (in case the municipality is the purchaser, within three years), he forfeits all claim to the land, and to the money paid at the time of sale, and to any subsequent taxes he may have paid on the land.

Surplus. Most provinces provide that where a surplus remains, after deducting from the amount for which lands were sold the amount of the taxes together with the percentages and costs, such surplus shall be paid into court to be paid out to the persons entitled to such surplus. If such surplus funds are not claimed, they become the property of the municipality after six years in Ontario and Manitoba and after three years in Alberta.

Acquisition of tax sale lands by municipalities. Municipalities may acquire lands which are offered for sale for arrears of taxes either by default or as a result of action on the part of the council. Thus, in Alberta at the expiry of one year after a tax sale, every parcel against which a tax recovery notice remains shall be finally acquired by the municipality, and in British Columbia if no bid is equal to the upset price the municipality is declared to be the purchaser.

Several provinces provide for action on behalf of the municipality to enable it to acquire lands at such a sale, subject to statutory conditions. In Charlottetown the city clerk may bid up to the amount owing on any parcel and if no bid is made on any parcel he may purchase it for the city. Similarly, in Nova Scotia, the treasurer at the adjourned sale may bid up to the amount owing where no other bid of equal amount has been made[13] and in New Brunswick the county treasurer may bid up to the amount owing, plus 10 per cent. A Quebec municipality, if authorized by council, may bid up to the amount owing plus any amount sufficient to satisfy privileged debts of a rank higher than municipal taxes. An Ontario municipality may only bid if an appropriation therefor has been made in the municipal budget and only at the adjourned sale if no bid has been made equal to the amount owing.

Manitoba provides that the municipality shall have a prior right to purchase at a sale at the amount owing, even though there may be other and higher bids, and Alberta municipalities may bid, either at the public auction or at any subsequent private sale of such lands, for any lands which the municipality wants for any purpose for which it is authorized to acquire lands, but each such purchase must be approved by the Minister.

[13]The Halifax treasurer may bid up to the amount for which the parcel is being sold, plus the amount of any subsequent taxes.

Disposition of lands acquired by municipality at tax sales. Before the expiry of the redemption period, land acquired by a municipality at a tax sale may be resold in both Manitoba and British Columbia. In Manitoba, however, the sale or transfer of a tax sale certificate by the municipality for less than the land was bought in for requires the approval of the Minister; and in British Columbia a council may sell lands thus acquired at any time within nine months of the sale for not less than the upset price, plus interest at 6 per cent per annum, but such sale does not in any way interfere with the right of redemption.

In most instances, the disposition of such lands, after title is finally acquired by the municipality, is left to the discretion of the council. There are, however, a few exceptions which might be noted. If Charlottetown resells lands so acquired after more than six months from the date of the tax sale it can only do so after public notice, and in Quebec cities and towns lands so acquired must be sold either by auction or by private sale within a year after expiry of the redemption period, although the Minister may grant an extension of time. The proceeds of the sale or other disposition of such lands usually form part of the general funds of the municipality but the Halifax Charter requires that such proceeds be applied to the taxes owing and any balance then remaining be applied to the reduction of losses on other properties purchased by the city at tax sales. The money received from the sale of tax sale properties in British Columbia may only be used for making up sinking fund deficiencies, for reduction of debt, or for expenditures of a capital or other special nature.

Registration, Tax Lien, and Caveat Procedure

A much simpler procedure for collecting arrears of taxes occurs in Ontario and Saskatchewan. The procedure in Ontario is known as "registration of tax arrears certificates" and applied originally in those municipalities which in the thirties were in financial difficulties and came under provincial supervision as defaulting municipalities. The procedure then established has been continued in those municipalities even though they have ceased to be under supervision and it may be ordered by the Department of Municipal Affairs to be put into effect in other municipalities.[14] Under this plan, vacant lands on which taxes are in arrears at December 31 of the year following that in which they were levied, and improved lands on which taxes are in arrears on January 1 of the third year following that in which they were levied are vested in the municipality on registration of a tax arrears cer-

[14]The policy of the Department has been to await a request from the municipalities before ordering this procedure to be used. In 1949 it was in use in 4 cities, 59 towns, 27 villages, and 117 townships.

tificate in the registry office, subject to the right of redemption. Before registration the certificates must be approved by the Department of Municipal Affairs. The lands may be redeemed within one year of registration by payment of the arrears, with interest, plus certain costs and the taxes accrued since the date of registration. The use or disposition of the lands so acquired and the application of the proceeds from their use or disposition is subject to the approval of the Department.

Where taxes on land are unpaid in Saskatchewan municipalities more than six months after December 31 of the year in which they were levied the Tax Enforcement Act applies. The treasurer submits a list of such lands to the head of the council for his approval after which the list is published together with public notice that unless the taxes are paid within sixty days the treasurer will register a tax lien. Not later than December 31 the treasurer is required to forward to the Land Titles Office a tax lien respecting all properties included in the list, and on which the taxes have not been paid. The tax lien may be discharged at any time within two years on payment of the arrears and costs. At any time within a year after two years from the date of filing the tax lien, the municipality may apply for title to the land if the arrears have not been paid, unless an extension order is secured from the Provincial Mediation Board.

On receipt of application for title, the registrar directs the treasurer to notify all persons interested in the property. The treasurer, within six months after being directed by the registrar, notifies the assessed owner and other interested parties that the municipality has requested the issue of a certificate of title after thirty days from the date of such notice and that unless the lands are redeemed the registrar will issue a certificate of title. The municipality must notify the Provincial Mediation Board of the municipality's intention to make final application for title and the Board may order a stay of proceedings. If no prohibition order is issued the interested parties are again notified. If the municipality fails to apply for a certificate of title within the year after the expiry of two years from the registration of the lien or if it fails to make final application for title within two years of its first application for title it forfeits all claim to the land and the registrar cancels the lien.

Foreclosure Procedure

In Newfoundland, taxes imposed on any person in respect of any property attach to the property for a period not exceeding six years from the due date. Failing payment of the taxes, the council can proceed by foreclosure in the same manner as if the council held a mortgage on the property, ranking in priority to all other encumbrances on the property.

Compromise and Consolidation of Arrears

In three provinces, Ontario, Saskatchewan, and Alberta, provision is made for a compromise of arrears under certain circumstances. A compromise means an arrangement under which the municipality undertakes to accept a settlement on terms for payment of tax arrears different from those which would otherwise apply. Such a compromise may involve a reduction of the amount to be paid, or an extension of time within which payment must be made. A compromise with respect to arrears may be subject to certain conditions such as the prompt payment of the current taxes.

Where, in Ontario, a municipality is in default and as a result is under supervision by the Department of Municipal Affairs, the Department may authorize a compromise of arrears between the corporation and any ratepayer providing for an extension of the time for payment of arrears, or a reduction of the amount to be paid, or both. In Saskatchewan cities, where an area has been subdivided and assessed in lots and it appears to the council that the portion of the area upon which taxes are in arrears will not be developed in the immediate future, the council, with the approval of the Local Government Board, may compromise the municipality's claim and remit as much as they deem expedient.

The provision for compromise in Alberta is more comprehensive than in the two previous cases. Any council, by by-law, may make the provision of the Local Tax Arrears Consolidation Act apply for the current year in the municipality. The by-law is not binding until approved by the Minister and if any municipality, other than a city, declines to pass such a by-law the Minister, if he considers it proper to do so, may order the provisions of the Act to apply in the municipality.

Under this Act the owner of land against which there is a notification under the Tax Recovery Act may apply, before December 1 in any year, to consolidate the arrears on all the properties owned by him and must accompany the application with a deposit equal to one-fifth of the amount of the arrears. If the application is granted, the deposit is applied against the arrears and if refused, is returned to the applicant. The council may grant or refuse the application, but there is an appeal from the council's decision to the Minister.

Where the application is granted, the owner enters into an agreement with the municipality under which he undertakes to pay all the arrears in five instalments, of which the deposit is the first instalment, and one-fifth is payable by December 15 of each of the following four years. The completion of the agreement acts as a stay of proceedings under the Tax Recovery Act but the agreement only remains in effect if the instalments and the current taxes as well are paid by December 15 of each year. The amount of the arrears so consolidated are reduced by such discount as may be prescribed by the Lieutenant-Governor in Council who may classify taxes according to the number of years in arrears and may prescribe a rate of discount, not exceeding 25 per cent, by which any particular kind or class is to be reduced. A city in which the Act applies may modify its provision to adapt it to the city's special conditions, subject to the approval of the Minister, but not so as to grant greater relief than is provided for by the Act, except that the instalments may be extended from five to ten years. Where the instalments are extended, however, the arrears may not be reduced by any discount.

This Act further provides that in the case of crop failure, or under other proper circumstances, a council on application, from which there is an appeal to the Minister, may extend a consolidation agreement for one year and may waive payment of the instalment of arrears and payment of the current taxes for any one year. The waived instalment becomes payable by December 15 of the fifth year, with interest at 6 per cent per annum. If default is made in payments under the agreements or in payment of the current taxes, except where payment has been waived for one year as mentioned in the previous paragraph, all discounts previously given on any instalment and on the current taxes are cancelled and the current taxes and the unpaid balance of the consolidated taxes and penalties, which, but for the agreement, would have accrued since the application for consolidation, become due and payable.

APPENDIX A

STATUTORY PROVISIONS RE PENALTIES TO BE IMPOSED ON OVERDUE TAXES

Province	C or O[a]	Statutory provision for added interest
Newfoundland	C	At rate of 6% per annum commencing one year after due date
Nova Scotia		
Towns	O	At rate not exceeding 7% per annum
Municipalities	O	At rate not exceeding 6% per annum

APPENDIX A—*Continued*

Province	C or O[a]	Statutory provision for added interest
New Brunswick	O	At rate of ½% per month
Quebec		
Cities and towns	O	At rate not exceeding 5% per annum
Ontario	O[b]	At rate not exceeding 1% per month
Manitoba	C	At rate of ½% per month after Oct. 31
Saskatchewan	C	5% added after Dec. 31 and an addition of 5% of such combined amount at end of each succeeding year
Alberta		
Cities	O	6% in year of levy and 6% in each following year
Towns and villages	C	4% added Dec. 15; 4% added the following July 1 on the tax and penalty; 4% added each succeeding Dec. 15 and July 1
Municipal districts	C	4% added July 1 of year following levy; 4% added each Dec. 16 and July 1 thereafter
British Columbia	C	10% added July 1 of year taxes are levied[c]; interest at rate of 6% per annum after Dec. 31 of year levied

[a]C means compulsory, O means that it is optional whether or not the penalty provisions are used but if they are, they must be in conformity with the statute.

[b]Optional until Dec. 31 of year in which taxes are levied; compulsory after that date.

[c]The council before sending out of tax notices may alter date on which the penalty is to be added or direct parts of penalty to be added at different dates but 10% must be added by Dec. 31.

APPENDIX B

MORE IMPORTANT CONDITIONS FOR REDEEMING LANDS SOLD AT TAX SALES

Province	Period after sale within which land may be redeemed	Amount of money to be paid to redeem lands sold
Prince Edward Island		
Towns	2 years	Purchase price plus interest at 4% per annum plus value of improvement made by purchaser
Charlottetown	see below[a]	Purchase price plus interest at 10% per annum plus expenses
Nova Scotia		
General	1 year	Purchase price plus interest at 6% per annum
Halifax	1 year	Purchase price plus 10% plus taxes subsequent to sale, less net revenue received by purchaser from the property
New Brunswick		
General	1 year	Purchase price plus 15%
Saint John	1 year	Purchase price plus 10%, plus purchaser's expenditure for repairs not in excess of 15% of value of building

APPENDIX B—*Continued*

Province	Period after sale within which land may be redeemed	Amount of money to be paid to redeem lands sold
Quebec		
Cities and towns	1 year	Purchase price plus 10%, plus cost of certificate of sale[b]
Other municipalities	2 years	If redeemed from the municipality, purchase price plus 10%, plus taxes imposed since date of sale; in other cases, purchase price plus 10%, plus costs[c]
Ontario	1 year[d]	Purchase price plus 10%, plus accrued taxes; if municipality was purchaser also pay expenditures incurred to keep land in repair and insured, with interest; if sold for less than amount owing, full amount of taxes and costs plus 10%, plus accrued taxes
Manitoba		
General	1 year	Arrears plus costs, plus 10% and, if purchaser has paid taxes subsequently imposed plus amount of taxes so paid, plus 10%
Winnipeg	2 years	Arrears and costs plus ½% per month from date of sale, plus taxes paid by the purchaser subsequent to the sale
Alberta	1 year	All taxes owing, other than current taxes, plus costs
	4 years	Where lands were acquired by the municipality and have not been disposed of—amount of arrears and costs
British Columbia		
General	1 year[e]	Purchase price plus interest at 6% per annum
Vancouver	1 year	Purchase price plus interest at rate to be fixed by council but not exceeding 10%

[a]Right of redemption is limited to lands purchased at sale by city and only possible in interval before city resells the land.

[b]If a third party redeems for the benefit of the original owner he is entitled to be reimbursed by the owner the amount paid, with interest at 8%.

[c]Purchaser may compel person redeeming to reimburse him for necessary repairs plus 10% and may retain possession until such claim is paid.

[d]Where after the redemption date land which was sold to the municipality has not been resold or conveyed and has not been declared by by-law to be required for the purposes of the municipality it may be redeemed with the approval of the Department of Municipal Affairs within a period of ten years on payment of full amount that would have been payable for taxes, penalties, etc., plus expenditures with interest for repairs, insurance and costs of sale.

[e]Council may extend the time for redemption for a period not exceeding one year if authorized prior to the sale or for a similar period in the case of lands acquired by the municipality and not subsequently sold, if authorized by council prior to the expiry of the statutory redemption period.

CHAPTER XVII

PROVINCIAL-MUNICIPAL RELATIONS

ONE OF THE PRESSING and fundamental problems of local government is that of the relationships between the provinces and their municipalities. Its urgency results from the increasing pressure on the limited municipal finances; its importance lies in the necessity of preserving the reality of local self-government in a democracy. On the surface, the problem appears to be a financial one, but the political aspects, in the long run, may be of even greater significance. The importance and complexity of the problem is suggested by the attention which it has received in recent years, for it has been the subject of formal inquiry in several Canadian provinces[1] and in some of the states of the United States.[2] The problem is not confined to this continent, as evidenced, among others, by the inquiry in New Zealand in 1945, and the ill-fated Local Government Boundary Commission in England in 1946–9.

THE PROBLEM

Put briefly, the problem consists of resolving the conflicts involved in endeavouring to attain several ends at the same time, viz: (*a*) the execution of functions which provincial authorities consider essential for their citizens and, in doing so, to attain for all at least the indispensable minimum standard of performance; (*b*) the provision of facilities and services demanded by the citizens in the local municipalities through their local government; (*c*) the strengthening of the financial position of the local authorities, to enable them to carry out the purposes of (*a*) and (*b*) above; and (*d*) the maintenance of that degree of effectiveness and self-reliance in the local government institutions which is essential to the preservation of a democracy.

Before discussing these main ends and the difficulties involved in attaining them, it is desirable to review the changes which have taken place in the Canadian economy in more recent years and which affect and form, in part, the setting within which the problem must be worked out.

[1]Alberta in 1935 and 1948, Saskatchewan in 1936 and 1950, British Columbia in 1947, Nova Scotia in 1949, and Ontario and Manitoba in 1951.
[2]New York in 1945–6, Maine in 1945, Massachusetts in 1948, etc.

In the middle of the nineteenth century Canadian municipalities were, much more than now, the local units in the economy; they were more on a subsistence, and therefore self-sufficient basis, and the functions of municipal governments were local in the most direct sense of the term, arising in each case out of the particular circumstances and desires of each community. Municipal boundaries were more realistic—each town was a clearly recognizable entity, and the rural areas were also for the most part separate and distinct regions, each with a highly developed local character. Trade was chiefly between the town and its hinterland. Industrial activity was not great and mass production was unknown. Industry was dispersed, and within each community small factories, mills and home handcraft provided most non-agricultural goods. There was a frontier to be pushed out by the discontented or those unable to prosper, as prosperity was then known, in their original area. . . .

Both the local consciousness and the absence of marked economic differentiation or interdependence between local areas, as well as the relative simplicty of the whole economy, were conducive to the concept of a separate local government for each area: each looked after its own affairs and was not greatly interested in or affected by the affairs of others.[3]

Such was the economic setting at the time when the existing pattern of municipal institutions in the various provinces was originally drawn and when the major sources of municipal revenue were determined. These institutions were designed to serve a population predominantly rural and an economy largely agricultural. That these institutions have continued to serve as effectively as they have with little fundamental alteration through a century of rapid and radical changes in the economy is a tribute to the soundness of their original conception.

Since the turn of the century, and more particularly during and following the two World Wars, Canada has to a material degree changed from an agricultural to an industrialized economy and the greater part of the population, which in 1871 was largely rural (80.42 per cent), by 1951 was to be found in urban communities (61.5 per cent). As industrialization increased, local self-sufficiency decreased. Industrial specialization, technological advances, mass production and the concentration of industries in urban centres, and widespread expansion of trade, both domestic and foreign, made the economic welfare of each community more dependent upon the policies and welfare of all. An inevitable accompaniment of increasing industrialization was increasing urbanization, the concentration of population which provides the large labour force and the mass markets upon which mass production methods depend. This increased concentration of population in turn gave rise to an increase in the problems of the local governments, in-

[3]H. Carl Goldenberg, *Municipal Finance in Canada: A Study Prepared for the Royal Commission on Dominion-Provincial Relations* (Ottawa, 1939), p. 26.

creases both in degree and kind. The decline of individual self-sufficiency, characteristic of an industrial economy, forced the citizen to rely more and more upon the community organization to protect him against forces which individually he was well-nigh powerless to resist.

At the same time, influenced in part by the changing economy, there occurred a radical change in the thinking of the citizens on the function of government. The attitude that the government governs best that governs least, gave way to the idea of the welfare state. Government ceased to be regarded as an institution primarily concerned with protective and regulatory functions, and at the local level to provide essential physical services. It came to be considered as an institution that should be concerned with positive programmes for the benefit of the citizens, to protect them against social and economic hazards, to compensate them for personal and economic handicaps, and to assure to each what, at any given period, is assumed to be a reasonable standard of living. Pursuant to this changing political philosophy, local governments, as well as those at other levels, have greatly enlarged the scope of their activities in the field of the social services.

(*a*) *Provincial Policies*

The provincial governments have done much to develop more positive programmes in the interests of their citizens. Not the least of the influences bringing this about has been the changing view of the electors in regard to the responsibilities of governments and the realization of the political possibilities, in a democracy, of redistributing the wealth of the citizens. Other factors have made municipal actions and policies of increasing concern to the provinces. Many functions originally assumed to be exclusively of local concern have become provincial responsibilities as a result of changing conditions. Thus, roads, which were long considered to be a municipal problem, have increasingly been taken over by the provinces.

The advent of the automobile resulted in a need for a progressively rising standard of highway construction and a continuous extension of improved highways far beyond the financial resources of the municipalities. As so frequently happens, the rural municipalities in which the need was greatest were those least able to bear the expense. If adequate avenues for trade and commerce were to be available for the use of the new medium of transportation, it became expedient for the provinces to assume the responsibility for the main highway routes and, in addition, to see that subsidiary roads were brought up to a sufficiently high standard to be effective feeders to the main highways.

Public health, except in major epidemics, was also long considered to be of purely local concern but with increased knowledge of communicable diseases and the possibilities of their control, resulting from discoveries such as those of Koch and Pasteur in the nineteenth century, the interdependence of all communities in protecting themselves against disease became apparent. The provinces came to appreciate their responsibility for seeing that the majority was not placed in jeopardy by reason of lagging preventive measures in some municipalities. The hazards were multiplied by the growing mobility of the population as motor transportation continued to develop. This increased travel also resulted in a growing realization by the citizens of progress being made in other communities and gave rise to demands that the provincial authorities should do something to raise the local standards of performance in their home communities.

Increasing urbanization developed new and urgent problems and demands for more and better municipal services. The response to these demands brought rising municipal expenditures and consequent appeals to the provinces for financial assistance. To help the municipalities straighten out their financial problems, to guard against future financial difficulties, to see that provincial programmes were being carried out, and to assure themselves that provincial revenues being expended through municipal channels were being properly applied, the provinces were driven more and more into the position of directing, supervising and controlling many municipal activities.

When a provincial government has a programme of service which it wishes to carry out for the benefit of its people it may choose between the alternatives of organizing a staff of its own to administer the programme or of using the facilities of the established local government institutions. For certain purposes it has been considered expedient to organize the service on a provincial basis, as with the provincial police forces or provincial liquor stores. For other purposes the provinces have used the established municipal bodies, such as school boards, health boards, or councils, or have created new types of joint-municipal bodies, such as health units or conservation bodies, to implement provincial programmes. If a province chooses the latter of these alternatives it wishes to see that the programme is being carried out and that performance is at least up to the standard which the provincial authorities consider to be essential. It is often necessary to encourage the local bodies to obtain the desired results by making grants toward the particular service desired. Such grants are usually on a percentage basis designed to increase the expenditure by the local authorities for the particular purpose; the more local money that is spent, the more money they can obtain from the province. These grants are frequently accompanied by conditions respecting the quality or extent of the work to be done, for a reluctant municipal body can be induced to attain the desired minimum standard under threat of losing the grant. It would, of course, be legally possible for a province to require the local authorities, under threat of a penalty, to provide the desired services up to the standard fixed by the province. But when governments are freely elected from almost identical electorates, it is a more feasible approach, politically, to offer something which may be withheld, rather than to impose an obligation to be enforced by a positive penalty. If the programmes which a province wishes to promote through the medium of the local authorities are beyond the financial resources of many of the municipalities it may make unconditional grants to strengthen the basic financial position of the local government as an alternative to making additional sources of revenue available to the municipalities.

In more recent years, there has been an effort by the provinces to equalize the burden imposed by the standard of services which the provinces require the local authorities to maintain. As those standards are raised, and as the disparity in resources between municipalities increases, it becomes more difficult for the financially weaker municipalities to provide the service except under an overwhelming burden of taxation, and in extreme cases it may be quite impossible. It is for that reason that the provinces have introduced the equalizing factor in the grants which are made toward education, health, and highways, for if a uniform standard is to be maintained the burden bears unequally upon those with less resources. The burden can be equalized by subsidizing the service out of the general revenues of the province with the amount of assistance varying inversely to the local financial capacity. One difficulty is to find an acceptable standard for the measurement of relative financial capacity or fiscal need.

(*b*) *Provision for Locally Determined Programmes*

Members of locally elected bodies tend to hold the view that their first responsibility is to their electorate and to the local taxpayers who supply the greater part of the funds which they expend. They believe, and in so doing reflect the popular opinion in their communities, that their first concern is to supply the services and facilities and to adopt and carry out the policies which are desired by the local citizens. There are many services which it is generally conceded are matters of varying degrees of provincial concern, such as education or health, but there is also a wide and ever growing range of services which are exclusively of local concern, services which are desired by the citizens and are to be maintained up to standards demanded by the citizens. Such, for instance, would be the provision of street lighting, fire protection, parks, tree trimming, snow removal, the provision of sidewalks, recreation programmes, refuse removal and disposal, building inspection, etc. The range of such services increases as population increases and as the standard of public service expected by the citizens continues to rise.

The local taxing authorities are caught between two millstones. The upper one consists of the top limit of the burden of taxation which it is feasible to impose upon the taxpayers, and still leave them intact financially and leave their representatives intact politically. The position of the nether stone is progressively raised as the amount of the total municipal expenditure which is imposed by provincial policies and by uncontrollable special purpose bodies increases. Thus, the play between the two is continuously reduced and the capacity of the taxing authority, the council, to provide the services demanded by the public is narrowed. Caught as they are in this squeeze, councils are driven to continuous appeals to the provinces for financial assistance or additional sources of revenue. But there is likely to be a reluctance to make available to municipalities any really productive sources of revenue, for most provinces are themselves sufficiently desperate for additional funds that they would hesitate to release them to a subsidiary level of government.

(*c*) *Strengthening the Financial Position of Local Authorities*

The major source of municipal tax revenue, real property taxation, was designed to serve municipalities having a much more limited sphere of activity than that which now obtains. As suggested above, the use of local authorities to implement provincial programmes, the increase in uncontrollable expenditures through special purpose bodies, together with the rapid expansion of services in response to citizen demands, particularly in the field of social services, has placed the municipalities in a basically unsound financial position. In times of prosperity and full employment they are able to keep going but they have not the resources to weather the storm under adverse economic conditions. The problem is a more acute one with the larger centres for in these municipalities the overhead of irreducible public services is proportionately greater and the individual citizen is more dependent on continued community services.[4] As urbanization increases the municipal structure as a whole tends to become more vulnerable.

The financial plight of the municipalities became glaringly apparent in the 1930's when, as a result of economic depression, many municipalities found it imperative to make drastic reductions in normal services, to skimp maintenance of their physical plant, and, in the case of over fifty Canadian municipalities, to default on their obligations to their bondholders, in order to meet the cost of welfare and assistance to the unemployed. So acute was the problem that the provinces were forced to come to the assistance of the municipalities to keep them functioning, and to protect the provinces' own credit, and the Dominion, in turn, was compelled to come to the aid of the provinces. Although there had been occasions previously, as in western Canada before World War I, when financial difficulties brought provincial intervention, the problem had never previously been as widespread nor on such a large scale. One result was the close provincial supervision of the defaulting municipalities and the extension of provision for permanent provincial control of all municipal capital financing as a preventive against a repetition of such defaults. If a province is to assume responsibility for extricating municipalities which get themselves into financal difficulties, it is a logical step to take preventive measures against a recurrence of a similar situation.

Following the depression years came an accelerated trend toward urbanization accompanied by a growing need and demand for increased social services. The rapidly expanding urban population had to be accommodated within a supply of housing which had been practically static for a decade, for there had been little building during the depression and both labour and materials were in short supply during the war years. Among the results of this over-crowding, combined with other factors such as disturbed family life owing to war conditions and the rising age level of the whole population, was the need for expanded institutional facilities such as hospitals and homes for the aged, and increased expenditures for child care and protection. The prevailing tendency to look to governments to solve many social problems may have been strengthened by the experience of a substantial portion of the population during the thirties. Many of the social or welfare problems with which the municipalities were met, however, were beyond the resources or the capacities of the individual.

[4]There are, of course, special cases of extreme financial difficulty in some rural areas, as in the drought areas of the western provinces.

Where municipalities were reluctant to meet these needs they were in some cases encouraged by the provinces to act and in others were obliged to do so. The provinces in turn were forced to come to the financial assistance of the municipalities to enable them to carry the burden. In some instances the provinces assumed the whole cost of the service,[5] in others they shared in the cost, or increased the share which they had previously been paying.

With increased provincial assistance came increased supervision and direction. This, in turn has been accompanied by the irritations and bickering which so frequently occur where one level of government raises money and another spends it. The municipalities have resented provincial inroads on local autonomy at the same time that they have realized its inevitability and its justification. They have seen that ever growing provincial contributions will mean loss of local control and at the same time have been forced by their financial plight to make persistent appeals for more and more assistance.

The provinces, on the other hand, have been forced into giving greater financial assistance to the municipalities if their policies are to be carried out. If the job is to be done, the local authorities must be kept in business and, unless the provincial administration is to be overwhelmed with minor matters of primarily local concern, they must be kept in business with sufficient power of initiative and freedom of decision to attract the services of competent elected representatives and paid officers. If the local authorities are to be strait-jacketed in the interests of immediate efficiency and uniformity, the power of local self-government may atrophy with fatal long-run results. A fundamental necessity for effectiveness in any level of government is a substantial degree of financial independence.

(*d*) *The Maintenance of Effectiveness and Self-reliance in Local Government*

It is generally accepted that, in a country as vast as Canada or even as extensive as most of the provinces, local units of government are indispensable to effective administration. It is also generally believed by students of government that if a democratic form of government is to survive at the national level it can only do so if it is built upon a foundation of local autonomy. Such a system of local governments must be one in which the municipalities are not merely agencies of a higher authority but rather units which have ultimate responsibility within their sphere of jurisdiction. This sphere must be of sufficient

[5]As in the case of old age pensions and sanatorium care for tuberculosis patients.

scope to make the local authority significant in the esteem of the citizens and thus attract into public service a high quality of men and women in both elected and appointive office. Without the assurance of reasonably adequate resources commensurate with its responsibilities and without a reasonable degree of self-determination as to the extent and the avenues of expenditures, local self-government and the responsibility of the local elected representatives to their electors becomes a sham. A unit of government which has not the power of final decision but which must carry the responsibility for the financing and administration of policies which are not of its making is contrary to the fundamental principle of responsible government and places the elected representatives in an untenable position.

There are those who hold that the carrying out of policies of higher levels of government must take precedence over the desires of local authorities and that the implementing of those policies is the major if not the sole purpose of local government. This viewpoint is expressed by Professor Finer in discussing the changing attitude of local authorities toward the central authorities in England:

> . . . local authorities and central government are part and parcel of one governmental system, and that their relationship is one of a partnership and collaboration in a single organism possessing one common ultimate purpose and an integrated system of institutions for the purpose. This, we are sure, is the lesson of the facts: that the local governing bodies are integrated parts in a governmental structure and a corpus of functions larger and more important than themselves. They have practically no functions or purpose outside this context, and they and their problems are recognizable only within it.
>
> This does not mean that our local authorities have no entirely self-regarding functions, or that their only importance is derived from their collaboration, usually enforced collaboration, in an integrated arrangement. They have self-regarding functions, but, as we shall show presently, they are few and relatively unimportant. But neither the development of English local government, nor its main problems, especially that of finance, are comprehensible unless we recognize that local authorities are but cells in one living organism.[6]

Aside from the difficulties with which a province would be met in the field of Dominion-provincial relations, if it took such a position in the provincial-municipal field, it would be argued by some that granting the importance of implementing the policies of the higher authorities it may still be necessary to allow a wide measure of municipal independence lest the "ultimate purpose" of the preservation of the democratic system be frustrated in the pursuit of some less vital short-

[6]Herman Finer, *English Local Government* (London, 1933), pp. 9–10.

run purpose. It may be that it is necessary for the higher levels of government to tolerate some frustration of their immediate aims in the interests of strengthening municipal institutions if the political system is to be maintained.

This may be claimed to be an over emphasis of the importance of local self-government in the maintenance of a democratic system. Yet, with respect to Newfoundland, Powell argues that the failure of self-government there was due in great part to the lack of municipal organization. There was no body to deal with local problems at the local level and as a result so much of the time of members of the House of Assembly was taken up in lobbying in the interests of their political districts that they had little left to devote to the interests of the island as a whole. The national interests were sacrificed for local interests, and, in his opinion, largely through the failure to organize municipal government, democratic government was lost.[7]

Before discussing proposals for clarifying and improving the relationship between the provinces and their municipalities it is desirable to consider the development and extent of existing controls and supervision of the municipalities by the various provinces.

Provincial Control and Supervision

The extent and nature of provincial control and supervision vary from province to province but the trend would appear to be for a general increase in supervision.[8] Provincial control in the legal and constitutional sense is absolute, for the legislative power of the legislatures within the municipal sphere is exclusive and supreme. It is obvious, however, that if provincial authorities are to exercise effective control and supervision over their municipalities the legislative power must be supplemented by administrative agencies and these agencies must be provided with some discretionary powers and with what amounts to a delegated power of legislation.

Two types of such agencies have been used by the provinces for the supervision of municipalities. Most provinces have established a de-

[7]C. W. Powell (Director of Local Government Affairs, Newfoundland), "Problems Arising from Lack of Organized Municipalities in Newfoundland," *Proceedings of the First Annual Conference of the Institute of Public Administration of Canada* (1949), p. 180.

[8]Professor L. D. White in his *Introduction to the Study of Public Administration* (New York, 1945), suggests there is a pattern to the development of central authority supervision in which he notes eleven steps, as follows: (1) advice and information, (2) co-operative administration, (3) periodic reports, (4) inspection and advice, (5) central review, (6) grants-in-aid, (7) fixing standards, (8) requirement of prior permission, (9) appointment and removal of officers, (10) issuance of orders, (11) partial or total assumption of an activity. Each of these phases of development applies in some provinces.

partment of municipal affairs, headed by a Cabinet member. The control exercised by these departments in the general municipal field is supplemented by the control exercised by other provincial departments in special fields such as education, health, highways, planning, etc. As detailed control over the municipalities has grown, the practice has developed, in this as in other spheres, of enacting general legislation which endows the responsible Minister with the power to make regulations under the Act, usually subject to the approval of the Lieutenant-Governor in Council. These regulations, which constitute a form of supplementary legislation, may be far more extensive than the original statute out of which they arise, and they may enable the Minister and his department, through the Cabinet, to materially alter the result from that which the legislature may have anticipated when passing the basic enactment. In addition to this Cabinet control, most provinces have established administrative boards of a quasi-judicial nature which are given powers of review over certain municipal activities.

The idea underlying the establishment of provincial departments of municipal affairs appears to have been to give leadership and guidance in municipal development and to provide for the continuous study of the problems of the municipalities. The need was first recognized in the western provinces, where a rapidly expanding population required a correspondingly rapid development of local government institutions where none had existed before. Manitoba, in 1886, created the office of Municipal Commissioner. The Commissioner was a member of the Executive Council and had under him the Department of the Municipal Commissioner. The Commissioner's Department was established to take over the county functions in providing for the administration of justice when the county system was abolished in 1886. Its responsibilities were extended in 1918 when the incurring of municipal debt was made subject to the Commissioner's approval, a responsibility which was transferred to the Municipal and Public Utility Board in 1932.

Saskatchewan in 1908, three years after the creation of the province, also set up a Department of the Municipal Commissioner headed by a Cabinet member.[9] The Department was to supervise municipal accounting and records and the conduct of the affairs of the municipalities by their officers, to adjust differences arising between municipal councils, to provide for an annual inspection of the records of each municipality, and, on petition of a council or order of the Minister,

[9]Subsequently the title of the Commissioner was changed to Minister of Municipal Affairs and the name of the Department to the Department of Municipal Affairs.

to make special inspections. Where a council failed within sixty days to deal with any matter which the inspectors reported required summary action the Department could deal with it and, if considered expedient, could dismiss the treasurer or other officers of the municipality. Three years later, in 1911, Alberta created a Department of Municipal Affairs under the direction of a Minister of Municipal Affairs with powers almost the same as those of the Saskatchewan Department, with the added provision that the Minister could authorize a special audit of a municipality on petition of the freehold electors (100 in cities and 25 in other municipalities).

At the time when these latter two departments were provided for, the west was experiencing a "boom" and the new departments "devoted a great part of their time to organizing new municipalities—giving advice, helping install accounting and record systems, explaining the law. All along the way the provincial inspectors seem to have warned the cities, towns and villages against plunging into debt and to proceed cautiously until the economic future of the area could be more clearly foreseen. But the advice fell upon deaf ears; 'expansion' and 'development' were the watchword."[10]

The municipalities of the western provinces have appeared to accept provincial supervision more readily than those in the east, which may be owing to several factors. Because the departments of municipal affairs were already functioning at the time when many of the municipalities came into existence, they have been accepted as a natural accompaniment of local government, whereas in the older provinces the municipalities which for many years carried on with little or no provincial supervision have tended to resent the growing infringement on their autonomy. The rapid expansion in the west and the higher standards demanded in the twentieth century when the west was developing which forced the municipalities to look to the provinces for assistance in dealing with problems beyond their resources, was in contrast to the much slower development in the east in the previous century.

The growing pressure of municipal problems resulted in the establishment of a Department of Municipal Affairs in Quebec in 1918 under the jurisdiction of the Provincial Treasurer.[11] The Minister was given the responsibility of overseeing the administration of the munici-

[10]Winston W. Crouch, "Administrative Supervision of Local Government: The Canadian Experience," *American Political Science Review*, June, 1949, vol. XLII, no. 3, p. 509.

[11]Subsequently under the Minister of Municipal Affairs, Trade and Commerce and presently under the Minister of Municipal Affairs.

pal system and of providing for the inspection of local records and books. Councils which failed within thirty days to remedy any condition which an inspector found warranted summary action could be compelled to do so by the courts, at the instance of a ratepayer. Municipal borrowings were made subject to provincial approval.

As early as 1914 British Columbia had an Inspector of Municipalities, under the Attorney General, who on complaint or on his own initiative could hold public hearings on municipal matters; any resulting order, if approved by the Cabinet, was binding on the municipalities. The province also could regulate the form of municipal accounts and reports, the management of sinking funds, and the provincial inspection of records. Following the default of a number of municipalities and the development of sinking fund shortages in the early thirties, a Department of Municipal Affairs was created in 1934 and the Inspector of Municipalities was placed under the Minister of Municipal Affairs. The Department was to be "the recognized medium of communication between the municipalities of the Province and the Lieutenant-Governor in Council." The following year provision was made that, where a municipality was not handling its sinking funds satisfactorily, they could be administered by the Minister.

The financial difficulties and extensive defaults of a number of municipalities in the depression of the thirties resulted also in the appointment of a Minister of Municipal Affairs and corresponding department in Ontario in 1935. The Department's duties were similar to those in the other provinces, including a general oversight of municipal affairs, standardizing municipal accounting, compiling statistical information, conducting special investigations, and assisting municipalities with advice. Where the Ontario Municipal Board so ordered, the Department had supervision of the administration of defaulting municipalities.

As early as 1909 Nova Scotia appointed a Municipal Sinking Fund Commissioner who could sue for any deficiency in the amount provided for a local sinking fund. A Department of Municipal Affairs was established in 1935 and the Attorney General for the time being was designated the Minister of Municipal Affairs.[12] An officer known as the Municipal Commissioner was appointed whose duty was to inspect and audit the records of the municipalities. All borrowing by the municipalities had to be approved by the Minister and the duties of the Municipal Sinking Fund Commissioner were transferred to the Municipal Commissioner.

[12]By 1950 there was a full-time Minister of Municipal Affairs.

A Commissioner of Municipal Affairs was appointed in New Brunswick in 1934. His powers were much the same as those of the departments of municipal affairs in other provinces, although in some cases their exercise was subject to Cabinet approval. In 1936 provision was made for a Minister of Education, Federal and Municipal Relations[13] and the Commissioner came under his jurisdiction.

The situation in Newfoundland was somewhat different than that in the other provinces. Instead of a provincial officer or department being set up to control and supervise the established municipalities, a Director of Local Government was appointed in 1944, a great part of whose work has been to encourage and promote the incorporation of municipalities. Prior to 1938 St. John's was the only incorporated municipality and by 1944 there were only three others, but by 1951 the number had increased to twenty-seven. The Director of Local Government presently functions under the Department of Supply.

Thus, by 1936, all but one of the provinces then in the Dominion had established departments of provincial government devoted to dealing with municipal matters and with a Minister at the head of the department who was in a position to concentrate his attention on and to advise his Cabinet colleagues with respect to municipal problems. Originally most of these departments were created to assist with a rapidly expanding municipal development or to deal with financial problems arising out of the crisis of the thirties. Space does not permit an outline here of the subsequent development of their powers. As is so often the case, however, once these departments were established, the scope of their activities tended to increase and expand and such expansion inevitably served to limit the unrestricted exercise by the municipalities of their powers.

Paralleling the development of these departments of municipal affairs was the creation of provincial administrative boards, the purposes of which were somewhat different from those of the departments. Several of these bodies in different provinces were originally formed to deal with the problems of public utilities and their relations with municipal authorities. As utilities came more and more into the hands of the municipalities this aspect of their functions declined in importance. However, as a product of the financial difficulties of the thirties, several of these administrative quasi-judicial bodies have been assigned the task of controlling and supervising municipal financing, particularly capital financing, as well as jurisdiction in other municipal matters such as zoning, assessment, etc.

[13]Subsequently a Department of Municipal Affairs was established.

Ontario, in 1897, authorized the appointment of a Provincial Municipal Auditor[14] to give leadership in improving the keeping and audit of municipal and school accounts. He could prescribe the method of keeping such records and on request of two councillors or on petition of thirty ratepayers could make an inspection and audit, and councils were under obligation to carry out any subsequent recommendations for improvements which he made.

The Ontario Railway and Municipal Board, composed of three members, was formed in 1906 and although the greater part of their duties concerned railway matters, which had previously been under the jurisdiction of the Railway Committee of the Executive Council, they were assigned duties respecting some municipal matters such as assessment appeals from county judges, alterations of municipal boundaries, and approval of municipal by-laws relating to debt, sinking funds, or utilities, where such required provincial approval. They also had the duty of inquiring into any proposed bill relating to municipal corporations on request of the Cabinet, the Legislature, or any of its committees. A Bureau of Municipal Affairs was created in 1917, headed by a Director, to superintend the accounting of municipally controlled utilities, other than electrical utilities, and in addition it appears to have been contemplated that it would serve as a research agency in the municipal field,[15] and in 1919 it was provided that a member of the Railway and Municipal Board might be the Director of the Bureau.

Under the impact of the depression the Board's powers were increased in 1932 at which time it was renamed the Ontario Municipal Board and it was given a general power to require or forbid the doing of any act which any municipality was required to do or not to do under any Act or order of the Board or under any agreement to which the municipality was a party. It was also given the power to inquire into and determine, on request of the Lieutenant-Governor in Council or by its own motion, any matter which it might inquire into or determine on application or complaint. At the same time the Bureau of Municipal Affairs was transferred to the jurisdiction of the Board and one of the members of the Board was designated Municipal Commissioner. The Commissioner on his own initiative or on request of a

[14]His jurisdiction did not extend to cities having a population of 15,000.

[15]Among its duties were to issue bulletins dealing with each branch of municipal affairs to secure uniformity, efficiency, and economy in such administration, to collect statistical information regarding municipal affairs, to study the operation of municipal affairs elsewhere and make recommendations arising from such study, and to report to the Minister, when requested, on any suggested change in the laws relating to municipal corporations.

council or fifty ratepayers could direct a provincial audit of the financial affairs of a municipality at the municipality's expense[16] and could order the carrying out of anything the audit indicated was necessary.

The Board was given extensive jurisdiction over defaulting municipalities. A new general control over the finances of municipalities was added in 1935, by a provision that no municipal expenditures to be financed by the issue of debentures was to be undertaken without the approval of the Board, which might hold public hearings on the proposal, and in 1946 a further tightening of the control required municipalities to obtain the Board's approval for any expenditure if any portion of the cost was to be raised in a subsequent year, whether by debentures or otherwise. While these developments in the supervision of municipal finance were taking place over the years an increasing number of council actions of a non-financial nature were made subject to Municipal Board approval. By 1947 the volume of work of the Board had increased to the point that it became necessary to enlarge the personnel to five, and by 1951 to seven members.

Saskatchewan in 1913 established a Local Government Board of three members to hold office during good behaviour for ten years, but removable on address of the Legislature for cause. Associated with the Board, in an advisory capacity, were two members, one appointed annually by the executive of the rural municipalities' provincial organization and one by the executive of the urban municipalities' group. Municipalities were required to obtain the Board's approval of their borrowings and the Board could supervise the expenditure of borrowed money and manage the local sinking funds when it considered this expedient. The Board was given wide powers over municipalities in default in 1916 and the following year its powers were considerably extended to empower it, in matters within its jurisdiction, to require municipalities to do anything which under any Act they were required to do or to forbid the doing of anything in contravention of any law, regulation, or order. The decisions of the Board were declared to be final and not to be questioned or reviewed, restrained, or removed by prohibition or injunction, except that an appeal was provided to the Supreme Court on a question of jurisdiction, conditioned on obtaining leave to appeal from a judge of the Supreme Court.

A Board of Public Utility Commissioners was provided for in Alberta in 1915. This Board of three members[17] was afforded the same

[16]The legislation under which the Provincial Municipal Auditor had functioned was repealed in 1932.

[17]The Board is not always kept up to full strength.

security of tenure as the Saskatchewan Local Government Board. The municipalities came under its supervision in so far as they operated municipally owned utilities or were dealing with private utility operators and they were also required to obtain the Board's approval for issuing debentures. The Board, as in Saskatchewan, at its option could manage local sinking funds and could supervise the expenditure of borrowed monies. By 1923 the Board had been authorized to deal with the financial affairs of defaulting municipalities, to order compromises of taxes, to deal with land subdivisions, and to initiate enquiries into and determine any matter within its jurisdiction with a limitation of appeal as in Saskatchewan.

The Municipal and Public Utility Board of Manitoba, created in 1926, was a three-member board with the usual tenure of office. It was given general supervision of the financial affairs of the municipalities other than cities, to ensure that they did not incur an undue amount of debt, nor impose taxes beyond proper limits, nor misapply money raised for a specific purpose. It was authorized also to supervise sinking funds which were not being properly managed, to deal with compromises of taxes and with plans for land subdivision. In 1932 the power of approval of municipal debenture issues was transferred from the Municipal Commissioner to the Municipal and Public Utility Board. A unique power of this Board was a general power of validation of any lawful by-law or resolution of a council where by inadvertence or error procedural irregularities had occurred and the Board was satisfied that they would be lawful but for the irregularity and that no person was likely to be injuriously affected thereby.

The Quebec Municipal Commission, which was set up in 1932, was given jurisdiction over all municipalities and school boards, except those which were subject to the Montreal Metropolitan Commission and certain Montreal school boards. It consisted of two[18] members appointed for ten years and removable for cause. All municipal borrowing, except for relief purposes and temporary loans, were made subject to the Commission's approval and it was given extensive powers over defaulting municipalities. The Commission on its own initiative or on request of the government could investigate the financial affairs of any municipality. By a 1935 enactment no municipality could enter into any agreement affecting its credit without the prior approval of the Commission.

The extent and significance of provincial administrative controls

[18]The Lieutenant-Governor in Council could appoint an *ad hoc* member to decide an issue upon which the two members could not agree.

vary greatly. The greatest degree of such control occurs under the general municipal legislation of Newfoundland[19] which requires the approval of the Lieutenant-Governor in Council for the appointment of officers, the annual budget, the borrowing of money, the enactment of regulations (by-laws), and, in most cases, the rate of taxation. The Cabinet has a general power to disallow work done or being done or proposed to be done by the council, or to direct that a work be not proceeded with, or to disallow any expenditure made or proposed to be made, or any salary paid or proposed to be paid, or any resolution or decision on any subject passed or made by a council, and any order made by or on behalf of the Lieutenant-Governor in Council must be entered in the books of the council and has effect as if it were a resolution of council.

In some other provinces, however, where municipal institutions have been much longer established, there still remain instances of extensive over-all control and direction. Nova Scotia provides that every municipal by-law shall be subject to the approval of the Minister of Municipal Affairs who, notwithstanding that his approval has been given, may subsequently revoke the approval, in which case the by-law ceases to have any force and effect. The Lieutenant-Governor in Council in Quebec also may disallow any municipal by-law.[20] The Minister in Nova Scotia has also a general power to make orders requiring a municipality "to carry out, put into effect, observe, perform or enforce such matters or things as may be deemed necessary or desirable in the interests of the municipality or with respect to the due accounting for, collection or payment of any of its assets, liabilities, revenues, expenditures, funds or money."

All the provinces except Prince Edward Island have provided that by-laws to incur debt must be approved either by the department of municipal affairs or some other provincial agency before being effective. Other types of by-laws in some provinces are subject to the approval of provincial departments before they become effective, as in Ontario where local by-laws relating to public health are subject to the approval of the provincial health department, those relating to traffic, to the highways department. Zoning by-laws in Ontario are subject to the approval of the Ontario Municipal Board, and in Alberta, zoning by-laws are subject to approval by the Minister of Municipal Affairs. In many instances the exercise of specific powers granted to municipal councils is, by statute, made subject to review or

[19]This does not apply to St. John's.

[20]This disallowance does not apply in the case of a loan by-law already approved by the Minister of Municipal Affairs.

to some control by a provincial authority. Such is the provision in Ontario that cities may license wheeled vehicles, other than motor vehicles, but the licence fee must be approved by the Municipal Board, or that a city may pay an annual allowance to members of the council, but the amount of the allowance is subject to approval by the Department of Municipal Affairs.

The model by-law plan has not been extensively used, but does occur in the public health field in Ontario. Under this plan the provincial Public Health Act includes a model by-law which is to be in effect in every municipality until the municipal council passes its own by-law relating to the matters therein referred to. The municipal by-law when approved by the Department of Health supersedes the statutory by-law to the extent that its provisions are not less restrictive or less onerous than those of the statutory by-law.

In addition to such controls over the legislative and administrative activity of councils, provincial authorities have gradually extended their control over the personnel and conditions of employment of councils' administrative staffs. The extreme case again is in Newfoundland where the province reserves the right both to approve of all appointments and to review the salaries paid. In other provinces there are instances of provincial standards of qualification for municipal appointees; requirements that the qualifications of certain appointees be approved by a provincial administrative agency, in some cases that the actual appointees be approved by a provincial authority; the limitation of the right of councils to dismiss certain employees except with provincial approval or for cause; the limitation of the right of councils to reduce salaries of employees in certain cases; and the transfer to the courts or boards of arbitration of the final decision as to rates of pay and other working conditions in some cases. In a limited number of cases the province retains the right to dispense with the services of municipally appointed and municipally paid officers and to appoint others in their places and fix their rates of pay. There are other cases, in the sphere of the administration of justice, where the provinces appoint officials who are not subject to municipal direction but whose salaries are to be paid by the municipality.

Some provincial authorities have the power, under certain conditions, to dismiss elected members of council and to declare their seats vacant and to provide for a new council. Thus, in Nova Scotia, if a council fails or in the opinion of the Governor in Council is about to fail or may fail to pay the principal or interest due on a debenture or the amount due to a sinking fund, or fails to pay any other liabilities when due, or fails to levy and collect the amount necessary to meet the expenditures required for any years, he may declare the offices of the members of the councils to be vacant and may appoint members of a new council. In Saskatchewan municipalities, other than cities, the Minister or, in the case of rural municipalities, the Lieutenant-Governor in Council may at any time appoint persons to act instead of the council and such persons shall have all the powers of the council.

A further check on the municipalities consists of the inspection or investigation of the affairs of a municipality. Some are inspections by provincial officers at regular intervals, the scope of the inspection being limited usually to the financial activities and an examination of the books, records, and methods being used by the municipal officers.[21] These regular periodic examinations are provided for in the provinces of Quebec, Saskatchewan, and Alberta. Drastic powers to enforce action to remedy defects found by the inspectors are provided in Saskatchewan and Alberta. Thus, in Saskatchewan the Minister may dismiss officials or put a controller in charge of the municipality, and in Alberta the Minister may dismiss the officials concerned or may dismiss the council or any member and order a new election.

Most provinces also provide for special surveys or investigations of the affairs of municipalities by the department of municipal affairs or some other provincial agency either at the request of the council, on petition of citizens or creditors, or, in some instances, on the initiative of the department or agency. These investigations are largely confined to financial matters. In addition, there are provisions for judicial investigations, at the instance of a council, of any matter connected with the good government of the municipality or the conduct of its business either by the council or by an appointed or elected commission.

It should not be inferred from the above outline of the means by which the provinces may exercise control and direction over the municipalities that where they are discretionary they are frequently used. Many of them are sparingly used, and some are rarely invoked, if ever, but they do exist to enable the province to deal with an acute

[21]That the purpose of such inspections may be changing is suggested by the Deputy Minister of Municipal Affairs of Saskatchewan who, in discussing the work of the municipal inspectors, stated recently that with the development of efficient methods of accounting, improved auditing, and regular reporting the greater need for the inspectors was in connection with the duties and responsibilities of the elected officials. His Department is undertaking a complete reorganization of the inspection services to the end that the inspectors will be available to meet with and advise local councils at their meetings. (*Western Municipal News*, vol. 45, no. 8, Aug. 1950, p. 236.)

problem should it arise. Some of the less drastic controls, by their very nature, are in almost continuous use, as in the case of obtaining provincial approval of municipal borrowings. Much more extensive controls are provided in most provinces to deal with the special problem of defaulting municipalities, for desperate cases call for drastic remedies.

Factors Complicating Provincial-Municipal Relations

We have noted above in general terms what constitutes the basic problem of provincial-municipal relations and also the extent to which provincial controls and direction have advanced. To understand the complexity of the problem it is necessary to note some of the factors which increase the difficulty of solution. One of the important factors in some cases is the lack of confidence of the municipalities in the intentions of the provinces with respect to the municipalities and their interests. This lack of confidence may or may not be justified but its effect, to the extent that it exists, is just as damaging as if it were justified.

Regardless of what may be the proper legal or constitutional position, the municipal elected representatives believe that the primary purpose of creating municipalities was to serve the people of the various communities. The representatives at the provincial level are elected for the same purpose. It would seem reasonable then to expect that the two groups, elected to serve the same people, should work in harmony to that end. If they are to do so, however, mutual confidence between the two is essential. Yet, in many instances, the municipalities feel that there has been a lack of frankness on the part of the province as to the ultimate purposes behind legislation affecting the municipalities and an absence of consultation with the municipalities before legislation affecting them is introduced. They feel that they are placed at a permanent disadvantage under a system whereby legislation is introduced by a government before consultation with the municipalities, for, once legislation is introduced, a government cannot afford to lose face by conceding changes in it in response to municipal pressure. Thus, the municipalities have to choose between the alternatives of accepting without protest legislation to which they object, or of putting themselves in the position of publicly opposing the policy of the government in power. The latter alternative becomes increasingly dangerous as the importance of provincial grants and controls increases.

The provincial authorities, in some cases, take the position that the parliamentary system makes such a procedure inevitable. Where there is an Opposition constantly looking for an opportunity to oppose, and to stir up public feeling against the Government, a Government in power may feel that it cannot afford to disclose in advance the measures which it proposes to submit to the legislature. To consult with the municipalities or to explain the administration's intentions would merely supply the Opposition with advance knowledge of the Government's programme. That such need not be the attitude is suggested by an advertisement which appeared in the *Western Municipal News* of February, 1947, over the signatures of the Minister and Deputy Minister of Municipal Affairs of Saskatchewan, inviting the views of municipal representatives with respect to seven questions ranging from the advisability of a three or four year concurrent term for reeves and councillors, to the establishment of a Rural Municipal Credit Union to finance member municipalities. The Hon. J. H. McQuarrie, K.C., then Minister of Municipal Affairs for Nova Scotia, at the annual convention of the Union of Nova Scotia Municipalities in 1944, expressed the situation as follows:

A procedure can be worked out whereby all municipalities can be familiar with proposed legislation and have an opportunity to express their views either directly to the Department or to a Committee of the Legislature or to a Committee representing the Union. . . . In some cases it is not practical for the Union or the municipalities to be heard before legislation is introduced, and whether heard before introduction of the legislation or not, in every case full opportunity should be and is given for a hearing before a Committee of the Legislature. You have a right to be heard, a very definite right, but it is a right to be heard, and not a right to decide—to decide is the responsibility of the Legislature. . . .

Yet in 1951 the Legislative Committee of the same Union was complaining of the "short time between the introduction of the Bills and the time at which they come on for hearing. It is impossible in that time to obtain the views of all the municipalities." In contrast the secretary-treasurer of the Union of Alberta Municipalities reported to his organization in the same year, 1951, "We have received every cooperation from Premier Manning, the Honourable Mr. Gerhart and Mr. Judge. They have consistently consulted us concerning proposed legislation and allied matters affecting urban municipalities, and they have listened to us with patience. The provincial government even went so far this year as to pay the expenses of one of our committee meetings. . . ."

In 1947 the President of the Ontario Municipal Association, Mr. E. J. Campbell of Brantford, in his annual presidential address expressed the municipal viewpoint, in part, as follows:

> If, however, the provincial authorities were to establish the practice of consultation with the municipal organizations before municipal legislation is introduced, other than that of major policy, many mutual benefits would be derived. There would be an improved relationship between the two levels of government and a greater spirit of mutual confidence established which would be of benefit to the people whom both governments are designed to serve; the experience of those in actual municipal administration could thus be made available to the province and thereby possibly avoid the enactment of unworkable legislation; representations with respect to legislation could be made on behalf of the municipalities at a stage when it would be much less embarrassing to all parties than is the case once legislation has been introduced. In many other countries and provinces with a parliamentary form of government it is found feasible to consult with the local authorities through their organizations with respect to proposed legislation affecting municipalities.

If a government feels that it cannot consult with all the municipalities, which might not be feasible, and yet hesitates to give official recognition to any one municipal organization as the group to be consulted on behalf of the municipalities, it could use the "white paper" technique of setting forth the principles of its proposals, leaving ample opportunity for representations to be made by individual municipalities before any final legislation is drafted. Even though no useful suggestions are received from the municipalities the procedure would go far toward establishing a greater spirit of confidence.

It may be argued that the viewpoint of the municipalities is restricted and insular and that it is their duty to co-operate with the province which, after all, is the senior authority. It may be that many demands of the municipalities are unreasonable and their resistance unjustifiable. The fact remains, however, that to get the best results in promoting their own policies the provinces need the co-operation of the municipalities and the generous gesture is more easily made by the party in the dominant position. It is the province which is ultimately responsible for the operation of the municipal system it has created and it is the province which is responsible for providing the legislation and the financial and other conditions that will permit the system to do the job for which it has been created.

The failure of a province to take its municipal councils into its confidence with respect to both immediate and long-range policies affecting them reacts to the disadvantage of the province in obtaining the results which it wants. The municipal councils, which are ever conscious of the inroads upon their independence, tend to look with suspicion upon any new proposal or departure by the province lest it turn out to be baited with a hidden hook. The result is a hesitation to take advantage of progressive policies lest the net result be more provincial control. An example of this attitude recently occurred in Ontario where for many years the municipalities had complained because the province would bear no share of the cost of administration of relief or welfare. In 1948 the province enacted legislation to provide for welfare units to be established by municipal councils to handle the welfare activities and where such units were established the province undertook to pay 50 per cent of the administration costs. However, under this Act the province, with the consent of the council, appoints the administrator and may make regulations governing such units. In spite of the opportunity to recover half the cost of administration the municipalities have failed to take advantage of the legislation.

Not the least important cause of the reluctance of municipalities to move in such matters is the wide power of supplementary legislation given to a Minister or the Lieutenant-Governor in Council. It is not an uncommon experience to find that the benefits anticipated as a result of announcements of policy or legislative enactments are greatly reduced, and local freedom of action restricted, by administrative interpretation or by the regulations which are subsequently drawn up by the provincial permanent staff and approved by the Cabinet.[22]

The provinces have not done an effective job of convincing the municipalities of the value to them of provincial guidance and leadership, or of the reasons for provincial policies. Continuous lip service has been paid to the importance of maintaining strong and autonomous local government at the same time that local government was being weakened and its autonomy whittled away by provincial action. Even the financial assistance that some provinces have given to their municipalities has had a weakening and limiting effect.

[22]Thus, an announced government policy of "payment to a city or separated town of a subsidy equal to 33⅓ per cent of approved unrestricted road expenditures" becomes, in legislation, 33⅓ per cent "of the amount of the expenditure which is properly chargeable to road improvement and where there is any doubt or dispute the decision of the Minister shall be final." In the administrative interpretation and application this is again restricted to mean that on streets which the Department of Highways classes as through highways the province will contribute 33⅓ per cent of the city's share of the cost of construction, although it will pay 33⅓ per cent of the cost of maintenance on all streets, with the Department exercising the right to place a limit for each municipality on the total amount toward which the province will contribute.

Toward a Solution

Having outlined something of the problem involved and the setting within which any solution has to be worked out, it remains to consider a solution. The fundamental problem of the municipalities is a financial one—the fact that the revenues which they can raise from the available sources are not sufficient to meet the mandatory expenditures and the optional expenditures which the local citizens want their councils to incur. Experience in the Canadian provinces, as elsewhere, suggests that so long as the municipalities are being subsidized by the provinces they will never be satisfied and will always be asking for more, for there is almost no limit to the capacity of a political body to spend money, if someone else carries the onus of raising it. To persist in a policy of progressively increasing provincial assistance means progressively increasing provincial direction and control of the municipalities, and a progressive weakening of local self-government to the point that it might better be abandoned and replaced by a system of local provincial agencies.

It is not generally considered desirable in public financing to have one level of government raising revenues to be expended by another level of government and it has been described as a "thoroughly vicious system."[23] However, in spite of its unsoundness, the facts are that the provinces spend substantial sums which are raised by the Dominion and the municipalities spend large sums which are raised by the provinces. It would be an ideal situation if each level of government were in a position to finance its operations without grants from another level but, so far as the municipalities are concerned, such would be a counsel of perfection under existing conditions and probably impracticable even under any foreseeable changed conditions. If, therefore, the systems of provincial financial assistance are to continue, as seems inevitable, the aim should be to devise a system which will least interfere with attaining the main ends as set out earlier in this chapter.

Assuming that it is desirable to retain and to strengthen local self-government, and to keep it financially responsible, some solution of the financial problem must be found, if possible, other than increased provincial assistance. There does not appear to be any probable new substantial source of revenue, at least which would be significant for

[23]"Anyone interested in financing whether of a municipality, a province, a Dominion, an Empire or a League of Nations will, I think, admit it is unwise, an unsound, a wrong principle for one body to have to do with raising the taxes and another to be concerned with the spending of the money so raised, that other body not having to account to the representatives of those who have paid the taxes." Prime Minister W. L. Mackenzie King, *House of Commons Debates*, April 30, 1930, p. 1237.

all types of municipalities, nor is it likely that if such a source were to develop it would be made available to the municipalities. One alternative would appear to be the reallocation of functions as between the provinces and their municipalities.

The functions should be so allocated that, as far as possible, the municipalities will be entirely responsible, financially and otherwise, for certain functions and at the same time as free as possible from provincial control and direction in the sphere for which the municipality is responsible. The provinces should be solely responsible for the financing and administration of certain functions now carried on by municipalities. And those functions with respect to which the province feels its policies must be given first consideration, but which can best be administered by the local municipality, should become the financial responsibility of the province. In the administration of these latter functions the position should be that the municipality is formally recognized as acting as a provincial agent and not, as in the past, that the function is a municipal function toward which the province is granting financial asistance. To work out such a reallocation will not be a simple task, nor is it probable that a completely satisfactory division can be evolved, but it would appear to be the most hopeful solution for the existing situation between the provinces and their municipalities, a situation which can only get worse if the present bases of provincial-municipal fiscal relationships are continued.

In considering which of the present municipal functions might be transferred to the provinces, there are some respecting which there would appear to be little argument. Such would be those in which discretion on the part of the local authorities is not a factor, but in which the local authority is merely a bill-paying agency. Thus, in the matter of hospitalization of indigents, the question of whether or not a patient is to be admitted to hospital is determined by a doctor, the question of whether or not the patient is indigent is a question of fact. The role of the municipality, aside from providing an officer to ascertain the facts of indigency and residence, is merely that of paying the bill. It would make no appreciable difference to the patient or to the hospital whether the cheque to pay for the service rendered came from the town hall or the provincial capital. The same situation applies where children are taken into care by a Children's Aid Society. Where the Society is a voluntary statutory agency the municipality merely pays a bill for maintenance of wards which under the legislation are its responsibility. The local discretion in administration, which is most desirable, in this case is exercised by the Society and not by the municipal authorities, and that discretion can be just as effectively exercised by the Society whether the payment comes from a province or a municipality. A province may take the attitude that if it pays the cost it cannot leave discretion in administration to the Society but if responsibility for the expenditure of public funds necessarily involves the actual administration of the service it is surprising that such a principle does not apply when it is a municipality, rather than a province, which is supplying the money. The maintenance of persons in public institutions such as mental hospitals, sanatoria, training schools, etc., are other instances, varying from province to province, where the municipality's function is solely to provide money. In many of these cases there would be a further advantage to the community as a whole resulting from the elimination of the waste of time and money expended by the municipalities in trying to determine what municipality is responsible for the maintenance in particular cases. This problem grows as the population increases its mobility, with the result that municipalities are frequently opposing one another before the courts in the endeavour to disclaim financial responsibility.

Another type of expenditure which it would seem reasonable to transfer to the provinces is that for the administration of justice, where these costs are wholly or in part imposed upon the municipalities. Considering the extent to which the officials involved are appointed by the provinces and the extent to which the administration is controlled by detailed provincial rules and regulations, about the only local discretion involved is the decision as to who shall supply the fuel to heat the buildings involved, or who shall get the manual labour jobs. The lack of local significance in the administration of justice has been recognized in Manitoba by having the province assume the administration and bill the municipalities with their share of the cost. So slight is the local discretion and so obviously is the administration of justice a service to our society as a whole, that it would seem to be a logical service to transfer entirely to provincial administration and financing.

In considering the remaining functions, the question arises as to the principles which should apply in determining whether a service which requires local organization is better administered by the province or by a local authority. Lythgoe,[24] in discussing the problem as related to the English situation, suggests the following principles or tests, although conceding that it is doubtful whether any set of principles can be laid

[24] J. Lythgoe, "Principles Which Should Determine Whether a Service Requiring Local Organization Is Best Administered by a Central Government Department or by a Local Authority," *Public Administration*, spring 1949, vol. XXVII, C.3.A.

down which are suitable for application as a whole to all services: (1) wherever a public service requires local organization it should be accepted as a first broad principle that some form of local authority control of the administration is desirable unless good reason can be shown to the contrary; (2) wherever the service is capable of being successfully administered within the financial resources available to the local authority responsible for its administration, and without undue dependence on central government for specific grants in aid, it should be left in the hands of the local authority; (3) wherever the service is linked and should be co-ordinated with existing locally administered service it is desirable to concentrate local services under the local authority unless strong reasons exist to the contrary; (4) wherever it is possible to allow considerable diversity in the administration of a service it should be left to local authority administration.

In dealing with the practical problem of allocating functions it is desirable to clarify the purpose of the allocation and some of the more important factors involved. What is aimed at is the maximum efficiency of administration of the various services at the lowest possible cost, keeping in mind the desirability of maintaining an effective form of local self-government and reducing to a minimum the friction between the provincial and the municipal levels of government. Two of the more important factors to keep in mind are that the taxation of real property, in most cases, constitutes the only substantial source of municipal tax revenues and that it is not possible to maintain an expanding programme of social services on this limited tax base. If the friction between the two levels of government is to be reduced, it should help toward this end to reduce the number of points of contact. As the provinces increase the number of municipal activities toward which they give financial assistance the points of contact tend to increase and conversely as the number of municipal activities in which the provinces have an active joint interest are reduced, the points of contact, the sources of possible friction, are correspondingly reduced.

It would seem reasonable, therefore, to assign to the municipalities, to be financed entirely by them without any assistance or direction by the province, those services or functions which may be considered to serve or benefit real property, the major source of municipal revenue, services in which there is room for diversity of standard in accordance with local ideas, and for which the costs are not beyond the capacity of the existing sources of municipal revenues. These would include such functions as were noted on page 340. These named functions, however, do not necessarily cover the entire range of functions which might be made the sole responsibility of the municipality.

There remains a group of functions such as health, education, welfare, etc., which for best results require local organization and administration but in which the provincial interest in the standards to be maintained is such as to involve a large measure of provincial regulation and control. The provinces give varying assistance in these fields at present but generally on a more substantial basis toward education and welfare. There is undoubtedly much to be gained by having these functions administered by locally elected or appointed bodies, but the difficulty is to work out some satisfactory method of financing them. A view commonly held by the provinces is that it is necessary to have a substantial portion of the cost of such services paid by the municipality for the purpose of inducing a sense of responsibility in administration. Heretofore, the provincial attitude has been that, although these functions are the primary responsibility of the municipalities, in consideration of the large and growing cost and of the provincial interest in the standards to be maintained the province is prepared to give financial assistance accompanied by varying degrees of provincial regulation, control, and direction. So long as these activities are considered as municipal functions receiving provincial assistance, there will be municipal resentment at detailed provincial control. If, however, these activities are accepted by the provinces as primarily a provincial responsibility, with the municipalities merely being assessed for a sufficient share of the cost to assure a sense of responsibility in administration and with the province paying the greater part of the administration and other costs, the attitude toward provincial direction and setting of standards should materially change. As will be noted, the classes of expenditure proposed to be included in this group are for social services which it is argued by the municipalities are not legitimate charges against real property in any case, and it is the prospect of rising levels of expenditure on these services that gives the municipalities concern for their future financial stability.

It may well be that such a programme of reallocation of functions is not politically feasible, for it is one thing to decide what should be done and quite a different thing to do it. Experience everywhere suggests that this is characteristic of the local government situation.[25] This reluctance to undertake major adjustments in the sphere of local government may be due in part to the large number of units of government involved and in part to the complex intergovernmental relationships

[25]"The problem of local government has been before the country for at least sixty years. Practically every government in power has at some stage of its term of office made proposals for reform or at least indicated that reform was necessary." *Report of Local Government Committee* (Wellington, New Zealand, 1945), p. 151.

which would have to be unravelled and the many vested interests which might be aroused. There is an understandable hesitation on the part of a political body to institute sweeping changes, the political repercussions of which cannot be accurately foreseen if, by a series of minor adjustments, the immediate pressure can be relieved. Political wisdom may suggest that it is better "to endure the ills we have than fly to others that we know not of."

If, then, some such substantial reallocation of functions between the provinces and their municipalities is not likely, even though desirable, it remains to consider what might be done in the fiscal field to gain some improvement. As has been suggested earlier, it is not an easy task to devise a system of provincial assistance which will attain the varied purposes desired, but in attempting to do so there are some general principles that should be kept in mind by those responsible for working out such a plan.

One most desirable characteristic of any grant is that the formula by which it is to be calculated be as simple as possible. If the municipal authorities and the local citizens are to be satisfied that they are being dealt with equitably, as compared with other municipalities, and that they are getting everything to which they are entitled under a grant plan, the basis of calculation must be such that they can understand it. In some instances very involved and complex formulae have been worked out with the aim of giving due weight to the widely varied needs and conditions obtaining in different municipalities. While the aim is commendable, the result may be unsatisfactory to the recipients who cannot understand the formula or its justification. That which they do not understand, they distrust, and that distrust is accompanied by the suspicion that a formula which is too complex is purposely so designed. Even if the local authorities can apply such formulae to their own municipality, they have not sufficient knowledge of the variables in other municipalities to feel any assurance that they are getting equitable treatment. It may be that what is lost in equity by not attempting too many refinements is more than offset by the more ready acceptance by the municipalities of crude but readily understandable measures of varying local needs.

Not only is it desirable that the formulae upon which individual grants are calculated be simple but it is almost as important that the whole structure or system of grants be kept as simple as possible. If the sole purpose of provincial grants were to relieve the burden upon the local taxpayers the problem would not be so difficult. In such a case there would only be one type of grant required, the amount being determined by whatever the provincial authorities deemed to be the best measure of need. But when the grants have the additional purposes of encouraging specific services and of equalizing certain burdens as between municipalities there evolves a most complex structure of grants.

So long as provincial grants are to serve a variety of purposes the system of grants is bound to be complex. There should, however, be a continuous effort at the provincial level to reduce the multiplicity of grants. Whenever a municipal need for assistance is to be met, preference, if feasible, should be given to increasing the amount of a grant on some existing basis rather than to institute a new basis of grant. The whole system of grants should be continuously under review with the aim that where special grants which have been established for a particular purpose have served their purpose, the special grant should be eliminated and, if considered expedient, an equivalent amount added to some other established grant.

A complex system of grants is further complicated for the municipalities where the bases on which the individual grants are calculated are themselves complex and designed to attain varying purposes. A municipality may find itself in the predicament that what is done for the purpose of benefiting under the provisions of one plan of grants may be detrimental under another. Thus, where grants are related to assessment or tax rates, but some vary directly with the assessment and some vary inversely, it requires a nice calculation for the municipal authorities to determine whether a particular local change will involve a net gain or loss. The more complicated the system of grants, the greater will be the likelihood of conflicting results within the grant structure. Such is the case where the aim of easing the over-all burden on the local taxpayer is offset by increased expenditures induced by incentive grants. Again, grants which are based on expenditures for a stated purpose, although not conditioned upon greater expenditures, are frequently used by local pressure groups as a justification for greater spending for that specific purpose.

Not the least of the irritations arising at the administrative level out of the intergovernmental grants is the cost of compliance in the matter of providing records and reports for the provincial authorities and adjusting accounting procedures to produce information required for a variety of provincial authorities and departments, and the inspection in detail by provincial officials who are not always slow to assert their authority and who are prone to forget that, even though in receipt of provincial grants, the municipalities are not merely agents of the provinces. This matter was the subject of study by a parliamentary committee in England, appointed in 1949, the main objective of which was "To simplify the methods of departmental supervision over local government activities, to reduce the need for and the extent of such supervision, and to ensure, wherever possible, that a greater measure of responsibility rests on local authorities."[26]

The committee outlined their general approach to the problem as follows:

> To recognize that the local authorities are responsible bodies competent to discharge their own functions and that, though they may be statutory bodies through which Government policy is given effect, and operate to a large extent with Government money, they exercise their responsibilities in their own right, not ordinarily as agents of Government Departments. It follows that the objective should be to leave as much as possible of the detailed arrangement of a scheme or service to the local authority and to concentrate the Department's control at the key points where it can most effectively discharge its responsibilities for Government policy and financial administration.

Much progress might be made toward reducing the conflict of aims involved in the various grant plans and toward eliminating duplication of effort and waste of time at the municipal level if all grants were handled through the departments of municipal affairs or if at least the basis of grants, the conditions attached, and the type of reports, forms, and records required were cleared with the municipal department before being put into effect. It is only reasonable to expect that the departments of municipal affairs will have a better understanding of the over-all local problems than will any of the other provincial departments. They should be able to assist in advising on the effect on the local authorities of conflicting grant aims and in eliminating some of the problems of compliance. The municipalities should have the benefit of the skills and experience of the municipal departments in this regard, even at the expense of interdepartmental jealousies at the provincial level.

A most desirable characteristic of any satisfactory system of grants, from a municipal viewpoint, is its stability. Municipal sources of revenue are so restricted that there is little reserve to compensate for sudden changes in grant policies. This problem is rendered more acute by the overlapping of the budgeting periods of the various levels of government. Radical changes in provincial grant policies, as well as in

[26]*First Report of the Local Government Manpower Committee*, Cmd. 7870 (1950).

provincially imposed expenditures, which result in reductions of municipal revenues or increases in expenditures, may have serious effects upon municipal budgets and at a time when it is too late in the year to make compensating adjustments. Some of the irritation and uncertainty resulting from such drastic changes in provincial policy could be eliminated if the provincial policy were that reductions in the bases of grants or increases in obligatory expenditures should not take effect until the next municipal fiscal year.[27] There is less objection, municipally, to increases in grants taking effect immediately.

As long as provincial grants are to be used as a means of encouraging municipalities to develop specific services there must be incentive and conditional grants. It is the conditions attached, rather than the grants, which usually give rise to friction. There is need, however, in any system of grants for an unconditional grant, the spending of which is left entirely to local discretion. A great part of the purpose of all provincial grants is to relieve the burden on the local taxpayer but if all grants are conditioned on the performance of certain services and the maintenance of set standards the net result is not likely to be any relief to the taxpayer. Relief can be obtained by the use of the unconditional grant or subsidy, and at the same time the relationship between the two levels of government can be improved by providing at least one form of assistance that does not have the ultimate effect of taking away as much as it gives.

If there is to be an unconditional grant the problem then is to determine the basis of distribution. Here, again, the formula should be kept as simple as possible so that the local authorities can readily ascertain the extent to which they will benefit and so that they may assure themselves that they are not being inequitably dealt with as compared to other municipalities. Inasmuch as the usual reason advanced in justification of such grants is that they are designed to relieve the burden on real property, it is also desirable that such grants should be based on some factor which is common to all municipalities, which gives some indication of the relative need for assistance, and which cannot be manipulated by local authorities in their local interests. A further desirable characteristic is that such grants should recognize that the burden of municipal expenditures weighs more heavily on some classes of municipalities than on others, as per capita costs tend to increase as population increases.

[27]This policy was followed in Ontario at the 1950 session of the legislature when it was provided that increased charges to be paid by the municipalities for indigent hospital patients would not come into effect until January 1951.

The Moore Commission of New York State,[28] after "many methods of distribution were tested in the search for a more equitable method of apportionment of the cash assistance to be furnished by the State," arrived at the conclusion that the per capita formula was the most fair "for its close correlation with the needs of our municipalities." They recommended an annual per capita state grant to cities, towns, and villages of $6.75, $3.55, and $3.00 respectively. A similar basis was adopted in New Brunswick in 1947 for grants to cities, towns, and counties of $12.38, $6.92, and $1.66 respectively. Among the advantages of such a basis are that it eliminates the almost insuperable problem of province-wide equalization of assessments which obtains where grants are based on assessments or tax levies and similar factors which do not mean the same thing in one municipality as in another, for the population of a municipality is a fact which can be reasonably accurately determined. It recognizes that the responsibilities, and consequently the costs of government, vary from one class of municipality to another; and it further recognizes that social service costs constitute a continuously increasing share of the municipal expenditures and that such costs tend to be related more closely to the population than to any other factor. Even where provincial grants are not on a per capita basis, it might be a forward step to have different formulae for grants to urban and to rural municipalities. So great is the divergence of needs, conditions, and other factors as between these two general classes of municipalities that it seems almost impossible to devise a satisfactory uniform formula to apply to the metropolis and the hamlet.

One means by which some senior governments have assisted local governments has been the shared tax. Shared taxes have been used in the past in England and are used extensively in the United States. As previously noted tax sharing occurs in the Quebec sales tax, the Ontario liquor licence fees, the Alberta gasoline tax, and the British Columbia sales tax and motor vehicles tax. It is claimed by some students of municipal finance that "state-collected municipally shared taxes" are sound in principle and "appear to be the only fiscal resource now available for meeting recognized urban requirements for the services and needs of the coming years."[29] The Moore Commission report, however, based on New York State's thirty years' experience with shared taxes, advised against shared taxes on the grounds that they

[28]*Report of the Commission on Municipal Revenues and Reductions of Real Estate Taxes* (Albany, 1946).

[29]Leo Day Woodworth, *Shared Taxes*, The American Municipal Association Report, no. 155, November, 1944, p. 17.

were unstable and inequitable,[30] that the revenues were consistently subject to abrupt drops in the local share when local needs are greatest and that the amount of shared taxes received by a municipality was measured neither by its needs nor by the nature and quantity of the services provided.

The problem of provincial-municipal relations is one which is a matter of constant concern to both the provinces and the municipalities. The working out of a solution is not parallel to the problem of working out the difficulties of Dominion-provincial relations. In the latter case it is a matter of working out a mutual agreement between two levels of government, each of which has an assured constitutional status. In the case of provincial-municipal relations the relationship is that between a superior and an inferior level of government. In some respects this relationship merely complicates the problem for the natural attitude of the inferior is to be on the defensive.

Without any suggestion that this is a case in which the blame for the prevailing situation should be assigned to either level of government, for there is some right on both sides, the nature of things would indicate that the responsibility for working out a solution rests primarily upon the provinces, for they are the only one of the two levels that has the power to do so. To argue that the local authorities are narrow in their views and unprogressive in their approach to the modern problems of government is but to emphasize the need for an even more tolerant provincial approach to the solution of the problem, for it is the party who in fact has the final decision who can afford to go more than half way.

The provinces enact the legislative framework within which the municipalities function. The provinces determine the powers with which the municipalities are to be endowed and the responsibilities which are to be imposed upon them. It is the provinces which determine the sources of revenue available to their municipalities to finance the latter's operations. It would appear to be a province's responsibility to so design that legislative framework, and to so adjust the revenue sources, that the municipalities may exercise their powers and carry out their responsibilities.

It is to be expected that there will always be certain difficulties in the relationship between these two levels of government. Only when

[30]The local share of state collected taxes in New York State dropped from $84 million in 1930 to $38 million in 1933, a fall of 56 per cent just at the time when municipal resources were strained to the utmost to meet the impact of the depression.

a society is completely static can we expect to eliminate all intergovernmental friction. The process of growth and evolution is inevitably accompanied by friction and conflict. New problems continuously arise and circumstances change to alter the conditions under which any mutual arrangements may have been worked out. Much can be done, however, to reduce friction, to establish a feeling of mutual confidence, and to permit each level of government to go about its major tasks with greater and more beneficial results, if there is the will to do so.

INDEX

(*The abbreviation* m. *is used for* "municipal")

ABBATOIRS, as m. enterprises, 250, 251
Acadians, 37
Acclamation, of m. candidates, 145
Act of Union (1841), 28–9
Addington County, Upper Canada, 24n
Administration: civic, 162–76, council organization of, 166–9, manager plan of, 169–71, by boards of control, 172–4, by city commissioners, 174–6; of justice, 194, 361; of poll tax, 258; local discretion in, 360–1
Administrative activities of m. councils, 119–20, 162–76
Administrative boards: review of m. activities by, 345; creation and development of, 348–51
Administrators: of unemployment relief (Ont.), 182; of welfare services (Ont.), 358
Ad valorem taxes, 307–12
Advance election poll, 148
Advance payment of taxes, 319
Age requirements: for voting, 141; for paying poll tax, 257
Agencies: of m. government, 65; municipalities as, 360, 366
Agents tax (Nfld.), 220
Agricultural societies, 287
Airports, as m. enterprises, 250, 251
Alberta, Province of: history of m. government, 43–6; composition of m. corporations, 49n; The Cities Act (1952), 52n, 175; extent of m. organization, 60; expenditures by government of, 60; types of municipalities, 61–7, number, 66; area adjustment of rural municipalities, 68; annexation in urban municipalities, 70; Board of Public Utility Commissioners, 70, 229, 350–1; dissolution of municipalities, 72, creation, 75–6; election of councillors, 83; appointive powers of heads of municipalities, 87; council meetings, 93; compulsory voting by councillors, 95n; composition of councils, 106; district hospital boards, 134; requirements for m. candidates, 138, 140, nomination, 14–16, withdrawal, 147; vacancies in councils, 152; "proprietary electors," 154; corporations in m. elections, 154; initiative by electorate, 158; qualifications of electors, 160; m. elections schedule, 161; manager plan, 169, 171; appointment of m. officers, 180–1; Department of Municipal Affairs, 180–1, 273, 293, 346; m. pension plans, 189; provincial inspection of m. finances, 201; m. taxes, 212; m. business tax, 214; real property assessment, 215, 279, 281–2, 288–93; personal property assessment, 215, 302, 304; business assessment, 215, 306, 310–14; debenture interest rate limits, 227; m. debt limits, 230; m. sinking funds, 233; loans to municipalities, 239; m. debt in, 240; Municipal Assistance Act (1951), 246; m. enterprises, 252; m. minimum tax, 257; appointment of assessors, 263; use of assessment of previous year, 265; assessment notices, 267; Assessment Commission, 272, 274, 276, 278; tax-exempt property, 288–9, 292; fixed assessments, 293; m. tax collection, 316, 321–2; tax sales, 325–6, 328, 334; compro-

mise of tax arrears, 331–2; penalties for overdue taxes, 333; provincial-municipal relations, 335n; approval of zoning by-laws, 352; Union of Alberta Municipalities, 356; gasoline tax as shared tax, 368. *See also* Cities (Alta.), Municipal districts, Towns (Alta.), and Villages (Alta.)
Alberta Assessment Commission, 272, 274, 276, 278
Aldermen: definition, 77; ward, 83; election (Ont.), 85. *See also* Councillors
Allocation of municipal and provincial functions, 360–4
Amalgamation, 70
American colonies, influence on Canadian m. development, 22, 33
American Municipal Association, The, 368n
Amherst, N.S., 299n
Amusement centres, as m. enterprises, 250
Amusement taxes, 212
Angus, H. F., 16n
Animals tax, 212, 215. *See also* Dog tax
Annapolis County, N.S., 36
Annexation, 68–71; in Montreal area, 135
Appeals: against assessment, 268–70; against equalization of assessments, 275
Appointments: by head of council, 87; and dismissal of employees, 180–6; method of, 182–3; party politics in, 183; "local son" rule in, 183; merit systems in, 183–6; of assessors, 263; provincial approval of, 353
Appraisers, 263n. *See also* Assessors
Arbitration: committees of council (N.S.), 133; of salaries of m. uniformed employees (Ont.), 188; retroactive wages (Ont.), 200n; of assessments, 277
Area: adjustments of municipal, 68–71; municipal, as factor determining expenditures, 202; of premises, as basis for business assessment, 310–11
Arena, as m. enterprise, 251
Army officers, m. candidature of (Que.), 140
Arrears of taxes: collection (Ont.), 117n; collection (general), 316–31; compromise and consolidation of, 331–2
Arvida, Que.: manager plan, 169n; sales tax, 217
Asselin, J. O., 135n
Assessment: definition, 209, 211n, 261; "special," 211n; taxable m. assessments table (1948), 215; local judgment in, 243; general, chap. XII, 261–78; capital value basis, 262; rental or annual value basis, 262; process, 262, 264–6; notice of, 266–8, 269; appeals against, 268–80; roll, 269–70; regular review of, 271–2; special review of, 271–2; equalization of, 273–6; real property, chap. XIV, 279–301; under-assessment, 281, 283–4; school, 283; manual of, 283; lag behind market values, 284; fixed, 287, 292–4, 299–300; statutory 299–300; of utilities, 299–300; personal property and business, chap. XV, 302–14
Assessment Act (Ont.), 265n
Assessment Commission (Alta.), 274, 276, 278; (Sask.), 267, 276, 278
Assessment Commissioner (Ont.), 188
Assessment department, 167, 168
Assessment roll: as basis of voters' list, 142, 143; in Quebec municipalities, 264; information required for, 265
Assessors: in Upper Canada, 25; in Lower Canada, 34; in United Canada, 35; supplier of assessment roll, 142; combined with other offices, 178; appointment, 180–1, 263–4; in Alta., 180, 273, 280; in N.B., 181, 263–4; judgment of, 262, 264, 273, 280; in Que., 262; duties of, 263–8; qualification of,

263; in Ont., 263–4, 274, 280, 283; appeals by, 268; at courts of revision, 269, 270; in Man., 280; in B.C., 280; tendency to under-assess, 281, 283–4; manual for (Ont.), 283; schools for (N.B.), 283; recognition of real property value changes, 285; National Association of Assessing Officers, 285n, 303n; in personal property assessment, 303

Assiniboia, District of, 41

Assistance to municipalities, by provincial governments, 246–7. *See also* chap. xvii, 335–70

Attendance, at council committee meetings, 102. *See also* Quorum

Auction, public, in tax sale procedure, 321, 326, 329

Audit department, as m. administrative unit, 168

Auditors: appointment, 177, 180; prohibited from combining duties, 179; licensing of, 181; dismissal (Ont.), 182; warnings against unauthorized expenditures, 202

Australia, assessment basis, 262

Authority, of m. officers, 177–8. *See also* Powers.

Auto camps, 310

Automobiles, 337

Autonomy, municipal, chap. xvii, 335–70. *See also* Local self-government

Auto supplies, business assessment of, 311

"Back-scratching," 84

Baie-Comeau, Que., 169n

Bailiffs, 140

Baillis, 20

Baldwin Act (1849), 30–1, 32

Baldwin, Robert, 29, 32

Ballot, 147, 150, 154

Bankers, 309

Bankruptcy, in disqualification from m. candidature, 140

Banks, assessment of, 309

Barbers, assessment of, 309

Beaubien, Joseph, 92

Belleville, Ont.: board of police, 26n; size of council, 78; remuneration of councillors, 103

Bicycle taxes, 215

Bidding, at tax sales, 326, 328

Biggar, C. R. W., 24n, 25, 27, 31–2

Black, N. F., 44

Board: of Commissioners of Public Utilities (N.S.), 294; of Examiners (B.C.), 181; of Public Utility Commissioners (Atla.), 70, 229, 350–1; of revision, 128, 184

Boards, administrative: review of m. activities by, 345; creation and development of, 348–51

of control: election, 82n, 85; frequency of meetings, 94; description, 172–3; review of budget by, 199

of works, provincial, 30

of health: in P.E.I., 40; as "special-purpose bodies," 65

of Police, 26

of school trustees (in P.E.I.), 40. *See also* Schools

Bonds, 224n. *See also* Debentures

Borrowing, municipal, chap. xii, 223–60; temporary, 223, 224–5; long-term, 225–41; sinking fund debentures, 233–6; instalment or serial debentures, 236–7; debt consolidations, 237–8; sale of debentures, 238–9; provincial loans, 239

Boston, Mass., 33

Boundary adjustments, 67–71

Bourinot, J. G., 20n, 21n, 33

Brady, Alexander, 16n

Brantford, city of, Ont.: creation by special act, 26n; council, 27n; remuneration of councillors, 103; member of The Grand River Conservation Commission, 136

Brantford Township, Ont., 79

Brick yards, business assessment of, 309

Bridges: local improvement taxes for, 213; debentures for, 228

British Columbia, Province of: influence of topography on m. government, 17; extent of m. organization, 60; types of municipalities, 61–6; number of municipalities, 66; creation and dissolution of municipalities, 72–6; term of office of councillors, 81, election, 83, 106; heads of council, 87, 89, 105n; frequency of council meetings, 93; Municipal Act, 96n; Department of Municipal Affairs, 105n, 347; composition of councils, 106; m. standing committees, 108; school boards, 130n; requirements for m. candidates, 139; nomination papers, 144n; withdrawal of m. candidates, 147; advance election polls, 148; resignation of councillors, 152; vacancies in councils, 152; recount procedure, 157; qualifications of voters, 160; schedule of m. elections, 161; Board of Examiners, 181; revenue debentures, 226–8; Inspector of Municipal Affairs, 229, 347; m. debt, 230, 240–1; expenditure of borrowed money, 231n, 232–3; m. sinking fund investments, 235n; shared taxes, 245–6, 368; m. enterprises, 252, 253n; revenue from fines, 255; poll tax, 257; road tax, 258; dog tax, 259; assessment, 265; assessment appeals, 269, 277–8; assessment basis, 279; real property assessment, 282, 290; tax-exempt property, 288–9; fixed assessments, 293; provincial-municipal relations, 295, 335n; Power Commission, 296; statutory assessments, 300; business assessments, 306, 309–10, 312, 314; special franchise taxes, 307; tax collection, 316, 321; statutory tax limit, 317; tax sales, 326–9, 334; penalties on overdue taxes, 333; sales and motor vehicles tax, 368. *See also* Cities, District municipalities, and Villages (B.C.)

British North America Act, 18, 49–51, 208, 221

British régime, m. government during, 20–2

Britnell Report, 295

Brittain, Dr. H. L., 82

Brockelbank, J. H., 71

Brockville, Ont., 26n

Brokers, business assessment of, 309, 310

Bruchési, Jean, 20n

Budget, municipal, 199–201, 223; relation to provincial budgetary period, 367

Buildings: as part of land, 279; assessment, 281; local inspection of, 340

Bureau of Municipal Research, 82

Burgesses (Sask.), 154

Business assessment, 306–14

Business tax: as common type of m. tax, 212; as a major tax source, 214; total assessment by provinces, 215; as occupiers' tax, 217; licences as a form of, 254

Businesses, real property tax exemptions on, 292

Bus systems, as m. enterprises, 250

By-laws: annexation, 68; money, 69; voting on, 95, 153–8; definition, 96; questioning of, in court, 98; powers of councils to enact, 100–1; assignment of committee powers by, 108; procedure, 113; passing of, 118; as a class of legislation, 119–20; as basis of action, 164; for adopting manager plan, 171; governing city commissioners, 174; to appoint m. employees, 182; designating employees' duties by, 186; to authorize issue of debentures, 226, 231–2; annual taxing, 315; to consolidate tax arrears (Alta.), 331; approval by provincial agencies, 352; model, 353

Bytown, Upper Canada (later, Ottawa, Ont.), 26n, 27n

CAB LICENCE, 254

Cabinet, non-existent in m. government, 55–6; provincial, 358

Calgary, Alta.: annual expenditures, 60; remuneration of councillors,

103; proportional representation, 148n; revenue, 207, 254; sinking fund trustees, 236; special franchise taxes, 307; business assessment, 309, 314
Campbell, E. J., 357
Canadian Legion (B.E.S.L.), property exempt from taxation, 287
Candidates, municipal: general, 138–41; disqualifications, 140–1; nomination, 144–6; qualifications, 145–6; election deposit, 146; withdrawal, 146
Canning Parish, N.B., 323n
Cap de la Madeleine, Que.: manager plan, 169n; sales tax, 217
Capital: working, not permitted for municipalities, 223; construction, borrowing for, 225–6; value, as assessment basis, 262, 307–8
Carleton County, N.B., 38
Carleton, Guy. *See* Lord Dorchester
Casual municipal employees, 179
Caucus, meeting of council, 113
Cemeteries: as m. enterprises, 250–2; exempt from taxation, 287
Census-taking, by m. assessors, 265
Central Mortgage and Housing Corporation, payments in lieu of m. taxes, 222
Certificates: sales tax, 327, 329; of tax arrears (Ont.), 329–30
Chairman: head of village or township council, 78; of council committees, 111–12, 163–4
Champlain County, Que., 62–3
Change of status of municipalities, 67–76
Charitable institutions, exempt from taxation, 287, 291
Charlottetown, P.E.I.: incorporation, 39; councillors, 77n, ward system, 82n; council quorum, 94n; councillor remuneration, 103; mayor, 115; electoral officer, 142n, 144n; m. candidates in, 145–7; poll tax, 257; assessors, 263; assessment procedure, 265, 267; assessment appeals, 269, 272, 277–8; tax exemptions, 292–3, 304; personal property assessment, 304; specific taxes, 306; business taxes, 313; tax collection, 316, 322–5; date taxes due, 318; tax sales, 328–9, 333
Charters, municipal, 52
Chatham, Ont., 169n
Chattels: as personal property, 304; seizure for unpaid taxes, 321
Chicoutimi, Que.: manager plan, 169n; sales tax, 217
Children's Aid Societies: m. expenditures for, 194, 360–1; provincial grants for, 259; exempt from taxation, 287; local discretion in administration by, 360
Children's Protection Act (Ont.), 259
Churches, exempt from taxation, 287, 289
Churchill, Rt. Hon. Winston, 122
Circus permits, 254
Cities: as a type of municipality, 61, 67; number by provinces, 66; erection of, from towns, 76; head of council, 77; size of councils, 78; council term of office, 80; employees, 178
in Alberta: Cities Act (1952), 52n, 175; annexation procedures, 70; creation, 76; election and composition of councils, 106; qualifications of electors, 160; m. elections schedules, 161; limit on temporary loans, 225; limit on debenture term, 228; debt limit, 230; sinking fund trustees, 236; "minimum tax," 258; assessment appeals, 277–8; real property assessment, 286, 290, 301; tax exemptions, 289; personal property assessment, 305; business assessment, 312–13; penalties for overdue taxes, 333
in British Columbia: dissolution, 73; creation, 76; powers and duties of mayors, 87, 89; payment of councillors, 102; election and composition of councils, 106; nomina-

tions for m. candidates in, 144; m. elections schedule, 161; real property assessments, 286, 290–1, 301; business assessments, 312
in Manitoba: creation, 76; payment of councillors, 102; election and composition of councils, 106; limits on temporary borrowings, 225; real property assessments, 286; railway assessments, 300n; personal property assessments, 305; business assessments, 312
in New Brunswick: creation, 76; term of office of councillors, 80; limit on short-term borrowing, 225; legislative approval of debenture issues, 229; real property assessments, 286; personal property assessments, 305; business assessments, 312; per capita grants to, 368
in Nova Scotia: equalization of assessments, 274; real property assessments, 286; fixed assessments, 293; personal property assessments, 305; business assessments, 312
in Ontario: creation, 76; term of office of councillors, 80; payment of councillors, 102; election and composition of councils, 106; advance poll, 148; council vacancies, 152; initiative by petition, 158; compulsory appointment of assessors and tax collectors, 177; revenue from fines, 255; poll tax, 256n, 258n; highway grants to, 259; public library grant to, 260; assessment appeals, 269, 277–8; real property assessments, 286, 291, 301; business assessments, 312–13; tax sales, 324; provincial payments to, 358n
in Quebec: creation, 76; powers and duties of mayor, 87–8; payment of councillors, 101n; election and composition of councils, 106; mayor as *ex officio* member of committees, 108n; qualification and disqualification of candidates, 139–40; nomination meeting, 144; clerk as returning officer, 144n; nomination meetings, 144n; nominators, 145; candidate's consent, 146; election deposit, 146; withdrawal of candidates, 147; counterfoil ballots in m. elections, 150; resignation of councillors, 152; electors' qualifications, 159; m. elections schedule, 161; city manager plan, 170; animal tax, 215; stock-in-trade tax, 215; rentals tax, 216; water tax, 220; limit on temporary borrowing, 225; debt limits, 230; revenue from fines, 255; assessment basis, 262, 265; assessors, 264; assessment appeals, 268; regular review of assessments, 271; real property assessments, 286; tax-exempt property, 287, 291-2; specific taxes, 306; business assessments, 306, 312-13; tax calculations, 316; statutory tax limits, 317; tax sales, 325–6, 329, 333; penalties for overdue taxes, 333
in Saskatchewan: The City Act, 45, 52; creation, 76; compulsory payment of aldermen, 101; remuneration of mayors, 103; election and composition of councils in, 106; registration of voters, 142; appointment of election officers, 144n; nomination meetings, 144n; advance poll, 148; void ballots, 150; electors' qualifications, 159; m. elections schedule, 161; city manager plan, 170; city commissioners, 174; cash revenues, 206n; rentals tax, 216; limit on temporary borrowings, 225; limit on debenture term, 228; debt limit, 230; sinking fund trustees, 236; m. enterprises, 253n; revenue from fines, 255; assessment appeals, 269, 277–8; boards of assessment, 271–2; real property assessment, 286, 301; tax exemptions, 289, 292; charges in lieu

of taxes, 296; business assessments, 312–13; tax calculations, 316; tax collection, 321, 322n; compromise of tax arrears, 331

Cities Act of 1952 (Alta.), 52n, 175

Cities and Towns Act, The (Que.), 78n, 255

Citizens: at council meetings, 95; as members of m. committees, 109; protection by councillors, 117; impressions of council meetings by, 118; right to examine m. records, 118n; variety of problems of, 186; demand for economy, 194; changing concepts of government, 337

Citizenship, as qualification for m. voting, 142

City Act of 1908, The (Sask.), 45, 52

City manager, the, 169–71

Civil Service Board (Man.): powers, 180–1; dismissal of m. officers by, 182

Civil service, municipal: in Man., 180–2; recruitment and appointment, 182–5; merit systems, 184–5

Clark, Robert M., 306n

Classification: of municipalities, 61–6; of civic employees, 177–80; of m. expenditures, 203–4

Clerk of the peace, 42

Clerks, municipal: in Upper Canada, 25, 31; in United Canada, 30; in Lower Canada, 34; as recorder of council minutes, 119; preparation of voters' list by, 142–3; duty to advise of council decisions, 164; as co-ordinator, 169; compulsory appointment of, 177; combination with treasurer, 178–9; in Man., 180–1; salary range of (Ont.), 188; warning against unauthorized expenditures, 202; receipt of assessment roll by, 266; transmittal of assessment notices by, 267; as clerk of court of revision, 269; as tax calculator, 316; as conductor of tax sales, 326; in Charlottetown, 328

Clerk's department, as m. administrative unit, 167, 168

Clerk-treasurer: as combination officer, 178; as statutory officer, 179; appointment (Sask.), 181

Climate, as factor determining expenditures, 202, 203

Closed meetings of council, 94–5

Coal mines: business assessment of, 309; tax collection from workers in (N.B.), 323

Coal tax: in Newfoundland, 221; on chutes, 256

Coaticook, Que., 115n

Cobourg, Ont., 26n

Colbert, Jean Baptiste, 20

Collection, tax: tax roll as basis for, 316; by distress, 321; by suit, 321; by collecting rents, 322; by claim on insurance, 322; by set-off, 322; by publication and execution, 322–3; by pay deductions, 323; by transfer of lien, 323; by impounding motor vehicles, 323; by tax sales and tax liens, 323–32; by compromise and consolidation of tax arrears, 331–2

Collector of taxes: in Lower Canada, 34; in United Canada, 35; combined with other offices, 178; roll computed by, 316–18; as conductor of tax sales, 326

Colleges, exempt from taxation, 287

Commercial agents (travellers), specific tax on, 306

Commission: of Inquiry into Provincial and Municipal Taxation (Sask.), 289–90, 295; on Municipal Revenues and Reductions of Real Estate Taxes (New York State), 368n. *See also* Royal Commission

Commissioners: definition, 77; city, 174–6; assessment, salary of, 188

Committee on Provincial-Municipal Relations (Sask.), 295–6

Committees of municipal council: standing, 58, 108, 111, 163–4; special (or select), 108–9, 129; of the whole, 112; system of, 117;

finance, 199. *See also* Boards of control
Common council, 26–7, 27n
Community spirit, 85, 104, 287
Composition, of m. councils, 106
Compromise of tax arrears, 331–2
Conditional grants, 244–7
Connecticut, State of, 37
Conservation: The Grand River Conservation Commission, 136; as joint-municipal unit, 338
Consolidation: of debenture debt, 237–8; of tax arrears, 331–2
Constables, police, etc., 25, 42, 188
Constitutional Act (1791), 24
Constitutional position of Canadian local government, 18, 196, 208, 344
Contracts: award by boards of control, 173; recommendations by city commissioners re, 175
Control, boards of. *See* Boards of control
Controllers, 77, 82, 83, 102, 354
Controls: by municipalities, over expenditures, 201–2; by licences, 254; by provincial governments over m. activities, chap. XVII, 335–70
Conventions (unwritten rules), 115–16
Co-ordination, municipal: at interdepartmental level, 168–9; by municipal clerk, 169; by city manager, 169–71; by board of control, 172–4; by city commissioners, 174–6
provincial: at interdepartmental level, 366
Cornwall, Ont.: incorporation, 26n; selection of mayor, 27n; size of council, 78
Cornwallis, Lord Edward, 36
Corporate bodies, 48–9, 51
Corporation: municipal, 48n, 77n; voting by, 154
Corry, J. A., 6
Council-manager plan, 169–72
Councils, district (Lower Canada), 34–5
Councils, municipal, chap. IV, 77–107; personnel, 77–80, 101; term of office, 80–2; election, 81–6, 106, 138–61; head, 86–92; powers, 92–3, 96–8; composition, 92, 106; meetings, 93; by-laws and resolutions, 96; payment of members, 101–5; committees, 108-12; organization, 108, 166–9; caucus, 113; procedure, 113–19; activities, 119–20; personal element in, 120–5; vacancies, 151–2; recall of members, 153; election schedule (by provinces), 160–1; administration by, 162–6; boards of control, 172–4; city commissioners, 174–6; appointments by, 177, 180–5; dismissal of officials by, 181–2; fixing of employees' salaries by, 188; authority over expenditures, 191–205; acceptance of additional responsibilities, 196; problem of providing revenues, 206; power to levy taxes, 208, 315; authority to issue debentures, 227; obligation to provide for debt charges, 232; use of sinking fund surplus, 234–5; "raiding" of sinking funds, 236; preparation of assessment roll, 265; barred from courts of revision, 269; pressure by, on assessors, 283; granting of tax exemptions by, 291, 292; fixing of tax rate by, 315; action in tax sales, 325, 328–9; appeal to province for finances, 340; dismissal of members by provincial authorities, 353. *See also* Counties
Council, Special (post-Rebellion period, Lower Canada), 34
Councillors, municipal: definition, 77; number, 78–80; demands upon, 191. *See also* Aldermen
Counties: as a m. unit, 24, 35; councils, 35, 42, 58, 77–80, 93–4; wardens' term of office, 92: under-assessment in, 283. *See also* Wardens

in Manitoba: abolishment of, 345
in New Brunswick: size of councils in, 78–80; term of office of councillors, 80; voting requirements on question of valuation, 95n; payment of councillors, 102; election and composition of councils, 106; special committee, 110n; form of ballot, 147; resignation of councillors, 152; electors' qualifications, 159; statutory clerk-treasurers, 179; provincial approval of debentures, 229; dog tax, 259; m. assessment, 264; appeals by assessor, 268; equalization of assessments, 274; real property assessment, 286; tax collections, 318, 322; tax sales, 328
in Nova Scotia: size of councils, 79–80; payment of councillors, 102–3; election and composition of councils, 106; m. elections schedule, 160
in Ontario: wardens of, 77n, 115; size of councils, 79–80; assessors and tax collectors, 177; road superintendents, 180–1; m. assessment, 263; assessment appeals, 269, 277–8; equalization of assessments, 274, 275; tax sales, 324
in Quebec: by-laws of, 156; clerk-treasurers, 179; debt limits, 230; assessment, 263, 274–5; tax sales, 324
Counting of ballots, 149–51
County Assessment Act (Man.), 42
Court, magistrate's, 255
Court houses: erection and maintenance, 194; loans for, 239; taxation of, 295
Courts: of General Sessions of the Peace, 37
of Quarter Sessions, 20, 22–3, 25, 27, 38–9
of revision: appointments to, 87; in Saint John, N.B., 220; powers, 269–70. *See also* entries under the various types of municipalities
Creation of municipalities, 67; rural, 74; villages, 75; towns and cities, 76
Crouch, Winston W., 346n
Crown companies, m. payments by, 221–2
Crown property, exempt from taxation, 287–9, 294–9
Cumberland County, N.S., 36
Curling, Nfld., 220

DALTON TOWNSHIP, Ont., 79
Dance halls, as m. enterprises, 250
Date taxes due, 318
Debate, rules in m. councils, 114
Debentures: definition, 224n, 226; market for, 224; revenue type, 226; provincial approval of, 229–31; sinking fund type, 233–6; instalment or serial type, 236–7; in debt consolidations, 237–8; sale of, 238–9
Debt, municipal, trends in, 240
Debt charges: definition, 232; obligatory provision for, 192–3; municipal expenditure for, 205
Debt consolidations, 237–8
Deed, tax, 327–8
Deficits: occurrence in m. financing, 200; provision for, 201; in sinking funds, 233
Denominations of debentures, 238–9
Department of Highways. *See* Highways
Department of Municipal Affairs. *See* Municipal Affairs, Departments of
Department of Municipal Commissioner. *See* Municipal Commissioner.
Departments, of m. government: service types, 163; internal types, 163; number and types, 167–9; heads of, 186
Deposit, by m. candidate, 146
Depreciation, allowance for, in m. assessment, 282
Depression (1930's): closing fire stations during, 194n; unemployment

relief, 200n, 226; sinking fund surpluses during, 235; effect on m. debt, 240; financial difficulties of municipalities during, 255; tax sales during, 255
Deputy, mayor or reeve, 92
Deputy returning officer, 147, 150–1
Deserted wives, 304
Director: of Assessments (Alta.), 273, 276; of Local Government (Nfld.), 348
Direct tax, 208, 209
Disallowance, power of: in United Canada, 30; in N.S., 100; in Que., 100, 352
Discounts on taxes for prompt payment, 319
Discretion, local administrative, 360–1
Disease, protection against, 338
Disincorporation of m. corporations, 72
Dismissal: of council, 99; of town or city manager, 171; of department heads, 173; of m. officers, 181–2
Disorganization of m. corporations, 72
Disqualification: from voting at council meetings, 95; from m. candidature, 140–1
Dissolution of m. corporations, 72–3
Distress, collection of m. taxes by, 321
Distribution of m. expenditures, 205
District: m. administrative unit, 23–4, 37; magistrates, 27; surveyor, 30; councils, 30–1, 34–5; clerk, 31
District Councils Act (1841), 29, 31
District Courts of Quarter Sessions. *See* Courts of Quarter Sessions
District hospital boards (Alta.), 134
District municipalities (B.C.): as basic rural unit, 62; dissolution, 73; creation, 74; redivision of wards, 86n; payment of council members, 102; election and composition of councils, 106; m. elections schedule, 161; real property assessment, 286, 290, 301
Dog tax, 209, 212–13, 259
Dominion Bureau of Statistics, Classification of m. expenditures by, 203
Domestic employees, exempt from poll tax, 257
Dominion Government: expenditures compared with m. governments, 59; largest tax source of, 209; as local property owner, 222; property exempt from m. taxation, 287, 289, 294; payments in lieu of m. taxes, 297–9
Dominion of Canada: Parliament, 50, 51; electorate, 58
Dominion-Provincial Conference on Municipal Statistics, 203n
Dominion-Provincial relations, chap. XVII, 335–70.
Dorchester, Lord (Guy Carleton), 24
Drain inspectors, 34
Drainage works, 239
D.R.O. *See* Deputy returning officer
Drumheller, Alta., 142n
Drunkenness, grounds for disqualification of candidate, 140
Dundas County, Upper Canada, 24n
Dundas, Ont.: incorporation, 26n; council, 27n
Durham County, Upper Canada, 24n
Durham, Lord (John George Lambton), 27, 28
Durham Report, 28, 33–4
Duties: of m. corporations, 54; of m. employees, 186

EARNINGS: of m. enterprises, 207, 249; from sinking funds, 233–5; from licences, permits, and privileges, 253–5; from fines, 255; from rents, 255–6
East Kildonan, Man., 127, 135
East Windsor, Ont., 70
Edmonton, Alta.: creation, 52; annual expenditures, 60; city commissioners, 175; distribution of m. expenditures in, 205; sources of revenue, 207; business assessment, 309, 314
Education: m. expenditures for, 124, 205; "frills," 202; classification of school health services, 203; tax rates for, 211, 293; debentures for,

228; building fund for (N.S.), 239; bonded debt for, 241; provincial grants for, 245–7, 260; assessment appeals re (Man.), 278; tax exemption of schools, 287, 289, 310; training schools, 361; allocation of functions of, 363
Efficiency of m. government, 203
Elections: of county councils, 79–80; effect of term of office of councillors on, 81–6; basis, 82, 106; campaign during, 84; provincial statutes governing, 98; councillors' desire for, 121; candidates, 138–41, 144–7; the electorate, 141–2; voters' lists, 142–3; electoral process, 143–51; acclamation, 145; candidates' deposits, 146; ballots, 147; declaration of result, 148; proportional representation, 148–9; voting procedure, 150–1; to fill vacancies, 151–2; schedule (by provinces), 160–1
Electorate, municipal: demands for increased services, 53, 191, 195, 340; difference at other levels of government, 58–9; role in annexation procedure, 69; representatives of, 79; power, 98; inertia, 121–2; voting habits, 121–2; identity, 126n; voting on questions and by-laws, 153, 230; qualifications, 159–60; voting on manager plan, 170–1; non-taxpayers in, 191; ultimate control of m. expenditure, 202; responsibility of councillors to, 339
Electricity: tax, 219; works, as m. enterprise, 250; as provincial enterprise, 296; transmission lines assessment, 300
Eleemosynary institutions, 50
Elora, Ont., 136
Employees, municipal, chap. IX, 177–90; appointments, 177; types of, 177–80; officers and servants, 177–8; statutory and non-statutory officers, 178; part-time and full-time, 178–9; permanent and casual, 179; range of, 179–80; appointment and dismissal, 180–5; "outside workers," 180; merit systems, 184–5; duties, 186; working conditions, 186–90; pay, 186–8, 195; pensions, 188–90
Encroachments, m. charges for, 256
Engineer, municipal: non-feasibility of combining with other offices, 179; in Fredericton, 181; salary range in Ont., 188
England: degree of local self-government, 17; tradition of m. government, 17; parliamentary supremacy, 51; cost of private legislation, 53; problem of area adjustments, 68; mayors, 90; disclosure of councillor's pecuniary interest, 96n; Lindsay Committee, 104; committees in municipalities, 108; councils' standing orders, 113; special purpose bodies, 130; all-purpose m. body, 131–2; election of council, 138; surcharge on council members, 201; distinction between "tax" and "rate," 211; m. sinking funds, 236; assessment basis, 262; Local Government Boundary Commission, 335; central-local government relations, 343; *Report of Local Government Manpower Committee*, 366; shared taxes, 368
Enterprises: municipally operated, 206–7, 249–53; operated by provincial or national governments, 295
Enumerators, of voters' lists, 143
Equalization: grants, 244–5, 247–8, 339; of assessments, 273–6, 368
Equity, in m. assessments, 261, 273–6, 283, 311
Erection of municipalities, 67
Esquimault, B.C., 299n
Essex County, Upper Canada, 24n
Estimates of m. expenditures. *See* Budget, municipal
Eston, Sask., 150n
Ethics, councillors' code of, 116
Examinations: for m. officers, 180–1;

of m. financial affairs by province, 201
Executive committee. *See* Boards of control
Exemptions: from m. service, 141; from m. taxation, 287–9, 294–9; from personal property assessment, 304; from business assessment (Vancouver), 310
Exhibitions: as m. enterprises, 251; exempt from taxation, 287
Expediency in council actions, 53–4, 97–8
Expenditures, municipal, chap. x, 191–205; provincial and Dominion compared with, 59, 192; for debt charges, 192–3; for other m. bodies, 193; to provide for statutory obligations, 193–4; for optional services, 194–5; uncontrollable, 194–6; of Kingston, Ont., 194–5; continuous increase, 195–8; precedents for, 198; the budget, 199–201; controls over, 201–2; comparisons of, 202–3; classification of, 203–4; distribution in certain cities, 205; capital, financing of, 224
Expenses, councillors', 103–5
Express companies: specific tax on (P.E.I.), 306; business assessment on (Edmonton), 309

Fabrique, 31
Fairs, as m. enterprises, 251
Falardeau, Jean C., 21
Family Compact, 24
Farmers, personal property assessment exemptions, 304
Fees, for licences and permits, 254–5
Fence viewers, 25, 34
Fergus, Ont., 136
Ferries, as m. enterprises, 250, 251, 252
Fertility, factor in land assessment, 281
Finance, municipal: real property as tax base, 123–4; use by special purpose bodies, 129–30; expenditures, chap. x, 191–205; committee on, 199; tax revenues, chap. xi, 206–22; table of sources of tax revenues, 210; borrowings and non-tax revenues, chap. xii, 223–60; comparison with provincial and Dominion finance, 232, 240; provincial loans, 239; subsidies, grants, and shared taxes, 242–9; enterprise earnings, 249–53; licences, permits, and privileges, 253–5; fines and penalties, 255; rents, 255–6; poll tax, 256–8; assessment, chap. xiii, 261–78, chap. xiv, 279–301, chap. xv, 302–14; a factor in, chap. xvii, 335–70; strengthening of, 340–2; during depression of 1930's, 341; need for independence in, 342; fundamental problem of, 359
Finance committee, jurisdiction over sinking fund, 235
Finance department, as type of m. administrative unit, 167
Financial institutions: specific tax on (P.E.I.), 306; business assessment of (Regina), 310
Finer, Herman, 343n
Fines, m. revenue from, 254, 255
Fire chief, 188
Fire department: as a m. administrative unit, 167–8; maintenance, 194; curtailment during depression, 194n; in port cities, 203; expenditures for, 228; provincial grants for, 260; as a local service, 340
Fire districts, 44
Firemen: salary range (Ont.), 188; retirement age, 190
Fiscal need, municipal, difficulty of measuring, 339
Fiscal policy, municipal. *See* Finance, municipal
Fiscal year, municipal, 199
Fishermen, personal property assessment exemptions, 305
Fixed assessments, 292–4, 299–300
Floors, area as assessment basis, 310–12
Foreclosure procedure, 330–1
Formulae, of provincial grants to municipalities, 364–5
Fort Garry, Man.: Court of Sessions

at, 42; member of Greater Winnipeg Water District, 135
Fort William, Ont., 10n
France, local government in, 16; influence of Revolution, 17; influence on local government in New France, 20; hierarchical system, 61
Franchise: as a right to use streets for business purposes, 155; taxes, 219, 307. *See also* Voting
Fredericton, N.B.: not represented on county council, 62; remuneration of councillors, 103; number of standing committees of council, 111; taxation payment requirement of m. candidates, 139n, 146; duration of m. elections, 143n; nominations, 145n; expulsion of councillor, 151n; dismissal of m. officers, 181; m. budget, 199n; occupancy tax, 216; limit on short-term borrowings, 225; poll tax, 256n, 257; assessment appeals, 277; personal property tax, 302–3; business taxes, 307–8, 313; tax collection, 322
French-Canadians, attitude towards m. government, 36
French régime (1608–1760), m. government during, 19–20
"Frills," educational, 202
"Fringe areas," 68
Frontage tax. *See* Local improvement tax.
Frontenac County, Upper Canada, 24n
Frontenac, Louis de Buade, Comte de, 20
Fuel yards: as m. enterprises, 250; business assessment, 310–11
Full-time m. employees, 178
Functions of m. corporations, 54, 360–4.

GALT, Ont., 136
Gaolers: disqualified from m. candidature, 140; exempt from m. service, 141
Gaols, 27, 38, 42, 64, 239, 321
Garbage collection and disposal, 194, 205, 228
Gas: tax, examples of, 219; works, as m. enterprises, 250–2; assessment of companies, 300
Gasoline: specific tax (P.E.I.), 306; business assessment (Alta.), 311; tax, as shared tax (Alta.), 368
General Sessions of the Peace. *See* Courts
General government, m. expenditures for, 205
General vote, compared with ward, etc., vote, 82–6
Gentlemen's agreement, on secrecy of caucus, 113
Geography, as factor determining expenditures, 202
Glengary County, Upper Canada, 24n
Gloucester County, N.B.: incorporation, 38; rating of electors, 160
Goldenberg, H. Carl, 9n, 14, 266n, 290–1, 295, 336n
Golf courses, as m. enterprises, 251
Grain brokers, dealers, and merchants, business assessment of, 309–11
Grain elevators, fixed assessment of, 293
Grand jury, 37, 47
Grand'Mère, Que., 169n
Grand Prairie County, Alta., 64n
Grand River Conservation Commission, 134, 136–7
Grand voyer, 21
Grants, Dominion: in aid of local taxes, 295, 297–9; to provinces, 359
provincial: as portion of m. revenue, 206–7; purposes of, 242, 338–9; types, 242–8, 339, 367–8; examples (Ont.), 259; in aid of local taxes, 295; continuing need for, 359, 369; need for simple formula, 364–5; changes in system, 366–7
Greater Winnipeg Sanitary District, 127–8, 317
Greater Winnipeg Water District, 127, 134–5, 317
Grenvill County, Upper Canada, 24
Grey County, Ont., 199n

HALIFAX, N.S.: problem of metropolitan area, 14; annual expenditure, 60; mayoral veto power, 88; mayor's term of office, 92n; remuneration of councillors, 103; commissioners of school board, 130n; revisal officers, 142n; nomination of m. candidates, 145; provision for plebiscite, 157n; manager plan, 169n; revenue sources, 207; business taxes, 212, 307–8, 313; household tax, 216; tax-exempt property, 288–9; Dominion government payments in lieu of taxes, 299; specific taxes, 306; real property taxes, 315; date taxes due, 318; tax collection, 321–2; tax sales, 326–9
Hamilton, Ont.: problem of metropolitan area, 14; board of police, 26n; selection of mayor, 27n; annual expenditures, 60; size of m. council, 78
Hampstead, Que.: member of Montreal Metropolitan Commission, 134n; manager plan, 169n
Harbours: as m. enterprises, 25; debentures for, 228; national, 298
Harrison, Samuel Bealey, 29
Hasluck, E. G., 53n
Hastings County, Upper Canada, 24n
Head of m. council: general, 77–8; powers and duties, 86–9; leadership by, 89–90; status, 89–91; vote of, 89; *ex-officio* duties, 91; deputy mayor as, 92; term of office, 92; remuneration, 102–3; signature on tax sale warrant, 325
Head of m. department, appointment of employees by, 182
Health: department of, as m. administrative unit, 167–8, 338; classification of school health services, 203; m. expenditures for, 205; provincial grants for, 246; allocation of function, at local level, 363; officer, *see* Medical officer of Health
Heating systems, as m. enterprises, 250, 251
Hesse, District of, 23
Highway Improvement Act. (Ont.), 259
Highways: Ontario Minister and Department of, 182, 358; m. debt for, 241; provincial grants for, 246, 358; impetus for improvement, 377. *See also* Roads
Hincks, Sir Francis, 31
Historic sites, exempt from taxation, 287
History of m. government in Canada, 19–47; Ont. and Que., 19–36; N.S., 36–8; N.B., 38–9; Nfld. 40–1; Man. 41–3; Alta., 43–6; Sask., 43–6; B.C., 46–7
Horses, tax on, 215
Hospital board: as type of special purpose body; 65; in Ottawa, 128; district (Alta.), 134
Hospitalization of indigents, 193–4, 360, 367n
Hospitals: as m. enterprises, 250; business tax exemption of, 310; mental, 361
Hotels: keepers disqualified as candidates, 140; water taxes paid by, 220; business assessment, 309, 310
Housewives, exempt from poll tax, 257
Housing: and need for area adjustment, 68; emergency provision of, 196; as m. enterprise, 250, 251, 255–6; tax exemptions for, 291; projects of Crown agencies, 297
Hudson's Bay Company, 41, 43
Hugg, J. B., 96n
Hull, Que.: size of council, 78; ward system, 85; fiscal year, 199n; sources of m. revenue, 207; amusement tax, 218; water tax, 220
Hydro Electric power, Ontario system, 251
Hydro Electric Power Commission of Ontario, taxation of, 296
Hypothecation of m. securities, 224

ICE MERCHANT, permit for, 254
Ideal size for municipality, 71
Illegal acts, of m. councils, 53–4
Incinerators, loans for, 239
Indian Head, Sask., 43
Indigents: hospitalization, 193–4, 360, 367n; sanatorium care, 196
Indirect tax, 208n
Industrial development, 71, 292, 336
Industries: tax exemptions for, 292–4; war, operated by Crown agencies, 297
Initiative of electorate by petition, 158
Inspections, of m. activities by provincial governments, 354, 365
Inspector of Municipalities (B.C.), 229, 347
Inspectors: of drains, 34; in Department of Municipal Affairs (Alta.), 181, 354; building, in Fredericton, 181; of municipal finances, 201; in Sask., 354; in Que., 354
Instalment: debentures, 236–7; payment of taxes by, 318–19
Institute of Local Government, The, 188n
Institutions: charitable, etc., exempt from taxation, 287, 291; maintenance of persons in, 361
Insurance: premium tax, 220; institutions, specific tax on (P.E.I.), 306; companies, business assessment of (Winnipeg), 309; claim on, for collection of taxes, 322
Intangibles of m. government, 120–5
Intendant, 20
Inter-county relations, 133
Interdepartmental co-ordination, problem of: at m. level, 168–72; at provincial level, 366
Interest: on debt charges, 192; restriction on debenture rates, 227
Intergovernmental grants, 248–9
Inter-municipal relations, 70, 132–7
International City Managers' Association, 169
Inter-urban area (Ont.), 134
Investigations, of m. affairs by provincial governments, 354
Investments: sinking fund, 233–6; business assessment of investment bankers, 309
Isle-Maligne, Que., 169n

JACKSON, W. Eric, 55n
Jails. *See* Gaols
Jennings, W. Ivor, 4n
Jobbing, 28, 29
Johnstown, District of, 23
Joint-municipal bodies, 338. *See also* Inter-municipal relations
Judge, J. W., 45n, 295, 356
Judges: exempt from serving on councils, 141; revision of voters' lists by, 142; in voting recounts, 151
Judgment, of assessors, 261–2, 264, 273, 280
Justice, administration of, 361
Justices of the peace, 23, 25, 30, 38

KENT COUNTY, Upper Canada, 24n
King, Rt. Hon. W. L. M., 359n
Kings County, N.B., 264
Kings County, N.S., 36
Kingston, Ont.: loyalist settlements, 22; incorporation, 26n; early council, 27n; as capital of United Canada, 29; size of council, 78; ward system, 85; remuneration of councillors, 103; council organization, 167; m. expenditures (1951), 195; tax-exempt property, 288
Kitchener, Ont., 136
Knaplund, Paul, 28n

LAND: definition, 279; assessment of, 281; sale of, for unpaid taxes, 323–31
La Salle, Que., 134
Laski, Harold J., 4n
Leeds County, Upper Canada, 24n
La Tuque, Que., 169n
Lauzon, Que., 299n
Leadership: by head of council, 89; by council, 123

Legal department, as type of m. administrative unit, 167
Legal niceties, councillors' regard for, 53–4, 97–8
Legislation, municipal, 119–20, 162. *See also* By-laws
Lenox County, Upper Canada, 24n
Lethbridge, Alta.: voting registration, 142n; manager plan, 169n
Levis, Que., 217
Libraries, public: petition for establishment, 158; funds for, 193
Licences: resemblance to taxes, 215; to sell alcoholic beverages, 245; for motor vehicles, 246; definition, 253; revenue from, 254; types, 254
Lien, tax, 323, 325, 329–30
Limitation: on m. taxation, 191, 198, 208; on m. expenditures, 201; on m. borrowings, 223–5; on debenture terms, 227–31; on powers of courts of revision, 270; statutory, on m. taxes, 317
Lincoln County, Upper Canada, 24n
Lindsay Committee, 104
Liquor Control Board of Ontario, 296
Liquor: stores, taxation of, 295; stores, as provincial service, 338; licence fees (Ont.), 368
Lists, voters', 142–3
Literacy requirements, for m. candidates, 138
Literary societies, exempt from taxation, 287
Little Current, Ont., 299n
Loans, provincial, 239. *See also* Borrowing, municipal
Local Administration Act of 1937 (Nfld.), 40
Local Government Act of 1933 (Nfld.), 40
Local government area (Nfld.), 74
Local Government Board (Sask.): dismissal of m. officers by, 182; approval of debentures by, 229; authority over sinking fund surpluses and investments, 234–5; approval of charges in lieu of taxes, 296; action in tax arrears compromise, 331; establishment, 350; powers, 350
Local Government Boundary Commission, 335
Local improvement districts: in North West Territories, 44; in Saskatchewan, 45
Local improvement tax, 209–13
Local municipality, special meaning in Que. and Ont., 79n
"Local son," rule, in making appointments, 183
Local Tax Arrears Consolidation Act (Alta.), 331
Local self-government, preservation of, 335. *See also* Self-government
"Log-rolling," 84
London, Ont.: suburban problem of, 14; incorporation, 27n; early council, 27n; annual expenditures, 60; size of council, 78; ward system, 85; remuneration of councillors, 103; membership of standing committees, 108, 111; organization of council, 167; revenue sources, 207; debt limitation, 229; miscellaneous revenues, 254; street encroachment charges, 256; assessment values, 280n; tax-exempt property, 289
London, Eng., 17, 26n
Louiseville, Que., 169n
Lower Canada: limited experience of m. government, 31; history of m. government in, 32–6
Loyalists, United Empire, 17n, 21–4, 33, 36n, 38–9
Lucas, Sir C. P., 28n
Luneburg (or Lunenburg), District of, 23
Lunenburg County, N.S., 36–7
Lythgoe, J., 361

MACDONALD, Austin F., 115n, 162
MacLennan Commission (Ont.), 302
Magistrates: district, 27; disqualified as m. candidates, 140
Mail order businesses, assessment of, 309

Maine, State of, state-municipal relations in, 335n
Maintenance, of persons in public institutions, 361
Maire, 78, 87. *See* Mayor
Malartic, Que., 169n
Malfeasance of m. officers, 88
Management of sinking funds, 235–6
Manager plan, 169–72
Mandamus, writs, 99
Mandatory powers of councils, 99
Mandatory poll tax, 256
Manitoba, Province of: history of m. government, 41–3, 46; m. law, 51–2; annual expenditures, 60; extent of m. organization, 60; types of municipalities, 61–6, number, 66; annexation procedure, 69; dissolution and creation of municipalities, 72–6; election of councillors, 83, 106; powers of head of municipality, 88; frequency of council meetings, 93; compulsory voting by councillors, 95n; composition of councils, 106; qualification and disqualification of candidates, 139; m. clerk as returning officer, 144n; candidates' consent to serve, 145–6; withdrawal of candidates, 147; advance poll, 148; proportional representation, 148; vacancies in councils, 152; "ratepayers," 154; qualifications of m. electors, 159; m. elections schedule, 161; manager plan, 171; Civil Service Board, 180–2; dismissal of m. officers in, 182; m. pension plans, 189; administration of justice, 194, 273, 361; types of m. taxes, 212, 214; taxable m. assessments (1948), 215; limit on short-term m. borrowings, 224n; limit on debenture term, 227–8; Municipal and Public Utility Board, 229, 317, 345; m. debt, 230, 241; sinking fund earnings, 233; m. enterprises, 252; poll tax, 257–8; dog tax, 259; assessment, 263, 265; assessment appeals, 268–9, 271, 277–8; "value" for assessment, 279; valuation of buildings, 281; real property assessment, 282; tax-exempt property, 288, 292; fixed assessments, 293, 300; Telephone System, 296; personal property assessment, 302, 304; business assessment, 306, 312, 314; tax collection, 316, 321–2; taxes due date, 318; tax sales, 325–9, 334; penalties on overdue taxes, 333; provincial-municipal relations, 335n, Municipal Commissioner, 345. *See also* Cities, Rural municipalities, Towns, and Villages (Man.)
Manitoba Civil Service Board, 180–2
Manitoba Municipal and Public Utility Board: approval of long-term borrowing, 229; authority to exceed m. tax limit, 317; transfer of duties to, 345
Manitoba Telephone System, 296
Manning, Hon. E. C., 356
Manning, H. E., 316n
Manual of assessment (Ont.), 283
Maritime Provinces, history of m. government, 36–41
Market values, relation to assessment values, 284–5
Markets, as m. enterprises, 250
Massachusetts, State of: settlers from, 37; state-municipal relations in, 335n
Mayors: in Lower Canada, 35–6; of Manitoba municipalities, 42; leadership by, 56, 89–90; title of, as head of council, 78; of Quebec local municipalities, 79–80; election, 82; powers and duties, 86–9; status, 89–91; *ex officio* duties, 91; term of office, 92; deputy, 92; remuneration, 101–5; as *ex officio* member of committees, 108; unwritten rules as to office, 115; as administrators, 168; relation to city managers, 170; as members of board of control, 173; as *ex*

officio city commissioners, 174. *See also* Head of council
McEvoy, J. M., 25n, 26n, 27, 31, 57
McInnis, Edgar, 21n
McQuarrie, Hon. J. H., 356
Mechanics, personal property assessment exemptions of, 305
Mecklenburg, District of, 23
Mediation Board (Sask.), 330
Medical officer of health: not combined with other offices, 178–9; appointment and dismissal (Ont.), 180–2
Medicine Hat, Alta.: control of council by electorate, 100; recall procedure, 153; rentals tax, 216
Meetings of m. council, 93–122; frequency of, 93; special, 94; quorum, 94; voting in, 95–6; committee of the whole, 112; caucus, 113; procedure, 113–19; minutes, 118–19; seating arrangements, 122
Members of Parliament: disqualified from m. candidature, 140; exempt from m. service, 141
Mental incapacity, grounds for disqualification from m. candidature, 140
Merit system, in m. employee appointments, 184–5
Meters, parking, 256
Metropolitan area: problem of, 133–5; Montreal Metropolitan Commission, 134–5, 351. *See also* Area adjustments
Middleton, Mr. Justice, 177–8
Mileage allowance, for attendance at council meetings, 102
Milk, for needy school children, 196
Mill, explanation of in tax rates, 214n
Mill, John Stuart, 208
Milltown, N.B., 133n
Minister of Municipal Affairs. *See* Municipal Affairs, Department of
Minutes, of council meetings, 118–19, 164–5
Misfeasance, of m. officers (N.S.), 88
Model by-laws, 353
Moncton, N.B.: incorporation, 38; elections, 82n; remuneration of councillors, 103; representation on county council, 133n; council organization, 167; rentals tax, 216; miscellaneous revenues, 254; tax-exempt property, 289; Dominion payments in lieu of taxes, 299n
Money by-laws, 69, 231
Money lenders, permits for, 254
Montreal, Que.: metropolitan problem of, 14; *syndics*, 20; incorporation, 33; annual expenditure, 60; city council, 77n, 78; remuneration of councillors, 103; Metropolitan Commission, 134–5; administrative departments, 167; executive committee, 173–4; merit system, 183; fiscal year, 199n; revenue sources, 207, 254; sales tax, 217; amusement tax, 218; telephone apparatus tax, 218; insurance premium tax, 220; water tax, 220; licences and permits, 254; tax-exempt property, 289; specific taxes, 306; business assessments, 308, 313
Montreal Civil Service Commission, 184
Montreal East, Que.: member of Montreal Metropolitan Commission, 134n; manager plan, 169n
Montreal Metropolitan Commission, 134–5, 351
Montreal West, Que., 134n
Moore Commission (New York State), 368
Moose Jaw, Sask.: creation, 43; city commissioners, 174–5; sources of revenue, 207; sales tax, 218; m. revaluation, 272n; business assessment, 310–11, 314
Mothers' allowances (Ont.), 196
Motor boat tax (Nfld.), 221
Motorists: demands upon councils, 202; parking meters for, 256
Motor vehicles: impounding for overdue taxes, 323; taxes on (B.C.), 368

Mount Royal, Que., 134n, 169n
Municipal Act (B.C.), 96n
Municipal (Baldwin) Act of 1849 (United Canada), 30–2
Municipal Affairs, Departments and Ministers of: in dissolution of municipalities, 72; Ont., 102, 283, 291, 297, 329, 330–1, 334, 347, 353; B.C., 105n, 347; Man. (as Department of Municipal Commissioner), 148, 263n, 345; Sask., 152, 272, 274, 276, 345; Alta., 180–1, 273, 293, 346; N.B., 229, 283, 348; N.S., 229, 347, 352; Que., 238, 346; establishment of, 344–8; Nfld. (as Director of Local Government), 348; co-ordination of m. affairs by, 366
Municipal and Public Utility Board (Man.): approval of m. debt limits, 230, 345; control over sinking funds, 235; report of, 285n; powers, 317, 351; creation, 351
Municipal assessment districts (Man.), 263
Municipal Assessment Equalization and Appeal Board (Man.), 274, 275–6, 278
Municipal Assistance Act (Alta.), 246
Municipal Clauses Act of 1892 (B.C.), 46
Municipal Code (Que.): as general m. act, 52; governs "local" municipalities, 79n; governing meetings of council, 94n, 95n; prohibiting payment to councillors, 101n; provision for oral voting, 138; exemption from service on council under, 141; limit of voting franchise by, 142n; filling council vacancies under, 152; county by-laws under, 156; appointment of assessors under, 264; annual assessment under, 265; review of assessments under, 271; assessment of electrical transmission lines under, 299–300
Municipal Commissioner: Alta., 148; Man., 148, 263n, 345; N.S., 233, 235, 347; Sask., 345
Municipal Commissioners Act of 1908 (Sask.), 45
Municipal corporations: description, 48–9; definition, 77n
Municipal councils. *See* Councils, municipal
Municipal districts (Alta.): creation, 45, 74; area, 62; area adjustments, 68; dissolution, 72n, 73; payment of councillors, 102; election and composition of councils, 106; delegation of powers to committees, 111n; nomination meeting, 144; electors' qualifications, 160; m. elections schedule, 161; appointment of secretary-treasurers, 181; temporary borrowings limit, 225; debenture term limit, 227–8; debt limit, 230; poll tax, 256; real property assessment, 286, 290, 301; business assessment, 313; tax roll, 316; penalty for overdue taxes, 333
Municipal Hospitals Act (Alta.), 64
Municipal organization, 59
Municipal powers, 49–54
"Municipalities" (type of municipality in N.S.): definition, 77n; elections, 82n; statutory meeting requirements, 93; payment of councillors, 101, 102n; nominators of candidates, 145; dismissal of clerks and treasurers, 181; highway tax, 208n; limit on temporary borrowing, 225; poll tax, 256; assessment notices, 267; assessment appeals, 269, 272, 277; equalization of assessments, 274; real property assessment, 286; penalties for overdue taxes, 333
Municipalities, district. *See* District municipalities
Munro, W. B., 81n

NASSAU, District of, 23
National Association of Assessing Officers, 285n, 303n

Navy officers, disqualified from m. candidature (Que.), 140
New Brunswick, Province of: history of m. government, 28n, 37; county corporations, 49n; as one of original Canadian provinces, 50; extent of m. organization, 60; annual expenditures, 60; types of municipalities, 61; cities, 67; dissolution and creation of municipalities, 72, 74–6; county councils, 77n, 80, 95n; size of councils, 79–80; term of office of councillors, 80; election of councillors, 83, 106; requirement for council meetings, 93; composition of councils, 106; nomination procedure, 144; withdrawal of candidates, 147; early use of ballot, 147n; "ratepayers," 154; electors' qualifications, 159; m. elections schedule, 160; manager plan, 169; licensing of m. auditors, 181; pension plans, 189; provincial grants and subsidies, 206n, 243, 368; types of m. taxes, 212, 214, 256–9; m. assessment, 1948, 215; m. enterprises, 252; assessment procedures, 267–8, 318; equalization of assessments, 274; assessment appeals, 277, 278; assessment basis, 279–80; real property assessment, 282; school for assessors, 283; tax-exempt property, 288; personal property assessment, 302–3, 305; business assessment, 312–13; tax calculations, 316; taxing procedure, 318; tax collections, 321–2; tax sales, 325, 327, 334; penalty for overdue taxes, 333; Minister of Education, Federal and Municipal Relations, 348. *See also* Cities, Counties, Towns, and Villages (N.B.)
New England colonies: influence on Canadian m. government, 22, 37; town meetings, 24
New Westminster, B.C.: incorporation, 46; business tax, 212, 310
New York City, 149n
New York State: state-municipal relations, 335n; Moore Commission, 368–9; shared taxes, 369n
New Zealand: physical factors in m. development, 16; assessment basis of municipalities, 262; relationship between central and local government, 335
Newcastle, District of, 23
Newcastle, N.B., 133n
Newfoundland, Province of: status of m. government, 14, 344; influence of topography on m. government, 17; history of m. government, 40–1, 50n; general municipal act, 52; extent of m. organization, 60; types of municipalities, 61–6, number, 66; creation of rural municipalities, 74; term of office of councillors, 81; vote of council chairman, 89; frequency of council meetings, 93; election and composition of councils, 106; candidates' qualifications, 139; m. electors' qualifications, 159; m. fiscal year, 199n; provincial grants, 206n, 244; types of m. taxation, 212–15, 218; m. assessments, 215, 265–8, 277–8, 302, 306, 312, 317; m. taxes peculiar to, 220–1; m. service fee, 257; statutory tax limits, 317; date m. taxes due, 318n; tax collection by distress, 321; foreclosure, 330; penalties on overdue taxes, 332–3; lack of m. organization, 344; Director of Local Government, 348; provincial control over municipalities, 351, 353
Newmarket, Ont., 151
Niagara, District of, 23
Niagara Falls, Ont.: manager plan, 169n; sources of revenue, 207; tax-exempt property, 288
Nomination of m. candidates, 144–6; number of nominators, 160–1
Non-feasance of m. officers (N.S.), 88
Non-statutory officers, 178

Norfolk County, Upper Canada, 24n
North West Territories, 43, 44
Northfield Parish, N.B., 323n
Northumberland County (Upper Canada), 24n; (N.B.,), 38
Note: promissory, 223; treasury, 223
Notice: required for special council meetings, 94; of assessment, 266–8; of taxes, 317-18
Nova Scotia, Province of: immigration of loyalists, 21; emigrants, to Prairies, 43; as one of original Canadian provinces, 50; annual expenditures, 60; extent of m. organization, 60; types of municipalities, 61–6, number, 66, creation and dissolution, 72–6; county and district wardens, 77n, 88; size of county councils, 79–80; election of councillors, 81; duties of town mayors, 86–7; power of wardens, 88; m. by-laws subject to Minister's approval, 100; payment of councillors, 101–2; arbitration committees of councils, 133; registration of m. voters, 142; m. nomination procedure, 144; withdrawal of candidates, 147; recount of votes, 151; "ratepayers," 154; m. electors' qualifications, 159; m. elections schedule, 160; manager plan, 169; dismissal of m. officers, 181; licensing of m. auditors, 181; m. pension plans, 189; Highway Tax, 208n; types of m. taxes, 212, 214, 257–8; m. assessments, 1948, 215; limit on debenture term, 227–8; approval of debenture issues, 229; Department of Municipal Affairs, 229, 347, 352; m. sinking funds, 235–6; school building fund, 239; m. loan fund, 239; m. debt, 240–1; m. enterprises, 252; annual assessment, 265; assessment appeals, 268–9, 271; equalization of assessments, 274; assessment basis, 279–80; real property assessment, 282, 286; fixed assessments, 294; personal property assessment, 302–5; business assessment, 312–13; m. tax collection, 316, 321; discounts for prompt tax payment, 319; tax sales, 325–8, 334; penalties on overdue taxes, 332–3; provincial-municipal relations, 335n; Municipal Sinking Fund Commission, 347; provincial control of municipalities, 352–3; Union of Nova Scotia Municipalities, 356. *See also* Cities, "Municipalities," and Towns (N.S.)
Nurses, salary range for (Ont.), 188

Obsolescence, allowance for, in real property assessing, 282
Occupancy tax: as common m. tax, 212; variations and examples of, 216
Official Opposition, 55–6
Officers, municipal: statutory, 165; and employees, chap. IX, 177–90; definition, 177–8; and servants, 177–8; non-statutory, 178; not elected, 180; dismissal and appointment, 181–5; duties, 186; salaries, 187–8; assessors, 263
Officials, municipal: as part-time and full-time employees, 163; contact with committee chairmen, 164; inherent conflict with council, 165–6; municipal manager, 169–71; control over expenditures, 201
Ontario, Province of: history of m. government, 19–32, 57; loyalist settlers, 21n; transplanting of institutions of, 42–3, 46; m. system of, as basis for Manitoba system, 42; immigrants to B.C., 47; as one of original Canadian provinces, 50; Municipal Act of, 51; creation of municipalities, 51–2, 74–6; supply of school funds by municipalities, 54; governmental expenditures, 60; extent of m. organization, 60, 67; types of municipalities, 61–6, number, 66; incomplete m. organization, 67;

amalgamation of municipalities by statutes, 70; dissolution of m. corporations, 73; election of councillors, 83; frequency of council meetings, 93; Department of Municipal Affairs, 102, 281, 283, 297, 329–31, 334, 347; tax collections, 117n, 316, 322, 329–30; suburban road commissions, 134; inter-urban m. areas, 134; m. candidates' qualifications and disqualifications, 139–40, 146; m. nomination meetings, 144; clerk as returning officer, 144n; nominators, 145n; nominee's consent, 146; withdrawal of candidates, 147; tie votes in m. elections, 151; councillor's resignation, 152; corporations voting in m. elections, 154; voting on granting a franchise, 155; qualifications of m. electors, 159; m. election schedule, 161; manager plan, 169; boards of control, 172–3; appointment of assessors and tax collectors, 177; combination of offices of clerk and treasurer, 179; medical officers of health, 180, 188; appointment of m. auditors, 180; dismissal of m. officers, 180–1; salaries of m. employees, 188; m. pension plans, 189–90; funds for library and parks boards, 193; old age pensions, 196; indigents' sanatorium care, 196; indigent hospitalization, 197n, 367n; m. arbitration awards, 200n; expenditure of funds from next year's receipts, 201; provincial grants and subsidies, 206n, 242–5, 259–60; types of m. taxes, 212, 258–9; assessment of utilities, 214, 299–300; m. temporary borrowing limit, 224n, 225; Public Parks Act, 226n; Public Utilities Act, 226n; limit on debenture term, 228; m. debt limit, 230; statutory inducements to provide for m. debt charges, 232; m. sinking funds, 234; loans to municipalities, 239; m. debenture debt, 240; hydro-electric power system, 251, 296; Hydro Electric Power Commission, 251, 296; m. enterprises, 252; assessment appeals, 269–70, 277–8; equalization of assessments, 274–5; assessment basis, 279; basis of building valuation, 281; real property assessment, 282, 291, 301; manual for assessors, 283; tax-exempt property, 288, 292; fixed assessments, 293; Liquor Control Board of, 296; payments in lieu of taxes, 297; business assessments, 306, 312–13; *ad valorem* taxes, 307–8; tax limit, 317; m. tax sales, 325–8, 334; compromise of tax arrears, 331; penalties on overdue taxes, 333; provincial-municipal relations, 335n; Provincial Municipal Auditor, 349; welfare administration units, 358; liquor licence fees, 368. *See also* Cities, Counties, Towns, Villages, and Townships (Ont.)

Ontario Municipal Board: area adjustments by, 68–9; dissolution of municipalities by, 72–3; changes in m. status by, 76; proposed as arbitrator in budgetary disputes, 130n; creation of inter-urban area authorities by, 134; and Grand River Conservation Commission, 136; approval of m. expenditures by, 201; approval of short-term borrowing by, 224n; approval of debenture issues by, 228–30; authority over sinking funds, 234; assessment appeals to, 278, 297; authority to raise tax limit, 317; relation to Department of Municipal Affairs, 347; establishment, 349; powers, 349–50; approval of zoning by-laws by, 352; approval of licence fees by, 353

Ontario Municipal Improvement Corporation, 239

Ontario Railway and Municipal Board,

349 (predecessor of Ontario Municipal Board, *q.v.*)
Open meetings of m. councils, 94–5
Opposition, 55–6
Optimum size for municipalities, 71
Optional powers of councils, 99–101
Optional services, expenditures for, 194–7
Ordinance for the Formation and Regulation of Municipalities in British Columbia, 46
Ordinances providing m. government in Lower Canada, 34–5
Organization: of councils, 108–25; of council committees, 108–9
Ottawa, Ont.: annual expenditures, 60; size of council, 78; civic hospital, 128; question submitted to electors, 156n; miscellaneous revenues, 254; tax-exempt property, 288; payments in lieu of taxes, 297, 299
Outremont, Que.: mayor, 92; member of Montreal Metropolitan Commission, 134n; manager plan, 169n; sales tax, 217
"Outside workers," appointment of, 180
Overdrafts, municipal: occurrence, 200; of previous councils, 201
Overseers: of highways, 25, 34–5; of the poor, 34; of villages (Sask.), 78
Owen Sound, Ont.: m. budget, 199n; sources of revenue, 207

Paris, Ont., 136
Parish and Town Officers Act, Upper Canada, 25–6
Parish Assessment Act (Man.), 42
Parishes: Upper Canada, 25–6; Lower Canada, 34–6; Que., 62–3, 73, 78, 106, 225; Ont., 62, 64; N.B., 79, 263–4; as voting areas, 82
Park boards: as special purpose bodies, 65; in Winnipeg, 127; in Ont., 128n, 193
Parks: debentures for, 228; national, 298; exempt from business tax (Vancouver), 310; as a local service, 340
Parties, political, in m. government, 55–7, 122, 183
Part-time municipal employees, 178
Paupers, exempt from poll taxes, 257
Payment: of councillors, 101–5; of m. employees, 186–8; in lieu of taxes, 221–2, 296–7; of taxes, 318–23
Penalties: for refusing to serve on councils, 141; for overdue taxes, 319–20, 332–3. *See also* Fines
Penitentiaries, payments in lieu of taxes for, 297
"Penny-pinchers," charge against councils, 202
Pensions: for m. employees, 188–90; old age (Ont.), 196
Percentage grants, 244
Permanent m. employees, 179
Permits: resemblance to taxes, 215; definition, 254; revenue from, 254; types, 254–5
Personal element in m. government, 120–5
Personal property assessment, 302–5
Personal property tax: as a general tax, 211; as common type of m. tax, 212; as major tax source, 214; assessment by provinces, 215
Personnel: of councils, 77–80, 101; of special committees, 109; of standing committees, 111; of special purpose bodies, 126, 129; municipal, control of, by provincial governments, 353
Peterborough, Ont.: remuneration of councillors, 103; void ballots, 150n; distribution of m. expenditures, 205; sources of revenue, 207; City Trust, 235–6
Petition: annexation, 69–70; for establishment of new rural municipalities, 74; for creation of villages, 75; for creation of towns and cities, 76; against by-laws, 100; for recall of councillors, 152–3
Picton, Ont., 26n
Pictou, N.S., 299n
Planning, municipal: increasing importance of, 56; long-range, 68; lack

of, 81, 115; community, 123; Winnipeg Town Planning Commission, 128
Planning department, as m. administrative unit, 167
Playgrounds: Winnipeg commission, 127; m. provision of, 196; debentures for, 228
Plebiscite: in Alberta counties, 65; precedent to dissolution of m. corporation, 73
Plewman, W. R., 94n
"Plumping," 150
Pohlman, F. W., 44n
Police: boards of, 26, 91; Board of Police Commissioners, Winnipeg, 127; conflicts with councils, 129; salaries, 188; retirement age, 190; m. expenditures for, 205; provincial grants for, 260; provincial, 338
"Political football," 131–2
Political parties, *see* Parties, political
Polling: divisions, 144; day, 148, 160–1. *See also* Voting
Poll tax: example of flat-rate tax, 209; as common type of m. tax, 212; as less important tax type, 213; definition and description, 256–8
Population: rural and urban classification of, 11–13; of m. wards, 85; density of, as factor determining expenditures, 202; as basis for m. grants, 243, 368
Port Hope, Ont., 26n
Post offices, taxation of, 295
Pound keepers, 25, 34, 141
Powell, C. W., 40, 344
Powers: of head of council, 88; of councils, 92–3, 96–101, 114; mandatory and optional, 99; of committees, 110–11; ultimate, of council, 163; of council to levy taxes, 208
Prairie Provinces, history of m. government in, 41–6
Precedents: in council practice, 116; importance in m. expenditures, 198
Prescott, Ont., 26n
Preston, Ont., 136
Prince Edward County, Upper Canada, 24n
Prince Edward Island: types of m. taxes in, 212; personal property of property from m. taxation, assessment, 214, 302–4; m. debt, 241; m. enterprises, 252; assessment basis, 279; real property assessment, 282; tax-exempt property, 288; business assessment, 312–13; tax collection, 323; tax sales, 326–7; redemption of tax sale land, 333. *See also* Towns and Villages (P.E.I.)
Private Acts, 52, 67
Private employment, compared with m. employment, 186–7
Procedure: of councils, 113–19; of tax sales, 326–7; of foreclosure, 330–1
Proceedings, of council meetings, 118–20
Processing tax (Nfld.), 220
Proctor, Frank B., 177n, 181n, 201n
Profit, from m. enterprises, 250–2. *See also* Surpluses
Pro-mayor, 92
Promissory note, as form of m. short-term borrowing, 223
Property qualifications: for m. voters, 142, 154–6, 159–60; for m. candidates, 146
Proportional representation, 148–9
Proprietors, as class of electors (Que.), 154
Provinces: extent of m. organization in, 59; tax resources, 209; exemption 287–8. *See also* entries after each provincial name
Provincial Board of Examiners (Sask.), 181
Provincial Departments of Municipal Affairs. *See* Municipal Affairs, Departments and Ministers of
Provincial governments: expenditures of, 59–60; exemptions from m. taxation, 289; payments in lieu of

taxes, 297; increased responsibilities of, 337–9; assistance to municipalities during Depression of 1930's, 341; intervention at m. level, 341–2; control and supervision exercised by, 344–55; lack of consultation with municipalities, 355; allocation of functions with municipalities, 360–4. *See also* chap XVII, 335–70, and Grants, provincial
Provincial legislation: general, 51–3; on area adjustments, 68, 70; regulation-making powers under, 345; purposes behind, 355
Provincial loans to municipalities, 239
Provincial Mediation Board (Sask.), 330
Provincial Municipal Assessor (Man.), 263, 265, 270
Provincial Municipal Auditor (Ont.), 349
Provincial-municipal relations, 14–15, chap. XVIII, 335–70; Committee on (Sask.), 295–6; in B.C., 295
Publication: of voters' lists, 142; of names of delinquent taxpayers, 322
Public health: changing concepts of, 338; local by-laws governing (Ont.), 352; Act (Ont.), 353
Public libraries. *See* Libraries, public
Public opinion: sensitivity of m. government to, 121–2; on area of m. responsibility, 123; public interest as source of, 124; and special purpose bodies, 131–2
Public ownership. *See* Enterprises, municipally operated
Public Parks Act, The (Ont.), 128n, 226n
Public Parks Board (Winnipeg), 317
Public schools. *See* Education
Public utilities. *See* Enterprises, municipally operated
Public Utilities Act (Ont.), 226n
Public welfare, 182

QUALIFICATIONS: of m. candidates, 138–40, 145–6; of electors, 141–2, 159–60; of assessors, 263
Qu'Appelle, Sask., 43
Quarter Sessions, Courts of. *See* Courts
Quebec City, Que.: suburban problem of, 14; *syndics* (during French régime), 20; incorporation, 33; annual expenditures, 60; remuneration of councillors, 103; manager plan, 169n; fiscal year, 199n; sources of revenue, 207; sales tax, 217; amusement tax, 218; water tax, 220
Quebec Hydro Electric Commission, 296
Quebec, Province of: history of local government, 19–21, 32–6; as one of original Canadian provinces, 50; Cities and Towns Act, 52, 78n, 255; annual governmental expenditures, 60; extent of m. organization in, 60–7; types of municipalities, 61, number, 66; m. organization, 67; urban boundary adjustments, 68; creation of rural municipalities, 74; county councils, 77n, 79–80; meaning of "local municipalities," 79n; election of councillors, 83, 106; qualification and disqualification of candidates, 139–40; exemptions from m. service, 141; filling council vacancies, 152; "proprietors," 154; voting on a franchise, 155; electorate approval of by-laws, 155–6; electors' qualifications, 159; m. elections schedule, 161; manager plan, 169–71; statutory clerk-treasurers, 179; provincial licensing of m. auditors, 181; dismissal of rural m. officials, 182; m. pension plans, 189; provincial inspection of m. finances, 201; types of m. taxes, 212, 215–19, 257, 259; Municipal Commission, 225, 229, 351; debenture term limit, 227, 228; m. debt limit, 230; m. sinking funds, 233; Department of Municipal Affairs, 238, 346; deben-

ture sale by tender, 238; sales tax shared with municipalities, 245–6, 368; m. enterprises, 252; m. assessing process, 264–5, 267; assessment appeals, 269–71, 277–8; equalization of assessments, 274; assessment basis, 279; real property assessment, 282; tax-exempt property, 288, 291–2; fixed assessments, 293; Hydro Electric Commission of, 296; assessment of electric transmission lines, 299–300; personal property assessment, 302–4; business assessment, 306, 312; tax calculations, 316; tax collection, 316–17; tax sales, 326–8; penalties on overdue taxes, 333; provincial control over m. activities, 352. *See also* Municipal Code (Que.), and Cities, Counties, Towns, Townships, and Villages (Que.)

Quebec Municipal Commission: approval of temporary m. borrowings, 225, of long-term borrowing, 229; establishment of, 351; jurisdiction of, 351

"Questions," submission to m. electorate, 153–8

Quorum at council meetings: definition, 94; necessity for, 93; lack of, 152

"RAIDING" of m. sinking fund, 236

"Railroading" of measures through council, 110

Railway: employees exempt from m. service, 141, advance election poll for, 148; street, debentures for, 228, as m. enterprises, 250; company, tax exemption of, 293; m. assessment of, 300

Rate book, 316–18

Ratepayers: as portion of m. electorate, 154; court action by, against m. corporation, 201

"Rates," municipal, meanings in Canada and England, 211n

Rates of pay: for councillors, 102–3; for m. employees, 187–8, competition with private employers in, 195, as factor determining m. expenditures, 202

Reallocation of provincial and municipal functions, 360–4

Real property: as m. tax base, 123–4, 191, 208–9; as m. tax revenue source, 212–14, 340, 362; total assessment, by provinces, 215; as security for m. debentures, 226; owned by municipalities, 255; assessment, 262, chap. XIV, 279–301; definition, 279; basis for valuation, 279–82; under-assessment, 281, 283–4; changing values, 284–5

Rebellion (1837), 31

Recall of councillors, 152–3

Recorder (Que.), 255

Recording, as function of assessing, 263, 264

Records: of council meetings, 118–19; of duties of senior m. officers, 186; scrutiny by provincial financial inspectors, 201; for provincial authorities, 365

Recount of votes, 151

Recreation: expenditures for, 205; as a local service, 340

Recruitment of m. employees, 183–4

Redemption of property sold for taxes, 327–8, 333–4

Red tape in m. administration, 164

Red River colony, 41

Reduction of m. status, 72

Re-election, desire of councillors for, 121

Reeve: in Manitoba counties, 42; definition, 78; in Ontario municipalities, 80; election, 82; powers and duties, 86–9, 91; vote of, 89; status, 89–91; term of office, 92; remuneration, 101–5

Refuse, collection and disposal of, 194, 203, 205, 239, 340

Regina, Sask.: creation, 43, 52; office of mayor, 115; city commissioners, 174–5; sources of revenue, 207; amusement tax, 218; debt limita-

tion, 229; sinking fund trustees, 236; real property assessment, 282; business assessment, 310–11, 314
Registration: for m. voting, 142; of tax arrears certificates (Ont.), 329–30
Registry offices, exempt from m. taxation, 287
Regulations, provincial, 98–9, 345, 358
Relations, provincial-municipal. *See* Provincial-municipal relations,
Relief recipients: disqualified as m. candidates, 140; in Ont., 194; budgetary problems associated with, 200n; financing costs of, 226, 341; provincial grants for, 247
Remuneration: of councillors, 101–5; of m. employees, 186–8
Renne, Ronald R., 16n
Rental tax: as common type of m. tax, 212; variations and examples, 216
Rental value: as real property assessment base, 262; as business assessment basis, 308–10
Rents: m. revenue from, 254; collection in payment of taxes, 322
Repeal of m. by-laws, 100–1
Reports: by m. committees, 118; need for more intelligible type of, 124–5; for provincial authorities, 365
Residence requirements for m. voting, 142, 159
Resignation of councillors, 151–2
Resolutions of councils: definition, 96; as basis for council action, 164–5. *See also* By-laws
Restrictions on m. long-term borrowing, 227–32. *See also* Limitation
Returning officer: m. clerk as, 143–4; deputy, 147, 150–1
Revenues, municipal: from utilities and other m. enterprises, 193, 249–53; from taxes, chap. XI, 206–22; main sources of, 206; compared with Dominion and provincial, 210; from borrowings and non-tax sources, chap. XII, 223–60; from subsidies, grants, and shared taxes, 242–9; from rents, 255–6; from poll tax, 256–8; from dog tax, 259
Revisal officers for voters' lists, 142
Rhode Island, State of, 37
Rimouski, Que., 169n
Roads: overseers, 25, 34–5; construction, 68; machinery, 71, 228; suburban commissioners, 134; inspectors (Que.), 141; superintendents (Ont.), 180–1; expenditures, 197; oiling of, 213; debentures for, 228. *See also* Highways and Streets
Roberts, Arthur, 18n
Robertson, R. W. W., 20n
Robson, H. A., 96n
Robson, William A., 4n
Roll, tax (or collector's), 316–18
Rolling mills, fixed assessment of, 293
Rouyn, Que., 169n
Rowat, Donald C., 133n
Rowell-Sirois Commission, 294
Royal Commission: on Rates and Taxes Act (N.B.), 267n; on Dominion-Provincial Relations, 294; on Taxation (Alta.), 295
Royal visit (1939), 53
Rules of procedure, 113–19
Rupert's Land, 41
Rural districts (Nfld.): as m. type, 61; creation, 74; election and composition of council, 106
Rural municipal corporations: table of, 63; number, by provinces, 66; problem of area adjustments, 68; ideal size, 71; creation, 74; size of councils, 79; payment of councillors, 102; part-time employees, 178; real property assessment, 291
Rural municipalities: in Manitoba: creation, 74; election and composition of councils of, 106; vacancies in councils, 152; debt limits, 230; railway assessments, 300n; statutory tax limit, 317
in Saskatchewan: The Rural Municipalities Act of 1909, 45, 52;

proposed area adjustments, 68; dissolution, 73; creation, 74; election and composition of councils, 106; delegation of powers to committees, 111n; qualification of candidates, 139; nominators, 145; qualifications of electors, 160; m. elections schedule, 161; dismissal of officers, 182; temporary borrowing limit, 225; debenture interest rate limit, 227; debt limits, 230; real property assessment, 286, 301; tax roll, 316; tax collection, 316; tax sales, 325

Rural Municipalities Act, The, of 1909 (Sask.), 45, 52

Russell, Lord John, 29

SABBATH, the, 54

St. Boniface, Man.: area adjustment exception, 69; as part of Winnipeg metropolitan area, 127–8; as part of Greater Winnipeg Water District, 135–6; sources of revenue, 207; assessment, 263n

St. James, Man.: as part of St. James–Winnipeg Airport Commission, 128; as part of Greater Winnipeg Water District, 135; proportional representation, 148

Saint John, City of, N.B.: suburban area problem, 14; Loyalist settlement, 21; incorporation, 38; annual expenditures, 60; repeal of by-laws, 100; representation on county council, 133n; recall procedure, 153; initiative of electors by petition, 158; manager plan, 169n; distribution of m. expenditures, 205; sources of revenue, 207; turnover tax, 219–20; miscellaneous revenues, 254; poll tax, 256–7; valuators, 274n; tax-exempt property, 287, 289, 292n; payments by Dominion in lieu of taxes, 299n; business taxes, 307–8, 313; tax sales, 326, 327n, 333

St. John County, N.B., 264n, 274n

St. John's, Nfld.: incorporation, 40, 348; insurance premium tax, 220; real property assessment, 262; court of revision, 277; tax exemptions, 292; business taxes, 308, 313

St. Lambert, Que., 169n

St. Laurent, Que.: member of Montreal Metropolitan Commission, 134n; manager plan, 169n

St. Pierre, Que., 134n

St. Stephen, N.B., 133n

St. Vital, Man.: as part of Greater Winnipeg Water District, 135; proportional representation, 148

Ste-Agathe-des-Monts, Que., 169n

Salaries: of heads of council, 102–5; of city and town managers, 171; recommendations on, by city commissioners, 175; of city commissioners, 175; as a m. expenditure, 195

Sales: of debentures, 238–9; for taxes, 255, 321, 323–31

Sales tax: as common m. type, 212; as shared tax, 245–6, 368

Saloons, 50

Sanatoria, 194, 361

Sandwich, Ont., 70

Sarnia, Ont., 169n

Saskatchewan, Province of: history of m. government, 43–6; provincial legislation for municipalities, 45, 52; annual expenditures, 60; extent of m. organization, 60; types of municipalities, 61–6; number 66, area adjustments, 68–70, dissolution and creation, 72–6; councillors' term of office, 81; election of councillors, 83, 106; appointive powers of heads of councils, 87; frequency of council meetings, 93; compulsory voting by councillors, 95n; composition of councils, 106; qualification for m. candidates, 137; candidates' disqualifications, 140; nomination meetings, 144; candidate's consent to serve, 145–6; withdrawal of candidates, 147; tie votes in m. elections, 151; Department and Minister of Municipal Affairs, 152, 272, 274, 276, 345; corporations' vote in elections, 154; "burgesses," 154; m. electors' qualifications, 159; provincial licensing of auditors, 181; Provincial Board of Examiners, 181; Local Government Board, 182, 229, 234–5, 296, 331, 350; dismissal of m. officers, 182; m. pension plans, 189, 190n; provincial inspection of m. affairs, 201; cash receipts of municipalities, 206n; public revenue tax on real property, 208n, 273; types of m. taxes in, 212, 214, 218, 257–8, 307; limit on debenture interest rates 227; m. debt limit, 230; funds for debt charges, 232; m. sinking funds, 233–4; debenture debt, 240; equalization road grants, 247–8; m. enterprises, 252, 253n; compulsory annual assessment, 265; assessment notices, 267; assessment appeals, 269, 277–8; boards of assessment, 271–2; provincial review of assessments, 272; basis of assessment, 279–80; valuation of buildings, 281; real property assessment, 282, 283n, 291; tax-exempt property, 288–9; Commission of Inquiry into Provincial and Municipal Taxation (1936), 289–90, 295; statutory assessments, 300; business assessment, 306, 310, 312–14; tax calculations, 316, 321; tax collections, 322, 329–30; tax sales, 325, 334; compromise of tax arrears, 331; penalties on overdue taxes, 333; appointments in place of councils, 354. *See also* Cities, Rural municipalities, Towns, and Villages (Sask.)

Saskatchewan Assessment Commission, 276, 278

Saskatchewan Tax Commission, 302

Saskatoon, Sask.: city commissioners, 174–5; amusement tax, 218; miscellaneous revenues, 254; business assessment, 310–11, 314

Schedule of m. elections, 159–60

School Act, The (Alta.), 64

School boards: in P.E.I., 40; provision of funds for, 54, 193; as a type of special purpose body, 65; in Winnipeg, 128; in Ont., 129, 130n, 140, 158; in Halifax, 130n; in B.C., 130n; provincial grants to, 207

Schools. *See* Education

Scrope, G. Poulett, 28n

Seating arrangements in m. councils, 122

Secondary schools, provincial grants to (Ont.), 260

Secret discussion by council, 113

Secretary-treasurers, municipal: in Lower Canada, 35; in Alta., 180–1; in Que., 181; in Man., 181–2; in Sask, 182; as tax calculator and collector, 316

Sectional representation, 85

Securities, hypothecating of, 224. *See also* Debentures and Bonds

Select (or special committees), 108–9

"Select men," 22

Self-government, municipal, 14–5, chap. XVII, 335–70; New England tradition of, 37; no prolonged struggle for, in Western provinces, 46

Selkirk, Lord (Thomas Douglas), 41

Senators: disqualified as m. candidates, 140; exempt from serving on councils, 140

"Separate schools": tax rates for, 211; provincial grants to (Ont.), 260; assessment appeals re (Man.), 278

"Separated towns" (Ont.): definition, 64n; not part of county system, 80; highway grants to, 259; provincial payments to, 358n

Serial debentures, 236–7

Servants, municipal, 177–8

Services, municipal: as factor determining m. expenditures, 202; quantity and quality of, 203; school health, classification of, 203; revenues for, 206; grants for, 339
Sewers: construction, 203; m. expenditures for, 205; local improvement taxes for, 212; debentures for, 228; loans for, 239
Shared taxes, 245–6, 368–9
Shawinigan Falls, Que.: manager plan, 169n; fiscal year, 199n
Sheriffs: role in 1859 Nova Scotia municipal Act, 37; participation in erection of Nova Scotia towns, 76; disqualified from m. candidature, 140; and revision of voters' list, 142; and tax sales, 325–7
Sherbrooke, Que.: remuneration of councillors, 103; number of standing committees, 111; office of mayor, 115
Shortt, Adam, 22, 26n
Sidewalks: local improvement rate for, 213; debentures for paving, 228; provision for, as local service, 340
Sidney Township, Ont., 289
Signs, m. charges for, 256
Simcoe County, Ont., 64
Simcoe, John Graves, 24
Simon, Sir Ernest, 4
Single tax, 289
Sinking fund: municipalities encouraged to levy for, 232; type of debenture, 233–6; trustees of, 235–6; management of, 235–6; "raiding" of, 236; reduction of, 237–8, 329
"Skul-duggery," 138
Snow removal: 197–8, 200, 202–3, 205, 225, 340
Social services: opinions on m. responsibility for, 123–4; expansion of, 197, 341; provincial grants for, 246; limit to, on real property tax base, 362
Social workers, 183
Socialism, 56
Soil, as factor in assessing real property, 279, 280
Solicitors: municipal, dismissal of, in Nova Scotia towns, 181; not required at courts of revision, 270
Sorel, Que., 217
Sources of m. tax revenues, 210
Sous baillis, 20
South Qu'Appelle, Sask., 43
Special Acts, 52, 67
Special (or select) m. committees, 108, 109
Special meetings of m. councils, 94
Special purpose bodies, 65, chap. VI, 126–32; mayor as *ex officio* member of, 91; use in Canada and England, 108; accounting practices for expenditures by, 203; provincial grants to, 207; increase in uncontrollable expenditures by, 340
"Spendthrift," charge against councillors, 202
Spoils system, lack of, in Canadian municipalities, 183
Stadium, as m. enterprise, 251
Standards: of m. services, 338–9; for determining provincial grants to municipalities, 339; of health, education, welfare, etc., 363
Standing committees: role of chairmen, 58; definition, 108; number and types, 111
Status of municipalities: change of, 67; annexation, 68–71; amalgamation, 70; disorganization, dissolution, and disincorporation, 72; reduction of, 72
Statute labour and fire districts, 44
Statutes. *See* Legislation, provincial
Statutory bodies. *See* Special purpose bodies
Statutory requirements: for change in m. status, 67–76; for council meetings, 93; for council action, 96, 98; for payment of councillors, 101–3; for m. officers, 178,

264; for m. expenditures, 193–4
Statutory tax limits, 317
Stock-in-trade tax: as form of personal property tax, 212; in Quebec, 215–16, 303; in Newfoundland, 215–16
Stocks, used in long-term m. borrowing, 226
Stockyard, as m. enterprise, 251
Storage business, assessment of (Alta.), 311
Stormont County, Upper Canada, 24n
Streets: maintenance, 194, 197; lighting, 194, 197, 340; m. expenditures for, 205; payments for flushing, sweeping, oiling, 213; encroachments on, 256. *See also* Roads
Subsidies: provincial, as part of m. revenues, 206n; m. to industries, 292. *See also* Grants
Suburbanization, 197
Suburban Development Act, The (Ont.), 133–4
Suburban municipalities, 68–71
Suburban road commissions (Ont.), 134
Suburban service board (Ont.), 133–4
Suffolk County, Upper Canada, 24n
Sugar factories, fixed assessment of, 293
Suit, collection of taxes by, 321
Summerside, P.E.I.: incorporation, 39; not covered by 1948 Towns Act, 40
Supplementary legislation, 98–9
Surpluses: from sinking funds, 233–5; from m. enterprises, 250–2; from tax sales, 328
Surveyor, district, 30–1
Suspensions: of m. employees by head of council, 87–8; of m. by-laws, 100
Switzerland: democratic tradition in, 17; municipalities under state jurisdiction, 18
Sydenham, Lord (Charles Poulett Thomson), 28–9, 34
Syndics, 20

TAVERNS: regulated by Courts of Quarter Sessions, 23; in s. 92 of B.N.A. Act, 50; keepers, disqualified from m. candidature, 140; water tax levied on, 220
Taxation, municipal: limit of, 191; revenues from chap. XI, 206–22; current, 208–21; limited number of sources, 208–9; direct, 208–9; base and tax rate, 209; shared, between province and municipalities, 245–6; sharing burden of, 261; rate of, 261; assessment for, chap. XIII, 261–78; exemptions from, 286–9; of special franchises, 307; *ad valorem* taxes, 307–8; general, chap. XVI, 315–34; roll, 316–18
Tax Commission (Sask.), 302
Tax deed, 327–8
Tax Enforcement Act (Sask.), 330
Taxes, municipal: immunity from, in Lower Canada, 34; in Quebec and Ontario counties, 64; collection of arrears (Ont.), 117n; real property base of, 123–4, 191; councils as collecting authority for special purpose bodies, 129–30; and qualification of candidates, 139, 146; school, 197, 211, 293; determination of, 199, 315; revenues from, 206–22, 315–34; as percentage of gross revenues, 207; direct, 208, 209; indirect, 208n; base and rate of, 209; general and special, 211; local improvement, 211–13, 293; real property, 211–14, 324; personal property and business, 211–12, 214; common types of, table, 212; dog, 212; rentals, 212, 216; amusement, 212, 218; occupancy, 212; sales, 212, 217–18; telephone equipment, 212, 218; water, 212, 220; stock-in-trade, 212, 215–16; animal, 212, 215; vehicle, 215; tenants and occupiers, 216; electricity and gas, 219; franchise, 219; turnover, 219–20;

insurance premium, 220; peculiar to Newfoundland, 220–1; billiard table, 221; bowling alley, 221; sales for, 255, 323–31; rates of, 261, 285, 315; notices of, 317–18; statutory m. limits on, 317; collection of, 318, 320, 332–3; due date of, 318; discount on, 319; compromise and consolidation of arrears of, 331–2; overdue, 318, 320, 332–3; real property, as major source of, 340, 362; shared, 368
Tax liens, 329
Tax Recovery Act (Alta.), 331–2
Tax Sales, 255, 323–31
Taxi licences, 254
Taxpayers: as part of m. electorate, 191; control over expenditures, 202; customary position of, 251; pressure of, on assessors, 283; penalties on, 319; responsibility of councillors to, 339. *See also* Electorate
Teachers, exempt from m. service, 141
Telegraph: m. assessment on lines, 299–300; specific tax on companies (Halifax), 306; business assessment on companies (Edmonton), 309
Telephone: equipment tax as m. tax type, 212, 218; systems, as m. enterprises, 250–2; system of Manitoba, 296; lines, m. assessment of, 299–300, 309
Temiskaming, Que., 169n
Temporary municipal employees, 179
Tenders, for debentures, 238
Term of office: of council members, 80–2; of mayors, reeves, wardens, chairmen, 92
Terms, debenture, 227–8
Terrain, as factor determining expenditures, 202–3
Thomson, Charles Poulett. *See* Sydenham, Lord
Three Rivers, Que.: *syndics* in, 20; manager plan, 169n; sales tax, 217; water tax, 220
Tie vote, breaking of, 95, 155
Topography, as factor determining expenditures, 202–3
Tories, 29
Toronto, Ont.: metropolitan area of, 14, 70; incorporation, 26n; under special Act, 52; annual expenditures, 60; council, 78–9, 82; ward system, 85; debate on "Waterfront Grab," 94n; remuneration of councillors, 103; municipally operated transportation, 128; administrative departments, 167–8; range and number of m. employees, 180; merit system, 185; sources of revenue, 207; debt limit, 229; debenture redemption, 234n; range of permits and licences, 254; tax exemptions, 292
Total number of municipalities, 66
Town Act, The, of 1908 (Sask.), 45, 52
Town halls, 239
Town meeting, New England type, 24, 26, 33, 37
Town planning: Winnipeg Town Planning Commission, 128; by special bodies, 134
Towns: number of, by provinces, 66; change of status, 72; erection from villages, 76; erection to cities, 76; head of council of, 77; number of councillors in, 78; managers, 169–71
  in Alberta: creation, 76; annexation procedures, 70; payment of councillors, 101n, 102; election and composition of councils, 106; qualifications of voters, 160; m. elections schedule, 161; manager plan, 170; appointment of secretary-treasurer, 181; limit on temporary borrowings, 225; limits on debenture terms, 228; debt limits, 230; sinking fund investments, 235n; "minimum taxes," 258; basis of valuation of buildings, 281; real property assessment, 286, 301; tax exemptions, 289; personal property tax, 305; busi-

ness assessment, 312–13; penalties for overdue taxes, 333
in British Columbia: not a municipal type, 61
in Manitoba: dissolution, 73; creation, 76; payment of councillors, 102; election and composition of councils, 106; limit on temporary borrowings, 225; real property assessment, 286; railways assessment, 300n; personal property assessment, 305; business assessment, 312
in New Brunswick: creation, 76; election and composition of councils, 106; requirements for candidates, 139; clergy disqualified from candidature, 140; qualifications for electors, 159; m. elections schedule, 160; limits on temporary borrowings, 225; dog tax, 259; assessors, 263; real property assessment, 286; personal property assessment, 305; business assessment, 312; tax collection, 318; per capita grants to, 368
in Nova Scotia: dissolution, 73; creation, 76; councillors' term of office, 80; duties of mayors, 86–7; election and composition of councils, 106; payment of councillors, 101n, 102–3; requirements of candidates, 139; clergy disqualified from candidature, 140; m. clerk as returning officer, 144n; breaking tie vote, 151n; approval to issue debentures by, 155; m. elections schedule, 160; dismissal of clerks and solicitors, 181; appeal of officers to courts, 188; limitations on temporary borrowings, 225; poll tax, 256; assessments, 267, 277, 286, 293, 305, 312; penalties on overdue taxes, 332
in Ontario: "separated," 64n, 80; creation, 76; election and composition of councils, 106; initiative by electoral petition, 158; compulsory appointment of assessors and tax collectors, 177; real property assessment, 286, 301; business assessment, 312–13; tax sales, 324
in Prince Edward Island: number of councillors, 78; election and composition of councils, 106; candidate's election deposit, 146; qualifications of electors, 159; m. elections schedule, 160; personal property tax, 214; limit on temporary borrowings, 225; limit on debenture terms, 228; provincial approval of debentures not required, 229; debt limit, 230; debenture reissue, 232; poll tax, 258; notice of assessment, 267; courts of revision, 269; assessment appeal courts, 277, real property assessment, 286; tax exemptions, 292; personal property tax, 303; business assessment, 306, 312; tax collections, 322; redemption of land sold at tax sales, 333
in Quebec: creation, 76; payment of councillors, 101; election and composition of councils, 106; mayor as *ex officio* member of committees, 108n; requirements for candidates, 139; disqualifications from candidacy, 140; fixed date for nomination meetings, 144; m. clerk as returning officer, 144n; nomination meetings, 144n; nominators, 145; candidate's consent, 146; candidate's election deposit, 146; withdrawal of candidates, 147; use of counterfoil in ballots, 150; resignation of councillors, 152; qualifications of electors, 159; m. elections schedule, 161; manager plan, 170; animal tax, 215; stock-in-trade tax, 215; rentals tax, 216; water tax, 220; limits on temporary borrowings, 225; debt limits, 230; revenue from fines,

255; assessment basis, 262, 265; assessors, 264; appeals against assessment, 268; regular review of assessments, 271; real property assessment, 286; tax exemptions, 291–2; personal property assessment, 306; business assessment, 306, 312–13; tax calculations, 316; statutory tax limits, 317; tax sales, 325–6, 329, 333; penalties for overdue taxes, 333
in Saskatchewan: creation, 76; The Town Act, 45, 52; term of office of councillors, 81; mayors required to vote, 89; payment of councillors, 102; election and composition of councils, 106; registration of voters, 142; advance poll, 148; void ballots, 150; m. elections schedule, 161; cash revenues, 206n; rentals tax, 216; limits on temporary borrowings, 225; limits on debenture terms, 227; debt limits, 230; sinking fund trustees, 236; m. enterprises, 253n; revenues from fines, 255; poll tax, 256; courts of revisions, 269; real property assessment, 286, 301; real property tax exemptions, 289, 292; business assessment, 312–13; tax calculations, 316
Towns Act of 1948 (P.E.I.), 39–40
Towns Incorporation Act of 1888 (N.S.), 38
Townships: in Upper Canada, 25; in United Canada, 29, 35; in Lower Canada, 34, 36; in Prairie Provinces, 44n; as rural m. unit, 62–3; number of councillors, 78, 80
in Ontario: creation, 74; number of councillors, 78, 80; election and composition of councils, 106; appointment of assessors and tax collectors, 177; real property assessment, 286, 301; tax sales, 324
in Quebec: dissolution, 73; creation, 74; number of councillors, 78; election and composition of councils, 106; real property assessment, 286
Transcona, Man.: in Greater Winnipeg Sanitary District, 127; in Greater Winnipeg Water District, 135
Traffic, guards for school children, 196
Training schools, m. responsibility for, 361
Transmission lines, assessment of, 300
Transportation commission, 65
Transportation systems, as m. enterprises, 251, 252. *See also* Railways and Bus Systems
Treasurers, municipal: in municipal districts, 30–1; compulsory appointment, 177; statutory responsibilities, 178; combination with clerk, 178; in Manitoba, 181–2; in Nova Scotia "municipalities," 181; in Fredericton, 181; in Saskatchewan, 182, 330; in Ontario, 188; warnings against unauthorized expenditures, 202; as tax calculator and collector; 316; action in tax sales, 325–6, 328, 330. *See also* Clerk-treasurer
Treasury department, as m. administrative unit, 168
Treasury note, as form of m. short-term borrowing, 223
Tree trimming, as a local service, 340
Trois-Rivières, Que. *See* Three Rivers
Trustees, of m. sinking funds, 235–6
Tunnels, 256
Tuxedo, Man., 135

Ultra vires action of councils, 53–4, 97–8
Unconditional grants: general, 339; in Ontario, 243–4
Under-assessment, 281, 283–4
Unemployment relief: m. budgetary provisions for, 200n; financing of, during Depression, 226, 341; taxes for, 293

Uniformed forces, rates of pay of, 187–8
Unincorporated townships, 64n
Union Bill. *See* Act of Union
Union of Alberta Municipalities, 356
Union of Nova Scotia Municipalities, 356
United Empire Loyalists. *See* Loyalists
United States: influences on Canadian m. government, 16n, 82, 126, 131, 169; local government, 18; municipal incorporation, 49; jurisdiction of states over m. government, 50n; powers of mayors, 87, 90; term of office of mayors, 92; salaries of mayors, 105; special purpose bodies, 131; manager plan, 169; sale of debentures, 232; capital value assessment, 262; national-state relations, 335; use of shared taxes, 368
Unwritten rules of procedure, 115–16, 118n
Upper Canada, history of m. government in, 22–9
Urbanization, 9–13, 123, 127, 336, 338, 341
Urban municipalities: number of, by provinces, 66; problem of area adjustments, 68–71; ideal size, 71; size of council, 79; election of councillors, 84; and special purpose bodies, 127
Utilities, assessment of, 299–300, 306–7
Utility commissions, 65

VACANCIES IN COUNCILS, 151–2
Val-d'Or, Que., 169n
Valleyfield, Que., 169n
Valuation: for taxation, 261; of real property, 279; of buildings, 281; of personal property, 304. *See also* Assessment
Valuators: in N.B., 274–5; in Ont., 275
Value: assessed, tax levy on, 211; capital, of real property, 262; rental, of real property, 262; definition of, 279
Vancouver, B.C.: metropolitan area problem in, 14; annual expenditures, 60; size of council, 78–9; remuneration of councillors, 103; distribution of m. expenditures, 205; District Joint Sewage Board, 205n; sources of revenue, 207; standing committees, 108; business tax, 212; franchise tax, 219; water tax, 220; debt limitation, 229; miscellaneous revenues, 254; real property assessment, 282; business assessment, 310; tax limit, 317; redemption of land sold at tax sales, 334
Vehicle tax: fiscal significance, 215; in Nfld, 221
Verdun, Que.: ward system, 85; member of Montreal Metropolitan Commission, 134; manager plan, 169n; sources of revenue, 207; sales tax, 217; amusement taxes, 218
Veterans' properties, exempt from taxation, 291
Veto power of heads of council, 88
Victoria, B.C.: suburban problem, 14; creation, 46; polling places, 144n; manager plan, 169n; sources of revenue, 207; miscellaneous revenues, 254
Village Act, The, of 1908 (Sask.), 45, 52
Villages: number, by provinces, 66; change of status, 72, 76; creation, 75; head of councils, 78; number of councillors, 78, 80
in Alberta: dissolution, 73; creation, 74–5; payment of councillors, 101n, 102; election and composition of councils, 106; qualifications of voters, 160; elections schedule, 161; appointment of secretary-treasurer, 181; limit on temporary borrowings, 225; limit on debenture terms, 228; debt limits, 230; sinking

fund investments, 235n; "minimum tax," 257; tax exemptions, 280; real property assessment, 286, 290, 301; personal property assessment, 305; business assessment, 312–13; penalties for overdue taxes, 333
in British Columbia: dissolution, 73; creation, 75; number of councillors, 78; payment of council members prohibited, 101n; election and composition of councils, 106; real property assessment, 286, 290, 301; business assessment, 312
in Manitoba: dissolution, 73; creation, 75; election and composition of councils, 106; limits on temporary borrowings, 225; real property assessment, 286; railway assessment, 300n; personal property assessment, 305; business assessment, 312
in New Brunswick: dissolution, 73, 74n; creation, 75; head of council, 78; compulsory voting by councillors, 95n; election and composition of councils, 106; statement of candidate's eligibility, 145; withdrawal of candidates, 147; void ballots, 150; qualifications of electors, 159; elections schedule, 160; limits on temporary borrowings, 225; limits on debenture interest rates, 227; provincial approval of debenture issues, 229; debt limits, 230; dog tax, 259; real property assessment, 286; personal property assessment, 305; business assessment, 312; tax collection, 318, per capita grants, 368
in Ontario: creation, 75; number of councillors, 78; election and composition of councils, 106; appointment of assessors and tax collectors, 177; real property assessment, 286, 301; business assessment, 312, 313
in Prince Edward Island: creation, 75; number of councillors 78; head of councils, 78; election and composition of councils, 106; real property assessment, 286; business assessment, 312
in Quebec: creation, 75; number of councillors, 78; election and composition of councils, 106; debt limits, 230; real property assessment, 286; business assessment, 312–13
in Saskatchewan: The Village Act, 45, 52; dissolution, 73; creation, 75; payment of councillors, 102; election and composition of councils, 106; void ballots, 150; qualifications of electors, 159; elections schedule, 161; cash revenues, 206n; limits on short-term borrowings, 225; limits on debenture term, 227; real property assessment, 286, 301; business assessment, 312–13; tax roll, 316; debt limits, 230; tax collection, 316
Village Service Act of 1950 (P.E.I.), 40, 75n
Virginia, colony of, 22
Voters' lists, 142–3
Voting: of mayor or reeve, 89; casting vote to break tie, 89; in council meetings, 95–6, 119; compulsory, by councillors, 95; on repeal of by-laws, 100; on payment of councillors, 101; habits of m. electorate, 121–2; chap. VII, 138–61; The electorate, 141–2; voters' lists, 142–3; the electoral process, 143–51; ballots, 147; declaration of result, 148; by proportional representation, 148–9; counting the votes, 149–51; procedures, 150–1; "plumping," 150; tie vote, 151; recount, 151; m. election schedule (by provinces), 160–1

WAGES: as m. expenditure, 195, 202; reduction in, 195; rates of, 202
Walkerville, Ont., 70

Wallas, Graham, 4
Wardens: church, 25; town, 25; district (Upper Canada), 29–31; district (Lower Canada), 34; county, 36, 42, 77–8; in N.S., 88; rotation of, 92, 115
Wards: councils elected by, 78; as vote basis, 82–6, 150; in Toronto, 85; criticism of system, 150
Warrants, for tax sales, 325
Warren, J. H., 9n
Waterloo, Ont., 136
Water mains, 203
Water taxes: as payment for services supplied, 212–13; description of, 220
Waterworks: debentures for, 228; loans for, 239; as type of m. enterprise, 250, 251
Welfare: discretion of boards of, 129n; department, as m. administrative unit, 167; officer, combined with other offices, 178; provincial department of (Ont.), 182; m. expenditures for, 205; provincial grants for, 246; allocation of functions of, 363
Welfare state, concept of, 337
Welland, Ont.: salary of mayor of, 103n; council organization in, 166
Western provinces: history of m. government, 42–7; provincial departments of m. affairs, 344–6; provincial supervision of municipalities, 346
West Kildonan, Man.: member of Winnipeg and St. Boniface Harbour Commission and River Control Board, 127; member of Greater Winnipeg Water District, 135
Westmount, Que.: member of Montreal Metropolitan Commission, 134n; manager plan, 169n; sources of revenue, 207; sales tax, 217; amusement tax, 218; tax-exempt property, 289
White, L. D., 344
"White paper" technique, 357
Widows, exempt from m. taxation, 287, 304
Windsor, Ont.: suburban problem in, 14; amalgamation, 70; annual expenditures, 60
Winnipeg, Man.: corporation, 43; annual expenditures, 60; area adjustments, 69; size of council, 78; ward system, 85; remuneration of councillors, 103; civic boards, 127–8; candidate's election deposit, 146; proportional representation, 148–9; administrative departments, 167–8; distribution of m. expenditures, 205; sources of revenue, 207; utility sales tax, 212; electricity and gas tax, 219; sinking fund trustees, 236; miscellaneous revenues, 254; revenues from fines, 255; provincial government and assessment, 263n; tax-exempt property, 289; personal property assessment, 302; business assessment, 308–9; 314; tax limit, 317; redemption of land sold for taxes, 334
Withdrawal of m. candidates, 146–7
Wittke, Carl, 33n
Wolseley, Sask., 43
Woodstock, N.B.: representation on county council, 133n; manager plan, 169n; incorporation, 38
Woodworth, Leo Day, 368n
Working capital, not permitted for municipalities, 223
Working conditions: of m. employees, 186–90; pay, 186–8; pensions, 188–90
Works department, as m. administrative unit, 167–8
Wright, Frederick, 134n

York County: Upper Canada, 24n; New Brunswick, 38, 160
York Township, Ont., 10n
Young Men's Christian Association, 291
Young Women's Christian Association, 291

Zoning, by-laws, 352

CANADIAN GOVERNMENT SERIES

Edited by C. B. Macpherson

1. **Democratic Government and Politics.** By J. A. CORRY AND J. E. HODGETTS. Third edition.

2. **The Government of Canada.** By R. MACGREGOR DAWSON. Fifth edition, revised by Norman Ward.

3. **Constitutional Amendment in Canada.** By PAUL GÉRIN-LAJOIE.

4. **The Canadian House of Commons: Representation.** By NORMAN WARD. Out of print

5. **The Government of Prince Edward Island.** By FRANK MACKINNON.

6. **Canadian Municipal Government.** By KENNETH GRANT CRAWFORD.

7. **Pioneer Public Service: An Administrative History of the United Canadas, 1841–1867.** By J. E. HODGETTS.

8. **The Government of Nova Scotia.** By J. MURRAY BECK. Out of print

9. **The Office of the Lieutenant-Governor.** By JOHN T. SAYWELL. Out of print

10. **Politics in New Brunswick.** By HUGH G. THORBURN.

11. **The Public Purse.** By NORMAN WARD.

12. **Procedure in the Canadian House of Commons.** By W. F. DAWSON. Out of print

13. **The Canadian General Election of 1957.** By JOHN MEISEL.

14. **The Government of Manitoba.** By M. S. DONNELLY.

15. **The Modern Senate of Canada.** By F. A. KUNZ.

16. **Responsible Government in Ontario.** By F. F. SCHINDELER.

www.ingramcontent.com/pod-product-compliance
Lightning Source LLC
LaVergne TN
LVHW090800070826
844660LV00022B/1039
9781442639515